RETHINKING
HOME
ECONOMICS

Rethinking Home Economics

WOMEN AND THE
HISTORY OF A PROFESSION

EDITED BY

Sarah Stage *and* Virginia B. Vincenti

CORNELL UNIVERSITY PRESS

ITHACA AND LONDON

PUBLICATION OF THIS BOOK WAS MADE POSSIBLE, IN PART, BY A GRANT
FROM THE COLLEGE OF HUMAN ECOLOGY AT CORNELL UNIVERSITY.

First published 1997 by Cornell University Press.
First printing, Cornell Paperbacks, 1997.

Printed in the United States of America

Library of Congress Cataloging-in-Publication Data

Rethinking home economics : women and the history of a profession /
  Sarah Stage and Virginia B. Vincenti, editors.
      p.   cm.
   Includes index.
   ISBN 0-8014-2971-4 (cloth : alk. paper).—ISBN 0-8014-8175-9 (pbk : alk. paper)
   1. Home economics—United States—History—20th century.
   2. Women—United States—Social conditions.   I. Stage, Sarah.
   II. Vincenti, Virginia Bramble, 1946–
   TX23.R48   1997   96-29976
   640'.973'0904—dc21

Cornell University Press strives to utilize environmentally responsible
suppliers and materials to the fullest extent possible in the publishing
of its books. Such materials include vegetable-based, low-VOC inks and
acid-free papers that are also either recycled, totally chlorine-free, or
partly composed of nonwood fibers.

Cloth printing   10 9 8 7 6 5 4 3 2 1

Paperback printing   10 9 8 7 6 5 4 3 2 1

Contents

v

Preface

This volume originated in a series of informal and freewheeling conversations between two women, a dean trained in the home economics tradition and a faculty member who is a historian. We had a common starting point: both of us shared a deep concern because the home economics profession was ignored, misunderstood, and even maligned. As we talked over coffee and sandwiches about the ways in which woman's work was generally devalued, we realized that we needed to know more about home economics because we wanted to understand not only the painful trials and struggles but also the accomplishments and successes. In essence, we both wanted to learn more about the specific history of home economics within the larger context of the history of female professionalization in the United States.

From the start, we knew that any successful discussion had to involve both home economists and historians of women. One without the other simply would not do. Home economists needed the insights drawn from recent feminist historical scholarship to position and interpret their field in a wider context; historians needed to talk to "real" home economists about the work they were doing and the roads the profession had traveled in the twentieth century. As women often will, we envisioned a cordial blending of the two groups in which people would both talk and listen. We wanted to make home economists comfortable enough to speak honestly about the varied directions their field has taken, and we also wanted to attract historical scholars who were receptive to the potential of these professionals as living source material. We knew that Cornell was the perfect place for such a meeting because of the university's long and distinguished involvement in education, research, and extension in agriculture and home economics.

In October 1991, through the generosity of the New York State Council for the Humanities, as well as funds from the New York State College of Human Ecology, more than three hundred people attended a two-day conference at the New York State College of Human Ecology titled "Rethinking Women and Home Economics in the Twentieth Century." The essays in this volume provide a real sense of the excitement of the Ithaca meeting as well as the nature of the dialogue between history and home economics. The quality and interest of the scholarly work presented here will surely inspire more lively and animated conversations like our own.

Francille M. Firebaugh
Dean
New York State College of Human Ecology

Joan Jacobs Brumberg
Professor
New York State College of Human Ecology

Ithaca, New York

Acknowledgments

We would like to thank the many people who helped to bring this volume to fruition. First, we are indebted to Joan Jacobs Brumberg for putting together the conference at Cornell University, October 4–5, 1991, where most of the essays in this book were first presented. In addition, Francille Firebaugh, dean of the College of Human Ecology, played a critical role. Not only did she sponsor the conference, but she provided seed money that enabled us to work together collaboratively from opposite shores of the continent (California and Massachusetts in the early days of this project). Margaret Rossiter also deserves special mention. Her interest in home economics has been an impetus to our scholarship, and her willingness to share the fruits of her prodigious research has been a boon to our work.

The task of editing *Rethinking Home Economics* has been enlivened by the opportunity it has given us to get to know each other and experience personally the dialogue between home economists and historians that this book attempts to foster. When we first met at Joan Brumberg's house in Ithaca, our common interest in Ellen Richards created a rapport that developed into a rewarding and productive friendship. One of the joys of academic life is the opportunity, once in a while at least, to enter into intellectually stimulating discussion, even heated debate, with someone you respect. Our most productive and stimulating work occurred when we met for marathon weekends, sitting at the computer together, discussing and writing, reading and editing separately, then returning to reflect and write again. In the spirit of this equal collaboration, we have alphabetized our names as editors.

We dedicate this book to our children, Lisa Ann Vincenti and Twain Kenyon. Because of the work of courageous women, their mothers are different people today than they were at their children's ages. We hope Lisa and Twain can take value from our collaborative work and personal journeys as they make their own contributions in the twenty-first century.

S. S. *and* V. B. V.

RETHINKING
HOME
ECONOMICS

Introduction
Home Economics:
What's in a Name?

SARAH STAGE

Home economics has not fared well at the hands of historians. Until recently women's historians largely dismissed home economics as little more
than a conspiracy to keep women in the kitchen. For the generation of women
who grew up in the 1950s and 1960s, the words "home economics" still con-
jure up memories of junior high school classes in cooking and sewing—hours
spent making aprons and white sauce, twin symbols of prescribed middle-
class domesticity. The feminists of the 1970s cast off their aprons long before
they burned their bras. It was no surprise when Robin Morgan, speaking at
the American Home Economics Association convention in 1972, declared,
"As a radical feminist, I am here addressing the enemy."[1]

Most women's historians who treated home economics shared Morgan's
animus, not surprising since they generally relied on three negative frameworks: one that emphasized the work of Catharine Beecher and judged
home economics as part and parcel of the nineteenth-century cult of domesticity; a second that focused on the careers of Lillian Gilbreth and Christine Frederick and underscored the relationship between home economics
and scientific management; and a third, heavily influenced by Betty
Friedan, who in *The Feminine Mystique* (1963) charged home economics
with the creation of "the happy housewife heroine" of the 1950s.[2]

1. "What Robin Morgan Said at Denver," *Journal of Home Economics* 65 (January 1973): 13.
2. Betty Friedan, *The Feminine Mystique* (New York: Norton, 1963). For examples of negative treatments of home economics, see Barbara Ehrenreich and Deirdre English, *For Her Own
Good: 150 Years of Experts' Advice to Women* (Garden City, N.Y.: Anchor Press, 1978); Susan
Strasser, *Never Done: A History of American Housework* (New York: Pantheon, 1982); Ruth

1

Largely missing from historians' treatment of home economics has been an understanding of the significant evolution of the concept of Victorian domesticity championed by Catharine Beecher into the formal home economics movement launched by Ellen Richards in the early twentieth century. Home economics as it was practiced at the turn of the century focused more on careers for women than on domesticity and sheds light on the intersection of gender and professionalism.

The essays in this volume contribute to a rethinking of women and home economics in the twentieth century by scholars at every level, from the doctoral dissertations of Carmen Harris and Carolyn Goldstein, to the work of senior scholars such as Nancy Tomes, Ronald Kline, and Margaret Rossiter. The exploration of the ways in which race, class, and gender influenced women's options has moved the study of home economics toward a more complex rendering of the dynamics that gave rise to professional home economics and a greater understanding of the obstacles women encountered and the strategies they employed to gain legitimacy as the field developed in the twentieth century.

Central to the new scholarship on home economics has been the work of scholars who have approached the issues of politics and professionalization from the perspective of women's history. Paula Baker and Anne Firor Scott broadened the definition of politics to get beyond voting and officeholding and include the important work women have done organizing for change. Baker's pathbreaking article on the "domestication of politics" moved women from the periphery to the center of studies of U.S. political culture in the period before woman suffrage. Scott's book *Natural Allies* (1991) documented the way women's voluntary associations shaped America's social and political landscape.[3]

Home economics constitutes a classic case of the interplay of politics and domesticity in women's history. At the turn of the century home economists politicized domesticity by urging women to use their skills in "that larger

---

Schwartz Cowan, *More Work for Mother: The Ironies of Household Technology from the Open Hearth to the Microwave* (New York: Basic Books, 1983); Laura Shapiro, *Perfection Salad: Women and Cooking at the Turn of the Century* (New York: Farrar, Straus and Giroux 1986); Glenna Matthews, *"Just a Housewife": The Rise and Fall of Domesticity in America* (New York: Oxford University Press, 1987); and Bettina Berch, *The Endless Day: The Political Economy of Women and Work* (New York: Harcourt Brace Jovanovich, 1982). For a notable exception, see Dolores Hayden, *The Grand Domestic Revolution: The History of Feminist Designs for American Homes, Neighborhoods, and Cities* (Cambridge: MIT Press, 1981). Indispensable for an understanding of nineteenth-century domestic economy and its most significant exponent is Kathryn Kish Sklar, *Catharine Beecher: A Study in American Domesticity* (New Haven: Yale University Press, 1973).

3. Paula Baker, "The Domestication of Politics: Women and American Political Society, 1780–1920," *American Historical Review* 89 (1984): 620–47; Anne Firor Scott, *Natural Allies: Women's Associations in American History* (Urbana: University of Illinois Press, 1991).

household the city."[4]   Along with the settlement house movement, home economics moved women into public policy under the rubric of social and municipal housekeeping. Much more than "glorified housekeeping," home economics began as part of the broader movement for progressive reform.

At the same time women's history has promoted a new understanding of women's political culture, it has offered new insights into professionalization, an important framework within which to examine home economics. When Robert Wiebe first explored the move to set standards and establish professional organizations in the early twentieth century in *The Search for Order* (1967), he failed to grasp the centrality of gender to professionalization. Professional organizations are generally motivated by the desire to draw lines, as much to exclude as to include. The American Medical Association (AMA) was formed in 1847 by doctors alarmed at the growing competition from homeopaths, whom they sought to deny consultation and legitimacy by barring them from membership in the AMA. By the early twentieth century many other groups, from lawyers to historians, were setting standards and defining membership. Significantly, the movement for professionalization occurred precisely at the time a growing number of college-educated women were seeking entry into the professions. Some organizations defined themselves in ways that limited women's access and participation. Historians for example, increasingly hinged their professional status on employment at a college or university—institutions rarely willing to hire women faculty. Although not necessarily a strategy to exclude women, professionalism was gendered with a vengeance, down to its language of objectivity, science, expertise, and disinterested inquiry. Women, largely denied employment in male professions, developed parallel tracks to careers and sought to upgrade, standardize, and professionalize the fields in which they worked in an attempt to be competitive for jobs and resources and to gain legitimacy. The move from social settlements to social work is the most documented of the trends toward female gendered professionalism.

Historians who have examined women and the issue of professionalization have been of two minds. Some, notably Penina Glazer and Miriam Slater in *Unequal Colleagues* (1987), argued that professionalization disadvantaged women and was inherently conservative and antithetical to social reform. More recently Robyn Muncy, in *Creating a Female Dominion in American Reform* (1991), looked at the development of the Children's Bureau and outlined the way in which women's professional culture fused so-

---

4. "Report of the Special Committee on the Lake Placid Conference on Home Economics in Elementary and Secondary Schools, 1901," Appendix in Lake Placid Conference on Home Economics, *Proceedings of the First, Second, and Third Conferences* (Lake Placid, N.Y., 1902), pp. 8–9.

cial service and personal advancement. Professionalization, Muncy argues, did not stand in opposition to reform but rather formed an integral part of the ethos of a female dominion in American reform.[5]

The issue of women and professionalization, raised by Nancy Tomes and Joan Jacobs Brumberg in their significant 1985 article, remains central to studies of women's occupations in the twentieth century and has stimulated scholars to look closely at social work, nursing, and other gendered professions. Susan Reverby's *Ordered to Care* (1987), and Barbara Melosh's *"The Physician's Hand": Work Culture and Conflict in Nursing* (1982) have provided important models which treat nursing. More recently *Gendered Domains* (1992), edited by Reverby and Dorothy O. Helly, pursued the issue in the context of other fields and arenas.[6]

The new work in women's history dealing with politics and professionalization has established the larger ground in which to study home economics. As a preeminent example of a gendered domain, home economics is a significant area in which to evaluate the structures and strategies women employed in their efforts to expand the range of their activities in the twentieth century. As one of the primary areas in which educated women found professional employment in academia and business from the 1900s to the 1960s, the field of home economics can no longer be dismissed as domesticity prescribed.

The essays in this volume share a willingness to approach the subject of home economics from the perspective of these new frameworks. They seek to get beyond judgments on whether home economics "helped" or "hurt" women and to ask instead how and why it developed as it did and what we can learn from the successes and failures of these pioneering women professionals. This new spirit of inquiry has made it possible to begin a dialogue with home economists, a cooperative effort represented in this book by the coeditorship of a women's historian and a home economics teacher educator specializing in the history and philosophy of home economics. The reminiscences of four home economists further the interaction. By juxtaposing the life experiences of these four home economics practitioners

5. See Penina Migdal Glazer and Miriam Slater, *Unequal Colleagues: The Entrance of Women into the Professions, 1890–1940* (New Brunswick: Rutgers University Press, 1987), and Robyn Muncy, *Creating a Female Dominion in American Reform, 1890–1935* (New York: Oxford University Press, 1991).

6. Joan Jacobs Brumberg and Nancy Tomes, "Women in the Professions: A Research Agenda for American Historians," *Reviews in American History* 10 (June 1982): 275–96; Susan Reverby, *Ordered to Care: The Dilemma of American Nursing, 1850–1945* (New York: Cambridge University Press, 1987); Barbara Melosh, *"The Physician's Hand": Work, Culture, and Conflict in American Nursing* (Philadelphia: Temple University Press, 1982); and Susan M. Reverby and Dorothy O. Helly, eds., *Gendered Domains: Rethinking Public and Private in Women's History* (Ithaca: Cornell University Press, 1992).

with the historical interpretations, we hope that lived reality will enhance historical knowledge.

The history of home economics in the twentieth century is rich with insights into gendered domains in the professions, business, and academia. The home economics movement led by Ellen Richards that began with the Lake Placid conferences (1899–1907) and resulted in the creation of the American Home Economics Association (AHEA) in 1909 marked a very different direction from the domestic economy advocated by Catharine Beecher. During this period the pioneers of home economics struggled to define the field, a task that was and continues to be difficult, fraught with tension, confusion, and compromise. This struggle for definition bears close scrutiny as we seek to understand the nature of home economics and how it sheds light on the intersection of gender and professionalism.

Home economics has had a particularly difficult time defining itself. At the first Lake Placid meeting in 1899 a primary order of business was the selection of a name. Household arts, domestic economy, domestic science, home economics—each term indicated different goals and different emphases, and each had its champions.[7] "Household arts" implied cooking and sewing and was tied to manual training in the public schools and cooking schools like the one popularized by Fannie Farmer in Boston. "Domestic economy" harked back to Catharine Beecher, echoing the title of her influential *Treatise on Domestic Economy* (1842). As it was employed in the 1890s, domestic economy focused on the housewife and her problems, particularly the "servant problem." As immigration patterns shifted in the 1880s and 1890s, middle- and upper-class women found it increasingly difficult to find paid help. Many of the activities pursued under the rubric of domestic economy addressed the servant problem—trying to upgrade domestic work, provide better training for immigrant girls, and put employers in touch with employees. The concept of "domestic science" tied the kitchen to the chemical laboratory, emphasizing nutrition and sanitation. It was the term preferred by Ellen Richards, the "engineer" of the modern home economics movement. Richards, trained in chemistry at Vassar and the Massachusetts Institute of Technology, saw domestic science as a way to move women trained in science into employment in academics and industry. The term "home economics" borrowed its perspective from the emerging social sciences and most clearly positioned the home in relation to the larger polity, encouraging reform and municipal housekeeping.

---

7. See Emma Seifrit Weigley, "It Might Have Been Euthenics: The Lake Placid Conferences and the Home Economics Movement," *American Quarterly* 26 (March 1974): 79–96.

After much debate, the Lake Placid group selected the term "home economics." By neatly tying the notion of the home as woman's traditional sphere to the cachet of the new social sciences, it represented a compromise acceptable to the diverse factions that made up the early home economics movement.

A committee on nomenclature continued to search during the next decade for a better alternative—an indication that tension existed among those who viewed home economics as primarily sociological and economic, those who viewed it as more closely tied to the sciences and the laboratory, and those who judged it in more traditional terms as related to women's domestic duties. The scientific faction, led by Wilbur O. Atwater of the U.S. Department of Agriculture, pressed for "home science." Yet it is striking that in justifying the change, Atwater argued on religious rather than scientific grounds, stating that he objected to "economics" because it "related the work of the conference to a too material basis and left out the soul."[8] Ellen Richards, never happy with "home economics," tried unsuccessfully to substitute "oekology" and later "euthenics." In time, her choice of "ecology" would win support. In the 1960s and 1970s several prominent home economics schools, including the prestigious College of Home Economics at Cornell University, changed their name from "home economics" to "human ecology."

In practice, the Lake Placid group adopted a tripartite terminology: "household arts" described work in primary school, "domestic science" fit courses taught in secondary school, and "home economics" applied to college and graduate work. Thus the choice of "home economics" in 1899 as the umbrella term for the Lake Placid conferences actually grew out of short-term contingencies, establishing a troubling pattern of allowing short-term goals to influence the definition and direction of the field.

Ellen Richards, who preferred the term "domestic science," conceded on the issue of nomenclature and presided over "home economics" conferences. Her willingness to compromise had a great deal to do with her plans to get home economics adopted as part of the curriculum at the elite women's colleges in the East. As a graduate of Vassar and founder of the Association of Collegiate Alumnae (a precursor to today's American Association of University Women), Richards had little use for the household arts contingent or the middle-class clubwomen who championed domestic economy. She wished to move home economics beyond cooking and sewing and finding better servants. What she had in mind was a professional field for educated women. At MIT she championed domestic science, but she recognized that home economics better suited the liberal arts curriculum of the elite eastern women's colleges.

8. *Fourth Annual Conference on Home Economics* (Lake Placid, N.Y., 1903), p. 84.

Richards, who was instrumental in getting domestic science courses taught at Wellesley and Smith, was dealt a major setback in 1893 when Bryn Mawr College determined that "there are not enough elements of intellectual growth in cooking or housekeeping to nourish a very serious or profound course of training for really intelligent women."[9] M. Carey Thomas, the president of Bryn Mawr, thought home economics was too sex stereotyped to fit in a curriculum designed to replicate the rigors of the male Ivy League colleges. Further, home economics suffered from being confused in the public mind with household skills, deemed nonacademic, and from its association with the agricultural colleges in the Midwest (presumed inferior to eastern schools) and its lowly eastern precursors, the schools of cookery. Ellen Richards was stung by the rebuff, but she quickly recognized that before she could gain academic acceptance for home economics it must be standardized, upgraded, and professionalized. The Lake Placid conferences were her response.

Richards worked consistently and effectively through the Lake Placid conferences to move home economics toward rigorous research in the natural and social sciences. At the center of her plan was the "provision for the higher education of some selected young women who shall be fitted by the best training for a higher leadership."[10] She accepted the term "home economics" because she hoped that under that label the subject would "find a logical place in the colleges and university course [of study] and not be confused with the mere 'household arts.'"[11]

Not all segments of the home economics movement embraced Richards's vision of the purpose of home economics, however. As attendance at the Lake Placid conferences grew from eleven to over seven hundred, conflicting voices were raised. Ellen Richards pointedly absented herself from the fifth conference, held in the summer of 1903 in Boston. There the household arts contingent mounted a rear-guard action, insisting that "the day will come when it will be considered as dignified to help in housework as to master typewriting or stenography."[12] As Richards constantly pointed out, woman's primary role had shifted from production in the home to consumption in the marketplace. With commercial laundries, ready-made clothing, and bakery bread readily available in towns and cities, why, she asked, "should we try to keep all domestic industries under our own roofs at such disadvantage and expense?"[13]

9. Quoted in Isabel Bevier and Susannah Usher, *The Home Economics Movement* (Boston: Whitcomb and Barrows, 1912), pp. 15–16.

10. "History and Outline of the First Conference," *Proceedings of the First, Second, and Third Conferences*, p. 3.

11. Ibid., p. 7.

12. *Fifth Annual Conference on Home Economics* (Lake Placid, N.Y., 1904), p. 45.

13. Ellen Richards, "Domestic Industries—In or Out—Why Not?" *Sixth Annual Conference on Home Economics* (Lake Placid, N.Y., 1905), pp. 27–31.

The goals and objectives of the nascent home economics movement were never entirely clear or consistent. Home economics formed part of the broader movement for vocational training which gained adherents in the decades following the Civil War. Educational and social reformers demanded changes in the curriculum to move it away from classical Greek and Latin toward subjects better suited to train workers and farmers. Manual or vocational training for boys formed the core of the new practical curricula. But what about girls? Many argued that girls needed training to prepare them for the tasks of homemaking and should have the same opportunities afforded boys in manual and agricultural programs. Although at one time advocates urged cooking courses for boys as well as girls and woodworking for both sexes, manual training and home economics soon became sex segregated, much to the dismay of women labor leaders who urged that girls be trained in ways that would lead to paid employment in industry. Strong traditional beliefs concerning woman's place worked to further the most conservative and traditional view of home economics. Legislators appeared willing to fund training for girls only if it promised to reinforce gender stereotypes. As a result, midwestern land-grant schools established home economics departments intended to promote domestic roles for young women. Ironically, the departments they created provided career opportunities for college-educated women to be gainfully employed outside the home and to gain a foothold in academia. The home economics faculties at the land-grant schools prepared students more for careers in teaching and institutional management than for housekeeping. By 1910 literally hundreds of women had found employment teaching home economics at every level from grade school to the college and university.

Home economics never did gain acceptance at the elite women's colleges, as Richards had hoped. Ironically, her efforts to professionalize the field backfired by giving her opponents at the Seven Sisters schools the ammunition they needed to prevent the formation of home economics departments in the women's colleges. In 1905 the committee on collegiate administration for the American Collegiate Association (ACA) unanimously passed a resolution stating that "home economics as such has no place in a college course for women" and instead "belongs in a professional course . . . taken after leaving colleges."[14] The ACA thus kept home economics out of the classroom by arguing that it had in fact become a profession and thus belonged in the postgraduate curriculum. The tactic neatly sidestepped controversy over the intellectual rigor of the subject and instead reinforced the conclusion that home economics had become too specialized for a liberal arts program. Infuriated, Richards railed against the

14. *Proceedings of the Eighth Annual Conference* (Lake Placid, N.Y., 1907), p. 38.

"stupid blindness" of the ACA and insisted that home economics "must form a part of the educational equipment of all *live* institutions."[15]

Rebuffed by the elite eastern women's schools, home economics watched as its balance of power shifted perceptibly away from Richards and her disciples in Boston even before her death in 1911. The midwest land-grant colleges, which had embraced home economics enthusiastically, and the Department of Agriculture, which actively supported research in home economics through its experiment stations, had the jobs and resources and increasingly held the power.

The extent to which the field of home economics continued to allow itself to be defined by external pressures, whether Richards's determination to gain its acceptance in the elite eastern women's colleges or the desire of college presidents in the Midwest to segregate women students in home economics departments, demonstrates a chronic problem in the field. The very fluidity and lack of structure that helped home economics find adherents also kept it from developing a central core of identity. Home economics could be whatever anyone wished it to be—conservative or reform, traditional or innovative, scientific or domestic. Home economists allowed, if not encouraged, the confusion. In an effort to expand women's opportunities and gain some measure of gender equity, home economists proved willing to trade on traditional views of woman's place—to use traditional terms to cloak untraditional activities.

The benefits and drawbacks of this strategy became even more problematic with the passage of a series of legislative measures which set the agenda for home economics in the twentieth century. Ironically, as Rima Apple points out in her essay "Liberal Arts or Vocational Training? Home Economics for Girls," the legislation that most benefited home economics financially also disadvantaged the field in the long run. Land-grant laws tied training for women to traditional notions of domesticity. Early home economics educators acquiesced, seeing in their departments something very different from the buttress to traditional female roles envisioned by male legislators. Two major pieces of legislation passed in the 1910s further set the parameters for home economics. The 1914 the Smith-Lever Act, designed to improve life in rural America, provided funds for home economics through the extension program of the Department of Agriculture. Smith-Lever did much to improve the lot of farm women, but at the very moment when the country was becoming increasingly urban, the Act tied home economics to rural life. The Smith-Hughes Act, passed in 1917, provided funding for home economics training and made the education of home economics teachers for the primary and secondary schools a central

15. Ellen Richards, "Euthenics in Higher Education: Better Living Conditions," *Eighth Annual Conference*, p. 34.

part of the mission of collegiate home economics. Unfortunately, Smith-Hughes funds tied home economics to vocational training at a time when universities had begun moving toward "pure" research. As a result, departments of home economics were denigrated as little more than teacher-training programs.

Home economics also suffered from the very important role it played in popularizing and applying theories developed in the social and natural sciences. Nancy Tomes in "Spreading the Germ Theory: Sanitary Science and Home Economics, 1880–1930," demonstrates the important work home economists undertook in promoting sanitation and public health. In "Modernizing Mothers: Home Economics and the Parent Education Movement, 1920–1945," Julia Grant points to the ways home economics helped to familiarize mothers with new theories in child development. Parents' clubs set up by home economists introduced material on psychology and child development in an atmosphere that allowed mothers to examine critically the work of the "experts."

Increasingly, as universities stressed "pure" research over "applied" science, this emphasis on popularization led to the devaluation of home economics. Gender stereotyping and sex discrimination also sabotaged home economics in academia. The troubles the field encountered as a woman's enclave within the male academy are documented in Margaret Rossiter's essay and are borne out in the reminiscences of Marjorie East, head of home economics at the Pennsylvania State University.

Outside the academy, home economists pushed for a professional identity but once again encountered the twin obstacles of gender stereotyping and sex discrimination. Lynn Nyhart, in "Home Economics in the Hospital, 1920–1930," shows how hospital dietitians seeking to professionalize their field found themselves caught between doctors and nurses in a struggle for turf.

The history of home economics seems rife with strategies that produced short-term gains and long-term problems. Keeping the field flexible allowed home economics to ride whatever hobby horse society had taken up at the moment. Thus home economics began as part of the reform ethos of progressivism. As I show in Chapter 1, "Ellen Richards and the Social Significance of the Home Economics Movement," early home economists stressed social service and municipal housekeeping. In the more conservative 1920s home economics focused more on the individual and less on social ills. The inauguration of the Children's Bureau in 1912 created what Robyn Muncy has called "a female dominion in American reform," which encouraged home economics practitioners to shift their focus to the child. When scientific management came into vogue in the 1920s, home economics was quick to jump on the bandwagon. In the process, professionalization, once tied to social service, became increasingly defined in masculine terms and female

"experts" like Christine Frederick chastised the housewife for her ignorance and inefficiency.

Emphasis on professionalization not only worked to separate home economists from other women but took on distinct class and racial biases. Some
of this tension becomes evident in Kathleen R. Babbitt's essay "Legitimiz-
ing Nutrition Education: The Impact of the Great Depression." Yet extension agents like Hazel Reed worked to make a real difference in people's
lives, as she shows in her reminiscences. Joan Jacobs Brumberg's photo essay clearly demonstrates how home economists' desire to set standards and
define the "good life" sometimes stifled racial and ethnic diversity and promoted a culturally bland, "white bread" world. Yet the extent to which the
social control model fails to capture the reality of the interaction between
home economists and the women they served becomes apparent in Carmen
Harris's work on black home demonstration agents in South Carolina. These
"fairy godmothers and magicians" worked against the odds to make a better life for black families. The reminiscences of Genevieve W. Thomas, an
African American home economics educator who worked in Georgia and
Florida, confirm the pattern Harris outlines.

Home economists who entered business faced a particularly difficult
task. They sought to maintain a professional posture in a climate in which
their employers often were interested only in "Selling Mrs. Homemaker."
The proliferation of home economics departments and test kitchens in business and industry provided home economists with welcome employment
opportunities but threatened the professionalism they had struggled so
hard to win. Many employers assumed that any woman could act as a home
economist and hired untrained women to staff their kitchens and push their
products. As Ronald R. Kline shows, home economists working for utility
companies acted as unreflective "agents of modernity," selling electricity to
farm families.

The AHEA compounded the problem. In its desire to open the field to all
comers, the organization set no standards for membership at its founding in
1909. By the 1920s, newly minted corporate "home economists" could lay
claim to professional status by affiliating with the AHEA. No wonder the
general public came to see corporate home economists as little more than
company flacks.

Trained home economists who found employment in business sought to
carry the educational mission of the field into the marketplace. Regina Lee
Blaszczyk's study of Lucy Maltby's work at Corning Glass and Lisa Mae
Robinson's look at Mary Engle Pennington's struggle with the ice industry
demonstrate the tension between sales and research, education and public
relations, that home economists experienced in business. Carolyn Goldstein perhaps sums it up best when she argues that although home economists were "part of the package," they worked hard to maintain their

professional mission—to be diplomats in the marketplace, negotiating between the consumer and the company. The reminiscences of Satenig St.Marie, the first woman vice-president of the JC Penney Company, document the opportunities and difficulties encountered by home economists in the business world.

In the long run, home economics, like nursing and other gendered professions, could never define itself outside of gender stereotypes. The strategy of using traditional ideas of womanhood to further untraditional activities had its pitfalls. But more to the point, any gendered domain seemed destined to discrimination. In the academy, not even a scientist of the stature of Agnes Fay Morgan at the University of California, Berkeley, could gain resources and respect for her department. As Margaret Rossiter points out, not until men moved into home economics in the 1960s did the field began to gain funding and legitimacy. Rossiter's brilliant piece of muckraking scholarship demonstrates clearly that gender, not merit, was the key factor in getting grants and institutional support. In business Lucy Maltby's experience at Corning Glass testified to the pervasive influence of gender stereotyping and sex discrimination. Maltby's major role in the research and development of new products for Corning yielded her neither the recognition nor the salary commensurate with her significant role in the company.

As home economics found itself increasingly beleaguered in the 1960s and 1970s it is ironic that it did not benefit from the new wave of feminism. Antipathy existed on each side in an era when style was often confused with substance and young feminists, like other activists of the day, subscribed to the motto "Don't trust anyone over thirty." Home economists did make an overture by inviting Robin Morgan to speak at their conference in 1973. Morgan's speech to the AHEA, however, left very little room for alliance. She began by stating unequivocally that the best thing career home economists could do was to "quit your jobs."[16] Second, she demanded that the AHEA actively lobby to remove home economics as a requirement from the secondary school curriculum. As one home economist responded, "Robin Morgan's attack came as a great shock to me because we've been teaching dual roles for women for years; I just couldn't believe we had many members who felt the woman's place was in the home."[17] In response to Morgan's challenge, the AHEA initiated a Woman's Role Committee. President Marjorie East stated, "If home economics does indeed perpetuate this [traditional and limited] concept of women, we have some rethinking to do."[18]

16. "What Robin Morgan Said at Denver," p. 13.
17. "The Women's Role Committee Speaks Out," *Journal of Home Economics* 65 (January 1973): 10.
18. Ibid.

In the ensuing decades, home economics has continued to grapple with its stereotype of "stitching and stirring" and attempted to update its mission and redefine its goals. As Virginia Vincenti points out in "Home Economics Moves into the Twenty-first Century," the field is still searching for a common core identity and a name that will more accurately reflect the range of its concerns.

While home economists have grown more introspective and self-critical, feminists, notably women's historians, who by the 1990s have experienced firsthand the frustrations and exhilaration of creating women's enclaves in academia, have grown less dismissive of home economics. It has taken nearly twenty-five years for the realization that feminism, women's history, and home economics have something to say and something to learn from one another. This volume marks a significant first step.

Home economists' active role in food conservation campaigns during World War I brought them unprecedented visibility and laid the groundwork for their movement into new careers. Courtesy Division of Rare and Manuscript Collections, Carl A. Kroch Library, Cornell University.

More Than Glorified Housekeeping

Home economists advocated more than glorified housekeeping. As a significant link between science and society, home economics applied scientific principles to address concerns of importance to many Americans, whether by combating dirt and disease or by popularizing modern theories of child rearing.

Home economists participated actively in the reform tradition of the early twentieth century which challenged the rigid determinism of Social Darwinism with its emphasis on heredity and its insistence on laissez-faire. Substituting an emphasis on environment over heredity and social justice over the survival of the fittest, reformers attacked the social problems brought about by the rise of industrial capitalism. Science and efficiency became their watchwords. Early pioneers in home economics shared this reformist ideology and activism as they worked to apply current theories of science and social science to daily life.

Sarah Stage points to the broad reform goals of the early home economics movement and shows that early home economists never intended to keep women in the kitchen. Ellen Richards used the traditional ideology of woman's place to urge women to do untraditional things, promoting the concept of social service and municipal housekeeping.

The turn of the century witnessed an explosion of new scientific knowledge, along with the birth of social sciences such as psychology and sociology. Home economists were in the vanguard in accepting and popularizing new scientific theories and research findings in microbiology, child psychology, and sanitary science. Nancy Tomes points to the important role home economists played in championing the germ theory and in teaching women ways to prevent the spread of infectious disease. Sanitary science made sense in a period before asepsis and antibiotics. Home economists' concern with dirt and disease, judged in light of the scientific knowledge of the time, was not just "make work" for women but a serious attempt to apply science to daily life and fight disease.

After World War I the reform impulse of progressivism gave way to a new emphasis on individualism. As the nation turned inward, so, too, did home economics. By the 1920s home economics narrowed its focus from broad social reform to the improvement of individual families with a new emphasis on the child and the value of proper parenting. Julia Grant shows how home economists "modernized motherhood," transmitting the latest theories on child development from the newly formed fields of sociology and psychology. The parent education movement they promoted provided a forum for women to interpret child development theories in light of their own experience and to reflect on their marital relationships. While "experts" like psychologist James Watson decried the inadequacy of American mothers, the child study clubs established by home economists created a space where women not only learned the new theories but found their own voices, evaluating the experts' advice in light of their own experience as mothers.

1 Ellen Richards and the Social Significance of the Home Economics Movement

SARAH STAGE

At its founding in 1909 the American Home Economics Association underscored the breadth of the new organization's vision by inviting into its membership "students, investigators, housekeepers, institutional managers, social and municipal workers, interested housewives and homemakers [and] professional workers in allied fields." The inclusiveness pointed to the emphasis placed on what its founder, Ellen Richards, called "the social significance of the home economics movement." The AHEA explicitly acknowledged its sense of social mission by enunciating as its goal "the improvement of living conditions in the home, the institutional household and the community."[1] Clearly "home" to these pioneers in home economics was not bounded by four walls. In fact, the discourse on the home in the early twentieth-century home economics movement points to much broader definitions of home and home economics than historians have acknowledged, definitions that worked to open avenues for women in careers in academics and social reform.

Historians have for the most part dismissed the home economics movement as a force for expanding women's options. They have largely missed an understanding of the significant evolution of the concept of Victorian domesticity championed by Catharine Beecher into the twentieth-century

I would like to thank my fellows in the Gender and Difference focused research group at the Center for Ideas and Society at the University of California, Riverside—Judy Coffin, June O'Connor, Georgia Warnke, Chris Campolo, and Luanne Castle. Our shared work and discussions rekindled my enthusiasm for this project and brought to bear new insights.

1. "Announcement: The American Home Economics Association and the Journal of Home Economics," *Journal of Home Economics* 1 (February 1909): 1.

home economics movement led by Ellen Richards. Home economics, as Richards practiced it, emphasized municipal housekeeping and formed an important component of women's political culture in the Progressive era.

Until a decade ago the idea that women participated in politics before the passage of the Nineteenth Amendment in 1920 amounted to heresy in the historical field. Politics, narrowly defined as voting and officeholding, remained in the eyes of most historians exclusively a male domain. The field of women's history has worked to redefine politics. Paula Baker, in her classic article "The Domestication of Politics," broke new ground by broadening the definition to include "any action, formal or informal, taken to affect the course of behavior of government or the community."[2] By redefining politics to include activities beyond voting and officeholding, Baker pointed to the importance of gender and to the significance of women's involvement in the larger political culture of the United States.

Baker's work made it clear that even at the height of the cult of domesticity, when the activities of middle-class women were supposedly circumscribed to the home, a distinctly female political subculture had emerged. As Baker pointed out, politics and domesticity were not at odds; women's political activity was firmly rooted in domesticity. The movement toward municipal housekeeping which began in the 1880s and played a central role in the politics of the Progressive era constituted a case in point. As any number of recent works point out, women's organizations combined the investigating techniques of the social sciences with a new emphasis on professionalism to expand women's political activities. We are only beginning to rediscover and appreciate the work Mary Beard did to document this transformation in her book *Woman's Work in Municipalities* (1915). Women formed a major impetus for progressive reform in the United States. "In the Progressive era," Baker tells us, "social policy—formerly the province of women's voluntary work—became public policy."[3]

Though it illuminated the significant role women played in the larger contours of American political life, the concept of the domestication of politics left largely oblique the mechanisms that enabled women's concerns to move from the periphery to the center of American politics in the Progressive period. To understand more fully the process by which politics became domesticated, it might be well to look at the other side of the phenomenon—to see how domesticity became politicized—specifically, to examine the social significance of the early home economics movement. This essay,

2. Paula Baker, "The Domestication of Politics: Women and American Political Society, 1780–1920," *American Historical Review* 89 (1984): 620–47.

3. Ibid., p. 640. See Mary Ritter Beard, *Woman's Work in Municipalities* (New York: D. Appleton, 1915). For the best treatment of women's importance in emerging social reform, see Robyn Muncy, *Creating a Female Dominion in American Reform, 1890–1935* (New York: Oxford University Press, 1991).

then, explores how the early home economics movement led by Ellen Richards helped transform domesticity into a vehicle to expand women's political power and looks at the role language played in enabling women to broaden their domestic duties to include social reform. By examining the discourse on the home we can observe how the term itself was gendered and how women and men sometimes used the word "home" in such distinct ways as to create a dual discourse containing a sharply conflicting set of inferences. Finally, by looking at the direction home economics took in the 1910s and 1920s, we can see how professionalism, embraced by women in home economics as a mechanism for female empowerment, ultimately fostered a more conservative view of the home and women's role, a view at odds with the social goals advocated by Ellen Richards, the founder of the home economics movement.

Placed in this broader context, the history of the early home economics movement can tell us a good deal about the strategies women used and the obstacles they encountered as they entered the public arena.

AT the turn of the century home economic developed into a profession that enabled and encouraged women to expand their activities beyond the home and kitchen. By urging women to conceive of their housekeeping responsibilities in the broadest possible social context, home economics played an important role in the politicization of domesticity. Ellen Richards, the first woman to hold a degree from Massachusetts Institute of Technology, worked to enlarge women's opportunities for scientific training and careers by redefining the home, enlarging its scope in a manner that encouraged women to move out of the domestic sphere and into the arena of social and political action.

In 1899, a decade before the founding of the AHEA, the founders of home economics met at Lake Placid to launch a formal home economics movement. The record of thir conference demonstrates that the last thing they had in mind was to keep women in the kitchen, a charge that has been leveled at home economics by generations of feminist critics. They were themselves career women or women active in public affairs. Seven earned their livings as teachers, lecturers, or authors: Maria Parloa, founder of the Boston Cooking School; Maria Daniell, her protégée, manager of the Lake Placid Club and a lecturer who gave demonstrations on food preparation; Anna Barrows, a pioneer writer on practical cookery and editor of the *New England Kitchen Magazine*; Louisa A. Nicholass, a teacher and organizer of one of the first courses in household arts at the State Normal School in Framingham, Massachusetts; Emily Huntington, founder of the Kitchen Garden method of teaching housekeeping to children; Alice Peloubet Norton, supervisor of domestic science in the public schools of Brookline,

Massachusetts, and later member of the department of household administration in the School of Education at the University of Chicago; and Ellen H. Richards, instructor of sanitary chemistry at the Massachusetts Institute of Technology and organizer of the New England Kitchen and the Boston School of Housekeeping.

Two women active in public life joined the group—Mrs. William G. Shailer, a clubwoman representing the National Household Economics Association (NHEA), and Mrs. William V. Kellen, a wealthy Boston philanthropist who financed the first school lunch program in the country. The hostess and host of the group, Annie Dewey and her husband, Melvil, were the founders of the Lake Placid Club, a cooperatively run educational and recreational community. Melvil Dewey, best remembered today for the creation of the Dewey decimal system, served as director of the state library and of home education for the state of New York.[4]

Ellen Richards, who masterminded the Lake Placid conferences, best represented the new breed of women who had taken up the cause of domestic science or home economics. A member of the first generation of college-educated women in the United States, she fashioned home economics to suit the needs of educated women like herself who sought an outlet for their talents and energies. Her career illuminates the genesis of the home economics movement and helps to explain its focus and direction. Until her death in 1911, Richards was the leader, the central strategist, and the "engineer" of the movement.[5]

Three central themes dominated Richards's life: a passion for science, a commitment to furthering women's education and careers, and a belief in the home as a source for social change. Richards found in home economics a way to bring her interests together in a new vocation for herself and for other college-educated women.

Born Ellen Henrietta Swallow in 1842, she was the only child of two New England schoolteachers. Her parents encouraged her intellectual bent, moving from Dunstable, Massachusetts, where Ellen was born, to nearby Westford so that she could attend an academy that accepted female pupils. At the same time, her mother's invalidism required Nellie, as she was called, to take over the management of the household at an early age.

Ellen Swallow graduated from the Westford academy in 1862 and briefly taught Latin in a country school before returning home to nurse her ailing mother. During this period of her life, when she was in her early twenties,

4. "Outline and History of the First Conference," *Proceedings of the First, Second and Third Conferences* (Lake Placid N.Y., 1902), pp. 8–9.

5. Isabel Bevier, *Home Economics in Education* (Philadelphia: J. B. Lippincott, 1924), p. 149. Bevier described Richards as home economics's "prophet, its interpreter, its conservator and engineer."

she experienced the classic symptoms of neurasthenia, a vague nervous disorder, which left her weak and debilitated. "I lived for over two years in Purgatory really," she later wrote. "I was thwarted and hedged in on every side; it seemed as though God didn't help me a bit and man was doing his best against me and my own heart even turned traitor, and well—altogether I had a sorry time of it."[6] A vigorous and healthy woman in her later life, Richards would look back on her illness as strikingly uncharacteristic. The extent to which her physical problems stemmed from her lack of intellectual outlet became apparent when her father agreed to send her to the newly opened Vassar College for Women. Her nervous symptoms, intense for over two years, quickly subsided.

Ellen Swallow entered Vassar in 1868 at the age of twenty-five. She had mastered enough Greek and Latin to join the junior class. Always practical, she passed up the opportunity to become the protégée of Vassar's most illustrious scientist, astronomer Maria Mitchell. She chose instead to work with Charles Farrar, who related chemistry to everyday life. This approach pleased Ellen, who was acutely sensitive to the charge that study spoiled women and who was eager to find practical work to supplement the family's flagging finances. "Professor Farrar encourages us to be very thorough," she wrote to her mother in 1869, "as the profession of analytical chemist is very profitable and means very nice and delicate work, fitted for ladies' hands."[7]

But upon her graduation from Vassar in 1870, every chemical firm she approached turned her down. Merrick and Gay of Boston put her off with the suggestion that she apply to the newly founded Massachusetts Institute of Technology (MIT). MIT, then in its infancy, was hungry for qualified students but reluctant to accept a woman. The institute admitted her as a "special student" in 1871, a category that saved her tuition while at the same time allowing MIT to keep her name off its student roster and avoid the precedent of coeducation. Richards later claimed that she would not have gone to MIT had she understood the terms.[8]

At MIT she found herself segregated in a special corner of the chemistry laboratory, "very much as a dangerous animal might have been."[9] Aware that she was on trial for her sex as well as her scholarship, she wrote her

---

6. Ellen Richards quoted in Caroline Hunt, *The Life of Ellen Richards* (Boston: Whitcomb and Barrows, 1912), p. 34.

7. Ellen Richards's letters home, in "The Early Days of Vassar," Ser. 2, *Vassar Miscellany* 28 (February 1899): 201.

8. "Committee on the Schools Report, 1882," Records of the MIT Alumni Association, 1870–1909, Massachusetts Institute of Technology, Institute Archives, Cambridge, Mass. (hereafter MIT).

9. Ellen Richards to William Otis Crosby, n.d., in Crosby Collection, MIT.

parents, "I hope in a quiet way I am winning a way which others will keep open."[10] She made herself useful in traditional womanly ways, sewing on buttons for her classmates and sweeping out the laboratory. Throughout her life she would use the camouflage of domesticity, as she did at MIT, to advance women's education and careers.

Ellen Swallow provided the entering wedge for women at MIT. She received her B.S. in 1873, becoming the first woman in the United States to hold a degree from MIT. Ambitiously, she prepared for the doctorate. But MIT did not wish to grant its first Ph.D. in chemistry to a woman. The faculty quietly discouraged her doctoral studies. She stayed on at MIT, marrying the young professor of mining and metallurgy Robert Hallowell Richards in 1875.

After an unorthodox honeymoon that consisted of an expedition to Nova Scotia with Robert and his students, the new Mrs. Richards plunged into the role of wife and homemaker with characteristic vigor. She had no intention of giving up her work and prided herself on her ability to manage a household at the same time she pursued her career as a research chemist. During this period she undertook the first scientific test of the Massachusetts water supply, personally testing more than twenty-five hundred samples.

In her spare time she worked to further the cause of women's education. In 1873 she joined Boston's Woman's Education Association (WEA), a group that was angered at Harvard's refusal to provide access to women.[11] With tact and skill she used her position as a relative by marriage to William Rogers, then president of MIT, to push successfully for women's advancement at the institute. Her first major victory came in 1876, when she persuaded MIT to open a Woman's Laboratory. There she taught chemistry to local women who wished to pursue graduate work. Within three years after the lab opened, MIT allowed women to be examined for degrees on the same basis as male students. "I am seeing the realization of my hopes and wishes in all directions," Richards confided to a friend from Vassar. "At the Institute women now have their position and can take a degree. This is a great step which I have been waiting for."[12] In 1883 the Woman's Laboratory was torn down and women were permitted to join the men in MIT's classrooms. That same year Ellen Richards became the first woman faculty member at MIT when she was named instructor in sanitary chemistry, the position she held until her death in 1911.[13]

10. Richards quoted in Hunt, *Life*, p. 91.

11. See Woman's Education Association, Annual Reports, Massachusetts Historical Society, Boston (hereafter MHS).

12. Ellen Richards to Anna Mineah, [summer] 1879, Ellen Richards Papers, Vassar College, Poughkeepsie, N.Y. (hereafter VC).

13. Caroline Hunt does Richards an injustice in her biography by stating that Richards opposed coeducation (pp. 147–48). The MIT archives show that she actively worked for it. See

Although Richards never taught a single course in home economics during her long career at MIT, her early experience in the Woman's Lab initiated her interest in domestic science. In the lab she applied science to problems women encountered in everyday life. Her experiments led to the publication of *The Chemistry of Cooking and Cleaning* (1880) and *Food Materials and Their Adulterations* (1885). Writing to a friend, she described her new work in domestic science and remarked, "I seem to have got[ten] drawn into that track now and must follow it out whether or no."[14]

Richards's interest in domestic science formed a part of a broader movement just beginning in the 1870s and 1880s. The social and economic changes fostered by the rapid growth of industrial capitalism in the decades following the Civil War led to a clamor for educational reform. Critics attacked the classical Greek and Latin curriculum and demanded practical courses to prepare students for work in industry or on the farm. The founding of the Massachusetts Institute of Technology in 1865 provided simply one example of the influence of the industrial spirit on academia. Manual training institutes, industrial education in the public schools, and the agricultural colleges established by the Morrill land-grant laws of 1862 and 1890 provided practical education for boys. Training in domestic skills, considered the equivalent practical education for girls, began to gain adherents by the 1870s. The decade witnessed a proliferation of courses in cooking and sewing. The land-grant colleges of the Midwest led the movement by creating departments of domestic arts and science; in the East cooking schools became popular.

Ellen Richards, not surprisingly, championed domestic science. She had, as she would later confess, "faith in science as a cure-all."[15] In the 1890s she had already begun to put her scientific theories to work in two social experiments—the New England Kitchen and the Boston School of Housekeeping.

The New England Kitchen began as an experiment funded by Boston philanthropist Pauline Agassiz Shaw to provide cheap, nutritious food to the working class in the hope of reducing alcoholism among the poor. Shaw gave Ellen Richards a thousand dollars to equip and staff a model kitchen. Richards, more interested in scientific diet than in temperance, welcomed the chance to put her theories on proper nutrition into practice. In 1890 the kitchen opened its doors in downtown Boston. A "food depot" rather than a restaurant, the New England Kitchen sold soups, stews, and puddings to be carried home for consumption. Richards tested each dish

---

Ellen Richards to Emma Savage Rogers, April 24, 1882, and Records of the Committee on Instruction, September 29, 1883, MIT.

14. Hunt, *Life*, p. 163.

15. Ellen Richards, "Ten Years of the Lake Placid Conference on Home Economics: Its History and Aims," *Lake Placid Conference on Home Economics, Proceedings of the Tenth Annual Conference, Chautauqua, New York, July 6–10, 1908* (Lake Placid, 1909), p. 20.

at her MIT lab to ensure its nutritive value. Although the New England Kitchen established Richards as a pioneer in the scientific study of nutrition, it failed to change the eating habits of Boston's poor. After three years Richards concluded, "The very poor are of two classes—those who know how to live cheaper than we can feed them or can ever hope to feed them and those that do not care for clean, wholesome food."[16] The insistence on Yankee cuisine, with its New England boiled dinners and Indian puddings, no doubt accounted for some of the resistance. Boston's immigrant poor realized they were being sold more than just a dinner. A young Irish boy, when pressed to buy an Indian pudding, responded, "You can't make a Yankee of me that way!"[17]

Richards's failure with the New England Kitchen did not diminish her desire to take domestic science out to the community. She chose as her next practical experiment the Boston School of Housekeeping, which had begun in 1897 as an attempt to solve the vexing "servant problem." In the late nineteenth century, as factories, offices, schoolrooms, and stores attracted women from the older immigrant groups, middle-class women, who for years had relied on Irish domestics, complained that they could no longer find good help. The School of Housekeeping, which opened on St. Botolph Street in 1897, marked an attempt by the Women's Educational and Industrial Union (WEIU) to attract the "better class of immigrants" back into service by raising the standard of training and providing a certificate. But the school proved a dismal failure. Domestics, already in short supply, had no incentive to spend eight months without pay while learning the trade. Nor did employers wish to send their servants away for the protracted course. At this juncture, the WEIU invited Richards to revamp the school's curriculum.[18]

Richards, who had little patience with the servant problem, soon transformed the School of Housekeeping into a "professional school for home and social economics" designed to train educated women for household and institutional management. Already she looked forward to the day when the college woman would apply scientific principles "not only in her own

16. Ellen H. Richards to Edward Atkinson, November 22, 1894, Edward Atkinson Papers, MHS.

17. Ellen H. Richards and Mary H. Abel, *The Story of the New England Kitchen*, part 2 (Boston: Whitcomb and Barrows, 1893), p. 11. For a fuller treatment of Richards's role in the New England Kitchen see Sarah Stage, "From Domestic Science to Social Housekeeping: The Career of Ellen Richards," in *Power and Responsibility: Case Studies in American Leadership*, ed. David M. Kennedy and Michael E. Parrish (New York: Harcourt Brace Jovanovich, 1986), pp. 211–28.

18. "School of Housekeeping," Records of the Women's Educational and Industrial Union, Arthur and Elizabeth Schlesinger Library on the History of Women in America, Radcliffe College, Cambridge, Mass.

home, but in all work for the amelioration of the condition of mankind."[19] The revamped School of Housekeeping combined two of Richards's pet projects: it demonstrated the applicability of women's scientific education to daily life at the same time it promoted careers for women in home economics or domestic science. Marion Talbot, a Richards protégée and teacher at the school, demonstrated the importance of the School of Housekeeping as a training ground when she left to become dean of women at the University of Chicago. Just as Richards hoped, domestic science was turning into a vehicle to further careers for women in institutional management and academia.[20]

Richards's desire to professionalize home economics and mold it into a career track for college-educated women clashed with the ideas of those who viewed home economics in more traditional terms, either as a means to improve women's skills in cooking and sewing or as a device to train better servants. Already the emphasis on household skills had hampered Richards in her struggle to get domestic science or home economics accepted as part of the curriculum at her alma mater, Vassar, and at the other elite women's colleges. Domestic science suffered both from its confusion in the public mind with household skills, deemed nonacademic, and from its association with the agricultural colleges in the Midwest (presumed inferior to eastern schools). Bryn Mawr spoke for the Seven Sisters, concluding, "There are not enough elements of intellectual growth in cooking or housekeeping to furnish a very serious or profound course of training for really intelligent women."[21] Stung by this rebuff, Richards acknowledged that before she could gain academic acceptance for domestic science, it must be standardized, systematized, upgraded, and professionalized.

A woman of broad vision, Richards realized that she would have to seize control of the nascent home economics movement and move it away from its preoccupation with bread baking and better servants. To do so she needed to create a national professional organization. But this goal was complicated by the existence of the National Household Economics Association, an organization composed largely of middle-class clubwomen who had founded the group at the Columbian Exposition in 1893 to deal specifically with the servant problem. Its avowed purpose was "to secure skilled

19. Ellen Richards, "The Relation of College Women to Progress in Domestic Science," paper presented at the Association of College Alumnae, October 24, 1890, clipping in Ellen Richards Papers, VC.

20. See Henrietta I. Goodrich, "Practical Experiments in Home Economics: The School of Housekeeping," *Journal of Home Economics* 3 (October 1911): 366–67.

21. Quoted in Isabel Bevier and Susannah Usher, *Home Economics Movement* (Boston: Whitcomb and Barrows, 1912), pp. 15–16.

labor in every department of our homes."[22] With great diplomacy and tact, Richards set out to supplant the NHEA.

The meeting at Lake Placid in 1899 marked her first step. Characteristically, Richards chose to work by indirection; she hand-picked the participants and had Annie and Melvil Dewey issue the formal invitations. Rather than create an organization that might be seen as a rival to the NHEA, she asked ten women active in home economics to meet at Lake Placid with the understanding that they would "work through existing agencies."[23] The group was informal, with no constitution or bylaws, but it did elect Ellen Richards chair.

The agenda of the first Lake Placid meeting clearly demonstrated Richards's emphasis on improving women's education and upgrading the field of home economics. Ten of the fifteen topics under discussion dealt specifically with education. Perhaps the most significant statement, the boldest announcement of Richards's purpose, was contained in the call for "provision for the higher education of some selected young women who shall be fitted by the best training for a higher leadership."[24] What Richards advocated amounted to the training of a college-educated elite to serve as the vanguard of the new home economics movement.

Richards's plan was to emphasize the scientific nature of home economics by bringing together the best minds in the field for a yearly series of small, select meetings. Within five years the Lake Placid conference grew in numbers from the original ten participants to over seven hundred. Just as Richards had intended, it supplanted the NHEA. That organization collapsed in 1903 when the General Federation of Women's Clubs absorbed its local chapters. There was no longer any need for the organization, its last president acknowledged, "as the Lake Placid conference was now doing much better work along the same lines."[25]

Richards, who liked working with men as well as women, attracted to the Lake Placid meetings pioneers in the study of nutrition such as Wilbur O. Atwater of the Department of Agriculture's office of experiment stations. Atwater and his assistant, Alfred C. True, proved to be important allies. They cooperated with the early home economists, hiring their graduates, publishing their research, and generally testifying to the scientific respectability of their work.[26]

22. For a clear statement of the purpose of the NHEA see "Report of the National Household Economic Association," *American Kitchen Magazine* 4 (December 1895): 131–42.

23. "Outline and History of the First Conference," p. 3.

24. Ibid.

25. Linda Hull Larned, "The National Household Economics Association, 1893–1903," *Journal of Home Economics* 1 (April 1909): 185–86.

26. See Ellen Richards to Miss [Laura Drake] Gill, n.d., in the Ellen Richards Papers, Sophia Smith Collection, Smith College, Northampton, Mass.

Richards's emphasis on professionalism and education prevailed in the ten years of the Lake Placid conferences. The collapse of the NHEA opened the way for the creation of a new national organization. The American Home Economics Association was founded in 1909 and elected Ellen Richards its first president.

Richards's success in capturing the leadership of the home economics movement did not mean that she alone dictated its course. She dominated but did not control the coalition of interests which came together in December 1908 under the rubric of the AHEA. Her ability to compromise was evident in the name of the new organization. Richards, who preferred "domestic science," presided over a "home economics" association.

Twice Ellen Richards tried to coin a word to replace home economics. In the 1880s she had championed "oekology," freely translated as "the science of right living." But she abandoned the term when it became clear that it had already been appropriated as "ecology" by the biological sciences.[27] At the sixth Lake Placid conference in 1904 she tried unsuccessfully to substitute the term "euthenics," which she defined as "the science of controllable environment."[28] Richards meant to challenge Francis Galton's eugenics, which emphasized social control through breeding. Euthenics posited that social change could be produced by individuals acting decisively to alter their environment. Richards envisioned a vanguard of scientifically trained women and men who would act as social engineers. Euthenics looked forward to a new era which promised women a much more active role in the shaping of society. An amalgam of domestic science, economics, and sociology, euthenics fit squarely in the reform Darwinist tradition that informed the broader movement for social melioration contemporaries called the Progressive movement.[29]

The equation of domestic science with social housekeeping implicit in the concept of euthenics had emerged year after year at Lake Placid. "Municipal housekeeping" was first mentioned in 1900, when Henrietta I. Goodrich, Richards's assistant at the Boston School of Housekeeping, outlined her work and urged professional training for women as "social ser-

27. Robert Clarke conflates the two terms in his informative but eccentric study of Richards, *Ellen Swallow, the Woman Who Founded Ecology* (Chicago: Follett, 1973).

28. *Sixth Annual Conference on Home Economics* (Lake Placid, N.Y., 1905), pp. 64–65.

29. See Emma Seifrit Weigley, "It Might Have Been Euthenics: The Lake Placid Conferences and the Home Economics Movement," *American Quarterly* 26 (1974): 79–96. Marjorie Brown in *Philosophical Studies of Home Economics*, vols. 1 and 2 (East Lansing, Mich.: College of Human Ecology, 1985), has distinguished between Richards's emphasis on science and Talbot's on social science. She overlooks the extent to which Richards and Talbot were strong allies who worked against the household arts contingent. Certainly euthenics, as Richards defined it, partook equally of science and social science and was part of reform Darwinism, the ideology that emphasized environment over heredity and encouraged social activism.

vants."[30] The category of municipal housekeeping was given a prominent place in a home economics syllabus drafted that same year. And in a special report issued on elementary and secondary schooling, the committee on education underscored the expansion of the domain of home economics when it castigated the "ignorance of men and women together in the management of that larger household, the city."[31]

As early as 1902 Marion Talbot had summed up the broader view of the nature and purpose of home economics:

> The demand for home economics which will be met in time is a different kind. It is the demand which shows that the making of bread is not an essential part of the making of a home. . . . That the obligations of home life are not by any means limited to its own four walls, that home economics must always be regarded in light of its relation to the general social system, that men and women are alike concerned in understanding the processes, activities, obligations and opportunities which make the home and family effective parts of the social fabric.[32]

Apparent in Talbot's message was a call for women to move out from the home and to participate in the social activism of progressive reform, which her broad definition of the home made integral to home economics.

This insistence on the social significance of home economics prevailed. At its founding, the AHEA enunciated its purpose in terms indicating that home economics encompassed the larger community. "The object of this association shall be to improve the conditions of living in the home, the institutional household, and the community."[33] The organization's charge was at once a call to action and a rallying cry for women to move out from the domestic sphere to take on the task of municipal housekeeping. As such it was domesticity politicized, a view best summed up in Frances Willard's observation that "government was only housekeeping on the broadest scale."[34]

The social and political activism that was so much a part of the AHEA's charge in 1908 remained among its avowed goals for over twenty years. But ultimately, the AHEA narrowed its vision. In 1930 the AHEA changed its objective to "the development and promotion of standards of home living that will be satisfying to the individual and profitable to society."[35]

30. *Proceedings of the First, Second and Third Conferences*, pp. 29–39.

31. "Report of the Special Committee of the Lake Placid Conference on Home Economics in Elementary and Secondary Schools, 1901," Appendix in *Proceedings of the First, Second, and Third Conferences*, p. 3.

32. *Fourth Annual Conference*, p. 22.

33. Keturah E. Baldwin, *The AHEA Saga* (Washington, D.C.: American Home Economics Association, 1949), p. 21.

34. Frances Willard to Susan B. Anthony, January 26, 1898, Harper Collection, Huntington Library, San Marino, Calif.

35. Baldwin, *AHEA Saga*, p. 26.

Although the link between the betterment of the home and society was never entirely severed, a shift from social activism to scientific management became clear. Rather than training women for careers in social service and municipal housekeeping, home economics now trained professional experts whose job it was to promote "standards of home living," presumably for a legion of housewives to uphold in the home.

To a certain extent, Ellen Richards presaged the rise of scientific management and the emphasis on expertise apparent in the subsequent course of the AHEA. Certainly her faith in science contained the seeds of scientific management. Yet it is clear that Richards's conception of the home was much broader than that of the efficiency experts who followed her. Richards urged women to conceive of housekeeping in the broadest sense and to make careers of carrying the values of the home into the community at large. Christine Frederick, who best represented the new breed of scientific managers, rejected the social significance of home economics and sought to bring women back into the kitchen. "Our greatest enemy," she stated flatly in 1914, "is the woman with the career."

> Let such a woman come into the home and express her art through its decoration, its furnishings, and its color schemes; or instead of going into a narrow field of dietetics, let her come into her home and there plan balanced menus and study nutrition values for her own family. Let her find it just as interesting to care for her own children as it is to go down to the east side and take care of Annie Bulowski.36

Frederick's vision of the purpose of home economics was clearly inimical to that of Richards. To understand how the mission of home economics changed in the early decades of the twentieth century calls for a close examination of the discourse on the home at the turn of the century.

To say that "home" was (and continues to be) a heavily loaded term is certainly an understatement. Increasingly in the nineteenth century the word stood for an entire constellation of values and beliefs, a sentimentalized but nevertheless potent response to the threat to traditional patterns of living imposed by urban industrialism. Home took its meaning, as we learn from deconstruction, as much from opposition as from signification. In the nineteenth century, as industrialism separated work space and living space, home came to mean more than a simple domicile. It was instead a "haven from the heartless world," at once a physical place and an emotional state, where the clamor of the marketplace was to be muted by the nurturing

---

36. Christine Frederick, "Points in Efficiency," *Journal of Home Economics* 6 (June 1914): 280.

presence of the wife and mother. In nineteenth-century discourse, home represented the female, woman's separate sphere, while the world at large, the public, competitive domain of the market, became "a man's world." This symbolic bifurcation of the world into separate spheres, although by no means descriptive of actual experience, nevertheless served to empower women at the same time it circumscribed their activities.

The moral superiority ascribed to women as keepers of the hearth and home was soon appropriated by women who demanded a broader field of action. Women like Ellen Richards used the concept of the home, with its implicit challenge to the values of urban industrialism, to buttress female moral authority and to press for a greater role for women in social or municipal housekeeping.

Ellen Richards's conception of the social significance of home economics drew its force from the gendered nature of the discourse on the home. The conflation of femininity, domesticity, and morality formed the backbone of the nineteenth-century cult of true womanhood. By stretching the definition of the home to encompass "that larger household, the city," Richards was able to broaden woman's sphere into municipal housekeeping without directly challenging the doctrine of domesticity. Home, as Richards understood the term, became emblematic of woman's moral authority. Ultimately, she used the term as a code word for that power. In her lexicon, which she shared with members of the advance guard of home economics such as Marion Talbot, women's moral authority coupled with their domestic skills allowed them boldly to move into a male world and clean it up, as if it were no more than a dirty house.

Others took a less expansive view of the definition of the home. The remarks of the dignitaries who addressed the American Home Economics Association at its founding in 1908–9 hint at the way the male speakers consistently adopted a more literal definition that emphasized the home as a physical space presided over by a woman helpmeet yet firmly under the control of male authority. Conceiving of the home in these terms did not so much undercut woman's moral authority as circumscribe it, tying the moral force of women to a very concrete and specified realm, the "home." Thus the commissioner of education, Elmer E. Brown, rhetorically reduced the work of the AHEA to the merely decorative, stating that the "work of making more attractive and wholesome homes is work that is going to uplift the moral life of our people."[37] Alfred True of the Department of Agriculture saw the purpose of the organization as to "make better homes" and asked rhetorically: "Can we maintain them as the pure source and happy environment of a vigorous childhood; can we keep them as the satisfactory sup-

---

37. "Organization and First Meeting of the American Home Economics Association," *Journal of Home Economics* 1 (February 1909): 27.

porters and encouragers of manhood and womanhood; can we hold them as the sure solace and refuge of old age?"[38] The literalness of the male speakers' view of the home was perhaps most clear and concrete in the remarks of John Hamilton, supervisor of farmers institutes in the U.S. Department of Agriculture, who exhorted home economists to "go and tell country people how to put a bathroom in every house in the United States."[39]

These literal notions of the home may be contrasted with the broader vision enunciated by Richards and her disciple Mary Hinman Abel. In her introductory remarks, Richards insisted that "home economics demands a study of ways and means to maintain a training school for good citizens at a cost within the reach of all."[40] Her own work, which emphasized women's new role as consumers, focused on economic and social issues, not on housekeeping or decoration. Abel, who followed John Hamilton on the platform, reminded her audience that "we must remember the city woman as well as the country woman." She then went on to discuss not the betterment of individual homes but improved public facilities for entire communities.[41]

This simple comparison hints at the existence of a dual discourse on the home in the early twentieth century in which the word "home" itself contained an entirely different set of inferences from those Richards and other women activists drew upon to expand women's opportunities. A more restrictive discourse on the home, one that equated home with traditional housekeeping functions and circumscribed female activity, was carried on simultaneously with the discourse fostered by Richards and the vanguard of home economists. Although both men and women participated in this dual discourse (we must read carefully to understand what was meant by the term "home"), the speeches cited above clearly indicate the antithetical uses to which the gendered concept of the home could be put.

By the 1920s home economics lost much of its sense of social mission. The American Home Economics Association, spelling out its goals in 1930, emphasized "standards of home living . . . satisfying . . . to the individual . . . and profitable to society," managing in one sentence to incorporate the Hoover era's emphasis on standards, individuality, and profitability. The change in focus away from the progressive ethos of reform and municipal housekeeping indicated as well the changing position of women in society and the decline of a gender-specific notion of

38. Ibid., p. 31.
39. Ibid., p. 34.
40. Ibid., p. 25.
41. Ibid., p. 36.

woman's special mission. Already by the 1910s the moral authority women could command as a result of the conflation of femininity, morality, and domesticity was giving way. Progressivism, with its emphasis on efficiency, expertise, and professionalism (an emphasis personified by Christine Frederick), challenged assertions of female essentialism and undercut woman's moral authority.

Ellen Richards and the early advocates of home economics who championed professionalism did not seem to recognize that "professionalism," like "home" was very much a gendered term, in this case one that uncritically incorporated notions of male objectivity. The female professional, then, was anomalous, a contradiction in terms. To exist at all she had to fight for footing on male ground and in male terms. In home economics women professionals like Christine Frederick accomplished this fancy footwork by separating themselves from the rank and file of women. In the process, home economics moved away from being a force to expand women's opportunities toward a professional track in which a group of female experts dictated "standards of home living" to women whose job it was presumably to remain in the kitchen and carry out their commands.

Frederick's hostility toward the "career woman," expressed as early as 1914, marked the beginning of a backlash against women's reform work outside the home, paradoxically led by a new group of professional career women like those in home economics. Frederick would have dismissed as nonsense the idea that the home constituted a moral force for female activism and not simply a physical place where women labored. She conceived of her task as a scientific attempt to upgrade that workplace, much in the same way her male counterparts worked to streamline the shop and the factory. Already by the second decade of the twentieth century, politicized domesticity, with its emphasis on volunteerism, reform, and uplift, had no place in the professional discourse of home economics, just as concern for the Annie Bulowskis of the world was not only falling out of vogue but falling into the hands of a professional elite of social workers.

But to dwell on the conservative direction home economics took in the 1920s and 1930s is to miss the significant role the early home economics movement played in the Progressive era. Far from circumscribing women's activities to the home, the home economics movement led by Ellen Richards called upon the educated woman to apply scientific principles "not only in her own home" but "in all work for the amelioration of the condition of mankind."[42] Richards's politicization of domesticity encouraged women to undertake municipal housekeeping and enabled them to take a

42. Ellen Richards, "The Relation of College Women to Progress in Domestic Science," paper presented to the Association of Collegiate Alumnae, October 21, 1890, clipping in Ellen Richards Papers, VC.

prominent place in the vanguard of Progressive reform. As early advocates of home economics insisted, "Home is in the mind and the heart, not in the kitchen."[43]

43. *Fourth Annual Conference*, p. 61.

2 Spreading the Germ Theory: Sanitary Science and Home Economics, 1880–1930

NANCY TOMES

In search of scientific principles to uplift the American home, the founders of the home economics movement at the turn of the century derived powerful insights from the new germ theory of disease, which gained widespread acceptance in the late 1800s. Teaching American women to master the invisible workings of the microbe in everyday life became a central element of the "science of controllable environment" envisioned by Ellen Richards and her compatriots. Bacteriology figured prominently in the early discipline's teachings about a wide range of topics, including home sanitation, interior decoration, and food preparation. Home economists stressed that the American housewife, whether dusting or canning, planning her parlor decor or nursing a sick child, could make an important contribution to the war against deadly diseases such as tuberculosis and typhoid. As Ellen Richards explained, "Sweeping and cleaning and laundry work are all processes of sanitation and not mere drudgery imposed by tradition, as some people seem to think." What home economists variously termed "sanitary" or "bacteriological" cleanliness served as a prime example of the importance of truly scientific housekeeping.[1]

This essay is drawn from a chapter in my book, *The Gospel of Germs: Men, Women, and the Microbe in American Life, 1870–1930* (Cambridge: Harvard University Press, forthcoming). My research has been generously supported by the National Endowment for the Humanities (Grant No. RH-21055-92) and the National Library of Medicine (Grant No. R01 LM0579-01). Its contents are solely the responsibility of the author and do not necessarily represent the official views of either the NEH or the NLM. I want to thank Joan Jacobs Brumberg, Sally Gregory Kohlstedt, Emma Weigley, Sarah Stage, and Virginia Vincenti for their comments on earlier drafts.

1. Ellen H. Richards, *Sanitation in Daily Life*, 3d ed. (Boston: Whitcomb and Barrows, 1915), p. 3. For an overview of the early home economics movement, see Sarah Stage, "From Domes-

Perhaps no aspect of the early home economics movement has been more profoundly misunderstood than its promotion of these new standards of cleanliness. In the late 1960s, when the "second wave" of feminists began to criticize the ways scientific experts had fostered restrictive roles for women, home economists' teachings on the subject made an easy target. The most cogent of the new feminist critiques, Barbara Ehrenreich and Deirdre English's widely read book *For Her Own Good: 150 Years of the Experts' Advice to Women,* included a chapter tellingly titled "Microbes and the Manufacture of Housework," which argued that home economists employed pseudo-scientific information about disease prevention to busy American women with a fruitless pursuit of cleanliness. "The scientific content of 'scientific cleaning' was extremely thin," Ehrenreich and English asserted. "The domestic scientists were right about the existence of germs, but neither they nor the actual scientists knew much about the transmission and destruction of germs."[2]

Contrary to this point of view, I will argue that the doctrine of scientific cleanliness taught by early home economists was not only consistent with the public health practice of the time but also represented far more than busywork. In an era when infectious diseases were the leading cause of death and municipal public health services were still limited and unreliable, the lessons of what S. Maria Elliott called "household bacteriology" had some real utility.[3] Home economists played a particularly important role in extending useful knowledge about evading microbial harms beyond the sanitarily privileged urban middle classes to recent immigrants, African Americans, and farm families, who in the early 1900s had limited access to pure drinking water, efficient sewage systems, or safe food supplies. The significance of bacteriological cleanliness began to diminish only in the 1920s, as improving living standards and declining mortality rates from infectious diseases lessened emphasis on the domestic "battle with bacteria."[4]

---

tic Science to Social Housekeeping: The Career of Ellen Richards," in *Power and Responsibility: Case Studies in American Leadership*, ed. David M. Kennedy and Michael E. Parrish (New York: Harcourt Brace Jovanovich, 1986), pp. 211–28; and Emma S. Weigley, "It Might Have Been Euthenics: The Lake Placid Conferences and the Home Economics Movement," *American Quarterly* 26 (March 1974): 79–96.

2. Barbara Ehrenreich and Deirdre English, *For Her Own Good: 150 Years of the Experts' Advice to Women* (New York: Doubleday, 1978), p. 159. For a recent, less critical assessment of the home economics movement, see Suellen Hoy, *Chasing Dirt: The American Pursuit of Cleanliness* (New York: Oxford University Press, 1995), esp. pp. 153–56.

3. S. Maria Elliott, *Household Bacteriology* (Chicago: American School of Home Economics, 1907).

4. The phrase "battle with bacteria" appears in "Bacteriology of the Household," *Cornell Reading-Course for Farmers' Wives*, N.S. 1, no. 4 (February 1909): 89.

Placing the home economics movement in the context of the prevailing disease environment and public health ideology of the time helps to explain the changing salience of domestic cleanliness to its educational mission. The waxing and waning of attention to disease prevention in the household is particularly interesting in light of the current resurgence of anxieties about the threat of infectious disease. For a variety of reasons, including the worldwide epidemic of AIDS, the increase in drug-resistant tuberculosis, and the general weakening of the public health infrastructure, Americans in the 1990s have become less complacent about their safety from the invisible world of microorganisms. Home economists' efforts to foster a sense of mastery over the microbe earlier in this century suggest some intriguing parallels to contemporary confrontations with a new generation of "superbugs."[5]

In 1899, the year of the first Lake Placid conference on home economics, the United States was in the midst of a national crusade to control the spread of infectious diseases. Never before in American history had the public health movement been so focused on the dangers of such diseases or so confident of its ability to reduce their ravages by prevention alone. High rates of many communicable diseases, particularly tuberculosis; changes in the social order such as urbanization and immigration that made those diseases more visible and menacing; new forms of print culture which facilitated mass health education; and, last but not least, new scientific theories of contagion that made the prevention of disease seem more feasible all prompted Progressive-era campaigns against infectious disease.[6]

The public health crusades represented a response to a genuinely dangerous disease environment. Although the death rates from most infectious diseases began to drop in the late 1800s, for reasons that are still unclear, they still accounted for the majority of deaths in 1900. Tuberculosis led the list of fatal diseases, accounting for roughly 10 percent of all deaths; among people in the prime of life, aged twenty to forty, the death rate was even higher, an average of one in four people. Influenza, pneumonia, and typhoid added substantially to the death rolls. Rates of infant and child mortality from diseases such as diphtheria, scarlet fever, and nonspecific diarrheal infections remained high in large cities, even

5. Laurie Garrett, *The Coming Plague: Newly Emerging Diseases in a World out of Balance* (New York: Farrar, Straus, and Giroux, 1994), illustrates the growing concern about so-called superbugs, which include new viruses such as AIDS and known forms of bacteria that have become resistant to antibiotics.

6. For overviews of the nineteenth-century American public health movement, see John Duffy, *The Sanitarians: A History of American Public Health* (Urbana: University of Illinois Press, 1990), and George Rosen, *The History of Public Health* (New York: MD Publications, 1958).

among affluent families.[7] The menace of infectious diseases was compounded by the paucity of means available to combat them. As of 1900, physicians could offer patients only immunizations against smallpox and rabies, plus a diphtheria antitoxin. The Progressive-era medicine chest held no "magic bullets," that is, drugs able to destroy the invading microbes without also killing their unlucky human hosts. The discovery of effective antimicrobial drugs remained a scientific ambition rather than a reality.[8]

Given the limits on medicine's curative resources, prevention offered the best method to reduce the toll of infectious diseases. Although researchers had not yet produced effective cures, they had developed a useful body of knowledge about how those diseases originated and spread so that they could be better avoided by conscious public and individual action. The late nineteenth-century public health movement's robust confidence in the power of prevention reflected growing certainty about the fundamental causes of disease.[9]

Beginning in the 1830s and 1840s, Anglo-American public health reformers had developed a "sanitary science" that linked organic chemical impurities or "ferments" in the air and water to the rising incidence of diseases such as cholera and typhoid fever. In the 1860s and 1870s, a growing number of scientists, chief among them the French chemist Louis Pasteur, became convinced that the "ferments" of disease were in fact living microorganisms. The phrase "germ theory of disease" came into use around 1870 to denote the hypothesis that these organisms, variously called germs, bacteria, or microbes, were the cause of both human and animal diseases.

Many physicians accustomed to explaining disease as a complex product of individual and environmental factors initially found the germ theory of disease too simplistic. But from the late 1870s on, increasingly sophisticated laboratory work combining pure cultures, staining techniques, and animal experimentation gradually illuminated the complex ways that pathogenic microbes infected their human and animal hosts. By 1900, the germ theory of disease and the experimental science of bacteriology that supported and

---

7. On mortality rates, see Judith Walzer Leavitt and Ronald Numbers, "Sickness and Health in America: An Overview," in *Sickness and Health in America,* 2d ed. rev. (Madison: University of Wisconsin Press, 1985), pp. 3–10; Michael Teller, *The Tuberculosis Movement* (Westwood, Conn. Greenwood Press, 1988), p. 3; Richard A. Meckel, *Save the Babies: American Public Health Reform and the Prevention of Infant Mortality, 1850–1929* (Baltimore: Johns Hopkins University Press, 1990); and Samuel Preston and Michael Haines, *Fatal Years: Child Mortality in Late Nineteenth-Century America* (Princeton: Princeton University Press, 1991).

8. For a short summary of the early history of immunology, see Rosen, *History of Public Health,* pp. 304–10.

9. The best overview of the nineteenth-century public health movement is Duffy, *Sanitarians.*

elaborated it had been assimilated into the older discipline of sanitary science and widely accepted by the medical and public health establishments.[10]

Early bacteriological investigations confirmed that the soil, air, and water were all saturated with diverse microorganisms, including those responsible for human diseases. Experimenters found that most microbes could be killed with high heat or chemical disinfectants, but some species, such as the rare but deadly anthrax, had a spore form that could travel long distances and endure highly unfavorable environmental conditions, only to flourish again when given moisture and sufficient warmth. In whatever form, disease germs found many routes to reach susceptible hosts. Investigations in the 1870s and 1880s targeted fecal contamination of the air and water as the main sources of infection. After the German physician Robert Koch's startling announcement in 1882 that he had isolated the bacillus responsible for tuberculosis, a disease long thought to be hereditary, researchers looked more closely at the role of spitting, coughing, and sneezing in spreading respiratory ailments. Subsequent work in the 1890s implicated animal and insect vectors in diseases such as bubonic plague, typhoid, and malaria. Finally, bacteriologists became more aware of bacterial contamination of the food supply from tuberculous cows, dust, flies, and food handlers. Improper food storage or preservation was linked to food poisoning, particularly by the deadly *Clostridium botulinum* responsible for botulism.[11]

Armed with these new bacteriological insights, public health authorities agitated for the expansion of municipal and state departments of public health. From the 1880s on, these departments gradually improved the provision of sanitary services such as municipal water filtration, sewage systems, and garbage collection; they also acquired the legal powers to enforce an increasingly elaborate code of sanitary regulations concerning plumbing, food preparation, and other hygienic matters. At the same time, public health leaders emphasized popular health education and voluntary sanitary reform of the household. Recognizing that existing sanitary laws were still limited in scope and difficult to enforce, late nineteenth-century health reformers stressed that individual citizens had to be educated not only to guard their homes against disease but also to lend political support to their local health departments.[12]

10. For a concise summary of the arguments over disease theory, which I discussed in the above two paragraphs, see Lester King, *Transformations in American Medicine* (Baltimore: Johns Hopkins University Press, 1991), pp. 142–81.

11. This rough chronology is based on my reading of the public health literature. For a general overview written toward the end of this explosion of knowledge, see Charles V. Chapin, *The Sources and Modes of Infection* (New York: Wiley, 1910).

12. On the expansion of state power in the provision of public health, see Barbara Gutmann Rosenkrantz, *Public Health and the State: Changing Views in Massachusetts, 1842–1936* (Cambridge: Harvard University Press, 1972). On the importance of popular health education, see Nancy Tomes, "The Private Side of Public Health: Sanitary Science, Domestic Hygiene, and the Germ Theory, 1870–1900," *Bulletin of the History of Medicine* 64 (1990): 528–30. The arguments

The late nineteenth-century concern about deficient domestic hygiene was by no means focused only on the poor and uneducated. Although public health authorities tended to assume, as did most white middle-class Americans, that working-class, immigrant, and nonwhite households were the worst sanitary offenders, they did not view their own class as exempt from hygienic ignorance. In their experience, neither affluence nor education guaranteed an understanding of the simple but deadly errors of personal hygiene commonly found in American households. In light of the new scientific findings about how contagious diseases spread, public health reformers believed that all Americans stood in need of sanitary redemption.

Both sexes were included in the late nineteenth-century appeals for domestic sanitary uplift, but in practical terms, the growing emphasis on "house diseases" imposed heavier, more constant burdens on women than men. In the gendered division of sanitary labor, men were apportioned responsibility for the external and structural spheres such as the construction of the house and installation of the plumbing system. Although these matters could be time-consuming, they did not occupy a male homeowner's constant attention and, if he had sufficient financial means, could be contracted out to an architect, sanitary engineer, or plumber. The interior of the house was the woman's sanitary province. Public health authorities assumed that the housewife had a greater knowledge of domestic conditions and a stronger motivation to protect the family's health than her husband did. Thus the all-important daily minutia of sanitary cleanliness fell squarely in the female domain. Although middle- and upper-class women could hire domestic servants to do the heavy cleaning involved, they still had to maintain constant vigilance to make sure the work was done correctly or else suffer guilt over a loved one's illness.

The public health movement's equation of domestic hygiene with disease prevention offered the early leaders of the home economics movement a splendid field for action. Domestic disease prevention served as a perfect illustration of how science applied to the home could promote individual, familial, and social uplift. Here was a field in which women could naturally excel, as educators and researchers as well as wives and mothers. In addressing the deep anxieties about infectious disease common to their era, home economists found an issue made to order.

The career of Ellen Richards, the "mother of home economics," clearly illustrates the centrality of sanitary science to the emerging field. The first

---

in the following two paragraphs are also taken from this article. Two excellent recent works on England offer arguments about the "private side of public health" similar to my own: Anne Hardy, *The Epidemic Streets: Infectious Disease and the Rise of Preventive Medicine, 1856–1900* (Oxford: Clarendon Press, 1993), and Annmarie Adams, *Architecture in the Family Way: Doctors, Houses, and Women, 1870–1900* (Montreal: McGill-Queen's University Press, 1996).

American woman to get a science degree, Richards trained as a chemist at the Massachusetts Institute of Technology in the early 1870s and became affiliated with its new laboratory for sanitary research in 1884, where she helped pioneer methodologies for measuring water pollution. Although she was trained as a sanitary chemist, not as a bacteriologist, Richards realized how the latter discipline could contribute to securing safe water, air, and food supplies. As early as 1887, in a household manual coauthored with Marion Talbot for the Association of College Alumnae, Richards wrote, "The general acceptance of the germ theory of disease makes it imperative for every housekeeper to guard against all accumulations of dust, since such accumulations may harbor dangerous germs." In making sanitary science an essential building block of home economics, she included not only the older, chemical understanding of health and disease but also the newer insights of bacteriology.[13]

Among the slightly younger generation of women and men who joined Richards at the Lake Placid conferences in the early 1900s and helped found the American Home Economics Association in 1909—for example, S. Maria Elliott of Simmons College, Maurice Le Bosquet of the American School of Home Economics, Marion Talbot of the University of Chicago, and Martha Van Rensselaer of Cornell University—the appeal of sanitary science in general and bacteriology in particular was equally strong. The conception of the housewife as public health crusader nicely complemented the educational and political goals of early home economists.

In the first place, the threat of disease offered an effective way to challenge many women's unreflective attachment to traditional housekeeping methods. The Lake Placid conferees frequently complained that it was difficult to convince homemakers, especially those from the more affluent classes, to change their accustomed ways of cleaning or decorating in the name of some abstract ideal of science or utility. But if new housekeeping methods could be shown to safeguard their families against potentially fatal diseases, women would be more receptive to home economists' suggestions. As May Bolster noted in a talk at the 1902 Lake Placid conference,

---

13. Ellen H. Richards and Marion Talbot, eds., *Home Sanitation: A Manual for Housekeepers* (Boston: Ticknor, 1887), p. 9. On Richards's scientific training and career, see Margaret Rossiter, *Women Scientists in America: Struggles and Strategies to 1940* (Baltimore: Johns Hopkins University Press, 1982), esp. pp. 68–70. On her contribution to the public health movement, see George Rosen, "Ellen H. Richards (1842–1911), Sanitary Chemist and Pioneer of Professional Equality for Women in Health Science," *American Journal of Public Health* 64 (August 1974): 816–19; and Rosenkrantz, *Public Health and the State,* esp. p. 100.

The kind of chemical analysis Richards did in the laboratory was quite distinct from bacteriology. But though her conception of sanitary science and home sanitation remained heavily indebted to her chemical perspective, she seems quickly to have accepted the germ theory of disease and to have perceived the relevance of applied bacteriology to both home economics and health education.

even the most complacent clubwomen realized the importance of municipal sanitation, a point that could be used to interest them in the concept of
scientific housekeeping.[14]

Likewise, the stress on domestic disease control fostered the larger reform
agenda of home economics leaders. A basic education in bacteriology
would not only make American women better wives and mothers but also
more effective community leaders. Lessons about germs and disease mastered in the home could be applied to their dealings with storekeepers, milk
dealers, and local politicians. Household bacteriology provided an excellent example of how domestic science could serve as the rationale for the
broader forms of social housekeeping envisioned by Richards and other
Progressive-minded home economists.[15]

Thus discussions of germ life and household bacteriology figured prominently in their early attempts to delineate the field's educational mission.
In the various model curricula for domestic science courses drafted and debated by the Lake Placid participants, bacteriological perspectives were included at every level of teaching, starting from the basics of hygiene in the
primary grades, through the practical work offered in manual education
schools and the domestic science courses in the high schools, and culmi-
nating in the advanced courses in home economics at the college and graduate levels. Sanitary science and household bacteriology also became
favored topics for educational programs aimed at adult homemakers, including clubwomen and farmwives.[16]

Home economists' conceptions of what they needed to teach regarding
bacteriology and preventive hygiene varied depending on their audience's
class and geographic location. For upper- and middle-class women living
in large cities and towns, the worst dangers of infection seemed to lie in the
exchanges between their homes and the rest of the community. Women of
means could easily be instructed to make their domestic environments safer

14. May Bolster, "Standards of Living as Reflected through Women's Clubs," Lake Placid
Conference on Home Economics [hereafter LPC], *Proceedings of the Fourth Annual Conference,*
pp. 51–52.

15. For an excellent account of Richards's Progressive political philosophy, see Stage, "From
Domestic Science to Social Housekeeping." Historians are only beginning to appreciate how
central a role women played in Progressive-era sanitary reform in areas as diverse as tenement
house reform, water and air pollution control, and food and drug regulation. See, for example,
Suellen M. Hoy, "'Municipal Housekeeping': The Role of Women in Improving Urban Sanitation Practices, 1880–1917," in *Pollution and Reform in American Cities, 1870–1930,* ed. Martin
V. Melosi (Austin: University of Texas Press, 1980), pp. 173–98.

16. These generalizations are based on my reading of the Lake Placid Conference Proceedings, 1899–1909. See, for example, Mary Roberts Smith, "Report of Committee on Courses of
Study in Home Economics in Colleges and Universities," LPC, *Proceedings of the Fourth Annual Conference, 16–20 September 1902,* pp. 17–21; Maria Parloa, "Suggestions for Home and
Club Study," LPC, *Proceedings of Seventh Annual Conference,* pp. 95–97.

from microbial incursions by purchasing sanitary aids such as filtered water, good quality plumbing, certified milk, and iceboxes. Yet other common
experiences, such as riding in railway cars, staying in hotels, purchasing
factory-made clothing, or patronizing commercial laundries, exposed them
and their families to the sanitary misdeeds of the less enlightened. Complete safety from disease required enlisting affluent women to take action
beyond the household, such as supporting antispitting ordinances and
white-label campaigns.[17]

Home economists realized that poor women, whether they lived in urban
or rural areas, faced more fundamental difficulties in securing their homes
from disease. In cities, substandard housing, diet, and working conditions
predisposed working-class families to infectious diseases; yet their tenement homes were the least likely to have the clean, abundant water supply,
sanitary toilets, well-ventilated rooms, and wholesome food deemed essential to resisting such illnesses. Rural women faced another distinctive
set of sanitary hazards. Home economists recognized that in the early 1900s,
even relatively well-off farm households lacked the basics of safe sanitation.
On many farms, human and animal wastes polluted springs and outdoor
wells, flies carried germs from manure piles to milk pails, and food storage
and preservation were primitive.[18]

From city to countryside, then, the field of domestic sanitary science offered a mission made to order for the founding generation of home economists. Disease prevention was an issue bound to interest homemakers from
every walk of life. Instructing women in simple, effective ways to ward off
infectious disease brought science into the home in the most meaningful
way. Moreover, popularizing the rules of protective hygiene did not require
highly specialized medical knowledge or equipment. Most methods of disease prevention seemed well within the reach of the average housewife.
What she might lack in sanitary aids such as flush toilets or vacuum cleaners, she could, with the home economists' guidance, compensate for with
ingenuity and hard work.

Although their intended audience was varied, the thrust of the home
economists' turn-of-the century sanitary gospel was remarkably uniform:

17. Consumer groups began to organize white-label campaigns at the turn of the century to
encourage women to buy goods made in factories that provided decent wages, hours, and sanitation for their workers. To get a sense of these concerns, see, for example, "Railway Sanitation," LPC, *Proceedings of the Eighth Annual Conference, 15–22 September 1906*, pp. 101–2;
and "Cleanliness in Markets, Hotels and Restaurants," *Journal of Home Economics* 1 (June
1909): 289–90.

18. The tenor of home economists' concerns about the tenement dweller are nicely conveyed
in Mabel Hyde Kittredge, "The Need of the Immigrant," *Journal of Home Economics* 5 (October
1913): 307–16. Their sanitary critique of the American farm is epitomized in Martha Van Rensselaer, "Suggestions on Home Sanitation," *Cornell Farmers Wives' Reading-Course*, Ser. 3, no.
11 (November 1904).

dirt bred disease, therefore women of all classes had to keep themselves, their food, and their houses clean. In fact, much of the "science of controllable environment" hinged on the intelligent management of human wastes and other forms of organic dirt. But upon closer reading, home economists' conceptions of what dirt was dangerous and how bacteriology applied to the home were far more nuanced and complex than the simple equation of dirt with disease implies.

In their writings and lectures, home economists attempted to give ordinary women a radical new understanding of their environment: that they shared the world with an invisible host of microbes; that far from being universally dangerous, many microorganisms performed useful functions; that a basic knowledge of bacteriology was essential to distinguish germ friends from foes; and that careful habits could furnish protection against the latter. As S. Maria Elliott told readers in her 1907 text on household bacteriology, "If these lessons point out dangers of which you were before unconscious, they also suggest ways of escape from those dangers." From the science of bacteriology, modern society had learned that the "science of the infinitely small has become the infinitely important," she concluded.[19]

Early home economists believed that to appreciate the importance of sanitary cleanliness, women needed to understand both the germ theory of disease and the methods of bacteriology. To this end, they taught not only rules for disease prevention but also simple scientific explanations for why observance of those rules was so important. Their insistence that ordinary housewives should learn even the rudiments of bacteriology was a novel idea in the early 1900s.[20]

Martha Van Rensselaer's experience in preparing the first bulletins for the Cornell Farmers' Wives' Reading Course provides a case in point. Although she lacked a college education and had no special training in sanitary science or bacteriology, Van Rensselaer nonetheless felt that these subjects should be an essential part of the educational program for farm women she began in the early 1900s. When she approached a Cornell bacteriologist with the request, "I would like to learn about the bacteriology of the dishcloth so that I may explain to farm women the importance of its cleanliness," he responded, "Oh, they do not need to learn about bacteria. Teach them to keep the dishcloth clean because it is nicer that way."[21]

19. Elliott, *Household Bacteriology*, pp. [viii], 32.

20. The aim of popular science education itself was not novel, but rather its extension to housewives with limited education. See John C. Burnham, *How Superstition Won and Science Lost: Popularizing Science and Health in the United States* (New Brunswick: Rutgers University Press, 1987).

21. This incident is reported by Van Rensselaer's colleague Flora Rose in "A Page of Modern Education, 1900–1940: Forty Years of Home Economics at Cornell University," in *A Grow-*

Home economics educators emphatically rejected that approach in their early textbooks and circulars on the subjects of home hygiene and household bacteriology. While committed to making their explanations understandable to women with little or no formal education, they also tried to convey the complexity and fascination of bacteriology. For example, two of the standard books used in home economics course work, H. W. Conn's *Bacteria, Yeasts, and Molds in the Home* and S. Maria Elliott's *Household Bacteriology,* stressed the importance of conducting simple experiments using petri dishes so as to understand the vitality of bacterial life in the household. They encouraged students and housewives to seek access to a microscope so that they could see the invisible world for themselves. Even Van Rensselaer's short extension bulletins suggested that farm women grow their own "dust gardens" and observe the natural processes of decay and putrefaction that occurred in uncovered and unpreserved food items.[22]

Likewise, these early expositions of household bacteriology sought to convey a sense of the diversity of bacteriological processes in everyday life. Using drawings and photographs, they rendered the different classes of yeast, molds, and bacteria in substantial detail. Decrying the popular view that all microorganisms were bad, textbook authors emphasized the positive contributions that many species made to industry and agriculture. They contrasted the "bad" bacterial species that could spoil milk or even make it the agent of disease with the "good" species required for the manufacture of butter and cheese.

Such homely examples underlined the need for housewives to learn to discriminate between good and bad microbes and to keep the latter at bay. The exacting directions home economists gave about details of housecleaning, home decoration, food preparation, and the like grew out of this complex conception of the house's microbial environment. Three examples—the care of the toilet, the dangers of dust, and the hygiene of food—serve to illustrate the particularities of home economists' concerns about germs in the home.

In this era, no public health precept was better established than the role of fecal contamination in spreading diseases such as cholera and typhoid. Because disease germs throve in human sewage, it was assumed that food,

---

ing College: Home Economics at Cornell University (Ithaca: New York State College of Ecology, 1969), pp. 22–23.

22. H. W. Conn, *Bacteria, Yeasts, and Molds in the Home* (Boston: Ginn, 1903); Elliott, *Household Bacteriology;* "Bacteriology of the Household," *Cornell Reading Course for Farmers' Wives* N.S., 1, no. 4 (February 1909). Maria Elliott helped Van Rensselaer prepare this bulletin for the Cornell series. For all their good intentions, I suspect that home economists watered down the teaching of scientific principles when addressing their least educated audiences, such as immigrant women and sharecroppers' wives.

water, or air that came in contact with such wastes could become infected. Although by the early 1900s some public health experts had begun to question the disease-causing properties of sewer-contaminated air, or what was popularly referred to as "sewer gas," many health authorities continued to regard it as a potential source of danger.[23]

In line with prevailing public health opinion, home economists considered sanitary toilets to be the foundation of modern household hygiene. Without a safe system for disposal of human sewage, a housewife's efforts to have a healthy home were doomed. For town and city dwellers whose homes had the benefit of modern water closets connected to municipal sewer systems, protection against disease required understanding and maintaining a complex plumbing technology. Texts on home hygiene routinely included long, detailed expositions of the air- and watertight system of pipes, drains, and traps needed to prevent germ-laden sewage vapors from fouling the interior air supply. While counseling women to rely on experts such as plumbers or sanitary engineers to install household sanitation systems, home economists warned that only the housewife could keep those systems in proper sanitary order.

For example, toilets required exacting daily maintenance. S. Maria Elliott outlined a three-step procedure, which included soaking, brush-scrubbing, and cloth-scouring the water closet with disinfectant soap powder. Elliott also recommended that women periodically check to make sure their plumbing was airtight by using the peppermint test, which involved pouring oil of peppermint into the waste pipes at their highest accessible point and then sniffing the air in every room to see if its telltale odor escaped.[24]

Early home economists recognized that many American women still lived in homes that lacked indoor toilets and sewer lines and thus faced an even more extreme sanitary danger. Elliott expressed their collective sentiments when she declared in 1910, "The ordinary privy is a menace to health as well as an odorous disgrace." Home economists urged that urban housing codes be written to force landlords to install and maintain sanitary toilets and that municipal health departments provide inspectors to enforce those codes. Until the landlord and the state had fulfilled these obligations, the vigilance of the individual woman living in the tenement counted for comparatively little. Once tenement buildings had been brought up to code, housewives

23. From the 1890s on, public health authorities more systematically trained in laboratory methods, chief among them Charles V. Chapin of Providence, Rhode Island, debunked the sewer gas threat. On Chapin's career, see James V. Cassedy, *Charles V. Chapin and the Public Health Movement* (Cambridge: Harvard University Press, 1962).

24. S. Maria Elliott, *Household Hygiene* (Chicago: American School of Home Economics, 1910), pp. 192–93 (care of the water closet), 137–38 (peppermint test).

needed instruction in how to keep their toilets functioning properly by being flushed after every use and kept clean and free of rubbish.[25]

Home economists required rural women to be even more active agents in the pursuit of the safe toilet. Early home economics extension work aimed at educating farmers' wives about the many sanitary dangers of the unimproved farmstead: the little "babbling brook" from which they fetched wash water might carry fecal wastes from upstream, the family's old privy could be polluting the well from which they drank, and the flies attracted to human and animal manure could contaminate their milk and food. Fortunately, in comparison to tenement dwellers, it was easier for the farm household to rectify such conditions by constructing an inexpensive "sanitary privy," that is, a sewage-tight, disinfecting, and fly-screened toilet, or installing an indoor toilet connected to a cesspool. Although external improvements such as sanitary privies and cesspools were seen as the primary responsibility of the male farmer, extension workers stressed that farmwives had to be actively involved in getting their husbands to undertake such projects and maintaining the sanitary facilities once they were completed.[26]

Home economists' teachings about "dust dangers" offer another good example of the way concerns about disease shaped household practices. Bacteriologists' ability to culture pathogenic organisms from house dust and other forms of common dirt seemed incontrovertible proof that dusty, dirty environments fostered the spread of disease. Home economists often cited the work of an eminent New York bacteriologist, T. Mitchell Prudden, whose 1890 book, *Dust and Its Dangers*, laid out, "in simple language, what the real danger is of acquiring serious disease—especially consumption—by means of dust-laden air." Thus when home economists advised women to keep their homes free of germ-infested dust and dirt, they had the force of experimental science behind them.[27]

Methods of safe dust removal figured prominently in home economists' directives concerning scientific housecleaning. The use of a wet mop, "dustless" broom, and oiled dust cloth maximized the capture of potentially germ-laden dust particles. Housewives were taught to let several hours elapse between dusting the house and preparing food to allow those particles that eluded them to settle. Home economists hailed the vacuum

25. Ibid., p. 120. On instructing tenement housewives on toilet care, see Kittredge, "The Need of the Immigrant," esp. pp. 307–8.

26. For a typical sanitary critique of the farm, see Van Rensselaer, "Suggestions on Home Sanitation."

27. T. Mitchell Prudden, *Dust and Its Dangers* (New York: G. P. Putnam's Sons, 1890), p. [iii]. The dangers of dust were also popularized in the massive antituberculosis campaigns of the early 1900s.

cleaner not only as an energy saver but also as a hygienic boon because it sucked up dangerous dust far more safely and thoroughly than traditional carpet sweepers.[28]

Cautions about dust and disease also figured prominently in home economists' efforts to do away with the overstuffed furniture, room-sized carpets, wallpaper, and extensive bric-a-brac favored in late nineteenth-century decorating schemes. For example, they promoted finished wood floors covered with small area rugs as far less hospitable to germ life than the huge, difficult-to-clean carpets that graced most parlors. Women were urged to take down their wallpaper, which home economists regarded as a germ breeding ground, and tint their walls with paint containing germicidal agents. In the kitchen, easily washed surfaces such as enamel and linoleum provided the best stage for sanitary preparation.[29]

A final example of how a bacteriological perspective informed scientific housekeeping in the early 1900s can be seen in the area of food preservation and preparation. Home economists stressed that the safe preparation of meals required a clear understanding of microbial processes such as fermentation and decay. Their lesson plans taught the basic rules of sanitary food handling, beginning with the need to store food at precise temperatures to retard bacterial spoilage. Meats and homemade canned goods required lengthy cooking periods at high heat to destroy bacteria and their spores. Before and after cooking, dishes had to be kept carefully covered to prevent germ-laden dust and flyspecks from contaminating them. At every stage of food preparation, scrupulous cleanliness was necessary to kill germs; cooking and serving utensils had to be scalded in boiling water, dish towels must be boiled and dried before using, and the cook's hands and clothes must be washed with disinfectant soap.

Perhaps the most dramatic illustration of the importance of bacteriology to food preparation lay in the practice of home canning. Home economists advocated canning homegrown fruits and vegetables as an ideal way for farm women and girls to improve their diets and to make extra money to spend on home improvements. Teaching safe canning methods was a major focus of early extension work. Home canners learned what microorganisms were most commonly found on fruits and vegetables, why some

---

28. See, for example, the instructions for dusting in Elliott, *Household Bacteriology*, pp. 104–5.

29. For a characteristic critique of this sort, see Claudia Q. Murphy, "Wall Sanitation," LPC, *Proceedings of the Eighth Annual Conference, 15–22 September, 1906*, pp. 47–50.

As was true of many turn-of-the-century sanitary measures, the call to simplify furnishings predated the popularization of the germ theory. For example, the mid-nineteenth-century domestic reformer Catharine Beecher praised the virtues of simple, easily cleaned furnishings. See Catharine Beecher, *Treatise on Domestic Economy* (New York: Marsh Capen Lyon and Webb, 1841).

substances such as vinegar and salt retarded bacterial growth, and what precise temperatures and lengths of cooking were necessary to kill the pesky spores. The elaborate protocols of canning summed up the need for absolutely clean hands and utensils, sterile food containers, and exacting observance of cooking procedures. The penalty for failing to observe these bacteriological precautions was obvious: the food would spoil. Over all these proceedings hovered the specter of food poisoning, particularly the dread of botulism, a deadly form of bacterial food contamination associated with improper canning.[30]

Even as early home economists popularized greater bacteriological awareness in the home, new trends in the public health movement began to diminish the emphasis on domestic hygiene in disease prevention. In 1913, a Minnesota public health official named Hibbert Winslow Hill published a book entitled *The New Public Health,* which heralded an important shift in public health practice. At first glance, Hill's book seemed only to reinforce the emphasis on domestic sanitation so central to home economics. "The infectious diseases in general radiate from and are kept going by women," he declared in the preface. "To teach women, girls, prospective mothers, that they may practice in their household and in turn teach their children to war on invisible germ-foes is one of the functions of public health bacteriology."[31]

Yet Hill's conception of the new public health represented a significant change from the home economists' program of sanitary cleanliness. The latest bacteriological research, Hill insisted, showed that "dirty people are no more subject to disease than clean." He noted that even a person of immaculate habits could catch smallpox when exposed to its highly contagious virus; conversely, a person living in horrific filth would never get typhoid fever unless the specific germ was introduced into his digestive system. Therefore, isolating the sick was a more efficient preventive measure than ridding the environment of dirt. Exacting cleanliness might be sought for moral and aesthetic reasons, Hill conceded, but its pursuit was not the most scientific use of public health funds or energies. Rather, the state should concentrate on confining and regulating infected individuals and making

30. Some representative examples of early canning directives are Maria S. Parloa, "Canning and Preserving," *Cornell Reading-Course for Farmers' Wives,* Ser. 4, no. 20 (February 1906); and Ola Powell, *Successful Canning and Preserving,* 3d ed. rev. (Philadelphia: J. B. Lippincott, 1917). Although cases of botulism were recorded as early as the eighteenth century, the Belgian researcher Emile Pierre Marie van Ermengen isolated the microorganism responsible for this form of food poisoning in 1895. See James Harvey Young, "Botulism and the Ripe Olive Scare of 1919–1920," *Bulletin of the History of Medicine* 50 (1976): 372–91.

31. Hibbert Winslow Hill, *The New Public Health* (Minneapolis: Press of the Journal Lancet, 1913), p. 5. Hill anticipated the book's arguments about women's role in disease control in "Teaching Bacteriology to Mothers," *Journal of Home Economics* 2 (December 1910): 635–40.

sure their diseased discharges did not reach others through public water or food supplies.[32]

In the 1920s and 1930s, as the new public health became the guiding faith of the American public health movement, prevention of infectious diseases became more narrowly concerned with individual "case finding" and management on the one hand and improved municipal public health services on the other.[33] The housewife's contribution to the control of infectious disease diminished accordingly; her duties came to consist primarily of obeying the health department's quarantine regulations and obtaining immunizations for her children.

The "battle with bacteria" also became less salient within the maturing discipline of home economics. A new generation of home economics leaders realized that consolidating the field's legitimacy required strengthening its base in the university, which in turn necessitated placing more emphasis on original research. In the late 1910s and early 1920s, nutrition and textiles emerged as the most promising fields for home economics research and employment opportunities. In contrast, the technically sophisticated, medically dominated field of bacteriology offered few avenues for home economists to pursue independent research or to find jobs.[34]

As popularizers of public health information, home economists also faced increasing competition in the 1920s. After World War I, the field of health education, especially with children, expanded rapidly. Local and state health departments, voluntary health organizations, and professional societies launched a dizzying variety of educational initiatives. The home economists' educational agenda overlapped significantly with those of other female-dominated fields, particularly nursing. School nurses and visiting nurses effectively dominated areas of instruction with children and adult women that home economists otherwise might have claimed. As the ideal of "positive health," as opposed to mere freedom from disease, came to dominate health education in the 1920s, the home economists found their skills in nutrition to be more in demand than their expertise in household sanitation.[35]

32. Ibid., p. 122.

33. The best single account of this transition is Rosenkrantz, *Public Health and the State.*

34. These generalizations are based on my reading of the *Journal of Home Economics* in the 1910s and 1920s. See, for example, Agnes Fay Morgan, "Physical and Biological Chemistry in the Service of Home Economics," *Journal of Home Economics* 13 (December 1921): 586–91. Other essays in this volume survey the interwar job opportunities home economists found in fields associated with nutrition and textiles; bacteriology is conspicuously absent.

35. In the 1920s, articles in the *Journal of Home Economics* suggest that home economists were feeling the competition from other professions, particularly nursing, and that they saw nutrition as their best hope of aligning with the "new public health." See Martha Koehne, "The Health Education Program and the Home Economist," *Journal of Home Economics* 16 (July

Meanwhile, mortality rates resulting from infectious diseases declined steadily. By the late 1920s, heart disease and cancer had replaced tuberculosis, influenza, and pneumonia as the leading causes of death. As the number of hospitals and hospital insurance plans proliferated, those people who did contract serious infectious diseases were less likely to be cared for at home, diminishing the need for painstaking home nursing and sanitation procedures. Starting with the sulfanilamides in the mid-1930s, the discovery of effective antibiotics further reduced the threat of infectious diseases.[36]

Other long-term changes in the standard of living decreased the personal precautions individuals needed to take against their germ foes. Municipal water and sewer services gradually extended to all neighborhoods in American cities. Farmhouses lacking indoor plumbing or running water became increasingly rare except in the poorest parts of the country. Increased regulation of the dairy industry resulted in a safe, relatively cheap supply of pasteurized milk. Commercial processing techniques and "sanitary packaging" steadily decreased the likelihood of microbial contamination of foodstuffs. More homemakers acquired labor-saving appliances such as refrigerators, vacuum cleaners, and washing machines, which facilitated domestic cleanliness.[37]

The maxims of bacteriological cleanliness continued to be handed down from teacher to student, mother to daughter, but the fear of infectious diseases that had given them their original urgency gradually disappeared. The association between sanitary science and dread disease faded with each generation reared in greater safety from the killer diseases of the early 1900s, leaving behind only a vague conviction that cleanliness promoted health. By 1976, when Barbara Ehrenreich and Dierdre English conducted an informal survey of home economics professors, none could clearly articulate the relationship between cleanliness and good health.[38] Rather

---

1924): 373–80; Margaret Sawyer, "American Home Economics Association and the Health Program," *Journal of Home Economics* 16 (December 1924): 679–83.

36. On changing disease patterns, see Leavitt and Numbers, "Sickness and Health in America," esp. the chart on page 8. On the expansion of hospitals and changing health care patterns, see Rosemary Stevens, *In Sickness and in Wealth: American Hospitals in the Twentieth Century* (New York: Basic Books, 1989). Although the sulfa drugs were discovered in the late 1930s and penicillin came into clinical use in the 1940s, widespread antibiotic use became common only in the 1950s.

37. On changing American living standards, see Ruth Schwartz Cowan, *More Work for Mother: The Ironies of Household Technology from the Open Hearth to the Microwave* (New York: Basic Books, 1983); and Harvey Levenstein, *Revolution at the Table: The Transformation of the American Diet* (New York: Oxford University Press, 1988). The increasing difficulty middle- and upper-class women had in securing live-in domestic servants also contributed to their declining enthusiasm for rigorous housecleaning. See David Katzman, *Seven Days a Week* (New York: Oxford University Press, 1978).

38. Ehrenreich and English, *For Her Own Good*, pp. 160–61.

than read their confusion as evidence of the unscientific nature of early twentieth-century home economics, as Ehrenreich and English did, we might better see the atrophy of knowledge about domestic hygiene as a reflection of the lessening threat of infectious diseases over the last century.

To argue that early twentieth-century home economists provided American women with a bacteriologically informed perspective on household hygiene is not to claim that everything they taught was correct. In light of modern knowledge, some of the practices they advocated did indeed protect families against infectious diseases but others did not. For example, improvements in rural sanitation systems undoubtedly contributed to the decline in rates of typhoid, hookworm, and other diseases spread by human wastes. Thus the home economics movement's championship of the sanitary privy constituted a significant public health reform. The menace of microbial contamination of house dust, it turned out, was not so well founded. Scientists later discovered that the tubercle bacilli cultured from dust lacked infective power; the live bacilli expelled in droplet form by coughs and sneezes proved to be far more important to the spread of tuberculosis.[39]

The precepts early home economists taught have proved most enduring in the area of food preservation and handling. In an age when refrigeration was very expensive, when supplies of milk and water were liable to bacterial contamination, and when drinking glasses and utensils were frequently shared, we can only begin to guess what percentage of the gastrointestinal diseases so commonly suffered by Americans were the result of unsanitary food handling. To teach women that food needed to be stored at certain temperatures or that the surfaces and utensils used for preparing and serving food had to be kept scrupulously clean was neither busywork nor pseudoscientific. Such precautions remain the foundation of modern health departments' regulation of the food service industry.[40]

Through its educational outreach programs, the early home economics movement played an important role in acquainting women of all classes and races with such precautions. Affluent women had access to this information through a variety of channels, including women's clubs, popular magazines, and private physicians, whereas poor women had many fewer such educational opportunities. By including immigrant and rural women

39. Charles-Edward A. Winslow produced an exhaustive bacteriological study refuting the dangers of sewer gas in 1909. See the National Association of Master Plumbers of the United States, *Report of the Sanitary Committee, 1907–1908–1909* (Boston: The Association, 1909), pp. 39–95. On the importance of the sanitary privy in relation to the hookworm problem, see John Ettling, *The Germ of Laziness* (Cambridge: Harvard University Press, 1981). The point about the tubercle bacillus was explained to me by Barbara Bates.

40. The continuity in food-handling directives is strikingly evident in the course materials used in the Food Manager Certification Program for Suffolk County, New York, made available to me by Elizabeth Roberts Daily.

in its extension programs, the home economics movement helped democratize the spread of potentially valuable hygienic information.

Historians and demographers cannot gauge precisely how much such campaigns actually contributed to the fall of mortality rates from infectious disease in the decades from 1880 to 1930. But enlisting the housewife's help in preventing fecal contamination of water supplies and ridding food and milk supplies of harmful microbial life may have made a significant contribution to that decline. Only from the insulated perspective of a society grown used to the protections guaranteed by safe water and food supplies, sewage systems, and the like could these efforts be dismissed as mindless makework.[41]

Unfortunately, the heightened sense of responsibility for preventing infectious diseases promoted by home economists and other health reformers probably brought in its wake a new intensity of guilt. They tended to overemphasize the efficacy of individual hygienic measures, thus leaving women vulnerable to shame and grief when their efforts at disease prevention failed. A poignant letter written by a farm woman who had completed a correspondence course on home hygiene given by the Cornell extension service suggests the hard contours of such responsibility: "Men, men, mud, mud, and my cellar," she wrote. "I wonder we are alive. Poor me. I know if everything had been kept properly my children would be alive and well."[42]

Limitations on income and resources severely constrained the ability of very poor women to implement the ideals of bacteriological cleanliness. Without running water, convenient to use cleaning supplies, or sanitary toilets, even superficial cleanliness could be obtained only with backbreaking labor. In this sense, the home economics movement's emphasis on domestic hygiene may have worked to reinforce oppressively personal solutions to the perceived threat of diseases. Here as in many other areas of American reform, individual adaptation and blaming the victim often proved easier than changing the inequities in income and housing which underlay the unequal distribution of illness.[43]

41. Two recent works that argue for the importance of change at the personal and household levels are Douglas C. Ewbank and Samuel H. Preston, "Personal Health Behaviour and the Decline in Infant and Child Mortality: The United States, 1900–1930," in *What We Know about Health Transition: The Cultural, Social and Behavioural Determinants of Health*, ed. John C. Caldwell et al. (Canberra, Australia: Australian National University Press, 1990), pp. 116–49, and Hardy, *Epidemic Streets*.

42. "Reading Course Testimonials," Box 25, folder 16, Division of Rare and Manuscript Collections, Cornell University Library, Ithaca, N.Y. The author of the letter was not identified, nor was a specific date given, but it was written sometime between the early 1900s and the mid-1910s.

43. S. K. Kleinberg, *The Shadow of the Mills: Working-Class Families in Pittsburgh, 1870–1907* (Pittsburgh: University of Pittsburgh Press, 1989), provides an excellent overview of the poor health conditions common in working-class neighborhoods.

The legacy of these early twentieth-century efforts to spread the germ theory can still be seen in contemporary attitudes toward germs. Older Americans who remember the "bad old days" when siblings and friends died of typhoid or tuberculosis or polio, and who were first taught the rules of sanitary safety at an impressionable age, often have much stronger germ phobias than do Americans born in the postantibiotic era. Oral histories suggest that immigrant women raised in the 1920s and 1930s in very poor homes without the modern conveniences of toilets and refrigerators regarded exacting standards of housecleaning as a sacred duty to protect the family from disease. But their daughters and granddaughters proved harder and harder to convince that housecleaning is a prerequisite to good health. The oft-noted decline in the number of hours American women spend cleaning house may in part reflect the gradual weakening of the association between dirt and disease.[44]

The AIDs epidemic and growing concerns about environmental threats to health may reverse this more casual view of domestic hygiene. The appearance of deadly new viral diseases that have no cure, along with the resurgence of tuberculosis, a bacterial disease thought long under control, have reawakened many of the old fears associated with the spread of contagion. Widely publicized incidents of bacterial contamination of water and meat supplies have drawn attention to the vulnerability of existing hygienic protections. Confronted by a new generation of "superbugs," many Americans have begun to recall dimly remembered lessons about sterilizing dishes and cooking meats at high temperatures.

Rising concerns about new environmental threats to health have also focused attention on domestic hygiene. Worries about "sick" houses and buildings are couched in terms strikingly similar to earlier fears about "house diseases." Today people test their homes for radon gas instead of sewer gas and install water filters to remove chemicals, not bacteria, from their drinking water. Yet the impulse behind these individual efforts to protect the household against environmental dangers has many parallels to the early home economists' preoccupation with domestic disease prevention.

When we see these parallels between their concerns and our own, the history of the home economics movement serves to educate rather than to anger or to amuse. As we struggle in the late twentieth century to become

---

44. Nancy Tomes, "The Wages of Dirt Were Death," paper presented at the Annual Meeting of the Organization of American Historians, April 1991. On the decline in time spent housekeeping, see Molly O'Neill, "Drop the Mop, Bless the Mess: The Decline of Housekeeping," *New York Times,* April 11, 1993, I-1, 18. As O'Neill suggests, this decline reflects women's growing participation in the work force and men's reluctance to take up the slack in domestic chores. But it has been facilitated by the absence of fear that the rising tide of domestic dirt would harm family members' health.

more aware of the health consequences of our own interactions with the environment, to realize the limits of modern medicine in reducing our vulnerability to disease, and to appreciate the ways that race and class prejudice destroy health, the home economists' "battle with bacteria" provides an instructive historical precedent. In the wake of frightening new diseases, broken water mains, and tainted food, we may find ourselves turning to those old texts on household sanitation and bacteriology for more than historical insight.

3 Modernizing Mothers: Home Economics and the Parent Education Movement, 1920–1945

JULIA GRANT

In an address to the 1904 Lake Placid conference, Ellen Richards contended that "Home Economics stands for the ideal home life for today unhampered by the traditions of the past; the utilization of all the resources of modern science to improve the home life."[1] As society increasingly became mechanized, the understanding and application of scientific principles appeared to be vital to modernizing and professionalizing the homemaker's job. Although home economists are often thought of in connection with their championship of traditional womanhood, their efforts to modernize women's roles have only recently begun to receive attention.[2] This is particularly true in the case of child rearing, a central aspect of women's work that greatly concerned home economists during the 1920s and 1930s, when

The author gratefully acknowledges the financial assistance of Rockefeller Archive Center, the Cornell University College of Human Ecology, and the Boston University Humanities Foundation. I also appreciate the editorial comments and suggestions of Joyce Antler, Susan Mizruchi, Ann Lane, Sarah Stage, and Virginia Vincenti.

1. Quoted in Cora Winchell, "Home Economics at the Crossroads," *Journal of Home Economics* 18 (October 1926): 554.

2. Valuable accounts of the home economics movement in relation to gender issues and women's education include Joyce Antler, "Culture, Service, and Work: Changing Ideas of Higher Education for Women," in *The Undergraduate Woman: Issues in Educational Equity,* ed. Pamela J. Perun (Lexington, Mass.: Lexington Books, 1982), pp. 15–41; Maxine L. Margolis, *Mothers and Such: Views of American Women and Why They Changed* (Berkeley: University of California Press, 1984), pp. 124–47; John L. Rury, "Vocationalism for Home and Work: Women's Education in the United States," *History of Education Quarterly* 24 (Spring 1984): 21–45; Margaret Rossiter, *Women Scientists in America: Struggles and Strategies to 1940* (Baltimore: Johns Hopkins University Press, 1982); Barbara Miller Solomon, *In the Company of Educated Women* (New Haven: Yale University Press, 1985); Emma Seifrit Weigley, "It Might Have Been

they lent their considerable skills and energies to the burgeoning parent education movement.[3]

Parent education was a logical extension of the home economics agenda, which sought to scientize homemaking. Initially concerned with applying scientific principles to life in the home, Richards argued that women must become household engineers, evoking that popular icon of the 1910s—the engineer—who signified efficiency, inventiveness, and expertise.[4] Home economists aimed to diminish the boundaries between the old-fashioned mother in the home and a masculine technological society by supplying mothers with the tools of modern science. Mothers were urged to rely on the tenets of the behavioral sciences for their child-rearing strategies rather than on their natural instincts. Seeking to lessen the invidious distinctions between home and work, home economists reconceptualized mothering as professional labor requiring education and expertise. The modernization of mothering promised to usher traditional women's work into the twentieth century, making it a more enticing and intellectually challenging undertaking for the educated woman.[5] The new emphasis also provided vocational opportunities for home economists as experts in child development and parent education.

During the early years of home economics, the physical sciences dominated the educational agenda, partly because of the relatively recent, and hence uncertain, origin of the behavioral sciences. Child care occupied a minor place in the curriculum at first; the primary emphasis was on the physical care of infants. The subject of child care and training was rarely addressed at the early meetings of the American Home Economics Association, in which conference sessions on nutrition, textiles, and household management and technology held sway. The few public school home economics programs that included child care in the curriculum were primarily geared toward the poor, who, it was assumed, had much to learn about hygienic methods of caring for children. Thus, in spite of scattered efforts to educate girls and young women in scientific child-rearing methods, a

---

Euthenics: The Lake Placid Conferences and the Home Economics Movement," *American Quarterly* 26 (March 1974): 79–96.

3. This essay is based in part on chapter 2 of my dissertation, "Modernizing Motherhood: Child Study Clubs and the Parent Education Movement, 1915–1940" (Boston University, 1992), and my forthcoming book, *Raising Baby by the Book: The Education of American Mothers, 1890–1960* (New Haven: Yale University Press, forthcoming).

4. Rury, "Vocationalism," p. 26.

5. Jane Bernard Powers, in her study *The "Girl" Question in Education: Vocational Education for Young Women in the Progressive Era* (London: Falmer Press, 1992), has noted that "home economics is both traditional and feminist, it contains continuities and contradictions" (p. 4).

sample syllabus produced by the AHEA in 1913 completely neglected the care of children.[6]

In ensuing years, child development came to occupy a more prominent place in the home economics curriculum as the behavioral sciences joined the ranks of the legitimate sciences and home economists recognized the advantages of addressing a topic that had widespread societal appeal. Americans were becoming increasingly absorbed with the physical and psychological care of the young, as exemplified by the first White House Conference on Children held in 1909 and the establishment of the U.S. Children's Bureau in 1912. This period was also marked by the ascendancy of such child-centered professions as pediatrics and child psychology, which originated in response to both institutional pressures and parental demand. Advances in infant health and feeding had led to an unprecedented decline in the level of infant mortality and contributed to the belief that the incorporation of scientific principles into child rearing might enable parents to raise uniformly healthy, well-adjusted, and law-abiding citizens. By the 1920s child training and psychology had become a national obsession.[7]

Women were also dissatisfied with the standard home economics curriculum. In a 1917 study of the curricular needs of college-educated women, 80 percent of the women surveyed proposed that home economics programs include a child study component. One woman suggested, "If I were planning home economics courses, I would omit much of textiles, etc., and get right at the child business. . . . Women do not know how to care for themselves or their babies after the babies arrive—and they do not know how to train children from a physical or ethical standpoint."[8] Increasing numbers of college-educated women were marrying and having children, and home economists realized that their profession's success would hinge on their ability to devise a curriculum to serve the needs of this constituency.[9] In her 1926 presidential address to the AHEA, Katherine Blunt admitted that "in the future American Home Economics Association, the married home economics graduate will be a potent force." She advised

6. Elizabeth C. Jenkins, "The College Course in Home Economics," *Journal of Home Economics* 9 (July 1917): 305.

7. Richard A. Meckel, *Save the Babies: American Public Health Reform and the Prevention of Infant Mortality, 1850–1929* (Baltimore: Johns Hopkins University Press, 1990), p. 94, and Christina Hardyment, *Dream Babies: Three Centuries of Good Advice on Child Care* (Berkeley: University of California Press, 1988), p. 14. On the U.S. Children's Bureau, see Molly Ladd-Taylor, *Raising a Baby the Government Way: Mothers' Letters to the U.S. Children's Bureau, 1915–1932* (New Brunswick: Rutgers University Press, 1986).

8. Jenkins, "The College Course in Home Economics," pp. 309, 311.

9. Mary E. Cookingham, "Combining Marriage, Motherhood, and Jobs before World War II: Women College Graduates, Classes of 1905–1935," *Journal of Family History* 9 (Summer 1984): 178–95.

home economists to continue to develop courses of study in areas such as child training that directly influenced adult homemakers' lives.[10]

The organization finally lent its support to the parent education movement at the 1924 convention, when it resolved to place the development of a curriculum in child care at the top of its educational agenda, affirming that "the Association include a program of child study which represents all phases of child care and management, as a fundamental part in all programs." More concretely, it also planned to "work actively for the establishment of courses in child care management in public schools, colleges, and through extension agencies."[11]

Home economists took advantage of the connection between home economics and agriculture to bolster their case for the inclusion of child care in the curriculum. In 1926, Dean Anna Euretta Richardson of the Iowa State College of Home Economics proclaimed: "The newer Home Economics . . . must include child development and parent education if it is to function as training for the great vocation of homemaking on anything like the same breadth of lines as is modern agriculture."[12] The comparison with agriculture underscored the scientific component of child development work and questioned the validity of providing public funds for agricultural research while neglecting the study of children. Believing that the inclusion of parent education courses would enhance the appeal of home economics both within academia and with the general public, home economists lobbied successfully in 1925 to have the Land Grant College Association recognize child care as a key element in the home economics curriculum.[13]

Proponents of the integration of child rearing into the home economics curriculum found a useful ally in Lawrence Frank, a professional philanthropist with the Laura Spelman Rockefeller Memorial (LSRM), who used his position to channel crucial funds into the fledgling parent education movement. Frank was a graduate of Columbia University in economics. He had studied the conditions of New York's poor and was intrigued by the notion of applying the findings of the behavioral sciences to social problems. In 1923, Frank was asked to develop a plan to subsidize programs for children, which would attack the underlying causes of childhood problems. Frank responded with a proposal to provide funds for both the development and the dissemination of scientific information on children, reflecting a

10. Katherine Blunt, "President's Address: The Unity of the American Home Economics Association," *Journal of Home Economics* 18 (October 1926): 552.

11. "Seventeenth Annual Meeting, American Home Economics Association, June 30–July 3, 1924," *Journal of Home Economics* 16 (September 1924): 472, 474.

12. Anna Richardson to Lawrence K. Frank, December 18, 1926, Ser. 3, Box 26, no. 274, Laura Spelman Rockefeller Memorial Papers, Rockefeller Archive Center, Tarrytown, N.Y. (hereafter LSRM).

13. Edna Noble White to Lawrence K. Frank, January 25, 1925, Ser. 3, Box 32, no. 349, LSRM.

prevalent belief that many social problems—such as delinquency, maladjustment, and even poverty—could be traced to the improper care and nurture of children in the home.[14]

What was unique about Frank's plan, however, was his vision of a fortuitous combination of researchers and practitioners, professionals and laypeople, working to improve American homes. Frank maintained that women had a central role to play in reforming the home, not only from their position as mothers in the family but as clubwomen, educators, and researchers. Thus his plan included fellowships for women in child development and parent education; funds to support women's clubwork in parent education; and a central position for home economists in disseminating the insights of the child development movement to the American public.[15]

In 1925 Frank met with Anna Richardson, Katherine Blunt, and Agnes Fay Morgan, head of the Home Economics Department at the University of California, to discuss the possibility of LSRM funding for the AHEA'S work in parent education. Frank foresaw the possibility of using Smith-Lever (1914) and Smith-Hughes (1917) federal funds for work in home economics as a means of spreading the "gospel" of child development to American families.[16] He was especially intrigued with the concept of making use of the rapidly growing network of home demonstration agents working in rural areas with the Agricultural Extension Service. The agents were organizing and educating local homemakers, dispensing information about a variety of female enterprises, from sewing to gardening. With proper training, Frank reasoned, they could also function as parent educators. By providing seed money for child development projects in states with major land-grant universities and established extension services, the LSRM might ensure that parent education would be sponsored by state educational institutions.[17] Such a plan provided obvious benefits for home economists, who

14. Emily Cahan, "Science, Practice, and Gender Roles in Early American Child Psychology," in *Contemporary Constructions of the Child: Essays in Honor of William Kessen,* ed. Frank S. Kessel, Marc H. Bornstein, and Arnold J. Sameroff (Hillsdale, N.J.: Lawrence Erlbaum Associates, 1991), pp. 231–33.

15. Ibid., pp. 232–33.

16. I am in debt to Steven Schlossman's "Philanthropy and the Gospel of Child Development," *History of Education Quarterly* 21 (Fall 1981): 275–99, for this terminology. See also Steven Schlossman, "Before Home Start: Notes toward a History of Parent Education in America," *Harvard Educational Review* 46 (August 1976): 436–67; Christine Mary Shea, "The Ideology of Mental Health and the Emergence of the Therapeutic Liberal State: The American Mental Hygiene Movement, 1900–1930" (Ph.D. dissertation, University of Illinois at Urbana, 1980); and Hamilton Cravens, "Child-Saving in the Age of Professionalism, 1915–1930," in *American Childhood: A Research Guide and Historical Handbook,* ed. Joseph Hawes and N. Ray Hiner (Westport, Conn.: Greenwood Press, 1985), pp. 415–81.

17. Lawrence K. Frank to Mrs. Clifford Walker, June 6, 1924, Ser. 3, Box 44, no. 458, LSRM.

envisioned greater professional possibilities and societal influence for themselves as leaders in parent education if the plan worked.

As a result of the meeting, the AHEA was afforded a four-year grant from the LSRM—$10,000 for 1926 and $8,000 annually for the next three years— to provide for the appointment of Anna Richardson as a consultant in child study and parent education for the association.[18] Anna Euretta Richardson was born in South Carolina and held a bachelor's in science from Peabody College, Tennessee, and a master's from Teachers College, Columbia University. She worked as a federal home economics agent in the South after the passage of the Smith-Hughes Act in 1917, which provided funds for the training of home economics teachers; in 1919, she was appointed head of home economics for the Federal Bureau of Vocational Education. From 1923 to 1926 Richardson served as dean of home economics at Iowa State College. A major player in the AHEA, she was considered to be highly qualified to move home economics into the forefront of the parent education movement.[19]

To accomplish this task, however, she and her colleagues had to convince home economists, the Smith-Lever and Smith-Hughes specialists, and university administrators of the necessity of expanding the conception of home economics. Genevieve Fisher, who served as dean of home economics at Iowa State College after Richardson left to work with the AHEA, expressed this concern in a memo to President Raymond Hughes. "I appreciate," she admitted, "that it is difficult for us to live down the well established tradition that we are primarily interested in cooking and sewing."[20] Frank was pleased to note that many home economists were willing to include parenting as part of their scientific agenda, which he viewed as the homemaker's most important subject matter, suggesting that home economists had a "conviction of sin" but were willing to "remedy their mistakes as soon as possible."[21]

By enlarging the scope of home economics to include the care of children, proponents concluded that their discipline should ultimately appeal to

18. "Progress Report—American Home Economics Association, 11/15/29," Ser. 3, Box 26, no. 274, LSRM.

19. American Home Economics Association, *Home Economists: Portraits and Brief Biographies of the Men and Women Prominent in the Home Economics Movement in the United States* (Baltimore: American Home Economics Association, 1929), p. 60. One of Richardson's tasks was to provide an account of the extent to which child development had infiltrated the high school and college curricula. The results of her research were published in Anna Euretta Richardson, *Child Development and Parental Education in Home Economics: A Survey of Schools and Colleges* (Baltimore: American Home Economics Association, 1928).

20. Memo from Genevieve Fisher to R. M. Hughes, November 25, 1929, Ser. 3, Box 32, no. 341, LSRM.

21. Memo by Lawrence K. Frank, re: American Home Economics Association, March 15, 1925, Ser. 3, Box 26, no. 273, LSRM.

adults as well as high school students, men as well as women. This conception fitted nicely with the popular credos of the progressive education movement. But home economists anticipated an added benefit to the association of home economics with child development: an alliance with the increasingly respectable disciplines of psychology and sociology. Frank projected that home economists would work closely with the child welfare research institutes funded by the LSRM and associated with several major universities in disseminating the ideas developed by child developmentalists to the public.

Yet the growing interest of home economists in child development was met with skepticism and sometimes even opposition by male academics, who were reluctant to ally themselves with such an undeniably female discipline. Frank wrote to Richardson: "I have heard criticism that the Association is engaged in promoting interest and activity among its members for work in child study and parent education and that this promotion is causing some embarrassment to the educational people. . . . I imagine they are as usual rather disturbed and worried by signs of activity and determination on the part of the feminine members of staffs."[22] Some of the male scientists who staffed the child research institutes feared that the association of parent education with home economics would subvert their efforts to elevate the prestige of child development research. Bird Baldwin, director of the Iowa Child Welfare Research Station, repeatedly asked his colleagues, "Why are the Home Economics people trying to break into this field of child study and parent education?"[23] And Harold Jones, a prominent behavioral psychologist at the California Institute of Child Welfare, complained to Frank that they were "getting a little too much cooperation from Household Science."[24] Child developmentalists were still struggling to be recognized as legitimate scientists within the disciplines of psychology and medicine, and they feared that connections with a gendered discipline such as home economics would "taint" their bid for professional recognition. For home economists the opposite was true; they stood to gain prestige by affiliating with disciplines inhabited primarily by men. But they were conversant with the fears of their male colleagues in the social sciences and in their exchanges with them underscored that home economists were primarily to be the disseminators, rather than the producers, of information in the behavioral sciences.[25]

22. Lawrence K. Frank to Anna Richardson, March 26, 1927, Ser. 3, Box 26, no. 274, LSRM.

23. Quoted in Lawrence K. Frank, memo of interview with Dean Anne Richardson of School of Home Economics at Iowa, March 2, 1925, Ser. 3, Box 32, no. 341, LSRM.

24. Harold Jones to Lawrence K. Frank, September 28, 1928, Ser. 3, Box, 43, no. 452, LSRM.

25. In a memo to New York's educational commissioner, Flora Rose, who together with Martha Van Rensselaer headed Cornell's College of Home Economics, argued, "Just as physics, chemistry or economics are taught in other departments at the university and application made

Opposition from male academics did not prevent home economics departments in conjunction with state agricultural extension services from achieving notable success in popularizing the ideas of the child development movement. Child welfare institutes initiated at the University of California, the University of Minnesota, and the University of Iowa cooperated with home economists in moving education beyond the confines of academia and into America's rural villages and small towns. Other institutions, such as Cornell University, Georgia State College, and the University of Cincinnati, combined state and federal funding with support from the LSRM to promote curricula in child development, organize nursery schools, and train extension workers in parent education. In these and states such as Massachusetts, Michigan, and Oklahoma, home demonstration agents were key participants in the transmission of knowledge about children to American homemakers.[26]

New York State serves as a case study for the work of home economics extension in parent education at its best. The state boasted both a Bureau of Parent Education, established with a grant from the LSRM in 1928, and an exemplary model of extension education in child development sponsored by Cornell University. This extension program, housed in Cornell's Department of Family Life in the College of Home Economics, effectively exposed thousands of New York families to new theories of child development, beginning in the late 1920s and continuing through the 1940s.

The care of children was incorporated into home economics at Cornell in 1919, when a practice house for undergraduates was established where students could apply their home management and child-rearing skills.[27] In 1925 Cornell receive a four-year grant from the LSMR to institute its De-

---

in home economics so also application is made in the College of Home Economics with reference to environmental conditions in the governing of family life and with special reference to children." See "Confidential Report of the Home Economics Conference in Albany—November 21, 1929," Box 2, Folder 2, College of Home Economics, Division of Rare and Manuscript Collections, Cornell University Library, Ithaca, N.Y.

26. Accounts of the various statewide parent education programs in the 1920s include Cravens, "Child-Saving in the Age of Professionalism"; Dorothy Bradbury, *Pioneering in Child Welfare: A History of the Iowa Child Welfare Research Station* (Iowa City: State University of Iowa Press, 1933); Edith A. Davis and Esther McGinnis, *Parent Education: A Survey of the Minnesota Program* (Westport, Conn.: Greenwood Press, 1939); Gertrude Laws, *Parent Education in California* (Sacramento: California State Printing Office, 1937); and University of State of New York, State Education Department, Child Developmental and Parental Education, *Report of Work in Child Development and Parental Education Supported by Grant from the Spelman Fund to the State Education Department* (Albany, 1933). The White House Conference on Child Health and Protection also produced a comprehensive overview of parent education efforts entitled *Parent Education: Types, Content, Method* (New York: Century, 1932).

27. Ethel Bushnell Waring, "History that led up to the College of Home Economics and to the Department of Family Life in 1925," p. 2, Box 1, Ethel Bushnell Waring Papers, Division of Rare and Manuscript Collections, Cornell University Library.

partment of Child Development and Parent Education (which would later be called the Department of Family Life), with an affiliated nursery school for research and parent education.[28] Shortly after the establishment of the new department, Margaret Wylie, extension specialist in child study, instituted the Cornell Child Study Club Program as a component of the Agricultural Extension Service. Wylie had received her Ph.D. in psychology from the University of Michigan and engaged in postdoctoral work at the Illinois Institute of Juvenile Research, studying preschool children. Her academic competence was unquestioned, but Wylie was also a superb educator of adults. She both empathized with the problems of ordinary mothers and respected the insights and experiences that mothers garnered through caring for children.[29]

Wylie and her colleagues used home economics extension workers, trained by specialists in child development, to create educational opportunities for mothers throughout the state. Cornell's service to mothers had begun with the popular study courses for farmers' wives implemented by pioneer home economist Martha Van Rensselaer in the early 1900s.[30] The success of the venture indicated that the state's homemakers were eager for educational opportunities, and it paved the way for the Cornell Child Study Clubs.

The College of Home Economics instructed home demonstration agents, whose work had previously concentrated on household and farm management techniques, in the content and methods of parent education, with particular emphasis on the organization of child study groups. The agents, in turn, instructed local homemakers in the techniques of leading a child study group because the number of agents available to lead groups was limited. The groups were provided with course syllabi, pamphlets, and a lending library. The Department of Family Life sponsored annual conferences at the Ithaca campus for study group mothers, especially leaders, who were instructed both in the methods of leading discussion groups and in the latest theories in child development and family life education.

Beginning with the study of texts on the physical and psychological care of infants and preschool children, the groups combined discussions of academic subject material with interchanges about everyday problems with children. The extension staff assumed that adult homemakers needed an opportunity to connect learning with living and encouraged group members to integrate their experiences as mothers with course materials. Cornell requested that group meeting minutes include evaluations of particular

28. Ibid., p. 20.

29. For biographical information on Wylie, see Mary Ford et al., "Margaret Wylie," in *Necrology of Cornell Faculty, 1963–1964* (Ithaca: Cornell University Press, 1964), pp. 41–42.

30. Morris Bishop, *A History of Cornell* (Ithaca: Cornell University Press, 1962), p. 380.

readings, along with an analysis of the successful and unsuccessful aspects of each meeting. As a result, the club records reveal the processes by which mothers mediated between child development expertise and their own child-rearing practices. Although membership in a child study group might appear to indicate a reverence for scientific expertise, the groups actually often enabled mothers to define themselves as experts and to debunk or question prescriptions that seemed at odds with maternal practices.[31]

Groups were formed in up to fifty New York counties, and their memberships ranged from farm women to middle- to upper-middle class women in villages and cities.[32] Many groups clustered around Buffalo and Rochester; others were centered in rural villages scattered throughout the state, such as DeKalb Junction in St. Lawrence County and Sandy Creek in Oswego County. Although the economic status of the women varied, they were overwhelmingly white, native-born, and tended to have intact, medium-sized families, with two to four children. They also appeared to have been better educated than their non-study-group counterparts; most had some high school education and often a year or two of college, while the mean level of education for most rural New York women was between eight and ten years.[33]

The structure of the child study groups encouraged mothers to make intelligent choices as consumers of the behavioral sciences. For example, mothers were almost unanimously enthusiastic about materials on sex education, which had been denied to many of them as young women. Many women also found the concept that children pass through developmental stages to be both intriguing and reassuring. They regarded as impractical, however, the experts' suggestion that they adopt the scientific practices of nursery school teachers in rearing their children, insisting that the many household duties that competed for their attention complicated their jobs. The configuration of the typical child study group, which consisted of and was run almost entirely by mothers themselves, helped to ensure that the group developed a community voice that could be counterposed to the

31. I am currently investigating the ways in which the Cornell groups functioned as "interpretive communities," using the theories developed by Stanley Fish, *Is There a Text in This Class?: The Authority of Interpretive Communities* (Cambridge: Harvard University Press, 1980), and Janice Radway, *Reading the Romance: Women, Patriarchy, and Popular Literature* (Chapel Hill: University of North Carolina Press, 1984).

32. New York State College of Home Economics at Cornell University, *Sixteenth Annual Report* (Ithaca, 1941), p. 20.

33. W. A. Anderson finds that only 5 percent of Home Bureau members had less than eight years of education in his "Farm Women in the Home Bureau: A Study in Cortland County, New York, 1939," in *Cornell University Agricultural Experiment Station Bulletin, Department of Rural Sociology* 3 (October 1941): 3. On the average educational level of adult females in New York, see *Sixteenth Census of the United States: 1940 Population, Vol. 3, Part 5: New York–Oregon* (Washington, D.C., 1943).

voice of the expert. Such a community voice could be used to further expert advice, but in either case, groups mediated the impact of professional expertise on women's child-rearing practices.

The Cornell child study clubs originated in the late 1920s, a period when hyperbole concerning the dangers of incorrect early child training permeated popular culture. A virtual avalanche of child-rearing advice was unleashed on American parents, which confusingly blended both developmentalist and behaviorist approaches to child rearing. The most memorable figure of the period is the renowned behaviorist John B. Watson, who characterized children as human machines, whose conduct and behavior could be shaped by maternal technicians. Watson's influence was profound; his theories informed the popular *Infant Care* pamphlets dispensed by the U.S. Children's Bureau and numerous publications directed at parents during the period. Watson contended that children should be placed on regular schedules of eating, sleeping, and elimination, and he sternly rebuked mothers about the dangers of too much maternal affection.[34] The fascination with behaviorism epitomizes what has been termed the "scientific utopianism" of the period, which was central to the home economics philosophy: the faith in the possibilities of science for solving social problems.[35]

Simultaneously, theorists such as John Dewey and G. Stanley Hall advanced a developmentalist notion of child rearing, which enjoined mothers to discern the motivations behind children's actions and advised them to manipulate children's behavior through intelligent guidance rather than punishment.[36] Whereas behaviorists attempted to counteract the increasingly child-centered tendency of the American family, developmentalists

34. The most influential of John B. Watson's works include *Ways of Behaviorism* (New York: Harper & Brothers, 1928), and especially *Psychological Care of Infant and Child* (New York: Norton, 1928). Another popular behaviorist of the period was Douglas Thom, who authored several Children's Bureau pamphlets and wrote many child-rearing texts, including *Everyday Problems of the Everyday Child* (New York: D. Appleton, 1927). On Watson and behaviorism in the 1920s, see John M. O'Donnell, *The Origins of American Behaviorism* (New York: New York University Press, 1985); Dora Halperin, "The Changing Perceptions of the Nature of the Child in the Context of Early Childhood Education (Ph.D. dissertation, Nova Scotia University, 1986); Lucille C. Birnbaum, "Behaviorism in the 1920s," *American Quarterly* 1 (Spring 1955): 30–55; and Kerry W. Buckley, *Mechanical Man: John Broadus Watson and the Beginnings of Behaviorism* (New York: Guilford Press, 1989). Two Cornell faculty members, Ethel Bushnell Waring and Marguerite Wilker, published a prescriptive text following behaviorist principles, which was often used in study groups, *The Behavior of Young Children* (New York: C. Scribner's Sons, 1929).

35. Fred Matthews, "The Utopia of Human Relations: The Conflict-Free Family in American Social Thought, 1930–1960," *Journal of the History of the Behavioral Sciences* 24 (October 1988): 343.

36. See Dorothy Ross, *G. Stanley Hall: The Psychologist as Prophet* (Chicago: University of Chicago Press, 1972); Herbert M. Kliebard, *The Struggle for the American Curriculum, 1893–1958* (Boston: Routledge & Kegan Paul, 1986); and John Dewey, *Democracy and Education* (New York: Macmillan, 1916).

sought to facilitate the trend.[37] Behaviorists and developmentalists had in common a contention that the early years were a pivotal stage of life and that parental mishandling could have potentially disastrous consequences, resulting in later maladjustment or worse. The experts also uniformly decried the inadequacy of the typical mother, whose child-rearing philosophy derived from the questionable wisdom of family and friends rather than the empirical findings of the social sciences.

The task for child study mothers was to sift through conflicting theories and come to their own decisions about how best to raise their children. The records of the Cornell clubs show that most mothers were skeptical of extreme expert prescriptions of any persuasion and were just as likely to question the harsh injunctions of the behaviorists as they were the champions of the "democratic family" who dominated the curriculum in the 1940s and 1950s. Despite the experts' characteristic disregard for the experiences and insights of mothers in their formulations of optimal child-rearing strategies, mothers stubbornly clung to maternal experience as a valuable source of knowledge.

The majority of mothers in Cornell's child study clubs were curious about the findings of the behavioral sciences, while simultaneously skeptical about child-rearing prescriptions that appeared to be constructed in laboratory settings with little understanding of the demands and values of the typical homemaker. They might be sympathetic to some of the principles of Watson's philosophy of regularity and routine, for instance, while resisting strict enforcement of his mandates. For example, members of the Oakfield Child Study Club discussed Watson's admonition that mothers ignore crying children and put them to bed without the usual bedtime rituals to prevent the development of "bad habits." One mother admitted, "I just can't stand it to hear Johnny cry and it only takes 10–15 minutes to rock him to sleep so we do it."[38] Such ideas could encounter opposition from Cornell personnel, however. One county agent reported to the college: "One woman ruined meeting by insisting on giving her ideas about kindness to children, which was thoroughly sentimental and selfish. . . . Her main idea was that if a baby cried it needed picking up, that it was lonely!"[39] Of course, the humanistic notions of child rearing expressed in 1928 by this mother would be resurrected by child development professionals in the 1940s and 1950s.

Believing that nurturance and affection should take precedence over strict routines, mothers were unwilling to let science invade every aspect of

37. Paul Fass argues that America's attraction to behaviorism may have been a reaction to the emergence of the child-centered family in *The Damned and the Beautiful: American Youth in the 1920s* (New York: Oxford University Press, 1977), p. 106.

38. Oakfield Child Study Club Notebook, Genesee County, 1929–30, n.d., Margaret Wylie Papers, Division of Rare and Manuscript Collections, Cornell University Library (hereafter MW).

39. Oakfield–Batavia County Report—1928–29, n.d., MW.

the child-rearing process. After reading Watson's *Psychological Care of Infant and Child,* which denounced the kisses and caresses that mothers dispensed to their children, a Southold child study club secretary recounted that "most mothers agreed that while it could be overdone the child who was not given much affection always suffered."[40] The Penfield Child Study Group objected to the view expressed in one of its readings that deviations from a child's routine constituted an "immoral practice."[41] Although mothers agreed that some scheduling benefited both mother and child, they also recognized the need for flexibility in mothering, a concept notably absent from the behaviorist dogma.

Perhaps the most influential aspect of the behaviorist philosophy was its disavowal of heredity as a component of personality and behavior. According to Watson's schema, children were made, not born, and improper early training could lead to later maladjustment and worse. But many mothers were reluctant to accept the concept that children were born with a neutral character that could shaped at will. A reporter from a Sandy Creek, New York, group noted that "we all seemed to differ with some authors with regard to heredity. We claim it plays a large part in character."[42] Mothers also often questioned those who insisted that a child's future character was formed by the first six or seven years of life; such a precept could be discouraging to a young mother consumed with the mistakes made during the early years of child rearing.

Most groups entertained diverging views on the relative importance of heredity versus environment in the rearing of children, and discussions about this topic were often heated. One reported noted: "War was almost declared during the discussion of: 'The product that comes out of the home is the test.' "[43] A club from New Paltz enjoyed a spirited debate in response to Watson's declamation: "The vocation your child is to follow in later life is not determined from within, but from without—by you—by the kind of life you have made him lead."[44] These mothers questioned and at times resisted the experts' contention that mothers must accept total responsibility for children's propensities, temperaments, and abnormalities.

These discussions vividly reveal the impact of maternal thinking on women's attitudes toward environmentalist explanations of child behavior.

40. Southold Home Bureau Child Study Club Notebook—1929–30, Suffolk County, May 14, 1930, MW.

41. Penfield Child Study Club Report, Monroe County—1944–45, November, 7, 1944, MW.

42. Sandy Creek Child Study Club Report, Oswego County—Mrs. W. J. Potter—1933–39, December 8, 1936, MW.

43. Family Life Report, Syracuse–Salem Hyde Unit—Mrs. Jas. F. Solar, Syracuse City, Home Bureau Units Report 1938–40, April 30, 1940, MW.

44. Walkhill Valley Child Study Club Report—New Paltz, New York—Ulster County—1929–30, December 9, 1929, MW.

Mothers of more than one child were often struck by the differences between their children and remained convinced that individual character was
not as malleable as the behaviorists made it out to be. The experience of maternal practice could modify the extent to which mothers accepted the psychologists' belief that childhood was a "plastic" period.

While mothers often thought the behaviorists had gone too far in their insistence on unstinting discipline, they were equally dubious about the concept of "democracy" in child rearing which infused child study texts of the
late 1930s and 1940s, a precursor to the "permissiveness" that characterized child care advice in the 1950s. Drawing on the political ideology of
World War II, experts of this era characterized the family as the breeding
ground of democracy and advocated that parents yield to the intrinsic needs
of children, substituting "self-demand" feeding, for instance, for the regularity and routine of the behaviorists.[45] According to a prominent parent
educator, Sidonie Gruenberg, "When democratic tendencies are in the as-
cendant, children's needs and wants are given as much consideration
as those of their parents."[46] But during a course of readings entitled
"Democracy Begins at Home," the mothers of the Lockport Parents Guild
negated the notion that children should be given an equal voice in the affairs of the home, stating in their minutes that it was "the general opinion
that small children could be given too much voice in family problems."[47]
Unwilling to relinquish their authority either to experts or their own children, mothers in a Henrietta, New York, group warned against the dangers
of too much democracy, asserting that "we also decided that to abolish a
young dictator from the family we must be dictators to do it."[48]

Ironically, although the clubs were ostensibly formed to instill mothers
with expert advice, it was commonly the mothers who emerged as the experts. In discussions about discipline, mothers disregarded the precept
commonly voiced by parent educators that they refrain from saying "don't"
to their children, arguing that with small children about and many household chores, this word was crucial to survival. Mothers also insisted on the
need to use physical punishment to discipline toddlers and infants, who
had not yet developed the capacity to reason. One leader was chided by the
members of her group when she related Cornell's belief that mothers should
refrain from physically punishing their children, writing to Wylie, "I was

45. See especially Arnold Gesell and Frances Ilg, *Infant and Child in the Culture of Today*
(New York: Harper & Row, 1943).

46. Sidonie Matsner Gruenberg, "Family Life—Then and Now," *Child Study* 16 (November
1938): 44.

47. Lockport Parents Guild, Niagara County—Mrs. Raymond Schryner—1940–45, September 19, 1944, MW.

48. Henrietta Child Study Club, Monroe County—1940–45, February 17, 1942, MW.

told that every wrong deed should be punished."[49] Wylie respected the insights of mothers, and although she regularly read club meeting minutes and responded to requests for information, she rarely intervened in controversial group discussions. Her only exception to this practice appears to have been when groups advocated punishments that served to frighten, shame, or harm children, such as shutting a child up in a dark closet, which one group recommended to a mother with a disobedient child. In these instances, Wylie responded with a diplomatically worded letter, encouraging the group to reconsider its point of view. The opportunity to discuss problems of discipline with a group of mothers enabled women to reflect on their own practices and, in some cases, to modify the more severe punishments some of them had employed.

During the late 1920s and early 1930s, the Cornell groups concentrated on topics pertaining to the care and training of small children, with the mother-child relationship as the focal point. One ramification of the Depression was a shift in the parent education movement from an emphasis on the individual child to a broader concern with familial and societal relationships, including the father as a significant factor in successful family life.[50] Throughout their campaign, and increasingly during the 1930s, home economists had clamored to enlist men as well as women in parent education classes. Child study mothers and parent educators lamented the absence of fathers from family life and hoped that education in child development would remind them of their responsibilities to their families beyond breadwinning. Other educators had more grandiose hopes that the participation of fathers in parent education classes would contribute to the construction of a more egalitarian family.[51]

While studying the broader network of family relationships, child study mothers began discussing their marital relationships. Parent educators applied the concept of democracy to relationships between husbands and wives, and dictatorial husbands were criticized both in child study texts and in group meetings. Members were equally critical of absentee husbands

49. Natalie Campbell to Margaret Wylie, January 31, 1929, Elmira, New York, MW.

50. Writings from the period which exemplify this trend include Helen L. Witmer, *The Field of Parent Education*, Parent Education Monograph no. 1 (New York: National Council of Parent Education, 1934); Lemo T. Dennis, *Living Together in the Family* (Washington, D.C.: American Home Economics Association, 1934); Lemo Dennis Rockwood, *Teaching Family Relationships* (Washington, D.C.: American Home Economics Association, 1935); Esther McGinnis, *Home Economics and Education for Family Life* (Washington, D.C.: American Home Economics Association, 1932); and Eduard C. Lindeman, "Family Relatedness: A Basic Consideration for Parent Education," in *Papers on Parent Education Presented at the Biennial Conference* (Washington, D.C.: National Council of Parent Education, 1930).

51. Dwight Sanderson, "Trends in Family Life Today," *Journal of Home Economics* 24 (April 1932): 315.

and often commented on the indifference of fathers towards their families, complaining that they were sometimes apt to be no more than "pocketbooks" or "furnace tenders" in the home.[52]

There is little evidence that husbands modified their parenting behaviors in response to mothers' club work, but members were supported by each other and educational personnel in their quest for a more engaged fatherhood. Some child study groups were established for both mothers and fathers, but it was more common for mothers to arrange for special meetings attended by the fathers. Although many fathers were receptive to child study work, others found the meetings disconcerting. Mothers could use the so-called scientific component of child study texts as a weapon with which to defend their child-rearing strategies. A member of the Watertown Child Study Club reported that she had "explained to father, by having him read material given us, *why* I do as I do with five year old son and *why* his methods are wrong for him."[53] Mothers could gain allies for their child-rearing strategies and point of view in child study groups, which could subvert the traditional pattern of male authority in the family.

As a rule, the Cornell home economists were more critical of the structure of the traditional family than were child study mothers, who rarely challenged the sexual division of labor but sought to make changes from within the standard family structure. The study courses supplied to the groups sometimes took up feminist themes, which were sometimes met with angry or bewildered responses. For instance, the suggestion that children could be adequately cared for by individuals other than a mother was disconcerting to these women. In the words of the Benett Study Club, "*No* one *can* possibly take the place of a mother in the home."[54] The Greece Child Study Club furthered the assumption that the term "mother" implied a full-time commitment to children when its members discussed whether mothers could work and be successful parents: "Most agreed 'no,' at least while children are younger. After that . . . some thot mother could work. She could then be a successful *parent,* but [according to a few] not necessarily a successful mother."[55] Cornell, however, advocated female choice in this matter. A representative from a New Paltz group expressed her group's sentiment that mothers should confine their professional ambitions to parenthood in a letter to family life extension specialist Blanche E. Hedrick in 1941. Hedrick encouraged the women to continue their critical examination of ideas, saying, "We try to encourage a careful evaluation of

52. Child Study Club Report, Erie County—1931–38—Mrs. Daniel Fisher, March 10, 1937, MW.

53. Watertown Child Study Club Report, Jefferson County—1940–45—Mrs. Carl Shippee, n.d., MW.

54. Benett Study Club—Buffalo County, November 6, 1940, MW.

55. Greece Child Study Club—Monroe County, January 25, 1945, MW.

everything, in fact we are pleased when our people evaluate the things we ourselves teach because only as individuals weigh values for themselves do they come to have meaning and significance for them." But she also reiterated her contention that although being a good mother was of inestimable value, "the misfortune arises when an individual, who feels he or she has a real contribution to make, feels thwarted in doing so."[56] As a married educated woman working outside the home, Hedrick sought to further the notion that a good mother could also be an employed mother, a notion shared by many of her colleagues, married and unmarried.

During the 1930s Cornell developed courses tailored to the needs of the homemakers, many of whom had been participating in the clubs for some years and were approaching middle age. Groups plunged enthusiastically into such topics such as careers for women over forty, the empty nest syndrome, the happiness of the homemaker, and menopause. An overriding theme concerned women's need to develop themselves as individuals, separate from their identities as wives and mothers. In one group, the members were urged: "*Don't neglect yourself* as a member of the family. . . . Some mothers . . . when the children are grown they find themselves lacking; the husband and family having progressed. As you go along *train yourself for later life.*"[57] Almost every group reiterated this message to its members, suggesting that mothers were exceedingly conscious of the difficulty of maintaining their individual identities as they cared for their families.

Child study groups simultaneously buttressed women's position as wives and mothers in the family and supported their activities outside of the home. Mothers were encouraged to think of themselves as individuals with rights as well as responsibilities, although those rights were limited by the confines of traditional family life. For some women, child study work fulfilled intellectual and personal needs that could not be met by family life. Because child study groups promised to benefit children, mothers were able to justify the time spent developing their intellects and forging a spirit of community with other women. Nonetheless, women who became deeply involved with the work often experienced a conflict between studying and family responsibilities. Delia Huston, a group leader in Orange County, reported, "Thinking and studying about family life makes one see beneath the surface into the deeper meaning of one's family relationships—even at the very time the family is interfering with the freedom of the precious work and study hours."[58] Clearly, the primary benefits women derived from participation in these groups were personal rather than familial.

---

56. Blanche E. Hedrick, to Mrs. Gertrude Bevier of New Paltz, New York, August 7, 1940, MW.

57. Hilton Family Life Report, Mrs. Burritt—Monroe County—1940–41, March 21, 1940, MW.

58. Delia C. Huston to Blanche Hedrick, April 12, 1939, Home Bureau Unit Meetings—Orange County—1938–39, MW.

The minutes of the Cornell child study clubs speak movingly of the benefits of study group membership. Members relished the opportunity to cultivate their intellects and conversational skills in the company of other women. A leader of a long-lasting group from Hilton Company wrote to Wylie at Cornell: "My furniture never was so shabby, my wardrobe so nearly exhausted nor I so happy as I am now. At one time I felt as though I was stagnating. All I seemed able to talk about was housework and babies. Child Guidance was the turning point for me. Studying and reading books on psychology has given me an entirely different slant on life. My time is so occupied with worthwhile things that I don't have time to be small and petty. Things which used to make me fume and rage don't even sink under my new armor plate."[59] Some of the groups lasted for decades, with members joining in celebration of birthdays and anniversaries and comforting each other in the face of illness and death.

Child study groups also often fostered social reform efforts among their members. Some groups sponsored child health days, instituted school libraries, and provided recreational activities for youth. Discussions about the need for playgrounds, public health problems, and the impact of the faltering economy on youth often made their way into meeting minutes. The groups undoubtedly provided women with the opportunity to develop their leadership skills, as much testimony suggests. Although child study groups did little to promote feminist activism, there is no doubt that coteries of small town and rural women throughout New York State were motivated to work for improvements within their communities as a result of study group participation.

These communities of mothers reinforced women's sense of themselves as experts in their own right by providing a venue in which they could critically reflect on both their own child-rearing practices and the professional literature. The mothers' groups organized by home economists nationwide represent one of the earliest attempts to educate large numbers of homemakers and should be considered an important and successful demonstration of adult education. The campaign for parent education within home economics in fact may have quietly anticipated the discipline of women's studies, which seeks to make women's experiences the basis of a course of study. Although mothers' groups lacked an overarching feminist agenda and accepted the sexual division of labor, they nonetheless served to validate womens' experiences by making them a crucial part of the curriculum.

During the early years of parent education, home economists participated in a balancing act, trying to meet the needs of mothers as the primary caretakers of children, while simultaneously aiming to transform child rearing

59. Mrs. Walter Quinn to Margaret Wylie, November 17, 1933, MW.

into an enterprise worthy of the skills and talents of both men and women. Home economists hoped to make the definition of parenting more inclusive but ultimately failed in their effort to engage men in active and involved parenting. Reporting on a conference on household engineering held in 1927, a commentator observed the "universal dissatisfaction of the women with the authoritarian basis of family life and . . . the universal satisfaction of the men with it." This reporter also noted the women's "insistent demand" that men accept some responsibility for child rearing.[60] Another account of the conference reported that the "usual easy acceptance of differentiation of function—the woman as housekeeper, the man as wage-earner—was sharply challenged."[61] Unfortunately, the sharp demands of home economists to establish a more equitable division of labor in the home during the 1920s and 1930s became increasingly muted during the more complacent 1940s and 1950s.

Home economists appeared acutely aware of the paradox that their discipline held for women. The discipline assumed that a woman's primary allegiance was to home and family, yet home economists pursued careers. Home economists seemingly upheld traditional notions of women's place, while simultaneously seeking to de-gender traditional women's work by reformulating it for a masculine society. This tendency is reflected in the language they used to discuss child rearing. Parent educators championed the more gender-neutral term "parenting" as opposed to "mothering," reflecting in part an ideal of child rearing characterized by the involvement of both sexes. Yet parenting still was—and is—defined almost exclusively as women's work.

The 1920s ideology of scientific motherhood may have set the stage for the domestic conformity of the 1940s and 1950s. During the 1920s it was debatable whether the working mother would have a place in contemporary society, but the explosion of information concerning the complexity and magnitude of parenting provided new rationalizations for keeping mothers in the home. The modernization of mothering was pursued by scores of women, who viewed it as buttressing their roles from within the division of labor and who could not yet imagine a combination of motherhood and careers.

Modernized motherhood merged ideals of twentieth-century individualism and expertise with traditional conceptions of womanhood. Although

60. Phillip Youtz, "Report of the Teachers College Conference on Household Engineering" at the "Home Problems Conference held at Merrill-Palmer School, Detroit, April 18–20, 1927," p. 35, Ser. 3, Box 33, no. 354, LSRM.

61. Columbia University, Teachers College, *Homemaking as a Center for Research: Report of the Teachers College Conferences on Homemaking, March 2–April 20, 1927* (New York: Teachers College, Columbia University, 1927), p. 83.

the aims of parent educators may seem modest to contemporary sensibili-
ties, child study mothers had to struggle to acquire the benefits of modernized motherhood. Spouses were reluctant to participate in child rearing;
children were resentful of their mothers' outside activities. Child study
mothers complained about the propensity of other family members to stifle
their efforts to improve themselves and their families. Child psychologists
were reluctant to admit home economists into what was perceived to be a
masculine domain. Although both child study mothers and home economists were unable to transform a system that excluded women from the
larger society, child study groups provided a venue for the development of
the voices of those women who struggled to improve their situations from
within the stratified sphere of the traditional mother. In child study groups
women could wrestle with the problems of family life and find support for
their positions as wives, mothers, and individuals in a community of mothers. Home economists created these uniquely female educational institutions, which mediated between nineteenth-century maternalism and
twentieth-century scientific motherhood. In so doing, they opened a space
for mothers to interject their voices into the discourse of child development.

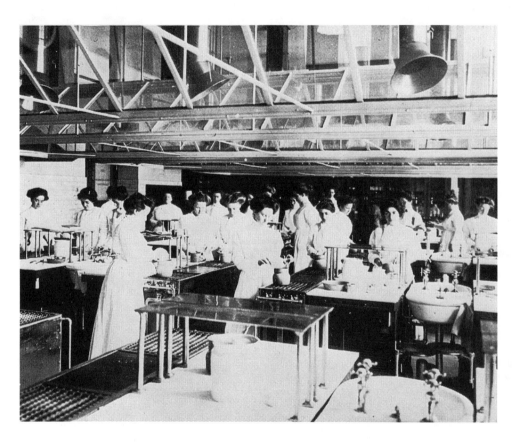

As higher education in home economics expanded in the 1910s, many administrators and professors modeled their curricula and their laboratories after those in place at leading institutions such as the School of Household Arts, Teachers College, Columbia University. Courtesy Division of Rare and Manuscript Collections, Carl A. Kroch Library, Cornell University.

Women's Place:
Home Economics
and Education

The gendered nature of home economics frustrated attempts to gain legitimacy for the field in academia and continues to inhibit the transformation of the field today. Historically women have had difficulty achieving equal treatment in higher education. In the 1870s the Ivy League schools in the East successfully resisted coeducation, leaving it to the elite Seven Sister colleges to create an equivalent education for young women. In the West and Midwest, where coeducation was more easily implemented as new institutions were established, women nevertheless often found themselves studying separately from male students. To college presidents such as Benjamin Ide Wheeler at the University of California, Berkeley, the creation of schools of home economics seemed an ideal way to segregate women students. The women faculty in home economics acquiesced to this state of affairs. Largely blocked from employment in traditional departments such as chemistry, economics, or sociology, they found that departments and colleges of home economics often provided their only opportunity for employment. In higher education separatism was not a strategy chosen by women as much as it was the only alternative to total exclusion.

Home economics may have opened opportunities for educated women when there were few, but as Rima Apple points out, increased emphasis on vocational preparation mandated by the Smith-Hughes Act (1917) undercut the status of the field of home economics at research universities. Male-gendered fields as decidedly vocational as mining and metallurgy, industrial engineering, and architecture suffered no similar stigmatization. Gender prejudice and discrimination appear to have played a significant role in the devaluation not only of home economics but of other women's fields such as nursing and library science. Margaret Rossiter shows that when men took over home economics, they received the respect and resources previously denied women home economics administrators. Marjorie East's reminiscences touch on the restructuring that took place at the Pennsylvania State Univerersity.

Home economics, designed by women to expand their options, has rarely been able to escape the limitations imposed by gender stereotypes, despite heroic attempts by generations of women to gain legitimacy for the field.

4 Liberal Arts or Vocational Training? Home Economics Education for Girls

RIMA D. APPLE

For many of us who passed through the U.S. public school system, the term "home economics" conjures up visions of girls learning to sew a straight seam and to prepare potato salad. Despite these memories, school-based home economics did not develop merely to teach girls to cook and sew; at its origins, dating back more than a century, it sought to elevate and enlarge women's roles in the home and in society, although some educators and home economists thought young women could be trained in the subject for paid employment. As a dynamic component of the school curriculum, home economics over the past century has been affected by social, pedagogical, demographic, and legislative developments that altered its perspective and content.

Beginning as early as the mid-nineteenth century with educational reformer Catharine Beecher, girls' schooling was intended to help students develop the critical thinking skills they would need in their own homes and in the wider community. For Beecher and her followers, the subject of domestic economy was not narrowly focused on technical household skills but rather was an integral part of a general science-based liberal arts education to prepare females for their professions as wives and mothers.[1] By the last third of the nineteenth century, developments in higher education furthered the idea of education for motherhood as part of the rationale for women's entrance into land grant colleges. For example, when the Iowa State Agricultural College opened in 1869, women were admitted to the

---

1. For the significance of Beecher, see Kathryn Kish Sklar, *Catharine Beecher: A Study in American Domesticity* (New York: Norton, 1973).

same courses as men. But even before the school opened, the Board of Trustees had declared that "if young men are to be educated to fit them for successful, intelligent, and practical farmers and mechanics, is it not as essential that young women should be educated in a manner that will qualify them to properly understand and discharge their duties as wives of farmers and mechanics?" By 1871, Iowa State offered domestic science courses.[2] The overwhelming majority of women attending coeducational land-grant colleges before 1915 were enrolled in home economics courses.[3]

By the twentieth century, the notion that all girls needed this training was a pedagogical given. Domestic science proponents continued to echo the themes of professionalism and science[4] and passed this assumption along to their students. A 1932 textbook asked, "Why study homemaking?" The answer is an updated version of Catharine Beecher: "Homemaking is a complicated job, involving many sorts of activities. . . . We need the benefit of the scientific study that has been made of various homemaking activities. . . . We need to think of homemaking as a business or a profession."[5] Two consistent assumptions underlay the calls for home economics education. First, that domestic tasks are women's work was consistently articulated and taken for granted but rarely explained. Second, that women need specific formal training for the domestic sphere justified domestic science in the schools. Yet changing demographics, developments in pedagogical theory, and political circumstances transformed home economics from a female version of general liberal arts and science education to skills-oriented vocational training.

For example, in the early twentieth century middle-class home economists viewed with alarm what they and many of their contemporaries saw as the breakdown of American family life. All around they saw a society disrupted by increased urbanization, industrialization, and immigration. Ellen Swallow Richards, founder of the Lake Placid conferences, in 1909

2. Ercel Sherman Eppright and Elizabeth Storm Ferguson, *A Century of Home Economics at Iowa State University: A Proud Past, a Lively Present, a Future Promise* (Ames: Iowa State University Home Economics Alumni Association, 1971), p. 4.

3. Linda Marie Fritschner, "The Rise and Fall of Home Economics: A Study with Implications for Women, Education, and Change" (Ph.D. dissertation, University of California, Davis, 1973).

4. Charlottte V. Gulick, "Introduction," in Mary L. Read, *The Mothercraft Manual* (Boston: Little, Brown, 1916), p. ix; Henrietta W. Calvin, *Principles and Policies in Home Economics Education,* U.S. Department of the Interior, Bureau of Education, Home Economics Circular 4, April 1918; Anna M. Cooley et al., *Teaching Home Economics* (New York: Macmillan, 1919), pp. vii, 14–17, 57–58; *Teacher's Guide in Planning Homemaking Education Programs for Secondary Schools in Alabama* (N.P.: Alabama Department of Education, State Board of Education, 1949).

5. Mabel B. Trilling and Florence Williams Nicholas, *The Girl and Her Home* (New York: Houghton Mifflin, 1932), p. 3.

confidently promoted home economics as "nothing less than an effort to save our social fabric from what seems inevitable disintegration."[6] This social reform outlook continued to influence the calls for home economics education. One writer in the *Journal of Home Economics* in 1919 declared, "Much of what is unwise in the rearing of children is due to the indifference, the inertia, and the lack of insight that arise from unpreparedness for the responsibility. Each generation of graduates from the eighth grade and high school courses in home economics should increase the number of homes in which babies and children will have better chances for survival and health."[7] Home economics courses would simultaneously train girls for their roles in the home and in the community. Through such schooling, girls would become responsible consumers and citizens; they would establish and run healthy households; they would be productive and confident homemakers.

Faith in the social benefits of home economics training also received support from the National Education Association, which clearly articulated the role leading educators envisioned for girls in American society. They explained that courses for girls should "enable them, thru [*sic*] the right sort of homemaking training, to enter homes of their own, able to assume the most sacred duties with an intelligent preparation, and to perpetuate the type of home that will bring about the highest standard of health and morals."[8] This rationale gave additional credence to the inclusion of home economics in the curricula of elementary and secondary schools, though it emphasized the technical aspects of homemaking while ignoring the larger "scientific" outlook of early twentieth-century home economists.

Clearly, however, such a major reform required an influx of money that local districts and state agencies could not provide. The Smith-Hughes Act of 1917 began federal provision of the financial wherewithal to fuel this transformation in American education. Yet despite calls by home economists and other educators for domestic science education in public schools, the initial debates over the funding of vocational education did not support home economics. This essay illustrates how political negotiations have shaped educational potentialities.

6. Quoted in *The Social History of American Education*, B. Edward McClellan and William Reese, ed. (Urbana: University of Illinois Press, 1988), p. 237.

7. Alma L. Binzel, "For the Homemaker: Making Children Worth While," *Journal of Home Economics* 11 (January 1919): 28; Eppright and Ferguson, *A Century of Home Economics*, pp. 86–87.

8. National Education Association, *Report of the Committee on the Place of Industries in Public Education to the National Council of Education* (N.P.: National Education Association, 1910), p. 110; Carlotta C. Greer, "When, How Much, and to Whom Should Home Economics Be Taught?" *Journal of Home Economics* 11 (June 1919): 235–41.

On January 20, 1914, Congress established a commission to report on the future of vocational education, partly in response to activities of the National Society for the Promotion of Industrial Education (NSPIE).[9] The panel included two women, Agnes Nestor and Florence Marshall, strong trade unionists committed to industrial vocational education, not home economics education, for girls. Nestor and Marshall fought against the inclusion of home economics in the drafted bill. As Nestor explained, they "foresaw difficulties when we found that some of the men wished to give girls more domestic science than opportunity to learn trades. . . . We felt that if domestic science were allowed the greater appropriation, it would be too easy to push all the girls into that field and not give them the technical training they were likely to find themselves in need of."[10] To these women, vocational training meant education for wage labor in industry, technical instruction that would prepare women for paid employment, which, they believed, home economics courses would not provide.

Other trade unionists who spoke before the commission voiced similar concerns. Leonora O'Reilly, vice-president of the New York Women's Trade Union League, declared that "so many of us have not anything like homes . . . and if we do make the mistake to get married we go back to the mill afterwards to help support the children which may come and can not be supported by the wages that are paid in the mills."[11]

Senator Carroll Page (R-Vermont), a member of the commission, reflected the prevailing ideology when he insisted that "the Almighty . . . has ordained that woman do the housework and the man do the work which he does."[12] He and Senator Hoke Smith (D-Georgia) and Congressman Dudley Mays Hughes (D-Georgia) represented rural states, where home economics was considered eminently practical for farm women. The strong connection between domestic science education and rural living was not new, as we have seen in the experience of land-grant colleges.

Eventually, the commission achieved a compromise between rural patriarchal interests embracing home economics education for girls and the trade unionists: it proposed funding the training of teachers of home economics, as well as those in agricultural, trade, and industrial subjects but

9. Gladys Alee Branegan, *Home Economics Teacher Training under the Smith-Hughes Act, 1917–1927* (New York: Teachers College, Columbia University, Bureau of Publications, 1929), p. 31.

10. Agnes Nestor, *Woman's Labor Leader* (Rockford, Ill.: Bellevue Books, 1954), quoted in Jane Bernard Powers, *The "Girl Question" in Education: Vocational Education for Young Women in the Progressive Era* (London: Falmer Press, 1992), p. 57; Greta Gray, "Vocational Training for Girls," *Journal of Home Economics* 11 (November 1919): 493–97.

11. U.S. Congress, *Report of the Commission on National Aid to Vocational Education*, vol. 2: *Hearings*, quoted in Powers, *The "Girl Question" in Education*, p. 58.

12. U.S. Congress, *Report of the Commission on National Aid to Vocational Education*, *Hearings*, quoted in Powers, *The "Girl Question" in Education*, p. 59.

funded only salaries of teachers of agricultural, trade and industrial subjects. Teachers of home economics were not to be supported except under the general category of agricultural education. In many ways, the commission's views on home economics were similar to those of earlier home economics advocates. Members did not deny the importance of domestic education for girls, but they saw it within the framework of a girl's general education, not as vocational education.

As significant as the Smith-Hughes Act (the legislation that eventually developed from the commission's report) has been for home economics education, it is ironic how little home economists were involved. Some evidence even suggests that the American Home Economics Association feared the effects of including home economics education under vocational education.[13] For example, Mary Schenck Woolman, a member of the association's Legislative Committee, believed that every girl, no matter what her plans for the future, should attend home economics classes "as an integral part of her general education in the elementary and high school." Since Smith-Hughes's support of vocational education was interpreted as technical education for paid employment rather than general liberal arts education for all schoolgirls, clearly home economics belonged outside the scope of the legislation. Fortunately, in Woolman's view, "the States believe in this [general home economics education] and are developing it, consequently national grants for this purpose are not required."[14] Home economists' general lack of interest in Smith-Hughes suggests that many of them agreed with her. Unless one was interested in the vocational (defined as training for paid employment) aspects of home economics, there was little reason to be involved with the development of the Smith-Hughes Bill.

The historical record does point to the pivotal role of the National Society for the Promotion of Industrial Education in the eventual passage of the legislation. Some members of the Legislative Committee of the AHEA participated in the deliberations of the NSPIE committee on Smith-Hughes. Yet their direct influence is difficult to gauge. It is crucial to note as well that the AHEA representatives who did speak at the NSPIE expressed strong support for the vocational aspects of home economics, not surprising considering the audience. As Helen Kinne, chair of the AHEA Legislative Committee, explained before the preliminary meeting of the NSPIE committee on the Smith-Hughes Bill, "Home making is a pursuit or a vocation, and has economic value. It does not bring in a wage to the worker, but while the woman at home is usually spoken of as a consumer, she is quite as emphatically a

13. For more on this point, see Phyllis Palmer, *Domesticity and Dirt: Housewives and Domestic Servants in the United States, 1920–1945* (Philadelphia: Temple University Press, 1989), pp. 90–92.

14. Mary Schenck Woolman, "The Smith-Hughes Bill," *Journal of Home Economics* 8 (May 1916): 241–46, quotation on p. 245.

producer in that she produces home conditions either for good or ill."[15] Similarly, when Woolman, a member of the NSPIE committee on Smith-Hughes as well as the AHEA Legislative Committee, called on members of the AHEA to write their congressional representatives and senators in support of the legislation, she emphasized the wage-earning, vocational facets of home economics, noting specifically the possibility for employment as "cook and housemaid, the dietitian, institution manager, and household decorator,"[16] a position in sharp contrast with that of Nestor and Marshall.

By the time the commission released its report, other proponents of home economics education were mobilized, though no home economics educator was called to speak.[17] Leaders of the General Federation of Women's Clubs testified to the importance of incorporating home economics in public schools. The organization's members, primarily middle- and upper-middle class women, consciously sought to improve the conditions of their "less fortunate sisters." Believing that industrial work was harmful to women physically and morally, they discouraged women's further employment in factories, shops, and offices and presented home economics in the public schools as "salvation through scientific investigation and cooperation."[18] Also heard at the hearings were representatives from government bureaus and departments, from the National Education Association, and from labor organizations.

The presence of home economics in the bill also attracted the support of various congressional members. Senator Page made an emotional speech in which he linked the decline of the American family, divorce, and infant mortality with insufficient training in homemaking: "Without this knowledge thousands of homes will be wrecked, thousands of lives ruined, and hundreds of thousands made unhappy for no other reason than that the homekeepers of our country have no adequate training in that most important of all duties, the making of a well-regulated, intelligently-conducted household. . . .

"It is coming to be more and more realized that we must give to our girls a training different from that with which we now provide them if crime, disease, divorce, and race suicide are not to continue to increase." Similarly, Representative Horace Towner, ignoring the many women who entered the paid labor force out of necessity, declared, "It will benefit the whole scheme

15. Helen Kinne, "Terminology and the Smith-Hughes Bill," *Journal of Home Economics* 8 (April 1916): 186–88, quotation on p. 187; Helen Kinne, "The Smith-Hughes Bill," *Journal of Home Economics* 8 (June 1916): 328.

16. Woolman, "The Smith-Hughes Bill," p. 245.

17. Branegan, *Home Economics Teacher Training*, pp. 26–27.

18. Mary Belle King Sherman, *General Federation of Women's Clubs Magazines*, March 1916, p. 17, quoted in Powers, *The "Girl Question" in Education*, p. 67. For more on this point, see ibid., pp. 65–67.

of home-making and home-keeping if you elevate the home in the mind of the girl who thinks too much about becoming a shop girl, or a factory worker, rather than of going to the home and becoming a mother . . . "[19] These comments received applause on the floor of Congress. Not surprisingly, then, the bill that passed the Congress included salaries for teachers of home economics.

During the debate over the Smith-Hughes Bill, very different definitions of vocational education had emerged, though opponents often seemed unaware that they were using the same terms for diverse curricular goals. On the one hand were those who promoted vocational home economics as technical training for future gainful employment. On the other hand were those who would place vocational home economics education in a girl's general liberal arts education as preparation for women's life work. The curricula institutionalized following the passage of Smith-Hughes combined elements of both, merging the orientation to technical skills with the view that each girl would in the future run her own home. As a result, home economics education stressed the preparation of girls for their future occupation of homemaker.

Though it focused on home economics instruction in the public schools, Smith-Hughes did much more than pay the salaries of a few teachers. By funding the training of home economics teachers for public schools, the act also affected home economics on college campuses. It encouraged the expansion of programs, but within a very narrow compass, which had contradictory results for university home economics. In the early twentieth century, women who wanted to pursue careers in scientific research were frequently counseled to study home economics. Though schools of home economics were less prestigious than other science departments on campus, they did allow women to develop scientific careers.[20] As home economics units became increasingly involved with teacher training for public school instruction, however, these schools could be more easily dismissed as vocational training departments, not science departments. Moreover, the growth of the administrative structures necessary to supervise the teacher training further lessened the perceived significance of the scientific aspects of home economics.[21]

---

19. Quoted in Powers, *The "Girl Question" in Education*, p. 68.

20. Margaret W. Rossiter, *Women Scientists in America: Struggles and Strategies to 1940* (Baltimore: Johns Hopkins University Press, 1982).

21. For some exploratory analysis on this point, see Rima D. Apple, "Science Gendered: Nutrition in the United States, 1840–1940," in *The Science and Culture of Nutrition*, ed. Harmke Kamminga and Andrew Cunningham (Amsterdam: Rodopi for the Wellcome Institute Series in the History of Medicine, 1995), pp. 129–57. Fritschner documented the increasing growth of the administrative structure of home economics schools in this period, but she ignored the science research–oriented components ("The Rise and Fall of Home Economics," chap. 4).

The Smith-Hughes Act institutionalized a particular view of home economics in elementary and secondary schools and on college campuses. Rather than the science-based orientation of the early proponents, the act fostered a more vocational outlook, a skills-oriented sequence of courses, with stress on "information and technique rather than on powers of thinking and judgment."[22] This emphasis strengthened a trend already apparent several years earlier. In 1913–14, Benjamin Andrews surveyed 288 high schools for the U.S. Bureau of Education, discovering that many offered some home economics classes, though of a narrow range. In 89 percent of the schools there were classes on food and nutrition, in 81 percent on aspects of sewing; only 25 pecent gave classes in broader areas of homemaking such as housekeeping and shelter. None of the schools offered the courses of a wider scope recommended by early home economists.[23] One university home economics instructor warned that since "men manage the schools" and "they are imbued with the idea that woman's place is in the home and because they like good food and conceive of home economics as being chiefly cooking," they would establish courses for specific skill development.[24] By 1923, observers could rightly conclude that "it is regrettable, though true, that home economics education is often judged by material and tangible results only," namely "numbers of garments made and quantities of foods served."[25] The social concerns of earlier home economics leaders were replaced with instruction in techniques of middle-class lifestyle.

The Smith-Hughes Act is a significant milestone in the history of the home economics movement because it cemented the relationship between home economics and the federal government. Though the act spread home economics education into school systems across the country, early proponents of home economics might have questioned the cost. The act's implementation undermined some of the basic principles espoused by home economics reformers, particularly scientific research as a basis for the continued development of the profession. Instead, it fostered the growth of an administrative structure necessary to realize the pedagogical goals of the legislation. Moreover, Smith-Hughes hindered the potential social reform

22. Mabel Barbara Trilling et al., *Home Economics in American Schools* (Chicago: University of Chicago Press, 1920), pp. 1–2.

23. Beulah I. Coon, *Home Economics Instruction in the Secondary Schools* (Washington, D.C.: Center for Applied Research in Education, 1964), pp. 23–24.

24. Gray, "Vocational Training for Girls," pp. 494–95.

25. Henrietta W. Calvin, *Home Economics Education*, U.S. Department of the Interior, Bureau of Education, Bulletin 6, 1923, p. 371; *Annual Homemaking Education Descriptive Report*, Wisconsin State Board of Vocational and Adult Education, to the U.S. Office of Education, 1953–54; *Home Economics Courses of Study for Junior High Schools*, U.S. Department of the Interior, Bureau of Education, Home Economics Circular 9, October 1920.

promised by early home economists because it promoted the skills-oriented, technical curriculum for girls in public schools.

The passage of the Smith-Hughes Act proved to be a necessary but not sufficient precondition for the development of home economics in the United States. Federal funding for home economics teachers expanded offerings in public schools throughout the country. The financial aid also fueled the growth of college home economics programs to staff the many teaching, supervisory, and administrative posts required to support this segment of a girl's education. The act itself, however, does not account for the form this instruction took or the rapidity with which the American educational system embraced home economics courses. The scope and content of home economics courses for girls were shaped by other factors, most notably changing demographics of the school population, pedagogical innovations, and cultural models. As we have seen in the fight for the Smith-Hughes Act, it was not the social reform arguments of home economics reformers or their call for home economics as a science-based liberal arts education for girls that swayed the votes for passage. Rather, it was the traditional image of woman as wife and mother in need of technical training to run her home efficiently and healthfully, an image that was already popular in American society and that focused on skills within the home rather than wider social concerns.

This concept of American domesticity had begun to affect public schools as early as the second decade of this century, when some schools and school districts made home economics education mandatory for girls. Fayette, Ohio, by 1914 required all seniors to take such a course. By 1915, all seventh- and eighth-grade girls in Indiana were required to take domestic science; Idaho required that home economics be taught in all rural high schools.[26] Educators were proud of their efforts. One state superintendent of public instruction confidently concluded: "The introduction of domestic science into the course of study has led to new interest in domestic pursuits, has increased the efficiency of young housewives, and has led to improvement in the general health."[27]

To progressive educators, science seemed the salvation for a disintegrating society; it would "teach children and youth exactly what they needed

26. Mrs. Frederic Schoff, "Education for Child Nurture and Home Making Outside of Schools," in *Report of the Commission of Education for the Year Ended June 30, 1914* (Washington, D.C.: U.S. government Printing Office, 1915), p. 368; "Home Economics," in *Report of the Commission of Education, 1915*, vol. 1 (Washington, D.C.: U.S. Department of the Interior, Bureau of Education, 1915), pp. 317–42.

27. Unnamed source quoted in *Report of the Commission of Education for the Year Ended June 30, 1914*, p. 319.

to know in order that they take their place as contributing members of society."[28] Curricular reforms such as vocational education reinforced the calls for home economics training for women. Proponents specifically linked effective home economics education and a citizen's civic responsibility: "Home economics in the schools of to-day . . . because of the nature of their content, afford just the right opportunity for the training of the girl as a member of society in her own home and in her community associations. They contribute, as all studies rightfully pursued should, towards the development of the social efficiency of the girl."[29]

Belief in the efficacy of education to alleviate social problems prompted contemporary curriculum reform movements during a time when the school population was changing. In 1900, only 59 percent of all children between the ages of five and seventeen attended schools; by 1928, this proportion had grown to 80 percent.[30] Several interrelated factors induced the sharp increase in school attendance. Before the turn of the century, secondary education was primarily college-oriented. In the twentieth century, the occupational structure of the U.S. economy created increasing numbers of jobs demanding high school education, if not graduation. Evolving elementary and high school curricula slowly, though unevenly, incorporated vocational education. The high school was no longer an elite institution for the college-bound; it was a popular institution with a pragmatic outlook: to prepare women and men for their roles in society.[31]

From early in the century, home economists had differentiated the form education should take depending on the age of the student. They did not dispute the need to train girls in the skills of housewifery. They targeted younger students for two reasons. Skills training at an early age could provide background for older girls to take more advanced courses. Moreover, despite increased accessibility, many girls did not reach high school, and those who did frequently sought occupational or academic training, not home economics. To enhance students' opportunities for domestic training, home economists spoke of tailoring the curriculum to the needs of the students, particularly "children of foreign parentage" living in "the poorer sections of the cities" who were likely to leave school early.[32] They rationalized that "since many children leave school by the end of the sixth grade," it was

28. Herbert M. Kliebard, "Psychology . . . The teacher's Blackstone: G. Stanley Hall and the Effort to Build a Developmental Curriculum for Youth," *Journal of Early Adolescence* 5 (1985): 467.

29. Cooley et al., *Teaching Home Economics*, pp. 37–38.

30. Barbara Brenzel, Cathy Roberts-Gersch, and Judith Wittner, "Becoming Social: School Girls and Their Culture between the Two World Wars," *Journal of Early Adolescence* 5 (1985): 480.

31. Rury, "Vocationalism," p. 252.

32. Calvin, *Principles and Policies in Home Economics Education*, p. 3.

necessary to begin "specialized work for girls in the fifth and sixth grades at least."[33]

A study of current problems in home economics, undertaken by the U.S. Bureau of Education in 1917 underscores home economists' concerns with school dropout rates. One home economics educator wrote poignantly, "When I think of the thousands of girls who leave school at the age of 12, I feel that if I had charge of that work, I should like to begin the very first year of school because at that age all girls love to play house. . . . Children of 5 or 6 can do nice work if properly taught."[34] Later in the century, increasing numbers of girls remained in school longer, but still home economics courses remained in the middle grades.

As a survey published in 1923 documents, students who attended high school often were reluctant to take home economics classes, though interest apparently differed from region to region. In eastern cities, only one in twelve high school girls enrolled in home economics courses; others followed an academic or commercial track. In the Pacific Northwest, however, conditions of the labor market did not encourage girls to enroll in commercial courses; local universities and colleges had more liberal entrance requirements, and "the inclination among high-school girls to marry young and take up actual housekeeping duties" influenced a greater proportion of the students to enroll in the home economics curriculum.[35] George S. Counts, a leading educational philosopher, explained the educational, social, and economic reasons why girls were disinclined to participate in high school home economics classes. They entered college preparatory classes if they wanted to continue their education and commercial courses to prepare themselves for the wage market. Girls believed that home economics, presented as preparation for wifehood and motherhood, would "avail [them] but little." He concluded that the students "probably reasoned, and reasoned wisely, that the college-preparatory and commercial courses would render larger immediate service in the matrimonial venture than the acquisition of the most expert skills in cooking and sewing."[36]

The low enrollment in home economics on the secondary level and the observation that many girls left formal educational institutions at a young age convinced educators that it was important to maintain and extend home

---

33. Agnes K. Hanna, *Home Economics in the Elementary and Secondary School* (Boston: Whitcomb and Barrows, 1922), p. 289.

34. *Current Problems in Home Economics,* U.S. Department of the Interior, Bureau of Education, Home Economics Circular 2, January 1, 1918, p. 7.

35. For example, Calvin, *Home Economics Education,* pp. 373–74, and *Present Status of Home Economics Education,* U.S. Department of the Interior, Bureau of Education, Home Economics Circular 10, November 1921, pp. 3–4.

36. George S. Counts, *The Senior High School Curriculum* (Chicago: University of Chicago Press, 1926), p. 103.

economics education below the high school level. Some attention was given to the early years of schooling, but most was directed toward the sixth, seventh, and eighth grades as more appropriate for technical training rather the abstract thinking of a general liberal arts education. As Carlotta Greer argued in 1919, "It is a fact that a greater number of pupils will be reached by placing home economics courses in the junior rather than in the senior high school. Since it is a subject of great importance in the life of all girls and since it fills an important place in democratic education, the matter of reaching the greatest number should be a consideration well worth regarding."[37] Thus, while despairing that high school girls often failed to avail themselves of the opportunity to study home economics, one 1921 survey of home economics education also proudly claimed that two-thirds of the larger school systems in the United States required all girls in the seventh and eighth grades to take the course.[38]

Enrollment in the lower levels of home economics did not abate. By the middle third of this century, the overwhelming proportion of girls in the United States attended home economics classes, the vast majority in the seventh and eighth grades. To learn more about the status of home economics, during the 1938–39 academic year, the U.S. Office of Education surveyed more than 70 percent of all students in junior high schools, junior-senior high schools, and senior high schools. It found that 76 percent of the girls in the seventh and eighth grades attended these classes, while only 23 percent of the twelfth graders participated in them.[39]

Courses in Muncie, Indiana, appear to have been fairly typical. Devised to meet the "the functional needs of the major group of the girls, who will be home-makers," the instruction began in the seventh and eighth grades, concentrating on food, clothing, and house planning. Optional courses on the high school level included dressmaking, millinery, hygiene and home nursing, household management, and food and clothing selection. This curriculum suggests that home economics education had been redifined. The broad societal outlook encompassing a girl's general education had been reduced to a narrow focus on the vocational skills necessary to maintain the individual household.

From its origins and throughout the nineteenth century, home economics had been promoted as a course of study to challenge girls' intellect and creativity, to educate women to think creatively about family life and social

37. Carlotta C. Greer, "When, How Much, and to Whom Should Home Economics Be Taught?" p. 236. See also *Home Economics Courses of Study for Junior High Schools*, U.S. Department of the Interior, Bureau of Education, Home Economics Circular 9, October 1920.

38. *Present Status of Home Economics Education*, pp. 3–4.

39. *Home Economics in the Public High Schools, 1938–39*, U.S. Office of Education, Vocational Division Bulletin 213, 1941, pp. 38–40; Powers, *The "Girl Question" in Education*; Fritschner, "The Rise and Fall of Home Economics."

problems, in short, a general liberal arts education. Before a student could appreciate these facets of home economics, however, she needed to develop a range of housewifery skills. This technical basis, it was emphasized, was only the minimal requirement *before* beginning more advanced aspects of home economics. Further study should greatly expand this foundation.[40]

Despite this expectation of additional advanced instruction, by the 1920s there was an undeniable trend toward a focus on the individual rather than the community and on the teaching of skills rather than of problem solving. Declared one 1921 analysis: "There is a general effort to insure that the school home economics education functions in the home life of the girl, that efficient methods of work are taught, and that the best standards of American living are maintained. Establishment of health habits and preparation for home helpfulness are the dominant motives now determining the courses of study and the methods of instruction."[41] Furthermore, though explaining that "*the primary objective of the intellectual training* that we give children in our school subjects is *a scientific attitude*" and despite concluding that home economics "provides the content for the application of scientific principles more thoroughly than does any other subject of study," surveys of home economics curricula and textbooks found that the subject had been reduced to "cookin' 'n' sewin'"—published recipes and commercial clothing patterns.[42] Later in the decade, in his survey of senior high school curricula in fifteen progressive school districts, Counts found that at least 85 percent of the home economics classes offered were cooking and sewing.[43]

Following the complaint that home economics had become merely a set of manual, technical skills, some textbooks consciously sought to emphasize the intellectual aspects of the topic. In *A Girl's Problems in Home Economics*, a popular textbook published in 1926, Mabel Trilling and Florence Williams explained that "throughout the book, every unit of subject matter has been treated so as to give the girls training in thinking out home economics problems as well as acquiring skill." The book's introduction, however, suggests that classroom teachers may have disagreed with this approach, for the authors found it important to remind them: "Emphasis has been placed on the intellectual content of problems selected for study as well as on the acquisition of technical skill. . . . Teachers should take

---

40. *Home Economics Courses of Study for Junior High Schools.*

41. *Present Status of Home Economics Education*, pp. 4–5.

42. Mabel Barbara Trilling et al., *Home Economics in American Schools*, supplement published in conjunction with *School Review and Elementary School Journal* 2 (1920).

43. Counts, *The Senior High School Curriculum*, pp. 104–5; Carter V. Good, "The High School Curriculum in Home Economics," *Journal of Home Economics* 19 (December 1927): 686–90.

pains to keep such lessons as those on the *problem-solving basis.*"[44] The text's title reflects another significant characteristic of home economics in the 1920s and 1930s: the subject was designed for girls, representing an important continuity with the field from the days of Catharine Beecher. Not surprisingly, given this attitude, in 1938–39 barely 1 percent of boys enrolled in home economics courses.[45]

Yet, throughout much of the twentieth century, many home economics educators, cognizant of the importance of including boys in these classes, attempted to broaden the curriculum. Thus, in their 1936 textbook, *Junior Home Problems*, Kate W. Kinyon and L. Thomas Hopkins explain: "Since the content of each unit is selected for the purpose of aiding junior high school pupils to meet their modern social problems more intelligently, emphasis is not placed upon specific facts to be learned nor specific skills to be acquired. Rather, the content treats the problem in its larger social relationships so as to derive the basic meanings and values which enable the pupil to improve *his* social behavior" (emphasis added).[46] This is in sharp contrast to the 1928 edition of this text, whose goals are "stated in terms of growth, attitudes, habits, knowledge, and skills" directed to "the needs of junior high school girls."[47] By 1936 the authors specifically claimed that problem-solving material was "as pertinent to the experiences of boys as to those of girls," and they used male pronouns to refer to students.

Although secondary school textbooks of the era reflected a renewed, widening vision of home economics education, home economists were slower to realize the need for direct involvement in constructing the legislation that also shaped the curriculum.[48] The Smith-Hughes Act had defined home economics education as vocational education, and from 1917 to 1963 all federal vocational education acts allocated specific categorical funding to home economics education. The 1963 Vocational Education Act, however, eliminated such funding. It allowed vocational funding disbursements for occupational home economics education leading to gainful employment but mandated no specific funding level. (Some earlier bills, such

44. Mabel B. Trilling and Florence Williams, "Suggestions to Teachers," in *A Girl's Problems in Home Economics* (Philadelphia: J. B. Lippincott, 1926), p. 2.

45. *Home Economics in Public High Schools, 1938–39,* p. 5.

46. Kate W. Kinyon and L. Thomas Hopkins, *Junior Home Problems,* rev. ed. (Chicago: Benj. H. Sanborn, 1936), pp. iii–iv.

47. Kate W. Kinyon and L. Thomas Hopkins, *Junior Home Problems* (Chicago: Benj. H. Sanborn, 1928), p. iii.

48. The history of these legislative efforts needs more detailed study. Material in the following paragraphs has been drawn from Letitia A. Combs, "Conflict and Resolution: 1976 Congressional Legislation for Consumer and Home making Education," *Journal of Vocational and Technical Education* 1, no. 2 (1985): 17–24. The interpretation is mine. I thank Wendy Way for discussing these issues with me.

as Smith-Hughes, were still in effect, and they continued to fund nonoccupational facets of the field.)

Understandably fearful that this gainful employment restriction presaged writing home economics out of the 1968 reauthorization bill, home economists became more active in lobbying Congress. At the same time, congressional representatives such as Albert Quie (R-Minnesota) and Claude Pepper (D-Florida), concerned that home economics programs did not address the social needs of the period, prepared an amendment to the 1968 bill that changed the name of the subject to "consumer and homemaking education" and mandated that a portion of its funding be allocated to depressed areas. Thus, while home economists involved themselves more directly in the legislative process, male legislators were still defining the field.

The 1976 Vocational Education Act confronted home economists with another serious legislative threat. For years their field had been funded within the broad area of vocational education; now representatives such as William Lehman (D-Florida) were denying the vocational (that is, occupational) aspects of home economics and seeking to classify it within the general curriculum of the public schools. The profession's reaction to the act demonstrates how far home economists had come in appreciating the legislative politics of home economics education. It also documents the continuing outside influences on the field.

During early congressional hearings, representatives learned that almost one-half of the females participating in vocational education courses were enrolled in homemaking and consumer classes and over 90 percent of the students in these classes were female. Representatives Quie, Lehman, and Shirley Chisholm (D-New York) concluded that home economics education promoted sex-stereotyped images of women as homemakers and of the homemaker as a woman. Thus they questioned the inclusion of home economics in vocational education. Most unsettling, Lehman introduced an amendment prohibiting funding for nonoccupational skills.

Home economists were not united in their reaction to this change. Some AHEA staff members worked with congressional staffers to construct an amendment that would be a compromise between Lehman's proposal and the provisions in the 1968 act. Unfortunately, this group consulted with only a few members of the profession and consequently seemed oblivious to the depth of resistance among home economists to this solution. Other home economics educators, representing the AHEA, the American Vocational Association (AVA), and the Home Economics Education Association (HEEA), instead issued a statement calling for the retention of the provisions in the 1968 act. Both groups seemed surprised they did not represent the consensus of the profession. The 1976 National Conference on Vocational Home Economics Education devoted much attention to this lack of agreement, consequently establishing a coalition of the AVA, the AHEA, and the HEEA to lobby Congress in support of the 1968 provisions and against any amendment. Shortly after arriving in Washington, however, the coalition quickly ascertained that there was much support in Congress for revising of the 1968 provisions and for the amendment limiting funding for home economics education. Taking a pragmatic approach, they worked with congressional staffers to prepare another amendment that reconciled their differences. Thus, with the passage of the 1976 act, home economics educators had learned to work with legislators and accepted modifications conditioned by political realities and social concerns.

The process of drafting of the Carl Perkins Vocation Education Acts of the 1980s and 1990s made home economics educators knowledgeable about consensus building and lobbying strategies. Rather than reacting to congressional proposals, leaders from organizations such as the American Vocational Association and the American Home Economics Association educated representatives and designed sample legislation even before the initial bills were drafted, thus ensuring that home economists had a say in the shape of home economics education in the American school system.

EARLY leaders in home economics saw the field as liberatory, extending the boundaries of domesticity beyond the individual household; women could and should use their education to improve the larger world. Unfortunately, the institutionalization of their hopes was mediated by legislative deliberations, gender stereotypes, patriarchal attitudes, curricular reforms, and bureaucratic machinations mostly beyond their control. Expanded courses in the public schools more often than not equated home economics with cooking and sewing. Rather than training girls in critical thinking and urging women to reach outside the domestic sphere, twentieth-century home economics in the public schools taught a narrow spectrum of domestic tasks. Moreover, until the last third of the twentieth century, it was a sex-segregated experience that reinforced the stereotypical middle-class patriarchal roles of wife and mother.

Today's situation is strikingly different in several important respects from that earlier in the century. Though the contemporary home economics curriculum is not the one proposed by early home economists, that is, science-based general liberal arts education designed for girls, neither is it the skills-oriented technical training familiar to so many of us even as recently as twenty years ago. No longer is home economics directed exclusively or even primarily to girls, especially in the lower grades. Current legislation, specifically the Perkins Act of 1990, mandates curricula that are much broader than cooking and sewing, encompassing consumerism, environmentalism, and family and community relationships. Though science is not a focus of contemporary home economics (also called family and consumer education, family and consumer sciences, human development, human ecology and family living, human science, and human ecology), textbooks do stress problem solving. And having learned the pitfalls as well as the benefits of federal funding, home economists continue to lobby through the coalition formed in 1976 for a more comprehensive vision of home economics education. Home economics continues to be a dynamic component of American schools, reflecting, responding to, and shaping educational opportunities for American students.

5 The Men Move In: Home Economics, 1950–1970

MARGARET W. ROSSITER

College-level instruction in home economics came under attack in the 1950s and 1960s, at a time when academia was experiencing a tremendous boom. Across the nation faculties were growing exponentially, new buildings were springing up, and whole campuses were proliferating. Instead of benefiting from the growth, however, the field of home economics found itself beleaguered and threatened from several directions for seemingly contradictory reasons. Administrators, all male then, held skeptical and hostile attitudes toward home economics, even as they expressed unabashed ignorance about the field.[1] Those at prestige-conscious universities confessed to a growing sense of embarrassment at the field's strong vocationalism and explicit links to teacher education (often required by state law). They pointed to the low proportion of doctorates among home economists and observed openly that most of its faculty consisted of women (usually 90–100 percent), especially older and single ones. To them such female domination constituted proof that the field was out of date.

One can sense a rising frustration and anger among the leaders in home economics, who not only had to fight losing battles for personnel and resources but also constantly had to define and defend the field's intellectual rigor and social importance. They tried repeatedly to convince skeptics of the field's legitimacy, not only on campus but also at the national level,

This chapter is drawn from my book, which has fuller documentation, *Women Scientists in America: Before Affirmative Action, 1940–1972* (Baltimore: Johns Hopkins University Press, 1995), chap. 8.

1. Jeanette A. Lee and Paul Dressel, *Liberal Education and Home Economics* (New York: Teachers College, 1963), p. 69.

where on numerous committees and commissions they attempted to garner greater research support. Nevertheless, despite some aid from the U.S. Department of Agriculture (USDA), especially "cooperative" research in home economics, the chief supporters of academic research in these years, other federal agencies such as the National Science Foundation, the National Institutes of Health, and the National Institute for Mental Health, refused to recognize home economics as a scientific field, although they did support such areas as nutrition and developmental psychology.

A practical and increasingly frequent remedy for the embattled position of home economics and one pursued by several of the remaining women deans was to hire men preferentially, especially those with doctorates in specialties such as child development. Such a plan, they reasoned, would attract new research funds and hence prestige. Only in this way could a dean hope to preserve her job and her college and salvage some vestige of her formerly respectable field, especially at the land-grant universities. But despite these women's best efforts, many of the larger programs actually shrank during these years of record growth. Several major programs, notably those at Chicago, Columbia's Teachers College, and the University of California, Berkeley, were discontinued, removed, or dismembered in some way. By the mid-1960s, when the Great Society provided substantial funding for subjects related to home economics, many women deans, often in ill health or near retirement age, proved unable to take advantage of the windfall. Predacious men, sensing both a big opportunity in an area they had formerly ridiculed as well as a moment of strategic weakness, seized the chance to take over. By 1968 the old college of home economics, built up over decades by a succession of devoted women deans, found itself forcibly, often brutally, renamed, restaffed, and reconstituted. To a large extent this set of "reforms" grew out of the ageism and misogyny of the time.

According to the United States Office of Education's (USOE) unpublished statistics, "Home Economics in Degree-Granting Institutions," which appeared biennially from 1939 until discontinued in 1963 (another sign of the decline of the field), the total number of institutions granting degrees in home economics increased modestly (4.6 percent) from 388 in 1947–48 to 406 in 1962–63, and the number of faculty (in terms of "full-time equivalents" or FTE) rose even more (7.1 percent) from 2,574 to 2,756.7. (Table 5.1.)[2] Four of the largest programs grew in size—those at the University of Minnesota, Pennsylvania State University, Texas Technological University, and most spectacular of all, Brigham Young University (BYU). At the latter institution, an expansionist president viewed home economics (or

2. U.S. Office of Education (hereafter USOE), Vocational Division, "Home Economics in Degree-Granting Institutions," in "Miscellaneous Publication" 2557 (mimeographed), 1939/40–1963/64, revised biennially.

TABLE 5.1 Largest home economics programs, by size of faculty, 1947–1948 and 1962–1963

Rank	Institution	Total FTE 1947–1948		Total FTE 1962–1963	Change	Percent
1	Iowa State	105	Iowa State	83	−22	−21.0
2	Cornell	101	Penn State	59.1	+13.5	+29.6
3	Michigan State	66.5	Cornell	50.	−51	−50.5
4	Kansas State	61	Brigham Young	38.3	+32.8	+596.3
5	Oklahoma A&M	51.5	Oklahoma State	36.6	−14.9	−28.9
6	Tennessee	47	Minnesota	36.3	+8	+28.2
7	Penn State	45.6	Texas Tech	35	+13.5	+64.2
8	Illinois	41	Kansas State	33.5	−27.5	−45.1
9	Ohio State	40.5	Michigan State	32.8	−33.7	−50.6
10	Oregon State	40.5	Purdue	32	−4	−11.1
11	Wisconsin	40.	Illinois	31.8	−9.2	−22.4
12	Purdue	36	Tennessee	31.8	−15.2	−32.3
13	Pratt Intitute	32	Oregon State	30.2	−8.3	−20.5
14	Syracuse	29	Ohio State	29	−11.5	−28.4
15	Minnesota	28.3	Wisconsin	29	−11	−27.5
	373 others	1,809.1	391 others	2,168.3	359.2	+19.9
TOTAL		2,574		2,756.7	+182.7	+7.1
Avg/Institution		6.63		6.79	+.16	+2.41%

Sources: "Home Economics in Degree-Granting Institutions, 1947–48," United States Office of Education, Division of Vocational Education, Miscellaneous No. 2557—Revised 1948, and American Home Economics Association, *Home Economics in Institutions Granting Bachelors or Higher Degrees, 1963–64* (Washington, D.C.: AHEA, n.d.), Table 25. Despite the title, most of the data are for 1962–63.

"family living," as he called BYU's department) as a way to promote traditional female roles among his thousands of Mormon women students. At BYU the home economics faculty exploded from 5.5 FTE in 1947–48 to 38.3 in 1962–66.[3] But this growth was exceptional. Many other departments suffered losses in these fifteen years of from 4 FTE at Purdue to 51 FTE at Cornell, where the male-dominated School of Hotel Administration seceded in 1954 to form an administratively separate school of its own.[4]

This striking drop in the size of the faculty at most of the nation's largest home economics programs between 1947–48 and 1962–63 was not accompanied by (and therefore partially explained by) a drop in the number of undergraduate or graduate degrees awarded. On the contrary, other data from

3. Ernest L. Wilkinson and W. Cleon Skousen, *Brigham Young University: A School of Destiny* (Provo, Utah: Brigham Young University Press, 1976), pp. 504–7, and 662.

4. Esther H. Stocks, "Part II, A Second Page, 1940–1965," in *A Growing College: Home Economics at Cornell University* (Ithaca: New York State College of Human Ecology, Cornell University, 1969), pp. 215–17.

these same reports indicate that most schools were turning out *more* graduates in 1962–63 than fifteen years earlier despite the loss of faculty. The total number of degrees awarded by the largest programs jumped from 1,628 in 1947–48 to 1,916 in 1962–63, a moderate increase of 17.7 percent.

What worried the home economics deans was that they were not holding on to their proportion of the student body. The USOE kept track of all "earned degrees conferred," and, more important, broke down its totals by sex. Data reveal that although some men heeded the call in the late 1940s to take courses in home economics, relatively few stayed to major in it. Only 97 men majored in home economics at the bachelor's degree level in 1947–48. That number doubled to 202 by 1967–68, but men still accounted for less than 2 percent of the total degrees awarded in home economics. Meanwhile, the number of women graduating from college nationwide almost tripled (from 96,165 graduates in 1947–48 to 277,116 twenty years later). The number majoring in home economics fields, however, did not even double (7,204 to 12,455). Put another way, whereas 7.5 percent of all women graduates in 1947–48 majored in home economics, by 1967–68 the percentage had fallen to only 4.5 percent, a substantial (40 percent) drop.[5]

To a certain extent, this slippage resulted simply from the breakdown of old forms of internal segregation long practiced at many of the land-grant colleges and the creation of new ones. Although officially coeducational for decades, several of these schools managed for quite a while to confine women to the college of home economics. At Iowa State University, where the trend was particularly noticeable, 64.5 percent of the women graduates of 1947–48 majored in home economics. By 1969–70 the percentage had dropped to 31.8. One reason for the precipitous decline was that the college of home economics had long taught women's physical education and "household art," as well as the more traditional home economics curriculum. In 1960, however, the university approved a new, separate major in physical education, and in 1968 the administration belatedly created a new, separate college of education. The college of home economics provided 630 of education's first 821 enrollees. Thus increasingly in the 1960s, as the land grant institutions diversified and new opportunities beckoned, women students moved into other parts of the university, and the formerly monolithic women's world of home economics splintered, even at Iowa State.[6]

Following a nationwide trend in the 1950s and 1960s, home economics placed a new stress on graduate degrees, particularly doctorates. The total number of such degrees awarded tripled between the late 1940s, when

5. USOE, *Earned Degrees Conferred*, 1947/48–1967/68.

6. USOE, *Earned Degrees Conferred*, 1947/48–1969/70, and Ercel Sherman Eppright and Elizabeth Storm Ferguson, *A Century of Home Economics at Iowa State University* (Ames: Iowa State University Home Economics Alumni Association, 1971), pp. 175–78, 258.

about fourteen were given annually, to about fifty in the mid-1950s, when it leveled off until starting to rise again in the early 1960s. Cornell University, by far the largest doctorate-granting program in the country, awarded about a fifth of all the Ph.D.'s in home economics during these years. Substantial programs also existed at Texas Woman's University, Pennsylvania State University, Teachers College, and Ohio State University. (Table 5.2.)[7] One reason why the number of Ph.D.'s awarded remained constant for nearly a decade, from 1954 to 1964, was the paucity of fellowships in the field. A 1954 survey by the National Science Foundation of financial aid for graduate students revealed that only thirty-two fellowships in home economics were awarded nationally, none by the federal government. In other fields, especially the biological sciences, the government, private sources, and the universities themselves funded hundreds of fellowships.[8]

TABLE 5.2. Largest producers of doctorates in home economics, by sex, 1947–48 to 1962–63

Institution	Total doctorates	Men receiving doctorates	Percent men
Cornell	112	30	26.8
Texas Woman's University	52	0	0.0
Penn State	48	3	6.3
Teachers College	45	17	37.8
Ohio State	42	0	0.0
Iowa State	37	0	0.0
Florida State	33	11	33.3
Wisconsin	33	0	0.0
Iowa[a]	28	14	50.0
California	24	9	37.5
New York University	19	1	5.3
Michigan State	18	4	22.2
Chicago	17	0	0.0
Purdue	16	0	0.0
Minnesota	15	3	20.0
Others	46	12	26.1
TOTAL	585	104	17.8

Source: U.S. Office of Education, Earned Degrees Conferred. 1947/48–1962/63.
[a]In child development and family relationships only.

7. Jeanette C. Gorman and Laura Jane Harper, "A Look at the Status of Home Economics in Higher Education," Journal of Home Economics (hereafter JHE) 62 (December 1970): 742.
8. National Science Foundation, Graduate Student Enrollment and Support in American Universities (Washington, D.C.: U.S. Government Printing Office, 1957), p. 742.

Despite the rising rhetoric about the need for more Ph.D.'s in the field, not even the top fifteen doctoral-producing programs in home economics persisted. In fact, there were some notable defections and retrenchments in the 1950s, starting with the distinguished program at the University of Chicago. Founded as a department of household administration in 1904 under Marion Talbot, a close friend of Ellen Richards, the program had later been relegated to the School of Education. In the 1920s under Katharine Blunt, home economics moved back into the colleges of arts, literature, and science and the graduate school and expanded its faculty to seventeen members. When the university reneged on the promise of a new building, Blunt, fed up with the lack of adequate facilities, resigned in 1929 and went to head the new Connecticut College for Women. Her protégée Lydia Roberts, an outstanding nutritionist and researcher (who later served on the first Food and Nutrition Board during World War II), succeeded her and trained many important women. When she retired in 1944, the university appointed Thelma Porter, one of her students, then at Michigan State College (later University), to head the program. The University of Chicago's home economics faculty was notable for its high proportion of doctorates, rare at that time. Among them were Hazel Kyrk, renowned in the area of consumer economics, Helen Oldham, and Margaret Davis Doyle.

In spite of the faculty's strong credentials and distinguished past, by the late 1940s President Robert Maynard Hutchins and other male administrators could find no funds or intellectual space at the University of Chicago for home economics. At a reorganization meeting in 1944, Hutchins decided to split the program among three separate faculties: biological sciences, social sciences, and humanities. In 1950 a new dean of biological sciences refused to administer his portion of the old home economics program. By 1952 the "department" was reduced to the level of a "committee" unable to make faculty appointments. This shakeup, as well as new tenure rules adopted about the same time, encouraged home economics faculty to leave or retire. By 1956, when Porter (one of only three remaining faculty members) resigned to accept the deanship at Michigan State University, the chancellor at the University of Chicago announced the program's termination. In his letter to the eight hundred home economics alumnae, Lawrence A. Kimpton disingenuously attributed his decision to the university's inability to compete with the land-grant schools in home economics. Three years later, the alumnae, still angry at the blow, asked Marie Dye to write a history of the defunct program. In it she praised Porter, who had "withstood the pressures brought to bear against the department with dignity and maintained her scholarly attitude and standards in spite of the temptation to find an easy way out." And she laid the blame for home economics's demise squarely on the shoulders of the administrators, who had skimped on funds for decades and refused to make a place for home economics's eminent program in the university's otherwise expanding postwar future.[9] Perhaps Porter, so long thwarted at the University of Chicago, got at least some revenge at Michigan State, where home economics grew rapidly under her leadership. But the fate of home economics at Chicago signaled that even a distinguished program with a high percentage of doctorates could not withstand the attacks of a male administration bent on its destruction. It remained to be seen what would happen at the land-grant colleges. Already the leadership at many of these institutions was showing signs of wanting to emulate their brethren at private institutions like the University of Chicago. The beleaguered home economists strategy of public stoicism and private revenge would recur all too often elsewhere in the decades to come.

A less dramatic restructuring—more of a retrenchment—took place in the late 1940s and 1950s at Columbia University's Teachers College. Before the deaths of Mary Swartz Rose in 1941 and her successor and protégée, Grace MacLeod, in 1944, home economics at Teachers College enjoyed a reputation as a leader in the field of foods and nutrition. Under Helen Judy Bond the program subsequently centered on the large department of household science and art. A series of reorganizations of the college in the late 1940s and 1950s relegated the nutrition program to a subordinate status within the department of science education. There the highest ranking of Rose's last followers was no more than a "lecturer." In later years the program moved into the area of "nutrition education" within a new division of health services, a compromise between the basic research in nutrition done in Rose's day and the new curricular needs at Teachers College.[10]

At Berkeley in the 1950s Chancellor Clark Kerr unveiled California's new master plan for higher education, which called for several new campuses. In 1955 the Berkeley academic senate voted to dump the department of household science and send it to the campuses at Davis and Santa Barbara. Most (but not all) of the university's male administrators saw home economics as an embarrassment to the prestige of the great university they hoped to build up at Berkeley. Home economists saw the move as a great blow to Agnes Fay Morgan, who had retired in 1954 after devoting more than forty years to establishing Berkeley's home economics program. Indeed, a long-delayed and expensive new building had been dedicated in her honor that same year at a ceremony attended by Kerr and a bevy of male agricultural administrators. Only the concerted action of many hundreds of California home economists

9. Marie Dye, "History of the Department of Home Economics, University of Chicago" (Chicago: University of Chicago Alumni Association, 1972), typescript, p. 177, copy in Special Collections, Regenstein Library, University of Chicago.

10. Orrea F. Pye, "The Nutrition Program at Teachers College, Columbia University," in *Conference on Education in Nutrition: Looking Forward from the Past, February 26 and 27, 1974* (New York: Columbia University, Teachers College, 1974), pp. 10–11.

and members of the American Association of University Women (whose strength administrators later admitted they had underestimated) brought about an eventual compromise: graduate work in nutritional sciences remained at Berkeley in Morgan Hall with its superb research facilities while the rest of the "household sciences" went to Santa Barbara and Davis. Thereupon Berkeley administrators, convinced that there was only one Agnes Fay Morgan, considered only male researchers to replace her as dean. When some candidates declined to come for unspecified reasons, the administration suspected that qualified men balked at working in a "home economics" unit. In the end George Briggs, a biochemist and former chief of the nutrition unit at the National Institutes of Health, took the deanship. Two years later, in 1962, he dropped the phrase "home economics" from the unit's title, leaving only the evidently gender-neutral term "nutritional sciences." The still active Agnes Fay Morgan kept a circumspect public silence. Even years later, when she completed a history of her department, she failed to mention the demise of home economics at Berkeley.[11]

During the 1950s more and more men earned doctorates in home economics. (Table 5.2.) Their proportion of the total degrees awarded reached its peak in 1957–58, when they received twenty of thirty-four, or 58.81 percent. Numerically they concentrated in a few programs, chiefly those at Cornell, Teachers College, Florida State, the University of Iowa, and Berkeley. At Cornell men's entrance was greatly facilitated, according to a history of the program, by a special W. T. Grant Foundation fellowship awarded twenty times between 1951 and 1962. Restricted to men, preferably married ones who held a master's degree in psychology, sociology, education, or some other field related to "family life," the generous fellowship provided the "substantial amount" a family man would need.[12]

Men's greatest inroads into the field of home economics concentrated in one area—child development and family relationships. Fully two-thirds (forty-two of sixty-three) of all the men earning Ph.D.'s in home economics in these years clustered in this specialty, where they composed nearly half (49.4 percent) of the total doctorates awarded. The rest were spread far more thinly over four additional fields. There were none at all in either general home economics or institutional management. (Table 5.3.)

11. For a much fuller version of the Berkeley story, see Maresi Nerad, "'Home Economics Has to Move': The Disappearance of the Department of Home Economics from the University of California, Berkeley" (Ph.D. dissertation, University of California, Berkeley, 1986), and her "Gender Stratification in Higher Education: The Department of Home Economics at the University of California, Berkeley, 1916–1962," *Women's Studies International Forum* 10 (1987): 157–64.

12. Stocks, "Second Page," pp. 242–43, 314–16; *Reports of the Grant Foundation, Incorporated*, 1948–62.

TABLE 5.3. Male doctorates in home economics, by specialty, 1955/56–1962/63

Field	Total	Men	Percent
Child development and family relationships	85	42	49.4%
Home economics education	83	9	10.8
Foods and nutrition	77	8	10.4
General home economics	53	0	0.0
Other home economics	35	2	5.7
Clothing and textiles	31	2	6.5
Institutional management	5	0	0.0
TOTAL	369	63	17.1%

Source: U.S. Office of Education, Earned Degrees Conferred, 1955/56–1962/63.

Certainly the field of foods and nutrition, in many ways the bedrock of home economics, remained almost totally feminized. Iowa State boasted the largest graduate program in the nation in this field, granting thirteen doctorates between 1955–56 and 1962–63 but none to men. Pearl Swanson and Ercel Eppright, two of a long line of Yale doctorates who studied under Lafayette Mendel, led the department and along with Wilma Brewer and others carried on a research tradition dating back to the 1920s. By outlasting the Teachers College program in nutrition, Iowa State's department of foods and nutrition continued the Mendel protégée chain into the 1960s and, through a second generation of doctorates, beyond.[13]

Although many home economics faculty during these years performed scientific work, especially what was known as "cooperative" research that was funded by the USDA and performed jointly by scientists at two or more agricultural colleges or experiment stations,[14] even this modest level of federal support never proved enough to satisfy the relentless demand on many campuses for ever more research. Women researchers at a few campuses, particularly Iowa State, Texas Woman's, and Cornell, supplemented USDA project funds with grants from the chemical and food industries, private foundations, the National Institutes of Health, and eventually even the National Aeronautics and Space Administration. Yet these funds were short-term, usually limited to foods and nutrition, and often had other restrictions on their use. Colleges of home economics and editorials and articles in the *Journal of Home Economics* increasingly recognized that research was necessary not only to improve the well-being of the nation's families in an in-

13. Eppright and Ferguson, *A Century of Home Economics*, chap. 14, pp. 187–97, chap. 16, p. 286.

14. Margaret A. Ohlson, P. Mabel Nelson, and Pearl P. Swanson, "Cooperative Research among Colleges," *JHE* 29 (February 1937): 108–13; Eppright and Ferguson, *A Century of Home Economics*, pp. 226–28.

creasingly technological age but also for the prestige and very preservation of the field itself.[15]

The AHEA, jolted by an attempted budget cut at the USDA (long the field's primary source of funds), and possibly spurred by the termination of the graduate program at the University of Chicago, moved to create its own committee in 1955 to consider ways to increase future federal aid for home economics research. This Committee on Federal Research Related to Home Economics consumed much of the time for the next seven years of several of the leading researchers and research administrators in home economics, including Agnes Fay Morgan, Pearl Swanson, Marie Dye, Helen LeBaron (dean at Iowa State), Hazel Kyrk, Helen Canoyer (dean at Cornell), and Grace Henderson (dean at Penn State). They drafted a series of reports, speeches, and grant proposals. In 1957 the group formulated an ambitious plan for a new federal agency, either a foundation like the National Science Foundation or an institute, perhaps like the National Institutes of Health, that would provide scholarships and fellowships to train much-needed new personnel and award grants to researchers at universities and elsewhere. Such funds were needed, they argued, to help combat continuing problems in American family life such as juvenile delinquency (then much in the news), unwise consumer spending, divorce, misuse of leisure, and bad diet. These problems were so pervasive and the government's response so scattered (across thirty-five agencies, according to a Library of Congress study) that the committee felt it imperative for government to create one new central agency.[16] Yet nothing came of the proposal. Five years later, the discouraged group recommended that the AHEA dissolve the committee. Much time and talent appeared to have gone for naught.[17]

But shortly thereafter the political tide began to turn for home economics. A midwestern home economist helped provide new research funds for the field with the passage of the Vocational Education Act of 1963. When Iowa State's Helen LeBaron served on the White House panel on vocational education that advised legislators on the act, she made sure that the bill in-

15. Eppright and Ferguson, *A Century of Home Economics*, p. 267; Joyce Thompson, *Marking a Trail: A History of the Texas Woman's University* (Denton, Tex: Texas Woman's University Press, 1982), pp. 157–58; and Stocks, *A Growing College, Part II*, pp. 248–57, 362–64, 394–404.

16. Grace Henderson, "Federal Research Related to Home Economics Given before Home Economics Division of the American Association of Land-Grant Colleges and State Universities, November 15, 1955," typescript in Grace Henderson Papers, Pennsylvania State University Archives, University Park.

17. After the first group dissolved, a new committee was formed, but it merely recommended that in light of the near impossibility of getting such an agency funded, the AHEA relegate this goal to its long-term wish list. Indeed, the association continued to pass resolutions recommending action at its annual meeting for several more years. See Helen Pundt, *AHEA: A History of Excellence* (Washington, D.C.: AHEA, 1980), pp. 288–89, 306, 328; Ruth Bonde, "Federal Research Related to Home Economics," *JHE* 52 (September 1960): 556.

cluded provisions for research funds for home economics. By 1965 the Vocational Education Act provided up to $12 million for research and by fiscal year 1967, $22.5 million.[18] Perversely, this sudden windfall backfired on the women home economists. Rather than helping them to do research and earn prestige, it signaled powerful men in academia that, however trivial "home economics" had once been, it was fast becoming a lucrative field, one worth taking over.

Meanwhile, home economics, even at the land-grant schools, came under siege as higher echelons within the American Association of Land-Grant and State Colleges and Universities (AALGSCU) hammered out a reduced, less visible status for the field. For a long time the association's division of home economics, composed of the deans and other administrators of instructional and extension home economics units at the nation's fifty-two land-grant universities, had struggled to find new sources for support of research. Over the years, especially since the passage of the Research and Marketing Act in 1946, the division (which contained many of the people on the AHEA's Committee on Federal Research) commissioned summaries of the status of research in the various fields and sponsored workshops for male and female administrators. Discussion there often generated a recommendation for still another attempt to define home economics in such a way as to convince others that the field merited more support.

In the spring of 1959, Dean Helen Canoyer of Cornell, the division's new representative to the association's imposing executive committee (half university presidents and half representatives of other groups, including home economics), presented the most recent definition (or defense) of her field. As she later recalled, she had expected that the men would be pleased with this latest effort because for years they had been badgering her to produce it. Instead, they received it in scornful silence. Then one university president (reportedly Eric Walker of Pennsylvania State) threw his unread copy on the table, denounced it as still inadequate, and moved that the association "request a study of the present status, objectives, and future of Home Economics in Land-Grant Institutions." Startled and aghast at the enormity of what was happening, the quick-thinking Canoyer stammered that any such request should first be approved by the home economics division. In 1960 that division acquiesced—but voiced misgivings that such a report by an outside "objective" group might misrepresent the field in an unsympathetic and even damaging way. For several years nothing happened because the association was unable to raise the money

18. Pundt, *AHEA*, p. 308; Eppright and Ferguson, *A Century of Home Economics*, pp. 262, 267; Mary Lee Hurt, "Expanded Research Programs under Vocational Education," *JHE* 57 (March 1965): 173–75.

for such an ambitious study. Finally, in November 1964 the Carnegie Corporation, just beginning its interest in the status of women in America, awarded $200,000 to fund the study.[19]

The Carnegie grant went to pay Earl J. McGrath and an associate, Jack T. Johnson, to complete the study in two years. McGrath, a former United States commissioner of education, was director of the Institute of Higher Education of Teachers College, where he had done similar studies of other areas of professional education in the past, including one on liberal arts and home economics. His task included processing questionnaires from the 75 institutions (of the 101 members of the newly expanded and renamed National Association of State Universities and Land-Grant Colleges, NASULGC) and thousands of home economists on their faculties (1,672 responded). McGrath and Johnson collected other degree data, interviewed as many home economists and administrators as necessary, and prepared a final report.[20]

The Changing Mission of Home Economics, the final 121-page report published in 1968, proved a remarkably inconsistent, internally contradictory document. It started out claiming that whatever purposes home economics initially filled, "the restraints of the past must be overcome." Even though the field had broadened its emphasis in recent years from "the home" to "the family," the authors judged it still too heavily dominated by the classic area of foods and nutrition. Moreover, they found home economics out of touch with recent work in the social sciences and thus "increasingly outside the mainstream of American undergraduate education." In summarizing their data, the authors made explicit the feminized nature of the field and hinted at concerns regarding age, sex, and marital status. Their data revealed that women constituted 90.2 percent of the faculty in the field. Over half were unmarried and 45 percent were over the age of forty-five. In the group as a whole, only 27.8 percent of the women versus 61.7 percent of the men held doctoral degrees, and most of these came from relatively few universities; fewer than ten universities accounted for three-fourths of the doctorates. Discounting the 533 projects home economics researchers reported they were engaged in, the report insisted that relatively little research was

19. The association first approached the Kellogg Foundation, but it was not interested (Helen G. Canoyer, "Report of the Home Economics Study Committee," *Proceedings of the American Association of Land-Grant Colleges and State Universities* 75, 1 [1961]: 182).

20. Lee and Dressel, *Liberal Education and Home Economics*; Earl J. McGrath and Jack T. Johnson, *The Changing Mission of Home Economics: A Report on Home Economics in the Land-Grant Colleges and State Universities* (New York: Teachers College Press, 1968), pp. i–iii, vii, x. See also C. J. Personius to Helen LeBaron, March 3, 1967, and Helen Canoyer, "Report of the Origin and History . . . ," Box 6, Personius Papers, Rare and Manuscript Collections, Division Cornell University Library.

being carried out in the field and that what little was done concentrated heavily at nine top universities.[21]

The report's accusatory tone did not change when it came to discussing the touchy topic of sex differentials in salaries. Although only 695 home economists reported their earnings, the data showed that women earned much less than did the far fewer men holding the same rank. This galling inequity must have been especially demoralizing to the women, who were generally older than the men. McGrath and Johnson immediately deflected attention from the striking differential, however, by stressing the positive fact that "salaries in home economics are particularly competitive and attractive at the lower ranks." Thus, rather than deploring the gender inequities their study revealed and calling for reform, the "objective" male experts minimized the discriminatory patterns revealed in their own data.[22]

After collecting and presenting all their demographic data, McGrath and Johnson offered conclusions and recommendations that proved not only anticlimactic and relatively muted but almost positive and thus a relief to the worried women in home economics. In fact, as McGrath admitted in an address at the AHEA's annual meeting in 1968, he had changed his impressions of home economics in the course of doing the study. He confessed that he began with the assumption that the report's recommendation would be to discontinue or dismember an outmoded field.[23] But in the course of the two years spent on the project, he and his associates became increasingly impressed with the strong corporate demand for home economics graduates here and abroad and the predictions of even greater employment prospects in President Lyndon Johnson's Great Society programs in the years to come. In fact, his staff had come to feel that home economics was so useful in so many ways to so many employers that training in this area should not be terminated but instead increased—at the community colleges, through "general education" courses for nonmajors in colleges, and even at the graduate level. Although earlier in their report McGrath and Johnson deplored the small number of universities training doctoral candidates in home economics as evidence of the field's narrowness and inbreeding, in their conclusion they stated almost the opposite: that because doctoral training was so expensive, the ten major existing programs would be sufficient if they and others expanded their enrollments. This proved to be the report's most controversial recommendation. Critics felt that if there were such a shortage of doctorates in the field, new programs were justified.

21. McGrath and Johnson, *Changing Mission*, pp. 2, 27, 29, 31, 32, 34, 58.
22. Ibid., p. 36.
23. For differing accounts compare ibid., p. ix, with Earl J. McGrath, "The Imperatives of Change for Home Economics," *JHE* 60 (September 1968): 505.

Moreover, they argued that a department without a graduate program could not attract top-quality staff and produce research.[24]

McGrath and Johnson recommended further that home economics programs should have more contact with other disciplines on campus, especially the social sciences. They judged it essential that home economics programs no longer be tied to the college of agriculture. Recognizing that experiment station funds provided important support for home economics research, they nevertheless insisted that the future of home economics lay in the cities and foreign nations, not in rural America.[25]

By the time the long-dreaded McGrath report appeared in late 1968, some of the very changes that the women home economists most feared had taken place or were under way on certain campuses. These changes could be brutal and humiliating, involving such deliberate ruptures with the past as name changes, appointment of male deans lacking qualifications in the field, reorganizations, terminations of some departments (especially home economics education), and a deliberate masculinization of the faculty and to a lesser extent the student body, accompanied by a dramatic increase in the level of funding. Such forcible change was evidently necessary to oust the women and to demonstrate that men were taking charge.

Already in the early 1960s several salvos had been leveled at women home economists by the upper levels of land grant education in two addresses at the AALGSCU annual meeting. Paul A. Miller, provost of Michigan State University, speaking in 1960, and Reuben Gustavson, professor of chemistry at the University of Arizona, speaking a year later, openly recommended that the colleges of home economics hire more men.[26] Finally, in 1965, as the result of a reorganization of the association arranged by Frederick L. Hovde, president of Purdue University, the division of home economics ceased to exist. Hovde argued that the new organization could compete more forcefully with other proliferating associations of "state universities" if it deemphasized its former land-grant, agricultural, that is, "cow college," emphasis. Though the new format eventually permitted the existence of a "commission for home economics," it eliminated the woman's seat (the uncomfortable one Canoyer had filled) on the executive

24. Following McGrath's presentation to the AHEA in June 1968, a three-member panel raised questions about the report, as summarized in "Question and Answer Panel," *JHE* 60 (September 1968): 513–14.

25. McGrath also urged some university to step forward and start the long-awaited home economics research journal, which Iowa State did in 1971. See *Home Economics Research Journal* 1 (September 1972).

26. Paul A. Miller, "Higher Education in Home Economics: An Appraisal and a Challenge," *Proceedings of the American Association of Land-Grant Colleges and State Universities* 74 (1960): 244–46.

committee. Effectively excluded, the home economists immediately formed their own separate but closely affiliated Association of Administrators of Home Economics and continued to meet annually with the NASULGC.[27]

West Virginia University became the first university since Berkeley to change the name of its home economics program and to hire a male head. In 1962, the trustees appointed as its new president the same Paul A. Miller of Michigan State University who only a year before had had the effrontery to tell the assembled deans of home economics they must hire more male faculty. Once at West Virginia, where the department of home economics constituted part of a combined college of agriculture, forestry resources, and home economics, Miller created a separate college of education and human resources with a new division of home and family studies. Before long it was headed by a man, William H. Marshall.[28]

At Pennsylvania State University, which had one of the largest and most rapidly growing colleges of home economics in the country, the change appears to have been even more brutal. Grace Henderson, director and dean since 1946, had built the department into a school and then a full college. In 1963 the university's president, Eric A. Walker, snubbed Henderson and her college when he appointed a committee on the university's future that included no one from home economics. The sense of betrayal increased when one of this committee's recommendations called for a new college of "human development," which would contain portions of the colleges of physical education and home economics. Ill with cancer, Henderson retired in 1966 and died five years later. Shortly after her departure, the college's name officially changed to "human development," its home economics education program shifted to the college of education, and a psychologist, Donald H. Ford, was appointed dean. By the spring of 1968, Ford had dissolved seven departments, added programs in nursing and criminal justice, and created four "problem-oriented divisions" within the new college. President Walker generously provided funds to add many new faculty members. The size of the faculty more than doubled from 78 in 1965 to 169 in 1972. Similarly, the size of the undergraduate student body expanded enormously (fivefold) from 882 in 1965 to 4,075 in 1972, and the number of graduate students grew from 135 to 160. Significantly, the proportion of women dropped strikingly at all levels during these years. With the new dean, the new mandate, and the new money, the percentage of women on the faculty also dropped from 78.2 in

27. See Frederick L. Hovde to Catherine Personius, April 30, 1964, and her reply June 22, 1964, both in Box 6, Personius Papers. Several other reports in this box indicate that she was instrumental in setting up the new organization.

28. Theodore Vallance, "Home Economics and the Development of New Forms of Human Service Education," in *Land-Grant Universities and Their Continuing Challenge*, ed. G. Lester Anderson (East Lansing: Michigan State University Press, 1976), pp. 88–91; Pundt, *AHEA*, p. 359.

1965 to a bare majority (50.3) in 1972. The proportion of women graduate students dropped substantially, from 91.9 percent to 62.1 percent, while that of undergraduates decreased from 76.4 percent to 58.0 percent (Table 5.4A) Thus the name change, reorganization, and hiring of a male dean constituted only the most visible tip of the drastic dismemberment and

TABLE 5.4. Comparison of men and women at two former colleges of home economics, 1965 and 1972

A. 1965

Pennsylvania State University

Name	College of Home Economics			
Departments	8 academic departments			
Administrative structure	1 dean, 3 assistant deans			
	Total	Men	Women	% women
Faculty	78	17	61	78.2
Graduate students	135	11	124	91.9
Undergraduates	882	208	674	76.4

Cornell University

Name	College of Home Economics			
Departments	7 academic departments			
Administrative structure	1 dean, 3 coordinators (women)			
	Total	Men	Women	% women
Faculty	108	19	89	82.4
Graduate students	145	17	128	88.3
Undergraduates	738	0	738	100.0

B. 1972

Pennsylvania State University

Name	College of Human Development			
Departments	4 academic divisions; 1 research institute			
Administrative structure	1 dean, 3 associate deans, 1 assistant dean			
	Total	Men	Women	% women
Faculty	169	84	85	50.3
Graduate students	153	58	95	62.1
Undergraduates	4,075	1,712	2,363	58

Cornell University

Name	College of Human Ecology			
Departments	5 academic departments			
Administrative structure	1 dean, 3 associate deans			
	Total	Men	Women	% women
Faculty	139	53	86	61.9
Graduate students	219	45	174	79.5
Undergraduates	1,162	63	1,099	94.6

Source: Theodore R. Vallance, "Home Economics and the Development of New Forms of Human Service Education," in *Land-Grant Universities and Their Continuing Challenge,* ed. G. Lester Anderson (East Lansing: Michigan State University Press, 1976), pp. 88 and 101.

systematic masculinization of home economics at Penn State in just seven years. Henderson's only public reaction was to lament that she wished she could have had ten more years to build up her college herself. It must have been infuriating to see all the resources long denied handed over so readily to her male successor.[29]

A few years later, another takeover, an academic mutiny by the male faculty abetted by the president, unfolded at Cornell University's New York State College of Home Economics. Everyone knew that Helen Canoyer, dean since 1954, would reach mandatory retirement age in 1968. In 1965 President James Perkins, formerly head of the Carnegie Corporation, appointed a committee to study the future of the college. Although Sara Blackwell of the college's department of home economics education chaired the committee, the majority of its members were men. The group met numerous times, collected some data (including the unflattering assertion that the women students in the college of home economics were weaker academically than those in the arts and agricultural colleges, which at that time restricted the number of women admitted). In its final report, dated December 1966, the committee recommended that the name of the college be changed to reflect its new, broader focus; men be admitted as undergraduates; graduate work be stressed even more; recruitment and research be more closely tied to the social science disciplines; and the college be reorganized into five departments rather than the current seven (with the termination, apparently, of textiles and clothing and Blackwell's own department of home economics education).[30] The report set the stage for a series of dramatic changes in 1968. In May of that year a new wing of Martha Van Rensselaer Hall was dedicated; in June Helen Canoyer retired to become dean of the college of home economics at the University of Massachusetts, Amherst; in July David C. Knapp, an administrator at the University of New Hampshire with no previous experience in home economics, became the new dean; and in November the remaining home economics faculty (there had been

29. "Dean Henderson Announces Retirement," *JHE* 57 (December 1965): 763; she died of cancer shortly after completing her term as president of Omicron Nu. See "In Memory," *Omicron Nu* 38 (Spring 1972): 4–5, and Rev. A. Jackson McCormack, "' . . . However . . . ,'" *Omicron Nu.* 38 (Spring 1972): 6–8; Obituary in *New York Times*, December 3, 1975, p. 48. Details of the reorganization are given by the victors in Vallance, "Home Economics," pp. 91–103, which cites various internal documents. There are also clippings and several relevant speeches in the Grace Henderson Papers, Pennsylvania State University Archives.

30. Most of the details of the multi-year reorganization are in Vallance, "Home Economics," pp. 83–88. See also [Cornell University], "Final Report of the President's Committee to Study the College of Home Economics, December 1966" (mimeographed). This episode is reminiscent of the coordinated takeover by male workers and male management of an established area of "women's work" after World War II analyzed in Ruth Milkman, *Gender at Work: The Dynamics of Job Segregation by Sex during World War II* (Urbana: University of Illinois Press, 1987).

a flurry of retirements) voted unanimously to change the name to the College of Human Ecology.[31]

The results of Knapp's first four years in office can be seen in Table 5.4B. He received resources to increase the size of the college, though not as dramatically as at Penn State. The faculty increased from 108 members in 1965 to 139 in 1972; the number of undergraduates from 738 to 1,162; and that of graduate students from 145 to 219. But every level the proportion of women dropped: on the faculty dramatically from 82.4 percent to 61.9 percent, with a decline in the actual number from 89 to 86. The decline was less precipitous in the student body, partly because of Cornell's long tradition of training men in home economics at the graduate level. Among the graduate students women's enrollment dropped from 88.3 percent to 79.5 percent, and that of women undergraduates fell from 100 percent to 94.6 percent. Knapp also upgraded the titles of the college's new administrators. Whereas Catherine Personius had insisted on being termed "coordinator" of research, her replacement was one of three administrators given the more impressive title of associate dean, presumably to enhance her status before fellow administrators at Cornell and elsewhere. Thus within seven years the men who had joined the Cornell home economics faculty beginning in the 1940s, and who still constituted less than 18 percent of the total college faculty in 1965, had managed to reshape the school to fit their image. Although the Cornell committee report barely mentioned any underlying gender issues, the results indicate the preferential recruitment of males. Canoyer, who acceded to the changes, was praised at her retirement in 1968 for graciously bowing to the inevitable.[32]

Similar changes took place at several other colleges of home economics in the late 1960s. The University of Wisconsin's School of Home Economics, long headed by Frances Zuill despite her lack of a doctorate, was reorganized in 1968. The name was changed to the School of Family Resources and Consumer Sciences and William H. Marshall, formerly of West Virginia University, became dean in the early 1970s. Similarly, in

31. Michael W. Whittier, "Part III: Epilogue, 1965–1968," in *A Growing College*, pp. 527–28. This very brief addendum to a five hundred-page volume that summarizes in great detail the college's achievements to the mid-1960s demonstrates the suddenness and distastefulness of the rupture.

32. Helen Canoyer, "The Changing Role of Home Economics," in *The Development of the Land-grant Colleges and Universities and Their Influence on the Economic and Social Life of the People*, West Virginia University Bulletin (Morgantown, 1963), pp. 109, 113; Urie Bronfenbrenner et al., "Helen Gertrude Canoyer, 1903–1984," *Memorial Statements, Cornell University Faculty, 1983–84* (Ithaca, 1984), pp. 7–8, which claims (erroneously) that she was one of the first women in the United States to earn a doctorate in economics. At least four had been awarded before 1900. Her Cornell obituary also applauded her enthusiastic encouragement of young men in the field over the years.

1970 the program at Michigan State University changed its name to the College of Human Ecology.[33]

Yet such changeovers did not occur everywhere or even at most institutions. A 1974 article in the *Journal of Home Economics* authored by AHEA president Marjorie East of Penn State and others reported that between 1962 and 1972, although name changes had seemed widespread, even epidemic, only 10 percent (22 of the 214 institutions reporting) had actually made a change. Of those half were small programs (with less than seventy-five majors) and half were among the 95 largest, most visible (generally land-grant) institutions. Among the 90 percent that made no change were the large, established programs at Iowa State, Kansas State, Purdue, and Minnesota, even though at these schools the number and proportion of men on the faculty may have approached the levels at Cornell and Penn State.[34] (Dean Precious Mabel Nelson had hired Iowa State's first male faculty member, Glenn Hawkes, in child development in 1950, and by 1970 there were 31 men, including 16 in "applied art" among a faculty of 185 members, or 16.8 percent.)[35] Thus even a relatively high proportion of men did not prove in itself sufficient to provoke a successful academic mutiny.

Instead the key factor in bringing on the painful forced break with tradition which occurred on a few campuses in the 1960s was the presence of an ambitious president (urged on by an aggressive board of trustees), anxious to remake overnight what had been perceived as a "cow college" into a prestigious university. Among the better-known university presidents trying to follow this path (though not always succeeding) in the 1950s and 1960s were Clark Kerr at Berkeley; Milton Eisenhower, first at Kansas State then at Penn State; John Hannah at Michigan State; Frederick Hovde at Purdue; James Perkins at Cornell; Eric Walker at Penn State; and Fred Harrington at Wisconsin. In the highly laudatory, even adulatory, official biographies that recount their many triumphs, home economics is treated anecdotally rather than analytically, if it is mentioned at all. In fact, these titans of academe found the field baffling and a bit of an embarrassment. Their instinct was to appoint a young male aide as dean "to straighten the college out." But unless they choreographed it

33. Marshall was, however, soon "fired for a lack of integrity" (Donna Taylor, "Interview with May S. Reynolds, Department of Home Economics, July 1977," tape index, p. 4, University of Wisconsin Archives, Madison); Paul L. Dressel, *College to University: The Hannah Years at Michigan State University, 1935–1969* (East Lansing: Michigan State University Publications, 1987), p. 70; and College of Home Economics, Michigan State University, "The Report of the Committee on the Future of Home Economics," January 1968, mimeographed, reprinted in 1980. (I thank Mary Grace for providing a copy.)

34. Susan Weis, Marjorie East, and Sarah Manning, "Home Economics Units in Higher Education: A Decade of Change," *JHE* 66 (May 1974): 11–15.

35. Eppright and Ferguson, *A Century of Home Economics*, pp. 259, 277, 279.

very carefully, setting up university-wide committees or commissions that deliberately left the women home economists out, such plans could be thwarted in various ways. At Kansas State the opposition of a strong dean, Margaret Justin, for years hampered Milton Eisenhower.[36] At Berkeley protest by the alumnae kept home economics from being totally abolished. And at Purdue, both in 1952 and 1962, the disapproval of the few women on the board of trustees kept Frederick Hovde from appointing a male dean.[37] These tactics sometimes stymied the presidents and forced them to endure a woman dean a little longer. She, in turn, feeling threatened and given new resources only to hire men, determined to stay on as long as possible in hopes of outlasting the hostile administration. Occasionally, as at Cornell, her long-postponed retirement became the focal point for a mutiny by the male faculty, aided and abetted by the president. Accordingly, when Helen LeBaron (who succeeded so well at Iowa State for over two decades and under three presidents) wrote in 1971 that much of the college's success had depended on having the right president, she was by no means indulging in modest understatement. By then the stress and turmoil the wrong president had caused her colleagues elsewhere was all too clear. Her success, however, proved hard to replicate: she married Iowa State's president James Hilton.[38]

FROM this vantage point the crux of the home economists' problems in the 1950s and 1960s can be found not so much in the numerical data on declining enrollments or lack of Ph.D.'s on the faculty, as was so often claimed at the time, but in the hostility and related lack of communication between a new breed of ambitious university presidents who wanted to get rid of home economics, whatever it was, and the many women deans who tried repeatedly and futilely to define the field and to improve and expand their programs with little outside support. If all else failed, the women deans might at least try to outlast the presidents. For a while the home economists exhorted each other to train more Ph.D.'s, and they worked very hard to

36. Stephen E. Ambrose and Richard H. Immerman, *Milton S. Eisenhower, Educational Statesman* (Baltimore: Johns Hopkins University Press, 1983), p. 89; for more on Justin, see James C. Carey, *KSU: The Quest for Identity* (Lawrence: Regents Press of Kansas, 1977), p. 214, as well as "Margaret M. Justin (1889–1967)," *JHE* 59 (September 1967): 488, and the Justin File, University Archives, Kansas State University, Manhattan.

37. E.g., Robert W. Topping, *The Hovde Years: A Biography of Frederick L. Hovde* (West Lafayette: Purdue University, 1980), pp. 381–82.

38. Helen LeBaron Hilton, "Foreword," in Eppright and Ferguson, *A Century of Home Economics.* LeBaron merits a biography. Before going to Iowa State in 1952, she had been an assistant dean at Penn State under Grace Henderson, an example of a protégée chain among home economics administrators.

garner more research funds. But when, in the mid-1960s, such support was suddenly forthcoming, many among even the strongest women deans were approaching retirement. Male administrators on several (but not all) major campuses seized the opportunity to reshape the formerly female bastion of home economics into the somewhat more gender-neutral subject of "nutritional sciences," "human development," or "human ecology."

Thus what had once been a female subject, home economics, taught for decades mostly by single women faculty to women students at all land-grant and many other colleges and universities in America—a classic tradition of "women's work" or a form of "territorial segregation"—had by the early 1960s become unacceptable to many: less interesting to the women students and intolerable to many administrators and many male faculty. This change came about not because of any great influx of male students, though there had been some. Rather, university presidents along with the male home economics faculty (generally less than 20 percent of the total and clustered within the subfields of child development and family studies) found their female dean and the school's reputation somehow embarrassing. With the help of a sympathetic male president, the mutinous men were sometimes able to replace the woman dean and much of the older female faculty with younger men. Thus home economics reverted to the more traditional and comfortable "hierarchical segregation" common in academia, with women faculty clustered in the lower ranks.

The ousted women rarely protested publicly. Some took to preparing scrapbooks or writing the history of the program as they had known it, often ending with an ambivalent chapter called "winds of change."[39] Even as late as 1968, when feminism arrived on campus and disciplines like sociology fueled recruitment in NOW (the National Organization for Women), hardly any home economists looked to the burgeoning women's movement for help in publicizing or protesting their imminent takeover.[40] Politically and stylistically the female home economists of the late 1960s were fairly far removed from most such groups. In fact, the men in home economics may have been more liberal than they, for when feminists at Cornell University offered the first course in "female studies" in 1970, it was sponsored

39. See Viola J. Anderson's *The Department of Home Economics at the University of Kansas: The First Fifty Years, 1910–1960* (Lawrence: University of Kansas Press, 1964), as well as college and department histories cited above. Some women home economists were less accepting of the new men than others, see Angelo M. Bentivegna, "Attitudes of Home Economics College and University Professionals toward Males Entering the Field" (Ed.D. dissertation, Pennsylvania State University, 1974).

40. The redoubtable Agnes Fay Morgan was an exception to this rule. One of her last articles for the Iota Sigma Pi newsletter mentioned the new movement. See Agnes Fay Morgan, "Women in Chemistry or Allied Fields and Professional Opportunities," *The Iotan* 27 (April 1968): 13–16. The whole subject remains to be explored.

by the College of Human Ecology and listed under Human Development and Family Studies 390, Professor Harold Feldman's course on the evolution of the female personality.[41]

41. Jennie Towle Farley, "Women on the March Again: The Rebirth of Feminism in an Academic Community" (Ph.D. dissertation, Cornell University, 1970), p. 243; Edward C. Devereux et al., "Harold Feldman, 1917–1988," *Memorial Statements, Cornell University Faculty, 1987–88* (Ithaca: Cornell University, 1989), pp. 23–24.

REMINISCENCES | *Marjorie East*

MAJORIE EAST headed the Department of Home Economics Education at the Pennsylvania State University from 1958 until her retirement in 1980. The author of several major textbooks on home economics, East has been a major force in home economics education. She served as president of the AHEA in 1972–73. In her reminiscences East recalls the years when the College of Home Economics at Penn State "was being dismembered."

Why did I choose home economics? Way back in 1932, Mrs. Larkey and Mrs. Ralston were my home economics teachers in high school. There was another choice. I was in love with mathematics and in high school courses in algebra, geometry, and trigonometry I liked the logic and abstraction, the "purity," and the sense of personal power that came from success. College math turned out to be something else, however. In pondering a new major, I thought of home economics because those teachers had touched me.

Mrs. Larkey was considered to be a sewing teacher, but she also taught home management with the accent on "home." She had us thinking of family and its importance as a nurturing center for children and grown-ups. We discussed marriage, responsibility for others, and the crucial importance of the home as the physical and emotional center for daily life. She got us self-centered adolescents to think about the pleasures of caring for people other than ourselves.

Mrs. Ralston was a cooking teacher but, again, with a focus on nutrition and experimental foods. She was always asking and answering "why" questions. If you eat this, this happens in your body. If you don't eat enough of this, this happens. If you use too hot a fire this happens to an egg, and so on. There was logic here, too. And she connected logic to people's welfare. Life could be better if people cooked and ate well and if they *thought* about what they did.

Then, too, teaching seemed like the best life. My father was a vocational agriculture teacher, probably one of the first in California, in 1919. My mother was an elementary school teacher. It seemed a pleasant, easy, cheerful life.

I went through college feeling not particularly challenged. I had a good teacher in food chemistry and in nutrition and textiles and another in foods who got me involved with the college club, the California Home Economics Association, and the American Home Economics Association.

My first teaching job was in a very rural, very small-town central high school with less than a hundred students. Part of my salary was paid by federal vocational funds which the government used to promote the teaching of agriculture and home economics and, gradually, other vocational areas by subsidizing the costs of secondary programs and teacher education programs. Homemaking was considered a vocation for women, important enough to be improved through education. Truly, a small school like this one could not have afforded the facilities and salary without such help. So I taught home ec and also art, mechanical drawing, typing, even shorthand. And I coached the school plays, put on the banquets, and published the school paper and yearbook. Did I know how to do any of these extras? No, but I learned enthusiastically.

As for home economics, those were my wake-up years. I made a difference in those kids' lives and in their families'. I was dizzy with excitement. Think of what I could do in the world! I found that I had learned *something*, but I had to know lots more to be a good home economist.

I joined the AHEA, attended some professional meetings, and read the *Journal of Home Economics*, but I needed more help. I thought I'd talk to a good, really first-rate home economist about my future. I picked out Agnes Fay Morgan, made an appointment and drove up to Berkeley, went into her office, and presented myself. She was absolutely mystified as well as disdainful. What did a home economics teacher want to talk to *her* about? Dismayed by the august presence, I couldn't explain my interests very well. She brushed me off quickly. My conference lasted about five minutes. So I'd seen a real home economist, but she was not very helpful.

During my schoolteaching years in California, I learned to work with boys as well as girls. Back in 1929, my junior high had a two-week exchange program with "shop" so the girls could learn to correct electrical problems and use tools about the house and boys learned to use a sewing machine for repairing clothes and familiarized themselves with basic recipes, kitchen tools, and techniques. Boys attended my classes in several schools but always as special people, to be remarked about. Only in recent years, though we knew it all along, have boys and girls been considered equally in need of education in nutrition, child development, money management, sex education, personal grooming, and clothing selection and equally interested in the arts of cooking, sewing, and interior design.

Graduate study with Laura Drummond, Helen Judy Bond, and Ernest Osborne, teaching at Simmons College and Antioch College, and working as a editor at Houghton Mifflin all educated me and prepared me for my most valuable educational experience. I went to Penn State in 1958 and retired in 1980. Through much of Grace Henderson's deanship I was part of a unified team with an excellent faculty and an excellent leader. Watching her think out problems, develop an espirit de corps among faculty and students, cope with and try to educate the university central administration, work with the McGrath committee that was established to review the place of home economics in the land-grant system, and so on was an education in leadership. Dealing with bitter defeat was part of the experience, too, as Gracie fought cancer while witnessing the renaming and absorption of her college; it had been dismembered and reconstructed by administrators who saw no place for home economics in a first-rate university. Even if Earl J. McGrath believed home economics to be important, Penn State didn't have to agree. The president at the time thought the real reason for coeducation was to provide coeds to attract male students.

So my department was tucked away in the College of Education, practically a unit unto itself with its own funding, again under the rubric of vocational money. Still, we thrived. We did our own thing with enthusiasm and developed what I believe was the most important home economics education group in the country with a great faculty and excellent graduate students, many from other countries. We graduated ninety-nine people with doctorates during my years at Penn State, three of whom were males. My high point, I think, was working with graduate students and seeing them develop. Yet the experience never did top the fun and sense of fulfillment derived from working with high school students. When working with graduate students you're about four years removed from adolescents. You're not with the kids or the teachers of the kids, but you're with the teachers of the teachers of the kids. So in most of my working life there's been a long distance and no feedback from the family lives I have tried to influence.

My life's work has been primarily focused on the profession of home economics and its improvement. I've tried to get each home economist to be aware of the importance of the field. There are many people in our field. Some of them are dopes. Some of them are brilliant. Some are sensitive to individual needs, others try to make elegant weddings important to all kids. They are not all working toward the same ends. I've been trying to bring order into the field and a sense of intellectual responsibility.

AHEA has certainly been an important part of my life. It allowed me to work with other professionals who inspired me and showed me there are great people in our field. All around the country they stick out like stars.

So I have no regrets about leaving mathematics behind all those years ago. If I could do it all again, there are some other fields that I'd consider, but I've been happy and proud to be a part of this group of professionals. I am dismayed, however, by my failure to make a profound difference in the field. Many other ways I might have shaped the field occur to me now. Could, should, ought, are words that haunt old age. Maybe my goals were too high, set up in the sky by hubris and youthful energy. I intended to change home economics and through it the world. I do believe still that it is important to help people to think about their dreams, to plan their lives, to shape their homes, to put meaning in the daily routines. I do believe in the importance of home economics.

Test kitchen home economists working in their spotless laboratory. *Left to right*: Helen Martin, Lilla Cortright, Mary Alice Dailey. "Where Mrs. Homeowner Is Never Forgotten: Consumer Products Division's Proving Ground for Corning Glassware," *Corning Glass Works Gaffer* 4 (October 1946): 4, courtesy of the Corning, Incorporated, Department of Archives and Records Management, Corning, New York.

They Cannot All Be Teachers: Forging Careers in Home Economics

Ellen Richards worried that the many women drawn to home economics as an avenue to a career at the turn of the century would saturate the market for teachers at a time when schools and colleges were the major employers of home economics graduates. "They cannot all be teachers," she lamented. Although women were still largely excluded from business and the professions, they proved to be inventive and creative in developing alternative work.

Women seeking opportunities to use their talents, however, rarely avoided drawing on traditional ideas of woman's place. Home economics in its many manifestations exemplified this pattern. Home economists proved resourceful in developing a variety of career paths in academia, institutional management, municipal housekeeping, and dietetics. But the new jobs they found remained gender specific. This section points to three of these new careers: careers in hospital dietetics, jobs in business and industry, and work as extension agents funded by the 1914 Smith-Lever Act to improve rural living conditions.

Because of the gendered nature of their work, home economists found their power circumscribed in hospitals and industry just as it was in academia. Regina Lee Blaszczyk demonstrates how at Corning Glass Works Lucy Maltby's significant contributions to industrial research, development, and sales were undercut by gender stereotypes that kept her from receiving adequate recognition and remuneration. Lynn Nyhart details how dietitians had to struggle for a place in a hospital hierarchy that privileged male doctors and put dietitians in competition with female nurses.

Human services, conceived of as a gendered "helping" field, also provided an outlet for home economists' expertise. Kathleen Babbitt explores the role home economists played in the New York State Temporary Emergency Relief Administration helping farm women make ends meet during the Great Depression of the 1930s. In her reminiscences Hazel Reed, a county extension agent in New York State, recounts her experiences helping women to "make over and make do" during the Depression.

The proliferation of jobs for home economists increased women's career opportunities and helped expand the influence of the field. But the creation of subfields with competing visions and missions would make it increasingly difficult for home economics to maintain a clear professional identity.

6 Home Economists in the Hospital, 1900–1930

LYNN K. NYHART

Much of the early history of home economics is closely allied with the history of women's education. From the turn of the century on, domestic scientists forged a place for themselves in public education at all levels from the primary school to the adult extension program. But Ellen Richards worried in 1906, "What are we to do with all our domestic science graduates? They cannot all be teachers."[1] Women trained in home economics in the first quarter of the century worked hard to find and develop new roles and new jobs for themselves, not just in the educational system but also in the private sector working in the food and consumer goods industries, in the public sector of food testing and regulation, and in the realm of what we today call food management—running cafeterias and dining halls for both public and private institutions. Several essays in this volume are devoted to the new roles home economists took on outside the sphere of education. I focus on just one: how hospital dietitians in the period between 1900 and 1930 created a place for themselves within the complex hierarchy of the hospital community.

Food has always been an essential part of home economics, forming one of the traditional core triad of subjects along with clothing and shelter. Cookery courses were among the earliest integrated into the home economics curricula, especially in the agricultural colleges of the Midwest, and healthful eating was a perennial concern of the field.[2] As the home

1. Quoted in E. Grace McCollough, "The Cooperation of Dietitian and Physician," *Journal of Home Economics* 4 (December 1912): 428–33, quotation on p. 428.
2. Emma Seifrit Weigley, "It Might Have Been Euthenics: The Lake Placid Conferences and the Home Economics Movement," *American Quarterly* 26 (March 1974): 80.

economics movement became more formalized around the turn of the century, "dietists" and "dietitians" working in hospitals and cafeterias participated in its expansion. At the second annual meeting of the American Home Economics Association in December 1909, for example, an entire session was devoted to hospital dietetics.[3] In its first volume, the *Journal of Home Economics* discussed the appropriate home economics course of study for hospital dietitians, and as we will see in more detail, home economics would continue to provide the formal educational base for dietitians even before standard educational requirements were established.

Dietetics consisted of more than just cookery or even the "science of healthful eating." A history extending back over millennia placed it in the realm of medicine: dietetics in the medical world concerned the uses of food and diet not only for maintaining health but also for healing. The use of food as an aspect of therapy had gone in and out of fashion numerous times. In the early twentieth century, dietetics was not very much in fashion among American physicians, who viewed it as a minor part of their therapeutic armamentarium. Most physicians considered it useful in treating only a few diseases and relegated the regular feeding of patients to nurses. But the possibility always existed that diet therapy would come back into vogue as a more significant part of the physician's sphere of expertise. Thus when dietitians began working in hospitals in increasing numbers in the early twentieth century, they found themselves carving out space in two realms: a women's realm of food and cookery, common to home economists and nurses, and an almost exclusively male physicians' realm of medical therapy.

The hospital context itself changed rapidly during the first thirty years of the century.[4] For the purposes of this essay, the most significant features were the boom in building new hospitals, the expansion and formalization of hospital-based nurses' training programs, and the growth of a middle-class clientele. The rapid creation of large numbers of new hospitals during this period meant that both buildings and administrative structures were being built from the ground up; this may have allowed dietitians to slip into the administrative hierarchy more easily than into an already fixed organizational structure. For the growth of dietetics the most important administrative change initially came in the nursing schools attached to hospitals. In 1900 the Federal Bureau of Education counted 432 such schools; by 1920 this number had more than tripled to over 1,750, and the number of nursing students attending them multiplied by a factor

---

3. "Provisional Program, American Home Economics Association Second Annual Meeting," [for Friday, December 31], *Journal of Home Economics* 1 (December 1909): 455.

4. Rosemary Stevens, *In Sickness and in Wealth: American Hospitals in the Twentieth Century* (New York: Basic Books, 1989).

of nearly five.[5] This rapid growth placed increasing demands on teachers of various parts of the nursing curriculum, including that devoted to diet. Dietitians initially entered the hospital hierarchy through this opening. By 1914, one writer could state that "about 50% of hospitals employ dietitians at the present time."[6]

The expansion of hospitals had other effects as well. The increase in the number of middle-class patients (who paid for their care) drew attention to services previously neglected in the hospital, including ones related to food. Administrators concerned themselves with the extent to which paying patients' eating experiences shaped their impression of the care given them in the hospital.[7] Dietitians played an important part in seeking to improve the overall hospital stay for such patients, striving to deliver food that was attractive, "dainty," hot when it was supposed to be hot, and cold when it was supposed to be cold.[8] Moreover, diet was an important part of a larger projection of the hospital as a model for community life. Dietitians and physicians repeatedly stressed that hospital fare should be not only nutritious but cheap, simple, and easily imitated by patients in their homes.[9]

As specialists in food and cookery, home economics–trained dietitians offered American hospitals three related areas of expertise: scientific knowledge of physiology and the chemistry of foods, practical knowledge of food purchasing and its aesthetic preparation, and the skill of translating between the two—of knowing how to make a "scientific diet" that patients would eat. But new social roles do not spring up just because people offer new expertise. The success of these food experts in establishing their position rested on their willingness to mold what they had to offer to fit the needs of the hospital and on their ability to take advantage of the opportunities provided by such events as World War I and the discovery of insulin.

5. Figures quoted in Committee for the Study of Nursing Education, *Nursing and Nursing Education in the United States* (1923; rpt. New York: Garland, 1984), p. 188.

6. Elmina White, "The Importance of Dietetics in Nurses' Training," *Pacific Coast Journal of Nursing* 10 (1914): 501.

7. See, e.g., Rena Eckman, "Institutional Economics Applied to Hospital Dietetic Problems," *Modern Hospital* 24 (1922): 175–78; Lulu Graves, "The Management of the Dietary Department of the Hospital," *Modern Hospital* 11 (1918): 394–98.

8. The amount of attention paid to the means of getting the food from kitchen to patient is remarkable. Hospital administrators and dietitians debated the merits of central kitchens versus ward kitchens; at conventions an assortment of food carts—designed to keep hot food hot and cold food cold at the same time—were displayed; and the responsibility for feeding the patient was hotly contested. See Graves, "Management of the Dietary Department," pp. 395–96; Renwick Ross, "The Kitchen," in *Hospital Management,* ed. Charlotte A. Alkens (Philadelphia: W. B. Saunders, 1911), pp. 251–52; Joseph B. Howland, "An Electrically Heated Food Truck," *Modern Hospital* 9 (1917): 301; and Helen Wallace, "Heated Food Boxes for Serving Hot Food from a Central Kitchen," *Modern Hospital* 9 (1917): 303.

9. Elliott P. Joslin, "The Hospital Dietary," *Modern Hospital* 9 (1917): 303 8 (1917): 57–60. Esther H. Funnell, "Nutrition Work in a Hospital Dispensary," *Modern Hospital* 18 (1922): 364–65.

The story of how dietitians secured their place in the hospital falls into three parts dividing roughly along chronological lines, each division signifying a new departure in dietitians' activities. Each phase also shows how dietitians defined their role in relation to a different group within the hospital community. Before about 1916 dietitians served primarily as instructors in practical cookery for nurses and as supervisors for the preparation of special meals for private patients. Between about 1916 and 1921 they rapidly added to these tasks the new managerial role of food administrator; this expansion brought dietitians into a closer, more powerful relationship with hospital administrators and assured them a stable (if not always comfortable) place in the hospital hierarchy. And in the third phase, starting about 1921, they began working more closely with physicians, both in carrying out "diet prescriptions" and in teaching physicians about the practical side of diet therapies. Indeed, by the mid-1920s dietitians had reason to hope that doctors might soon accept them as medical consultants and teachers to medical students on the basis of their expertise in therapeutic diets.[10]

None of these stages ended with the start of a new one; rather, at each point a new role was simply added to the previous ones. With this proliferation of roles came further expansion of the number of hospital dietitians. Although overall figures are hard to obtain, especially from the period before the founding of the American Dietetic Association (ADA) in 1917, the growth of the ADA gives some indication of the expansion of the field. Between 1925 and 1938, two dates for which figures are available, the number of dietitians increased dramatically. In 1925, 440 members of the ADA (out of a total of 660) worked in hospitals; by 1938 that number had multiplied over fivefold to some 2,400 (out of 3,800).[11] By about 1930 the "food departments" of many hospitals had expanded sufficiently to maintain two or more dietitians, who could now afford to specialize in either clinical work or administration.

As this overview suggests, dietitians *did* succeed in creating a firm place for themselves in the hospital structure, but their success was only partial, for their status as professionals remained precarious. Although the use of the term "professional" had become quite elastic during the Progressive era, expanding far beyond the traditional professions of law, medicine, and the-

---

10. A second important new task marking this last phase was the development of outpatient clinics, which catered mainly to lower-class and immigrant groups. They gave the dietitian less chance to practice her aesthetic skills than her practical ones of providing a "scientific diet" to people who either could little afford it or were not used to eating the suggested foods. This is in itself an entire chapter in the history of medical dietetics and public health and cannot be covered here.

11. Figures for 1925 are from Alberta M. MacFarlane, Quindara Oliver Dodge, and Mary deGarmo Bryan, "The Food Administrator: A Product of Modern Living," *Journal of the American Dietetic Association* (hereafter *JADA*) 25 (1949): 518. Figures for 1938 are from Lenna F. Cooper, "The Dietitian and Her Profession," *JADA* 14 (1938): 756. AHEA membership in 1938 was 12,000.

ology, it still conveyed mastery of a specific and unique area of knowledge and autonomous control over that territory. But as we will see, "scientific eating" remained an area in which claims to special expertise were hard to maintain, especially when the very concept of a woman professional still seemed like something of a contradiction in terms.[12]

THE role of the teaching dietitian, which emerged in the 1890's is intertwined with the history of nursing education, hospital development, and the growth of home economics itself. For even as Ellen Richards was wondering where to place the rapidly increasing numbers of women educated in home economics, the demand among hospital administrators for women with just such training was growing as well.

Hospitals had not always had dietitians. Traditionally, a chef, steward, or housekeeper controlled the food service of the hospital, planning meals to feed the many ward patients and hospital staff at a low cost. By the turn of the twentieth century, however, there were sufficient numbers of private patients and ward patients on specially prescribed diets to require someone to prepare individualized meals: higher-quality food for the private patients and special meals for sufferers of tuberculosis, nephritis, diabetes, typhoid fever, and a few other conditions. At the same time, hospital training schools for nurses increasingly sought teachers who could instruct pupil nurses in "invalid cookery" as a minor but necessary part of their education. This pair of needs opened up a new space in the hospital community for dietitians.

The first wave of hospital dietitians in the 1890s had little formal training; if they had any, it was likely to be from one the cooking schools of the Northeast, such as the Boston Cooking School or Mrs. (Sarah Tyson) Rorer's Philadelphia Cooking School or from one of the early schools of household arts. Biographical and institutional stories from the Philadelphia area give some indication of the role of these dietitians in the development of both nurses' courses and home economics education.

Martha Byerly of the Pennsylvania Hospital recalled in 1926 having read a magazine article in 1891 "on the crying need of trained women in hospitals to teach nurses to prepare food for the sick." She enrolled in Mrs. Rorer's cooking course that fall and spent the following year "studying chemistry and digestion, testing my recipes and teaching and lecturing when and where I could." By 1893 she had found employment as "superintendent of diet" at the Presbyterian Hospital of Philadelphia, teaching

---

12. On woman professionals, see Joan Jacobs Brumberg and Nancy Tomes, "Women in the Professions: A Research Agenda for American Historians," *Reviews in American History* 10 (1982): 275–96; and Daniel J. Walkowitz, "The Making of a Feminine Professional Identity: Social Workers in the 1920s," *American Historical Review* 95 (1990): 1051–75.

nurses and overseeing the preparation of all special foods. Significantly, too, in these same years the president of Smith College asked her "to work out a scheme for introducing a course of what would now be called Household Economics" at Smith.[13] Byerly's story suggests how a direct relationship between the cookery schools and nursing schools may have fed somewhat indirectly into the development of home economics.

In this same period, Anthony J. Drexel established the Drexel Institute, a college devoted primarily to vocational education, in Philadelphia. From its opening in 1892, Drexel offered a course in invalid cookery for nurses, along with a "normal course" aimed at future teachers of cookery. These two courses provided the foundation for the vocational courses in domestic science, which rapidly expanded. The normal course soon expanded to two years, and by 1914, when Drexel consolidated various courses into the School of Domestic Science and Arts, one explicitly intended clientele for the course was "those who wished to serve as dietitians or managers in charge of purchasing for hospitals and other institutions."[14] By this time, cookery courses for nurses had become more standard within the hospital-based training schools, and Drexel had moved out of the business of teaching nurses. Teaching future dietitians, however—the women who would teach the nurses at the hospitals—remained an important mission at Drexel. Nor did these teachers necessarily lack hospital cookery experience: Emma Smedley, an instructor in household economics at Drexel in 1909, when she was elected to the first AHEA Council, had graduated from Drexel's normal domestic science course and worked as instructor in dietetics at the Johns Hopkins University hospital before returning to Drexel to teach.[15]

Although the earliest dietitians may have been educated along lines similar to Byerly, the formalization of vocational schools like Drexel and the development of science education for women at the college level combined by the 1900s and 1910s to provide new sources of supply for hospital dietitians. Lenna Frances Cooper, one of Drexel's most distinguished graduates from this period, attended her first Lake Placid conference in 1907 and ten years later cofounded the American Dietetic Association. Cooper's career trajectory proved atypical among dietitians because of her close ties to John Harvey Kellogg's vegetarian Battle Creek Sanitarium, which was more of a health spa than a hospital. Her career nevertheless illustrates the close and complex relation of dietetics, nursing education, and home economics in the early part of the century.

13. Martha G. Byerly, "A Chapter in the History of Dietetics," *JADA* 2 (1926–27): 166–67. There is no indication of what happened to her sketch.

14. Edward D. McDonald and Edward M. Hinton, *Drexel Institute of Technology, 1891–1941: A Memorial History* (Philadelphia: N.p., 1942), pp. 187–200, quotation on p. 196.

15. "The Elected Officers," *Journal of Home Economics* 1 (December 1909): 90.

Cooper graduated from high school in Hutchinson, Kansas, and taught high school for two years before moving to Battle Creek, Michigan, where she attended the training school for nurses attached to Kellogg's sanitarium. Ella Kellogg, wife of the sanatarium's director, taught cookery there; she encouraged Cooper to go to Drexel. Cooper then moved to Philadelphia for a year, completing the Drexel course in normal domestic science in 1908. After graduating, she returned to Battle Creek, where she became chief dietitian at the sanitarium and subsequently head of a new training school for dietitians there. During this period she took time out to gain a bachelor's degree from Columbia University, a step probably unusual among the early dietitians as a group but not uncommon among the leaders of the profession. She also maintained close professional ties to home economics, serving as secretary of the AHEA from 1920 to 1923. When the dietitians' school became part of Battle Creek College, Cooper was named the college's dean of home economics, a position she held until 1926. She later also took a master's degree at Columbia (1926), again a step rare among hospital dietitians then but more in line with the other women leaders in dietetics and nutrition, who were among the pioneers in advanced scientific education for women. After finishing at Columbia, Cooper moved to Michigan State University as food service director, and then in 1930 she returned to New York City to become chief dietitian at Montefiore Hospital. Although Cooper moved back and forth throughout her career between practical food administration (mostly in hospital settings) and teaching, it appears that most women with advanced degrees in subjects related to nutrition remained in academia, whereas those who worked in hospitals usually held lesser degrees. Indeed, in the repeated discussions over the appropriate training for hospital dietitians, the vocational approach exemplified by Drexel's courses appears to have been viewed as a more suitable model for such practical work than an advanced degree.[16]

---

16. E. Neige Todhunter, "Biographical Notes from the History of Nutrition: Lenna Frances Cooper—February 25, 1875–February 23, 1961," *JADA* 47 (1965): 28. Todhunter gives Cooper's appointment as head of the training school as 1906 and states that it was after she took the Drexel course; Cooper's student record at Drexel, however, indicates that she completed the one-year curriculum of three courses in June 1908. It seems likely, therefore, that Cooper was appointed in 1908, not 1906. Information supplied by Drexel University, Office of Student Records, April 20, 1993.

A survey of hospital dietitians conducted in 1923, by which time presumably the standards were higher than in earlier years, revealed that of eighty-five responses concerning education, thirty-one dietitians had attended state universities or colleges, twenty had gone to private colleges, and thirty-four had attended non-degree-granting institutions. Seventy-four of the respondents had followed a general home economics curriculum. Only nine respondents had had more than four years of post–high school education. See Effie I. Raitt, "A Survey of the Status of the Hospital Dietitian," *Modern Hospital* 21 (1923): 631.

These anecdotes suggest that the earliest hospital dietitians had a range of education, which may or may not have been associated with formal home economics courses. The expansion of hospital nursing education, however, soon created a demand for dietitian-teachers who had more formal education, and home economics programs scrambled to meet the need. As an editorial in the opening issue of the *Journal of Home Economics* stated in 1909, "If we mistake it not, the professional dietitian has one of the most useful and promising fields open to workers in home economics."[17] An article in the same issue titled "The Training of Dietitans for Hospitals" confronted in more detail the problems of coordinating the requirements of hospital dietitians with the education provided by domestic science courses. Not the least of these problems was that both educators and students choosing careers perceived the job of dietitian as holding lower status than that of home economics teacher; to persuade her audience that this should not be the case, the article's author pointed out that the hospital had a great potential as a community model and that patients and nursing students were a valuable audience for spreading the gospel of proper food purchasing and preparation.[18] A somewhat darker message came from the physician William F. Boos, who gave an address titled "The Hospital Dietitian" to the first meeting of the AHEA's Section for Dietitians in December 1909. At the close of the speech, he noted that hospital dietetics was currently "woman's work, waiting for her, and offering fine inducements to her. This fact should be impressed upon young women in search of a professional career, for if there are no women available—and I fear there are not

---

The educational paths of nutrition researchers in academia tended to be longer and more science-oriented. Mary Swartz Rose, a contemporary of Cooper whose professorship in nutrition at Teachers College, Columbia (1921), was the first such in the country, received a bachelor of letters degree from Denison University in 1901 and a B.S. from Teachers College in 1906; she subsequently studied physiological chemistry under Lafayette B. Mendel at Yale, receiving her Ph.D. in 1909. Ruth Wheeler's bachelor's degree was from Vassar (1899); she, too, studied physiological chemistry and nutrition at Yale, receiving her Ph.D. there in 1913. Wheeler became instructor in nutrition at the University of Illinois in the faculty of household science; moved to Goucher College as professor of home economics in 1918; subsequently returned to the Midwest in 1921 to head the Department of Nutrition at University Hospital of the State University of Iowa; and completed her career at Vassar as professor of nutrition and physiology and chairman of the Division of Euthenics between 1928 and 1944. See E. Neige Todhunter, "Biographical Notes from the History of Nutrition: Mary Swartz Rose—October 31, 1874–February 1, 1941," *JADA* 29 (1953): 1013; Todhunter, "Biographical Notes from the History of Nutrition: Ruth Wheeler—August 5, 1877–September 29, 1948," *JADA* 47 (1965): 465. Rose, Wheeler, and Cooper were all close contemporaries, born between 1874 and 1877, and educated in that narrow window of time when science degrees were opening up for women. See Margaret Rossiter, *Women Scientists in America: Struggles and Strategies to 1940* (Baltimore: Johns Hopkins University Press, 1982).

17. "The Dietitian's Opportunity" [editorial], *Journal of Home Economics* 1 (February 1909): 73.

18. Florence R. Corbett, "The Training of Dietitians for Hospitals," *Journal of Home Economics* 1 (February 1909): 62–66.

many—it will not be long, in these days of overcrowded professions, before men will add dietetics to the list of callings for men, and women may realize too late what an opportunity they have lost."[19]

As the complex relations of supply, demand, and education for dietitians worked themselves out, dietitians were already at work in hospitals. In a special "diet kitchen" (often referred to as the "diet laboratory" to emphasize its scientific cleanliness, exactness, and control) the dietitian prepared the special menus and supervised the student nurses, who cooked individual dishes and prepared trays for the diet patients. In undertaking these tasks, the dietitian-teachers often fit into two overlapping administrative hierarchies, as part of the training school for nurses and also as part of the regular hospital staff.

From the point of view of the training schools, the main object of the dietitian was to provide student nurses with the knowledge and skills of scientific food preparation that would both help them pass their state board exams and serve them later in private nursing work. In the first decade of the century, such knowledge was not terribly esoteric. The New York State board examination of 1908 asked, "How should an egg be boiled? How should it be served to an invalid[?]" and "Give a recipe for lemon jelly, for creamy rice pudding." The more theoretical questions asked, "What are the uses of water in the body?" or "Give three examples of food containing fat."[20]

During the 1910s the core of knowledge related to dietetics expanded considerably and was reflected in the board exams for nurses. Beginning about 1915–16, questions began referring to the energy requirements of the body and the breakdown of the "energy value" of certain foods into water, fat, protein, carbohydrate, and ash or mineral matter. Nevertheless, such practical questions as "How would you make a) a cup of tea, b) a cup of coffee?" still filled up much of the exam.[21]

Dietitians gained prestige with the growing prominence of technical knowledge of dietetics in nursing education, but teaching nurses remained a fairly peripheral occupation in the hospital's larger scheme of things. Nor was it easy for dietitians to move beyond the diet kitchen, for doing so created tensions with the nursing staff. When dietitians wanted to visit patients to see how they responded to the diet, nurses sometimes objected to their presence on the wards as an invasion of both physical and professional territory. A. T. Atwood, dietitian at the Johns Hopkins University hospital, adjured dietitians in 1917 to adapt to the needs of the ward, while at the same time urging them to stay away so as not to complicate life for the

19. William F. Boos, "The Hospital Dietitian," *Boston Medical and Surgical Journal* 162 (March 24, 1910): 387.

20. Alida F. Pattee, ed., *State Board Requirements in Dietetics and State Board Examination Questions* (Mt. Vernon, N.Y.: Pattee, 1917, 2d ed. 1920), pp. 68–69.

21. Ibid., pp. 74–75.

nurses.[22] In 1925 a physician and a nursing educator from the Mayo Clinic protested that "a corps of dietitians who do all the work themselves pre-empt a field that belongs to the nurse, deprive her of a training that she has a right to demand, and leave her incapable of cooperating in the treatment of large groups of patients. . . . There is manifest injustice to the nurse in turning over to a newcomer, the dietitian, a problem in nursing as impor-tant as this."[23]

The tension between nurses and dietitians lasted through the 1920s and extended not only to the dietitian herself but also to the student dietitians who now received some practical training in the hospitals. A 1927 article titled "Ethics for Student Dietitians," written by a hospital dietitian, in-structed students venturing onto the wards that "the dietitian is an outsider in [the ward nurse's] domain, and that she is therefore entitled to know who you are and why you have come." And "it is never permissible to hold a conversation with anyone else on the ward without her consent."[24]

If nurses viewed dietitians as potentially dangerous usurpers of profes-sional territory, physicians during this early period did not share such pro-fessional anxieties; indeed, in the 1910s doctors seemed manifestly uninterested in dietitians' expert knowledge of nutrition and special diets. As one former hospital superintendent declared in 1917, "I am repeatedly in receipt of letters from dietitians throughout the country, women of high education, of elaborate special training and of intelligence and ability, who complain that they are given no work to do in the special feeding of cases in their institutions, and that their energies are confined, through no fault of their own, to 'making up the trays for patients.'" The same writer quoted a dietitian as saying, "I have been here a year . . . and I have not been asked by a single physician in the hospital to feed a patient specially, nor have the doctors, any one of them, taken the slightest interest in anything that I might be able to do."[25] This situation would change later in the 1920s, but in the meantime, dietitians chafed at the underuse of their skills.[26]

22. A. T. Atwood, "The Problems of the Dietitian and Her Relationship to the Hospital and the Training School," *Modern Hospital* 8 (1917): 285–88.

23. Russell M. Wilder and Florence H. Smith, "Teaching Nurses Diet Therapy," *Modern Hospital* 2 (1925): 243.

24. Mary W. Northrop, "Ethics for Student Dietitians," *JADA* 3 (1927–28): 30.

25. John A. Hornsby, "The Hospital Problem of Today—What Is It?" *Modern Hospital* 9 (1917): 326. For a similar comment, see Dr. Elizabeth Campbell, "The Relation of the Physician to the Dietitian," *Modern Hospital* 14 (1920): 397.

26. As late as 1923, a survey of 126 hospital dietitians yielded the following discouraging re-sults: twenty-six reported "no contact with physicians," six "very little," thirteen "less than 30 minutes a day," and sixty-four neglected to answer this part of the questionnaire. Only thirty-three, or just under a quarter of the total, reported any significant time in contact with physi-

Perhaps because of this situation, by the end of the 1910s dietitians were playing down their roles as teachers to nurses and as heads merely of the diet kitchen, looking instead to new areas into which they might expand. World War I propelled them into such a new area, with a vastly greater potential for power in the hospital. This new field was food administration.

ALTHOUGH the so-called managing dietitian, responsible for the food service of the entire hospital community, had existed from the early days of dietetics, it was only with World War I that she came into her own. Unlike the vast majority of home economics graduates, who went into teaching, the managing dietitian went into the hospital to become an administrator, *not* to teach. Initially this career path seemed to indicate lower professional ambition, but by 1920 many dietitians were interested in food administration. And by 1927, a survey of hospital dietitians showed that they had extensive administrative authority. More than half had control over the routine purchasing of food, over two-thirds had complete authority to hire and fire kitchen employees, and nearly all had entire supervision of the food department. Because the food department typically accounted for up to a third of a hospital's operating costs, food administrators held a considerable amount of power and responsibility.[27]

How did dietitians move so rapidly into administration? One can imagine that they understood well that in a bureaucratic institution power and prestige are conferred at least in part through the control of money; thus it made sense for a group seeking to secure and improve its status to try to gain some financial power. At the same time, home economics provided another rationale: home economists were trained for household management, and what was a hospital if not a large household? But because this shift in managerial authority meant a transfer of power away from hospital superintendents, we must also ask how the latter came to hand it over.

This shift in authority appears to have come during World War I. The war opened up new administrative positions, not only through the labor shortage created in the civilian realm but especially significantly through the introduction of dietitians into military hospitals as civilian employees. Through the Red Cross Bureau of Nursing, the Dietitians Service organized the training and recruitment of dietitians for work in military hospitals at

cians (Effie I. Raitt, "A Survey of the Status of the Hospital Dietitian," *Modern Hospital* 21 [1923]: 630).

27. Margaret Gillam, "The Hospital Dietary Department," *JADA* 3 (1927–28): 234–42. The 33 percent figure is given by S. S. Goldwater, M.D., "Economic Importance of the Dietary Department," *JADA* 1 (1925–26): 21.

home and abroad. There dietitians were charged with feeding all the patients, not just those with nutritional disorders and diseases. The Dietitians Service also established uniform standards of education, requiring a two-year course in home economics beyond the high school level and at least four months of practical work in a hospital before dietitians went to work for the military. A history of the ADA states that "by Armistice Day, 356 dietitians were assigned to military hospitals; 84 were serving overseas, and 272 were distributed among the 97 base hospitals, general hospitals, and post hospitals in the United States."[28] Despite the poorly defined status of dietitians in the military hospital hierarchy and the difficult conditions under which they worked, they became a permanent part of the organization. The war thus marked a significant step toward improving the status of the managing dietitian, for the higher educational standards and the heroic risks associated with working overseas during the war helped to forge a positive and patriotic image of the job of food administration. It also set a precedent for dietitians working in other federally funded hospitals: in 1919 the U.S. Public Health Service, which then controlled the hospitals for military veterans, established a dietetic section. Immediately some eighty-five dietitians went to work in these hospitals. As in the wartime military hospitals, they had extensive administrative responsibilities, controlling the purchase, preparation, and delivery of all food. The initial effort was judged a success, and by 1921 twice as many dietitians had found employment in these hospitals.[29] The war thus provided specific, highly visible opportunities for hospital dietitians to move into administration.

The war also precipitated the founding of the American Dietetic Association, organized by hospital dietitians to give themselves a professional identity clearly separate from that provided by the American Home Economics Association. When the AHEA canceled its annual meeting in 1917, Lenna F. Cooper, then director of the Training School at the Battle Creek Sanitarium (who would by 1918 become the supervising dietitian for the army), and Lulu Graves, supervisor of dietitians at the Lakeside Hospital in Cleveland, Ohio, hastily organized a meeting of dietitians to discuss how best to contribute to the war effort. Ninety-eight people attended, nearly half of them hospital dietitians. This group decided to form an association distinct from the AHEA or the American Hospital Association; thus was the American Dietetic Association born. Evidently concerned about their professional status, the founders of the ADA defined explicit educational requirements for mem-

---

28. Mary I. Barber, *History of the American Dietetic Association, 1917–1959* (Philadelphia: Lippincott, 1959), p. 204. For more on the dietitians in the military during World War I, see pp. 197–205. I thank Professor Bernice Hopkins for calling my attention to the importance of military hospitals and the Red Cross Nursing Service during and after World War I in the development of hospital dietetics.

29. Ibid., p. 254.

bership. The minimum for women educated before June 1917 was a one-year course in home economics beyond high school and a year of practical dietetic experience, and for those completing their education after 1917 the ADA mandated a two-year home economics course (already the standard requirement for teachers of home economics). The ADA requirements were clearly designed to improve the standing of dietitians and were, at least on paper, more exclusive than those of the AHEA, which invited membership from "all who are actively interested in home problems."[30]

Although the founding of the ADA was certainly an important result of the 1917 meeting, the more immediate aim was to discuss how dietitians could contribute to the war-related food conservation movement. This broader movement, which enlisted thousands of home economists in addition to the smaller group of hospital dietitians, helped to reinforce the idea that food management was an appropriate task for women in the workplace as well as in the home. By creating the U.S. Food Administration, which orchestrated the food conservation movement, the federal government conferred greater legitimacy on food management as a profession. And although the soldiers and even the officers on this front of the war were to be the home economists and housewives of America, the administration further underscored the importance of the food front by appointing as the Food Administration's first head a man, the prominent engineer Herbert Hoover.

"Food Will Win the War!" Hoover proclaimed, and in 1917 bulletins went out to every country outpost in the nation telling American women that the meat, butter, wheat, and sugar they conserved would fuel the Allied troops to victory. Hospital administrators embraced the reduction of food waste with enthusiasm. Hospital food departments conserved by serving smaller amounts to the patients, reducing the number of bread slices and size of milk portions, and distributing sugar in individually wrapped packets. Dietitians were encouraged to have their pupil nurses or kitchen employees weigh the garbage daily, keep a record of it, and make efforts to reduce it.[31]

Dietitians and other hospital administrators also used their institutional authority to impress upon patients the moral virtues of food conservation: "Patients should be taught economic habits in dealing with food. They

30. Quoted in Emma Seifrit Weigley, "Professionalization and the Dietitian," *JADA* 74 (1979): 318. Although the ADA's standards may have been higher than the official requirements of the AHEA, in practice it seems likely that most AHEA members had at least as much education as the dietitians. The contrast with the AHEA existed, therefore, to a greater degree at the level of rhetoric than that of membership.

31. Charles S. Pitcher, "Food Waste in Hospitals," *Modern Hospital* 11 (1918): 491–96; Lulu Graves, "The Effects of the Past Year's Events on Dietetics," *Modern Hospital* 12 (1919): 19; "Wrapped Sugar Economical," *Modern Hospital* 10 (1918): 206–7. Pitcher had advocated a detailed "waste accounting system" for food administrators as early as 1912 (Pitcher, "Waste Accounting Systems and Basic Dietary Ration Tables," *Journal of Home Economics* 4 [1912]: 460–68).

should not be allowed to see food wasted." Food administrators considered some foods inherently less wasteful than others and therefore encouraged their use in the diet. For example, "It would seem as if bananas might be used more. There is no more waste to a banana than to an egg. The caloric value is high. If suitably prepared, the banana is easily digested. It affords variety; it has a high moral value. Did you ever know an individual to commence a banana that he did not finish it?"[32]

High wartime prices provided an economic justification for conservation in addition to a patriotic one. Food costs had risen rapidly since the early 1910s and in 1916 alone increased 19 percent.[33] Managing dietitians *had* to pay attention to food costs as well as nutritional values. Administrators' concerns with food conservation and reducing of waste would persist in hospital management long after the war ended, although they would be justified later in purely economic terms, not on patriotic grounds.

The world war provided dietitians with more than simply the opportunity to show what they could do in administration. It also gave them an important new rationale for their claims of expertise for feeding the entire hospital community, not just the "special diet" patients. The war offered ample evidence that healthy people required a balanced diet just as much as sick ones. Tales circulated of the African unit stricken with scurvy because already inadequate rations of fresh vegetables were cooked for three hours before being served, or of British troops plagued with beri-beri because their diet was limited to "white bread, tinned meat, and jam." These stories lent weight to arguments that scientific eating was necessary for everyone.[34] Hospital dietitians successfully claimed that their expertise in translating food values into daily fare should be extended to all members of the hospital household.

The war therefore played a variety of crucial roles in expanding the territory of the dietitian. It created highly visible and valued administrative opportunities, most prominently in military hospitals, which allowed dietitians to move beyond the diet kitchen. It drove the food conservation movement, which highlighted the values of efficiency and management. And perhaps most important in the long run, it focused people's attention on the importance of a healthy diet, not just for those in need of specific therapies but for everyone. With this new intellectual basis, "managing" dietitians could claim to have elevated themselves above the class of shopkeepers, tea-

32. Elliott P. Joslin, "The Hospital Dietary," *Modern Hospital* 8 (1917): 58–59.

33. "The Advance in Food Prices," *Journal of Home Economics* 9 (April 1917): 184. See also Marion E. Smith, "Food Conservation at University Hospital, Philadelphia," *Modern Hospital* 10 (1918): 446; Lulu Graves, "Economical Preparation and Serving of Food," *Modern Hospital* 10 (1918): 357–58.

34. Katherine Blunt and Chi Che Wang, "The Present Status of Vitamines," *Modern Hospital* 14 (1920): 312–16.

house proprietors, and other tradeswomen. They now had a scientific, knowledge-based justification for their mission of healthful feeding.

EVEN as hospital dietitians were moving into the broader realm of general nutrition, other opportunities were opening up as well. Not long after the end of the war, diet therapy began coming back into medical vogue. In sharp contrast to doctors' desultory interest during the 1910s, their enthusiasm for diet therapy shot up dramatically after 1921, the year insulin was first synthesized and treatment of diabetes grabbed the medical headlines. Over the next few years insulin could be provided for only a tiny number of cases, and many physicians looked anew at the possibilities of diet therapy, the traditional form of treatment. The attention given to the physiology of the diabetic patient prompted new dietary treatments: whereas the traditional diabetic diet literally starved the patient to purify the system of sugar, in 1922 and 1923 physicians began to recommend high-fat diets for diabetics, to which, of course, dietitians had to adjust their menus.[35] At the same time, doctors began to demand that prescribed diets be much more precisely controlled, that accurate accounts be kept of patients' food consumption, and that dietitians see to it that the patient followed the diet exactly. This interest soon extended to other diseases as well, including new therapeutic diets for pernicious anemia, epilepsy, and tuberculosis, among others.

As medical interest in diet therapy increased, many physicians became aware of the embarrassing lacunae in their knowledge of dietetics. Dr. E. S. Gilmore, president of the American Hospital Association, wrote in 1925, "Occasionally, too, you meet doctors, and not always the older doctors, who have a very limited knowledge of dietetics. They know there are such things as carbohydrates and proteins and that in some way they are connected with food. . . . As to vitamins, some of these good men know nothing."[36] Vitamins had already become the object of laymen propagandists' attentions without the "protection" of medical authority: "The vitamin question has scarcely been touched from the therapeutic point of view except by purveyors of yeast and pills, and the pharmacologic research consists of accumulating testimonials from prize fighters and women of social prominence."[37] Another doctor worried about lay control over dietetics cautioned that if the medical community were not careful, "physicians will

35. A. D. Wickett, "Dietetics from the Medical Point of View," *Modern Hospital* 18 (1922): 546–48; Philip L. Marsh, "Application of the Laws of Metabolism to the Construction of Diabetic Diets," *Modern Hospital* 21 (1923): 76.

36. E. S. Gilmore, "The Place of the Dietetic Department in the Hospital from the Administrator's Viewpoint," *JADA* 1 (1925–26): 155.

37. Russell M. Wilder, "The Hospital Nutrition Expert," *JADA* 1 (1925–26): 120.

have another part of their legitimate field of practice painfully removed from them." He suggested as a countermeasure "to have the dietetic departments in hospitals throughout the country in the charge of well-trained dietitians working in harmony with physician and patient, incidentally educating both."[38]

Dietitians rejoiced that doctors were starting to value their special area of expertise. In rare instances, dietitians were actually invited to teach medical students. Of course, physicians continued to teach the theoretical subjects of metabolism, physiology, and blood chemistry, but for practical knowledge of food and food values, the dietitian proved a useful source. Some physicians were beginning to recognize that it took considerable skill to translate a "diet prescription" given in calories, fluids, and daily allowances of protein, fat, and carbohydrates, into palatable meals. This lesson was brought home to fourth-year medical students at Harvard in the mid-1920s. In a class co-taught by a physician and the chief dietitian at Boston City Hospital, students constructed menus out of abstract prescriptions for certain daily quantities of fat, protein, carbohydrates, and so forth and then ate the meals they planned. The dietitian teacher, Margaret McGovern, told of one medical student who created a high-fat meal for a diabetic (therapeutic according to the theory of the time) that included 30 grams of butter, 45 grams of mayonnaise, and 120 grams of heavy cream, in addition to steak, string beans, tomatoes, lettuce, and coffee. She then described how he coped with the monumental task of eating it:

> Some of the heavy cream he put in the coffee but was only able to use about one-third of the amount he had ordered. He whipped the rest and mixed it with the mayonnaise. Little realizing the volume of this amount of cream when whipped he was then faced with the problem of using over a half cup of this mixture. After completely covering the lettuce with it, he still had some left over. Determined to eat all the meal he had ordered, he had a second cup of coffee and put in the rest of the cream-mayonnaise mixture. His criticism was short but to the point. He suggested that anyone ordering such a diet be compelled to eat a similar meal. Later, however, he was shown that by more even distribution of fat among the three meals and by changing the foods about, the meal could be made palatable.[39]

One gets a sense that dietitians fortunate enough to be able to teach medical students in this way were taking revenge for years of impossible diets prescribed by ignorant interns and doctors. At the same time, of course, they

38. F. R. Nuzum, "Foods and Equipment for Food Service," *Modern Hospital* 22 (1924): 79–80.

39. Margaret McGovern, "Practical Problems in Dietetics for the Medical Student," *JADA* 3 (1927–28): 75–76.

took the opportunity to impress upon the medical profession the value of their expertise in the dietetic treatment of disease.

Although the increased interest in diet therapy in the 1920s allowed dietitians a much more visible role in medical work, doctors made it clear that the dietitian should view herself as merely an aid in carrying out the physician's orders and should in no way be recognized as an expert capable of independent diagnosis. "It is more than preposterous, it is idiotic, to turn over to a dietitian the care of a diabetic individual. . . . A dietitian is like a nurse, who should obey orders, and be a disciplinarian."[40] Experienced dietitians accepted this view as the way of the hospital. One dietitian writing in 1926 tried to convey this reality to her readers: "The general regime is semi-military for all but the scientific staff, that is, doctors and laboratory workers. . . . Most orders are given without explanation to be followed with unquestioned obedience." This subservience contrasted sharply with the life to which the college student of home economics was accustomed. "Her college education had developed her as an individual for leadership. . . . Her mind has been stimulated to question, wonder, and criticise constructively and destructively." In sum, "The college environment unfits the student for disciplined, circumscribed, cooperative work and living especially with disinterested and antagonistic groups." Rather than arguing for changing the hospital structure to accommodate a more independent-minded woman or suggesting that women seeking "leadership" roles find some other line of work, this writer urged that the college curriculum in home economics be shaped to prepare the new dietitian better for her future regimented life as a cog in the great hospital machine.[41] Women interested in independent research, it was assumed, would be better off in academia; although many dietitians hoped that their role would soon expand to encompass research, surveys and descriptions of what hospital dietitians actually did during this period generally omit any reference to research.[42]

40. See, e.g., Louis Frank, "Special Feeding of the Sick," *Modern Hospital* 15 (1920): 220–21.

41. Amalia Lautz, "The Adjustment of the College Graduate to Hospital Work in Nutrition," *JADA* 2 (1926–27): 114–15. The same picture, although with a more optimistic view of the future, had been presented over a decade earlier by E. Grace McCullough, "The Cooperation of Dietitian and Physician," *Journal of Home Economics* 4 (December 1912): 428–33.

42. For example, A. C. Bachmeyer, "The Place of the Department of Dietetics in the Hospital Composite," *Modern Hospital* 22 (1924): 178–79, in listing the duties of a dietitian, omits research entirely. A few university hospitals did enlist dietitians in research; more often what one finds is students conducting research as part of their college education, working in the hospital but answering to their professors. See C. P. Howard, "The Sphere of the Dietitian," *JADA* 2 (1926): 1–5, on the University of Iowa hospital and medical school, which established a dietetics department unusually early. Other scattered cases exist elsewhere as well: Helen Clarke, "The Dietetic Department of the Clifton Springs Sanitarium," *Modern Hospital* 21 (1923): 313–15, mentions the dietetics department's assistance in metabolic research (p. 315).

BY the end of the 1920s dietitians held an established base in the progressive hospital, having extended their realm far beyond the teaching of pupil nurses to include an expanded role for diet therapy as well as the management of food for the entire hospital community. Nevertheless, their status within the hospital hierarchy remained uneasy. This uncomfortable position may be partly explained by territorial imperatives: doctors, no less than nurses, jealously guarded their domain. But there was a difference between the territorial claims of physicians and nurses that accentuates the dietitian's position. The authority of physicians in the hospital was a given: by virtue of their power, physicians could assimilate any aspect of hospital life that they deemed "medical." If it had formerly fallen under the jurisdiction of some other part of the community, that was too bad; the latter group would be forced to accommodate. Nurses, by contrast, lacked that authority, at least vis-à-vis dietitians. Their jurisdiction remained much more open to serious challenge by dietitians, who were close to them in both the organization and the hierarchy of the hospital; hence the much tenser relationship between nurses and dietitians.[43] Gender differences reinforced these different relationships. The fact that the vast majority of hospital physicians were men strengthened their dominant position over both nurses and dietitians, reflecting the gender hierarchy at work in the broader society. Nurses and dietitians, as members of the same sex, had to work out their social relations on other grounds, without preexistent gender-based assumptions about which profession was "higher."

Dietitians sought to establish a clear basis for their own professional authority by working to raise and standardize the educational requirements for membership in their professional association (a task difficult to enforce in a period when the demand for dietitians constantly exceeded the supply). In 1926 the requirement for membership in the ADA increased from a two-year college-level course to a four-year degree with a major in foods and nutrition, and the following year the association recommended new standards for students' clinical training.[44] Some college educators and researchers in home economics and nutrition pushed for yet more stringent standards: Agnes Fay Morgan contended that dietitians would eventually require graduate-level education that emphasized the scientific and medical aspects of their work. As she pointedly put it, "The dietitian must speak

43. Dietitians who worked in outpatient clinics, where they had much greater autonomy, faced similar conflicts with public health nurses and social workers.

44. Weigley, "Professionalization and the Dietitian." This article also details several other criteria of professionalization, as set out by various sociologists up to about 1970. More recent discussions of professionalization have shown these criteria to be somewhat oversimplified. See Barbara Melosh, *The Physician's Hand* (Philadelphia: Temple University Press, 1982); and Andrew Abbott, *The System of Professions: An Essay on the Division of Expert Labor* (Chicago: University of Chicago Press, 1988).

the language and practice the suspended judgment of the scientists whose findings she is using practically before she can hope to be counted among those who rank with officers in the medical army." In case the lesson was not clear, she stressed the "cleavage of the dietitian to the physician's end of the hospital table, and away from the nurse's."[45] Despite the appeal this rhetoric must have had for dietitians, however, it reflected only poorly the reality of dietitians' hospital work, which, as we have seen, was far more concerned with the practical business of feeding the hospital household than with the aspirations of academic researchers.

In a social system in which scientific knowledge formed the prime cultural badge of professional authority, increasing the amount of education and stressing its scientific aspects constituted an understandable strategy (one taken by nurses as well, in addition to other groups seeking higher status). Food proved a particularly difficult area over which to establish claims of special authority, however, and knowledge of "scientific eating" turned out to be an extremely uncertain basis for demarcating a special sphere of expertise. The problem did not lie in something inherently "unprofessional" about working with food, but rather in its gendered associations. To the extent that they were defined as women's work, food therapy and nutrition research were by cultural consensus not considered "special" or authoritative areas of competence. All women were expected to know something about cooking and handling food, whether or not they did it "scientifically." For many, it must have seemed that dietitians just knew a little more about a basically pedestrian subject. Why should they be granted status higher than that of any other female household expert—which is to say, any woman? To the extent that dietetics was considered "medical" or therapeutic, however, it fell in the realm of the physician, and dietitians then had to subordinate their authority to that of physicians. This cruel Catch-22 of gendered definitions meant that dietitians' aspirations toward autonomy and professional authority, to the extent they were founded on special expertise, would always be thwarted.

Significantly, the areas into which dietitians moved with the least resistance during this period—food administration and general nutrition—had the lowest-status knowledge claims in the hospital community. Efficiency and good management, although certainly valued, did not compete with science for prestige. Nutrition was much more evidently based on scientific knowledge, but most physicians viewed educating patients to eat a healthful diet as an issue for normal life rather than illness (except in a few distinct cases such as diabetes); proper eating was therefore not generally a matter that trespassed on their own professional authority. It is perhaps not surprising, then, that the 1920s saw the beginning of a trend among

45. Agnes Fay Morgan, "College Education and the Food Specialist," *JADA* 1 (1926): 175–76.

dietitians toward a greater interest in outpatient education and food clinics. This new orientation followed the direction taken in nutrition work more generally over the 1930s and 1940s. The number of pages of the *Journal of the American Dietetic Association* devoted to special therapeutic diets, for example, decreased dramatically between the late 1920s and the late 1940s, from 18 percent to 6.5 percent, a fact accounted for by the growth of the view among dietitians and academic nutritionists that "corrective diets" had to be grounded in a more basic knowledge of a healthy normal diet.[46] Thus it was not in therapeutic diets, which would remain under the thumb of the physician, but in the scientific management of the healthy diet that hospital dietitians gained the greatest authority and autonomy.[47] Unfortunately, as academic nutritionists and other home economists came to learn as well, recognition of healthful eating as a realm of valuable expert knowledge would long be hindered by its designation as "women's work."

46. Corinne H. Robinson and Fairfax T. Proudfit, "Development of Positive Food Therapy," *JADA* 25 (1949): 497–503.
47. Public health nurses and social workers were also vying for authority over educating patients, especially outpatients, in dietary matters; women in all these occupations were striving for higher professional status.

7 Legitimizing Nutrition Education: The Impact of The Great Depression

KATHLEEN R. BABBITT

The new discipline of home economics advertised itself to its target population of young women during the 1910s and 1920s as vocational training. Home economics education was perceived by some of its most prominent proponents as an important component of women's rights, for no other area of women's education was so strongly committed to creating and finding jobs for its degree-holders. Students in home economics programs could prepare themselves for careers as social workers, factory inspectors, managers of large-scale institutions such as orphanages and private schools, nutritionists, and teachers. Women could of course arrive at these careers by other paths, but training in home economics was most welcome on the résumés of applicants for these positions.

One career option for the home economics student, however, mandated the training offered in departments and schools of home economics—a career in the Cooperative Extension Service of the United States Department of Agriculture. Because of the proximity of departments of home economics with colleges of agriculture, many of which fostered the new discipline of rural sociology in the 1920s, the land-grant institution provided an environment well-suited for women to learn about the rural populations they would serve as home demonstration agents in the extension service.

This essay examines the experience of women home demonstration agents and extension service specialists in the countryside of New York State during the period 1915–40, using the issue of nutrition education as

The research for this essay was partially funded by a Summer Research Fellowship in the History of Home Economics from the College of Human Ecology at Cornell University.

a lens. To what degree were Cooperative Extension Service home demonstration agents effective in educating the rural public? What resistance did they encounter and why? How did larger national events shape their work and change the ways rural and urban populations regarded them?

The extension service was the product of the momentum created by two government initiatives in the Progressive era. President Theodore Roosevelt's Commission on Country Life in 1908–9 brought to the attention of the public for the first time the economic and social problems of farmers in the United States. Five years later, in 1913, the United States Department of Agriculture mounted an extensive nationwide survey chronicling the many hardships of farm women, who worked long days inside and outside the house without running water, electricity, or hired help. USDA employees who compiled the results were pleased to note that a significant proportion of farm women asked for federally sponsored "traveling teachers" to teach them about domestic science. As one woman reported: "What is wanted in the farm home is a knowledge how to prescribe natural remedies and also a better and more rapid dissemination of information regarding disease prevention by health bulletins. Surely citizens are entitled to as much protection as cattle."[1] Many of the women who responded to the survey were concerned and frustrated at high mortality rates and chronic ill health in the countryside, which they felt could be reduced with proper education in nutrition, sanitation, and public health.[2]

These responses from farm women fit nicely with the agenda of agricultural scientists, who had been lobbying Congress for a federally sponsored program of agricultural education for years. When the Smith-Lever Act creating the Cooperative Extension Service was finally passed in 1914, it specified that education in home economics be provided for farm women. Overnight, a new career option was opened to women with degrees in home economics.

The entry of women into the countryside as home demonstration agents for the extension service was by no means smooth. It was, in fact, a bumpy ride. The experience of women home demonstration agents in New York State, who were administered by home economists at Cornell University, was typical of the many obstacles women in the extension service faced during the early years.

First, home economists were not prepared to provide the services mandated by Congress. Their male colleagues in colleges of agriculture had been

1. U.S. Department of Agriculture, Report 105, *Educational Needs of Farm Women* (Washington, D.C.: U.S. Government Printing Office, 1915), p. 58.

2. For more about the 1913 USDA survey of farm women, see Jane B. Knowles, "'It's Our Turn Now': Rural American Women Speak Out, 1900–1920," in *Women and Farming: Changing Roles, Changing Structures,* ed. Wava G. Haney and Jane B. Knowles (Boulder: Westview Press, 1988).

preparing for the birth of an entity such as the extension service for decades, through research in the Office of Experiment Stations and experiments in agricultural extension education.[3] In contrast, home economics was a brand-new field in 1915, barely established as a legitimate member of acad- eme. Home economists in land-grant institutions did not yet have access to research facilities, did not have the critical mass of students necessary to justify more faculty appointments, and were only beginning to articulate to each other an agenda of what they hoped to accomplish in academe and in society. In New York, although Martha Van Rensselaer had edited a very successful correspondence course for rural women for sixteen years before the advent of Cooperative Extension, the College of Agriculture was unpre- pared to give her the personnel she would need to place a home economist in each county, although the language of the Smith-Lever Act suggested that doing so was desirable. Van Rensselaer had an extremely difficult time find- ing enough women with home economics training to meet such a demand. The birth of the Cooperative Extension Service came perhaps five years too soon for home economists.

As a result, it was several years after the passage of the Smith-Lever Act before home economists in New York State could enter the field. When they did, it was because another set of circumstances was thrust upon them. The entry of the United States into World War I in 1917 generated an enormous effort by the federal government to reapportion the nonper- ishable food resources of the nation for the support of overseas troops through voluntary dietary substitutions by the general public. The govern- ment used employees of the only federal entity that had employees in every county—the Cooperative Extension Service—as its main conduit of information to the public. Many employees of the newborn extension ser- vice also served as representatives of the U.S. Food Administration during World War I and worked to educate the public about the voluntary dietary changes the government sought. The work of home demonstration agents during the war consisted largely of trying to persuade the public to stop eating the foods they were accustomed to in favor of foods most people considered distasteful.[4]

Rural women did not respond well to the admonitions of Food Adminis- tration female employees, and many of them resented the presence in their

---

3. See Charles Rosenberg, "Science, Technology, and Economic Growth: The Case of the Agricultural Experiment Station Scientist, 1875–1914," in Rosenberg, *No Other Gods: On Sci- ence and American Social Thought* (Baltimore: Johns Hopkins University Press, 1976), pp. 153–72. See also A. C. True, *The History of Agricultural Extension Work in the United States, 1785–1923* (Washington; D.C.: U.S. Government Printing Office, 1928).

4. See "An 'Uplift' Farm Adviser: The New Woman in a New Job," *Rural New Yorker,* April 18, 1917, p. 985. See also David Danbom, "The Agricultural Extension System and the First World War," *Historian* 41 (February 1979): 315–31.

neighborhoods of home economists, who presumably were there to tell them how and what to cook. One New York woman wrote: "Thrift and economy are not new elements in our affairs. We do not need to have new (and some of them entirely absurd and impracticable) recipes handed out to us by people who never baked a loaf of bread in their lives."[5] Young home demonstration agents working for the Food Administration sometimes got more than they bargained for when they tried to talk to rural audiences about wartime government nutrition recommendations. One young woman agent reported to her superiors at Cornell: "The farmers believe that our Government does absolutely nothing unless it is for graft and that every man is for himself and the whole business is rotten politics. Wilson ought to be in the trenches and get shot and so for the rest of the bunch if they can get rich off the farmer that is what they want. They are unpatriotic and they admit it saying that they won't be patriotic to a government like we have."[6] Farming people in New York reacted negatively to federal efforts to modify their nutritional habits during World War I. Government officials badly miscalculated the extent to which many farming families felt alienated from the government, which made the home demonstration agent's job during the early years of Cooperative Extension very difficult.

For several years after World War I, extension home economists in New York State spent a good deal of time undoing some of the damage done by government policies toward rural people during the war. Home demonstration agents were very vulnerable during these years. Because the extension service was partially funded by the federal government, many rural residents perceived its employees as government workers and thus part of the enemy.[7] The entry of home economists into the countryside as home demonstration agents of the extension service was a public relations debacle.

5. "A Housekeeper on Flour," *Rural New Yorker,* January 26, 1918, p. 116. This assessment was probably accurate in many cases. Martha Van Rensselaer and Flora Rose combed the state for enough young women with home economics training to place in each county. Most of the women they hired were extremely young, some of them were undoubtedly raised in the city, and none of them had experience teaching adults. See Flora Rose, Part I: "A Page of Modern Education, 1900–1940," in *A Growing College: Home Economics at Cornell University* (Ithaca: New York State College of Human Ecology, 1969), pp. 57, 62, and Kathleen R. Babbitt, "Producers and Consumers: New York State's Rural Women and the Cooperative Extension Service, 1900–1940" (Ph.D. dissertation, Binghamton University, 1995).

6. Anna Kerr to Claribel Nye, n.d. [ca. 1917], Records of the Dean of the College of Home Economics (hereafter RODCHE), Box 24, Folder 40. Division of Rare and Manuscript Collections, Cornell University Library, Ithaca, N.Y.

7. The comments of the home demonstration agent for Herkimer County during this period were typical: "In many sections of the county there exists an antagonistic feeling toward the work and the handling of the situation will demand its very tactful direction." Other agents reported a complete lack of interest among the women of their counties. See "Annual Report of Home Demonstration Agent Work in New York State, January 1, 1918, to January 1, 1919," *An-*

Throughout the 1920s home demonstration agents coaxed reluctant rural women to participate in extension service educational programs by joining the "voluntary" organization created by extension service employees, the Home Bureau.[8] Parallel with the more well-known Farm Bureau, the Home Bureau in New York State was a membership organization largely supported through dues and county funds. It was the only organization that home demonstration agents in New York State would work with, ensuring a certain degree of control over the delivery of curricula formulated at Cornell. Women from other organizations were welcome to join the Home Bureau as individuals, but home demonstration agents refused to accept other clubs into the Home Bureau as a group.[9] Home Bureaus existed to accept education from Cornell Cooperative Extension, and the female personnel of the extension service served that population only in New York State (see Table 7.1).

TABLE 7.1. Home Bureau membership as a percentage of New York farm households

Year	Home Bureau member	Farm households	Home Bureau membership as a percentage of farm households
1920	10,209	200,194	.05
1930	24,013	176,440	.14
1940	28,202	169,328	.17

Source: New York State College of Home Economics, *Annual Reports of Extension Service in Home Economics, New York State, 1920–1940*; Leon E. Truesdell, *Farm Population: 1880 to 1950* (U.S. Bureau of the Census Technical Paper No. 3, 1960), pp. 21, 23, 25.

---

nual Narrative and Statistical Reports from State Offices and County Agents, New York State, *1918*, National Archives Microfilm Series T-877, Reel 3.

8. The Home Bureau was a program of education in nutrition, home sewing, home decorating, and child care that was quite literally sold to women. The dues they paid bought them a curriculum formulated at Cornell. Women who joined had very little input in curriculum development or in the formulation of goals for the organization. The Home Bureau almost always served the needs of middle-class farm women, for these were the women with the leisure time, means of transportation, and money necessary to participate actively.

Home economists, however, always described the Home Bureau membership figures as evidence that there was a growing need for the education they offered to which they were merely responding. Actually, home economists, and not rural women, were defining what rural women needed. The small proportion of rural women who agreed with them made up the membership of the Home Bureau.

9. Apparently extension administrators were afraid that a club that joined the Home Bureau would replace extension service goals with its own agenda. See Helen Bull Vandervort Oral History, interviewed by Dolores Greenberg, February 7, 1964, p. 59, Division of Rare and Manuscript Collections, Cornell University Library.

In many communities, the Home Bureau created new demands on the time of middle-class rural women who were already active in the many women's groups that flourished in nearby towns and villages. Rural women were active in the Women's Christian Temperance Union, the Grange, and church-sponsored Ladies' Aid Societies. Some women were active participants in the Dairymen's League Cooperative, while others joined local committees that lobbied for consolidated rural schools. One farm woman wrote of the Home Bureau, "I, for one, would like to know how we are to be benefitted, or how we can help others through this new demand on our time and purses."[10] Many organizations interested middle-class rural women during the 1920s and provided serious competition for the Home Bureau.

At the same time, the dues required by the Home Bureau were prohibitive for women in more remote rural areas, who tended to be members of farm families who did not own their farms and were lower on the economic scale. Annual dues, which were one dollar, were too much for these women to spare. An ominous pattern was created by the presence of the Home Bureau, in which the women who could perhaps have been most helped by the extension service were unable to participate because of the financial barrier.

Despite these obstacles, home economists at Cornell formulated a program of education for rural women that focused on several key issues. Nutrition education emerged almost immediately as an important issue for rural populations. The rural diet was well-known for its reliance on starchy and fried foods and its absence of milk, vegetables, and fruits. Home economists felt that educating the rural public to modify their diets to include the latter foods would improve public health and prevent chronic gastrointestinal ailments that often prompted rural residents to resort to the patent medicine bottle.

Despite the evidence home demonstration agents in the field presented that an improved diet helped ward off colds, cured chronic constipation, prevented malnutrition in children, and drastically reduced disease among infants, rural women were slow to accept teaching in nutrition. As late as 1927, agents still had a great deal of difficulty interesting Home Bureau members in nutrition education, even when it was explicitly linked to preventive health care. In Delaware County, a project called "Food Selection in Relation to Digestion" failed miserably when five of eight Home Bureau clubs dropped the project after the first lessons.[11] And in 1931, the Cattaraugus County home demonstration agent wrote in her annual report, "It

10. Mrs. T. R., Wayne County, New York, "What of Home Economics Organization?" *Rural New Yorker,* August 24, 1918, p. 1003.

11. "Annual Narrative Report of Home Demonstration Work in Delaware County, 1927," *Extension Service Annual Narrative and Statistical Reports from State Offices and County Agents, New York State, 1927,* National Archives Microfilm Series T-877, Reel 25.

seems unfortunate that we cannot interest more people in so vital a subject as nutrition."[12]

Rural women remained skeptical of the validity of the nutrition education offered by extension home economics in part because of the newness of the field of human nutrition. Human nutrition research as a legitimate branch of scientific endeavor was only beginning to come to the attention of the American public in the 1920s, and press coverage of the new field was equally balanced between reporting legitimate discoveries in the laboratory and wildly inaccurate proclamations by would-be "experts" in nutrition. For example, the *New York Times* regularly reported the proclamations of so-called experts, who claimed that candy was necessary in the daily diet, overeating caused cancer or tuberculosis, and too much starchy food would cause poor jaw development. In this climate of misinformation, it was difficult for rural women to determine who was right and much easier for them to cling to old beliefs. Home demonstration agents patiently chipped away at folk wisdom, but change came slowly. One agent reported in 1927, "Many are still laboring under the prejudice that acid foods cause acid blood and rheumatism. They seem to understand better each year the relation of food to overweight, underweight and constipation but it takes longer to get over the prejudice that milk is fattening, cod liver oil something for Doctors to prescribe and tomatoes the cause of rheumatism."[13] If extension home economists had hoped to attain a certain status as experts in nutrition through their work as rural home demonstration agents, they were sorely disappointed. Home economists had a serious problem as educators in the 1920s—a significant gap existed between what they knew about nutrition and their ability to deliver that information to the public in an effective and convincing manner. Their failure was caused by lack of financial resources and personnel, competition among professionals for status as experts on nutrition, and public apathy about the need to change eating practices. All three of these trends would change in the next decade.

The Great Depression of the 1930s allowed extension home economists to come into their own in New York State as experts in human nutrition and as members of society who had valuable skills to offer. During these years extension home economists at Cornell and in the field were able to use nutrition education successfully and effectively in the extension service program. They did do so largely because of crucial support provided by New York State's newly restructured system of public welfare, the Temporary Emergency Relief Administration (TERA). Cooperation between TERA

---

12. "Annual Narrative Report of Home Demonstration Work in Cattaraugus County, 1931," *Extension Service Annual Narrative and Statistical Reports from State Offices and County Agents, New York State, 1931*, National Archives Microfilm Series T-877, Reel 37.

13. "Annual Narrative Report of Home Demonstration Work, Jefferson County, 1927," *Extension Service Annual Narrative and Statistical Reports from State Offices and County Agents, New York State, 1927*, National Archives Microfilm Series T-877, Reel 25.

administrators and extension service home economists produced institutions that educated the public about nutrition, fostered cooperation between rural and urban populations, and enabled families on relief to contribute important labor toward their own support. Neither the TERA nor the extension service could have achieved these accomplishments alone.

Professional social workers in New York State first began to address the seriousness of the economic depression that followed the 1929 stock market crash in the winter of 1931. By December of that year, an unprecedented sixty-two thousand families in the state were receiving relief of some form. (see Table 7.2).

New York State led the nation in creating innovative social welfare programs that broke sharply with the past and attempted to help the hundreds of thousands of its residents in need of assistance with the basics of survival—food, clothing, and shelter. In November 1931, Governor Franklin D. Roosevelt initiated the first state-level relief administration, the Temporary Emergency Relief Administration. The TERA ushered in a new era of state responsibility for the welfare of its citizens and was an untried experiment in cooperation of city, county, private, and state welfare organizations.

Although the state spent over $234 million over the course of the next seven years, it was never anywhere near enough to meet the urgent needs of a population caught in the throes of the worst crisis the capitalist system has known to date in this country. Relief administrators soon realized that what they could offer was ridiculously inadequate to meet the needs of unemployed people who were literally starving.[14] TERA officials, most of

TABLE 7.2. Number and percent of New York State families on relief

Month/year	Families on relief	Percent of all families
December 1932	247,037	7.8
December 1933	265,279	8.4
December 1934	559,235	17.7
December 1935	361,643	11.4
December 1936	278,439	8.8

Source: New York State Temporary Emergency Relief Administration, *Five Million People, One Billion Dollars: Final Report of the Temporary Emergency Relief Administration, November 1, 1931–June 30, 1937* (New York: Temporary Emergency Relief Administration, 1937), p. 55, *Fifteenth Census of the United States, 1930: Population* (Washington, D.C.: U.S. Government Printing Office, 1933), p. 902.

14. Temporary Emergency Relief Administration, *Five Million People, One Billion Dollars: Final Report of the Temporary Emergency Relief Administration* (Albany: Temporary Emergency Relief Adminstration, 1937). TERA director Harry Hopkins observed in frustration that

whom had social work backgrounds, realized that they needed the help of other professionals to stretch the relief dollar to provide the maximum benefit to human existence, particularly when it came to food.

Home economists in New York State, especially those at the College of Home Economics at Cornell, were uniquely qualified to assist social workers. Women who were employed by the Cooperative Extension Service had been working closely with the rural women of the state who joined the Home Bureau for over fifteen years and were well acquainted with the eating habits of rural and village families. Graduate students at the college had studied nutritional science intensively since 1927 and continued to do so throughout the Depression—no less than 40 percent of the theses for the master of science degree in home economics addressed issues of food and nutrition during the depression years. Faculty at the college had made food a priority as well. The findings of home economists Helen Canon and Faith Williams about the adequacy of the rural diet and the ability of rural women to provide good food for their families had been printed in nationally distributed extension bulletins in 1929 and 1930.[15] Perhaps no other group of professionals was as qualified to assist the social workers of the TERA as was the close-knit group of teachers, researchers, and field workers who made up the staff of the College of Home Economics at Cornell. For these women, the nutritional needs of unemployed workers and their families presented a rare opportunity to implement theories derived from nutritional research of the 1920s and 1930s.

Flora Rose, director of the College of Home Economics, prepared to work with the emergency administration in two ways. First, she could educate the public about the best nutrition for people in adverse circumstances. To do this, she prepared a food budget for families on relief, illustrating what foods were most nutritious and easy to prepare with meager relief food allowances. She also offered the use of a specialist in nutrition, employed by the Cooperative Extension Service, to teach the basics of nutrition adapted to relief allotments to public health nurses and social workers employed by the TERA. In this way the extension service was able to reach people on relief more directly because most relief recipients did not belong to the Home Bureau.

"among the almost innumerable criticisms we have experienced, the one most truthful allegation is never made except by the families who depend upon us. *We have never given adequate relief.*" Harry Hopkins, *Spending to Save: The Complete Story of Relief* (New York: Norton, 1936), p. 99.

15. Helen Canon, *Sizes of Purchasing Centers of New York Farm Families,* Cornell University Agricultural Experiment Station Bulletin 471, May 1928, described in detail the food purchasing habits of farm women in New York State; Faith M. Williams and Julia E. Lockwood, *An Economic Study of Food Consumed by Farm and Village Families in Central New York,* Cornell University Agricultural Experiment Station Bulletin 502, July 1929, measured the nutritional adequacy of the diets of rural people.

Second, Rose offered TERA administrators the services of the Home Bureau to cooperate with TERA programs or any other private or community relief program with which it was working. Throughout the Depression, Home Bureau clubs provided facilities and services for families on relief in an effort to help them improve and maintain a good standard of nutrition.

As the Depression lengthened, many New York State residents joined the ranks of the new poor. At the height of the Depression, nearly one in every five families received public assistance from the state. These people had exhausted every resource before applying for relief in hopes that their situation might improve and they could avoid "going on the dole." Not only was it a blow to a family's pride to be supported by the community, but the relief provided by the TERA was not adequate to support families accustomed to a weekly paycheck.[16]

The group everyone was most concerned about, parents and professionals alike, was the 625,000 children who were members of relief families in New York State in 1933. The question of how to feed these children and avoid permanent damage to their health became a serious issue. The United States Children's Bureau estimated that year that one-fifth of the nation's children "suffered definite injury" to their health because of lack of adequate nutrition.[17]

Flora Rose, drawing on her own training in nutrition under Mary Swartz Rose at Teachers College at Columbia University and on the research of Helen Canon, Faith Williams, and graduate student Janet

16. The TERA and other New Deal government agencies operated from a philosophy that represented a radical departure—that poverty stemmed from economic causes beyond the control of individuals. Although the builders of the welfare state may have held this belief, the vast majority of the public in the United States had been raised to believe in an older set of ideas—that poverty was caused by personal failings, usually alcoholism or laziness. See *The Family and the Depression: A Study of One Hundred Chicago Families* (Chicago: University of Chicago Press, 1938), p. 95.

Here I disagree with Lizabeth Cohen's analysis of the attitude of relief recipients toward accepting public assistance during the Depression (*Making a New Deal: Industrial Workers in Chicago, 1919–1939* [New York: Cambridge University Press, 1990], pp. 270–72). It is important to understand that rural/urban, ethnic, class, and occupational differences informed opinions about the New Deal among different segments of the population. Rural sociologists Carle Zimmerman and Nathan Whetten found that most rural families waited until three full years after the loss of income before applying for aid and then remained on the welfare rolls until the end of the Depression. This suggests that these families had exhausted every resource in an attempt to avoid accepting relief (*Rural Families on Relief* [Washington, D.C.: U.S. Government Printing Office, 1938], pp. 77, 79).

17. State of New York, Temporary Emergency Relief Administration, *Relief Activities of City and County Welfare Districts in Cooperation with the State Temporary Emergency Relief Administration, November 1931 to December 1933* (Albany: Temporary Emergency Relief Administration, 1934), p. 10; and "Diet and the Depression," *New York Times,* July 30, 1933, sec. IV, p. 4.

Bump, prepared an emergency food budget that was adopted by the TERA and later by the Federal Relief Emergency Administration. Careful homemakers who followed the budget could feed a family of five with slightly less than $5 per week.[18]

A typical daily menu in this food budget included whole grain bread, cooked cereal, and milk for breakfast; fruit, potatoes, a small amount of meat, milk, and whole grain bread for lunch; and bean soup, coleslaw, custard, and bread at the evening meal. The menus emphasized the consumption of milk, whole grains, and fruits and vegetables. Rose recommended small portions of meat, consumed only two or three times a week, instead of the daily meat servings most Americans considered mandatory. The food budgets distributed by the College of Home Economics enabled workers to remain healthy while dramatically reducing the amount of money spent on food.

Rose's emergency food budgets were popularized by her friend Eleanor Roosevelt. Rose had met Roosevelt through the New York State League of Women Voters in the early 1920s, and the two had been fast friends ever since. Roosevelt supported Rose's work with rural women in the state by guest lecturing at Farm and Home Week at Cornell each summer, and she shared the view that women's work in the home could make a crucial difference in the health and well-being of the family.[19] Eleanor Roosevelt pledged in 1933 to follow Rose's emergency diet for one week in the White House, and the *New York Times* ran stories each day telling what the president ate for lunch.[20] Roosevelt also printed a sample week's menus from Rose's food budgets in her popular depression-era book *It's Up to the Women*, cautioning, "Children can eat a great deal and still be undernourished and the adult in the family also may eat and not get the maximum amount of good out of their food, so the mother of a family should look upon her housekeeping and the planning of meals as a scientific occupation."[21] The Depression provided a context for housewives to accept human nutrition as an important component of family health.

As Flora Rose's diet became popularized, social welfare agencies sought out Cornell home economists for consultation. During the 1930s, extension nutrition specialist Lorna Barber worked closely with other professionals who saw hungry people on a daily basis. Barber's itinerary for June 1933

18. New York State College of Home Economics at Cornell University, "$5 for a Weeks Food for 5," typescript, March 4, 1933, Box 19, RODCHE.

19. Roosevelt credited Flora Rose in the chapter on the family budget: Eleanor Roosevelt, *It's Up to the Women* (New York: Frederick A. Stokes, 1933), p. 52.

20. See clippings, "7 1/2-Cent Economy Luncheon Served to the Roosevelts," n.d. [1933]; "Roosevelts Are Eating 'Low Cost Menus' to Publicize Plan and Aid Housewives," March 23, 1933; "New Low Cost Diet Ready for General Use," n.d. [1933], Box 19, Folder 17, RODCHE.

21. Roosevelt, *It's Up to the Women*, p. 64.

through September 1934 included lectures in eighty-two cities and towns to train public health nurses, welfare commissioners, TERA superintendents and employees, social workers, and civilians in organizations including PTA, the Grange, Home Bureau, and American Legion. Topics included "Use of TERA Food Budgets," "What the Home Bureau Can Do to Help in Relief Work," "Feeding the Malnourished Child," and "Preservation of Vegetables."[22] Barber always stressed the risk of permanent damage to the health of children who were inadequately fed. In response to those who criticized the scope and magnitude of relief distributed by the TERA, Barber said, "Let's not sacrifice the future of our children for a few millions of dollars. Instead, let's plan a recovery program that includes the children's health, for health is the backbone of the nation."[23] Like many other home economists who worked for the extension service, Lorna Barber was mainly concerned with human welfare.

Despite the best efforts of home economists like Lorna Barber to educate social workers and others about the importance of adequate nutrition, many counties did not provide enough for their relief recipients. Because the TERA was created quickly and was an innovation in poor relief, it was understaffed. Rather than hire professional social workers, county and town welfare commissioners often administered TERA dollars. Frequently these individuals were volunteers or were elected, and in some counties local politics sometimes influenced the decisions of town and county relief administrators. One upstate administrator claimed, "We have enough trouble relieving the Republicans, we can't bother with the Democrats."[24] TERA field representatives reported in 1933 that thirty out of fifty-four counties in New York provided food allowances that were "markedly inadequate" or "adequate on a minimum scale."[25] Local relief administrators could not be trusted to ensure that families on relief got enough income to prevent malnutrition or even starvation.

Distribution of low-cost but nutritious food budgets and consultation with other public officials who served the relief population of the state (such as the work nutritionist Lorna Barber did) are examples of the services extension home economists could provide to individuals. Yet the number of home economists specializing in nutrition was tiny compared to the vast and growing population of people on relief. Other, more collective efforts

22. Cooperative Extension Work in Agriculture and Home Economics, State of New York, *Annual Report: Home Demonstration Work in New York* (Ithaca: New York State College of Home Economics, 1934), pt. II: Appendix.

23. "Tells Value of Milk," press release, Cooperative Extension Work in Agriculture and Home Economics, State of New York, *Annual Report: Home Demonstration Work in New York* (Ithaca: New York State College of Home Economics, 1935), pt. 2: Appendix.

24. "Rural Relief Held Defective Up-State," *New York Times,* June 10, 1933, p. 15.

25. TERA, *Relief Activities of City and County Welfare Districts,* pp. 40, 41.

would be necessary if emergency nutrition education was to reach a suffering population on a larger scale.

Across the state, people realized the need to fill in the gaps left by inadequate relief. Rural women were eager to do what they could to help families increase their food supply. The Home Bureau of New York State provided the ideal vehicle for linking rural women with the needy families in cities and towns. Extension home economists helped Home Bureau members by providing information about food preservation processes and the economy that resulted from processing food at home rather than buying canned goods from the shelves of the grocery store.

Extension home economists tailored their programs to meet the emergency. More than ever they stressed adequate nutrition and helped rural women calculate the number of cans of each vegetable and fruit they would need to supply a year's worth of good nutrition for their family. The need for such education could not be overestimated, as correspondence from rural women reveals. In 1932, a Wayne County farm woman, mother of seven, wrote to thank Cornell home economists for providing the Home Bureau in her area, which had begun several months before.

> I can not resist writing you of the wonderful help I have received from our local Home Bureau. . . . I am very interested in nutrition. I do not understand calories or vitamins just what they are. I understand food changes when taken into the stomach, but what I want to know is this: What foods go together? . . . What is the difference in the stomach if coffee is mixed with milk before drinking or a cup of black coffee and a glass of milk taken separately. Milk I understand is the best food but does it not sometimes change to a harmful food with certain conditions of the stomach?[26]

This woman, genuinely concerned that she might feed her family food that did not "go together," was embarrassed that she could not answer the questions of her married daughters about nutrition. Nutritional information was not part of the common knowledge of the American public in the 1930s. More often than not, people aware of the importance of nutrition were confused by the misinformation fed the public by advocates of fad or quack diets, as this woman was. The extension service home economist became an important source of advice for those struggling to adopt healthy dietary changes in the difficult context of the Depression.

Home Bureau members felt a special obligation to their communities to keep their families off relief. County tax dollars had helped to support the

---

26. Madelene Klaeysen, Cornwell Dairy Farm, Palmyra, New York, to New York State College of Home Economics, January 18, 1932, Box 19, Folder 23, RODCHE.

Home Bureau–extension service educational programs for years. As one Home Bureau member wrote, "We believe that our recent struggle for existence has awakened the consciousness of many members in upholding higher home standards, because they are receiving help at public expense for that purpose."[27] Nutrition education through the extension service did, in fact, help some families avoid relief. One Home Bureau woman reported that after her husband lost his factory job, the family relied on her part-time income alone. She felt that they never could have survived without help had it not been for the inexpensive nutritious meals she learned about in the Home Bureau.[28] This experience was typical for many people, as the USDA noted at a special conference on food needs of the population in 1933: "Many thousands of borderline families, who might otherwise have become relief cases, have been helped through the live-at-home program initiated and promoted by the Cooperative Extension Service to produce the essentials of a balanced diet, and remain self supporting."[29] Flora Rose's emergency food budgets, distributed and popularized through the extension service, were an effective way for people to stay healthy even when their income was reduced significantly.

But strategies of self-reliance were not always sufficient to prevent disaster, and many families did not have the benefit of even the part-time work of one of their members. These families, forced to accept relief, were the ones who concerned relief administrators and home economists alike. Emergency conferences of home demonstration agents with Cornell personnel revealed that relief families spent most of the money disbursed by the TERA "very unwisely." Urban families tried to cook food procured with relief dollars on small two-burner oil stoves to save electricity and did not buy fruits or vegetables that would provide key vitamins and minerals.[30]

Relief income under the TERA allowed such a small margin for food that even though food purchases were the largest category of expense for those

27. "Annual Report of Extension Home Economics Work in Orange County, 1932," *Extension Service Annual Narrative and Statistical Reports from State Offices and County Agents, New York State*, National Archives Microfilm Series T-877, Reel 42.

28. Cooperative Extension Work in Agriculture and Home Economics, State of New York, *Annual Report: Home Demonstration Work in New York* (Ithaca: New York State College of Home Economics, 1933), p. 19.

29. "Safeguarding Family Health by Wise Use of Food in Relief Work: Report of Conference of October 7, 1933, at the U.S. Department of Agriculture, Washington, D.C.," p. 6, Box 19, Folder 28, RODCHE. The phrase "live-at-home relief" refers to a pre–New Deal extension service emphasis on greater self-sufficiency for rural residents.

30. "Summary of Emergency Conferences of Home Demonstration Agents and State Extension Service Leaders at Canandaigua, Watertown, and Syracuse, 1932," p. 1, Box 19, Folder 20, RODCHE. The agents who attended this conference were apparently concerned that a two-burner oil stove did not enable people to bake bread, which they considered an essential part of a survival diet. During the Depression, the extension service in home economics in New York

on relief, many individuals lacked adequate food. The average home relief allotment in upstate New York under the TERA was $28.87 per month. This was a disastrous cut in income for industrial workers, whose monthly earnings before the depression averaged $124.[31] Families usually spent 70 percent of this small relief allotment on food, which meant a weekly food budget of $5.05 for a family of five.[32] The inadequacy of relief money added to the despair of unemployed families, for many recipients were malnourished and too weak to work on the occasional odd job that presented itself. As one nutritionist said, the unemployed in the depression subsisted on a diet "forced below reasonable standards to bare essentials."[33] By 1933, the *New York Times* reported that members of relief families were more likely than members of nonrelief families to get sick and to suffer prolonged illnesses.[34]

TERA officials tried a variety of experiments to ensure that relief clients ate an adequate diet. For a short time they tried distributing food instead of money. The TERA purchased surplus foods from farmers and distributed them through local grocers. Welfare recipients could obtain selected foodstuffs at stores where the grocer cooperated with the TERA. But this system did not always work smoothly, and in one notorious error, the TERA distributed 50 million pounds of raw cabbage throughout the state. Part of the cabbage was supposed to have been distributed as sauerkraut, but relief officials ran out of vinegar.[35] Simply purchasing surplus food from farmers and distributing it to urban populations did not ensure that the food would get eaten. Most foods had to be processed in some way to prevent spoilage.

The most effective way of maintaining the health of those on relief in New York State was the subsistence gardens and canning centers jointly sponsored by the extension service and the TERA. During the Depression years of 1932–35, this strategy was employed in most New York State counties. The average value of TERA-supplied tools, seeds, and expertise to counties that participated in the subsistence garden program was $1,429. In counties like densely populated Nassau County, however, where many urban work-

---

State devoted a significant proportion of its time to bread-making classes. Relief food allotments often contained bags of flour because they were cheaper than baked foods.

31. Stanley Lebergott, *Manpower and Economic Growth: The American Record since 1800* (New York: McGraw-Hill, 1960), p. 527.

32. TERA, *Relief Activities of City and County Welfare Districts*, pp. 30, 31.

33. Henry C. Sherman in James Mickel Williams, *Human Aspects of Unemployment and Relief: With Special Reference to the Effects of the Depression on Children* (Chapel Hill: University of North Carolina Press, 1933), p. 53.

34. "Prolonged Illness Found among Idle: Survey Shows 40% of Sick on Relief Rolls in State Have Been Ailing for Year," *New York Times*, April 16, 1933, sec. 2, p. 1.

35. "226 Carloads of Relief Cabbage Reach Massachusetts by a Washington Error," *New York Times*, December 12, 1934, p. 8.

ers from New York City had recently joined the ranks of the unemployed, the TERA contribution was $3,652—more than twice the average.[36]

The TERA introduced the idea of subsistence gardens for Nassau County workers on relief in 1932. Like other counties with TERA emergency gardens, Nassau County was reimbursed by the TERA for the cost of tools, land, and seed it provided for unemployed workers turned gardeners. The first year of this experiment was very successful; just over thirteen thousand gardens yielded enough food for seventy-five thousand people. In 1933, the TERA sponsored sixty-five thousand gardens, and the number increased to sixty-nine thousand in 1934. Subsistence gardens proved to be the cheapest method of providing food for the huge population of unemployed workers during the Depression.[37]

The volume of food produced in these gardens created a new problem for TERA officials—how to help relief families preserve the food they had grown. Most of the gardeners were urban workers who did not own the equipment necessary to can fruits and vegetables. TERA administrators turned to extension service home economists for assistance in teaching subsistence gardeners how to preserve their harvests. In fact, harried staff members of New York State's TERA were only too glad to accept help from home economists in the extension service and at Cornell. As TERA administrator May Helen Smith wrote to one Cornell home economist: "In all probability, the Home Bureau Agent would be more conscious of the need than would our Field Representative who is obliged at this time to give so much time and thought to the subject of allocations, taxes, bonded indebtedness, etc., than she can give to subsistence gardens and food, important as are the two latter in the program."[38] Extension home economists and TERA administrators needed each other during the difficult years of the Depression; home economists benefited from the financial resources of the TERA, and TERA employees needed the expertise and knowledge of local conditions of the county home demonstration agents in the field.

Together, extension home economists and TERA officials planned public canning kitchens where subsistence gardeners could preserve their food.

36. Figures compiled from Table 2, "Detailed Report of Individual Gardens on Municipal and Home Projects in New York State in 1933," in W. A. Georgia, *Report on Subsistence Gardens in New York State for 1933* (New York: TERA, 1933), pp. 10–14. The total value of 1933 TERA contributions for subsistence gardens in New York State was $51,444. Georgia was the TERA's agricultural adviser to subsistence gardeners.

37. "Relief Gardens Aid 75,000," *New York Times,* November 3, 1932, p. 3. This was three times the yield TERA officials had predicted earlier in the summer. See "Gardens for Idle Flourish in State," *New York Times,* August 2, 1932, p. 14, and "Jobless in State Till 65,000 Gardens," *New York Times,* July 3, 1933, p. 6; "Relief Gardens Yield a $2,800,000 Harvest; Surplus Crop Being Canned by State Jobless," *New York Times,* September 24, 1934, p. 19.

38. May Helen Smith, TERA, to Martha Henning Eddy, Cornell University, n.d. (ca. July 1933), Box 19, Folder 16, RODCHE.

The TERA arranged with local businesses to donate space in idle buildings and equipment. County governments provided the money to purchase tin cans and other small equipment. Extension nutritionists, paid in part by the TERA and in part by the extension service, helped set up the kitchens and trained local workers in the intricacies of the canning process.

Once the kitchen was organized, local families brought in their produce and canned it under the watchful eye of an extension service employee. In some cases, large community gardens had been grown, and this produce was processed by men and women on work relief. Growing and processing their own food created a new sense of pride among dispirited unemployed workers, and the community canning kitchen became a place where men and women performed work that was important to their families and to the community. As Nassau County's home demonstration agent reported, "Men as well as women took a great deal of pride in the finished products. They supplemented the relief food order as well as conserved the surplus."[39]

Community gardens and canning kitchens were excellent ways to assist unemployed families without the shame that usually accompanied accepting relief. The gardening work done by volunteers and those paid by the TERA not only contributed to the support of their own families, but the surplus they produced assisted others in the community. Two thousand Nassau County families used the public canning kitchen in 1934, and in 1935, over $10,000 worth of surplus canned applesauce, beans, swiss chard, and tomatoes was produced by community garden and canning kitchen workers.[40]

The beans, beets, carrots, spinach, tomatoes, plums, pears, applesauce, and peaches that unemployed workers canned for their families in the relief kitchens of the Depression were crucial components of the emergency diets advocated by Flora Rose and other extension service home economists. In many cases women in the families of urban workers had grown so dependent on processed food that they did not know how to prepare fresh produce. One TERA report acknowledged the vital role extension service women played in educating the public about food preparation: "In connection with the gardens of 1933, the demand for teaching how to cook the vegetables for immediate use, with a minimum of fuel, was almost as great as the interest in methods of preservation, for raw vegetables presented new problems that a can opener could not solve in the emergency housekeeping

39. "Annual Report of Home Demonstration Work, Nassau County, 1934," *Extension Service Annual Narrative and Statistical Reports, New York State, 1934,* National Archives Microfilm Series T-877, Reel 49.

40. Ibid.; "Output of Seventeen Relief Kitchens and One Cannery, Nassau County, 1935," *Annual Report of New York State Extension Service in Home Economics* (Ithaca: New York State College of Home Economics, 1935), Appendix, pt. 2, p. 86a.

of the unemployed."[41] The expertise of Cornell home economists, combined with a minimal investment by state and local governments, ensured that a significant proportion of the state's unemployed workers received a balanced diet throughout the year even during the grimmest years of the Depression. The input from extension home economists was important in two ways—they provided both basic nutrition education and technical advice about the actual processing of the food—and was central to the success of community kitchens.

During the Depression years extension service home economists finally gained public recognition for their expertise in human nutrition. In contrast to the World War I years, when home economists were flatly rejected by the rural public, and the 1920s, when public attitudes toward nutrition softened somewhat but remained basically resistant, the social conditions of the 1930s provided an environment in which the knowledge and skills of home economists were valued and necessary. The many special efforts of extension service nutrition specialists and home demonstration agents during the Depression years—teaching basic nutrition to social workers, distributing emergency food budgets to unemployed workers, helping Home Bureau members avoid the relief rolls through careful management of scarce resources, supervising workers in emergency canning kitchens—indicate their willingness to respond to a crisis and adapt their educational program to meet new needs that arose.

This flexibility had many effects. Thousands of children of the unemployed—the population that so concerned experts during the 1930s—enjoyed better diets because of the community canning kitchens. The unequal distribution of relief so prevalent in areas where partisan politics determined the assistance a family could expect was partially equalized when workers learned to produce and process their own food. The limited resources of the Temporary Emergency Relief Administration were expanded so that a significant proportion of the relief population ate an adequate diet. Finally, the public learned that extension service home economists were indeed an important source of information about human nutrition. The Depression years taught extension home economists and state officials that combining their educational and economic resources could prove fruitful and effective.

41. Georgia, *Report on Subsistence Gardens for 1933*, p. 36.

8 "Where Mrs. Homemaker is Never Forgotten": Lucy Maltby and Home Economics at Corning Glass Works, 1929–1965

REGINA LEE BLASZCZYK

"What does Lucy think?"
—Corning Glass Works

In 1929, a home economics professor at Mansfield State Teachers College in Pennsylvania approached executives at nearby Corning Glass Works with her criticisms of Pyrex-brand baking ware, or Ovenware. Lucy M. Maltby contended that the company's kitchen glassware was impractical. Casserole-cover handles were difficult to grasp with potholders or mitts. Baking pans were made in sizes incompatible with many recipes and small, modern ovens. A perspicacious businesswoman with an unassuming bearing, Maltby qualified her assertions with sketches showing improvements that would make Pyrex more enticing to homemakers. Further, she avowed

Research for this article was funded by the Hagley Program in the History of Industrial America at the University of Delaware, the John E. Rovensky Fellowship in U.S. Business and Economic History, the Smithsonian Institution Predoctoral Fellowship Program, and the Rakow Grant of the Corning Museum of Glass. I extend thanks to David A. Hounshell, Anne M. Boylan, Glenn Porter, Lilla Cortright Halchin, Monique Bourque, Marguerite Connolly, Marie LaBerge, Steven Lubar, Robert Post, Nina de Angeli Walls, and William W. Walls for comments on earlier drafts. Special acknowledgments go to Michelle L. Cotton, Jerry E. Wright, Stuart Sammis, and other staff members of the Department of Archives and Records Management at Corning Incorporated, and to Lucy Maltby's family, who supported this research in innumerable ways. For a fuller study of product innovation at Corning Glass Works, see Blaszczyk, "Imagining Consumers: Manufacturers and Markets in Ceramics and Glass, 1865–1965" (Ph.D. dissertation, University of Delaware, 1995). The epigraph is from Earl Lifshey, "Home Economist Has Vital Role in Industry," *Home Furnishings Daily* (September 10, 1965), 28, clipping in Maltby Files, Corning Incorporated, Department of Archives and Records Management, Corning, N.Y. (hereafter CIDARM).

that Corning could enhance its sales of Pyrex Ovenware by systematically studying consumer needs and applying home economics to product development.[1]

Lucy Maltby visited Corning Glass Works, the corporation that dominated her hometown of Corning, New York, at a fortuitous moment. Since the early 1920s, sales of Corning's major consumer product, Pyrex Ovenware, had stagnated.[2] The popularity of Pyrex baking ware peaked shortly after its introduction in 1915. In 1920, Ovenware constituted over 25 percent of Corning's total sales, in 1922, 19 percent, and in 1926, about 13 percent.[3] While Ovenware performed poorly, sales of Corning's other products, including lamp components, railroad signal ware, and laboratory glassware, increased. By 1929, even before the stock market crashed, the future looked bleak for Corning's consumer products.

Concurrently, career opportunities had ripened for professional home economists in business. Expanding membership in the business section formed by the American Home Economics Association in 1924 testified to the burgeoning interest in corporate vocations among home economists. By 1929, the Kraft-Phenix Cheese Company, Ball Brothers Manufacturing Company, Sears, Roebuck and Company, Piggly-Wiggly Stores, and the Aluminum Goods Manufacturing Company were among a growing number of firms that employed graduate home economists in research, product development, sales, and publicity.[4] Since 1918, Corning managers occasionally had considered bringing "the woman's perspective" to their company by creating a domestic science department.[5]

1. Lilla Cortright Halchin, interview by author, October 7, 1992, Mansfield, Pa., tape recording, author's collection; Lilla Cortright Halchin, Mansfield, Pa., to author, December 2, 1993; George S. Maltby (Lucy Maltby's brother), interview by author, October 6, 1992, Corning, N.Y., tape recording, author's collection; and Donna Wirth, "Three Decades Teach Her Consumer Needs," *Milwaukee Journal,* January 14, 1965, p. 16, Maltby Files, CIDARM.

2. J. Walter Thompson Company, Minutes of Account Representatives' Meetings, July 23, 1929, J. Walter Thompson Archives, Special Collections Department, William R. Perkins Library, Duke University, Durham, N.C. (hereafter TA).

3. Corning Glass Works, Sales Turnover Sheets, 1922–1926, Vertical Files, Box G6, Folder: "Manufacturing Committee," CIDARM.

4. "Home Economics in Business: How an Expert Home Economist Helps Industry to Function Effectively," *Home Economist* 5 (December 1927): 208–9, 220, 222–24 (hereafter *HE*); Marjorie M. Heseltine, "Home Economics Women in Business," *HE* 6 (March 1928): 66, 80; Frances Weedman, "Home Economics and the Manufacturer: Home Economics Work with an Electric Appliance Company," *HE* 6 (June 1928): 159, 169–70; "Home Economics and the Manufacturer: The Home Economics Department of the Kraft-Phenix Cheese Company," *HE* 6 (August 1928): 223, 232, 234; Helen Robertson, "Home Economics Women in Business: The Home Cookery Department of the Piggly-Wiggly Stores of St. Louis," *HE* 7 (June 1929): 170–72.

5. Jesse T. Littleton, "Proposed Experimental Kitchen Laboratory," February 4, 1918; W. T. Hedges to Littleton, February 7, 1918; J. Frazier Shaw to William Churchill et al. [Response to "Proposed Experimental Kitchen Laboratory Outline"], February 12, 1918; Littleton, "Domestic Science Laboratory," March 4, 1924, Maltby Files, CIDARM.

Maltby's adroit presentation persuaded Corning's decision makers to transform their decade-old musings into corporate strategy. Convincing the glassworks to add a home economics department to its organizational chart, however, required more on Maltby's part than a few pencil sketches of pie plates. As the daughter of a prominent local family, Maltby certainly had the advantage of being a known quantity to the glassworks' managers. Most important, the credibility of Maltby's larger claims for home economics rested in large part on her superb qualifications, which included one of the best home economics educations of the 1920s and the vision this education had imparted to her.

Maltby approached Corning Glass Works with a B.S. in home economics from Cornell University, an M.S. in home economics from Iowa State College, and seven years' experience as a home economics teacher at the secondary and college levels. As a teenager, Maltby had elected to attend the state-supported School of Home Economics at Cornell University, which was inexpensive and close to her home in Corning. Like many contemporary home economists, Maltby came from an Anglo-American Protestant family that emphasized education for women. Her maternal grandmother had attended seminary and taught school before the Civil War. Her mother, Lucy Swingle Maltby, was a college graduate, a teacher, and an excellent cook who enjoyed homemaking. At Cornell under Martha Van Rensselaer and Flora Rose, Lucy Maltby translated a youthful admiration for her mother's dual commitments to education and homemaking into her own expertise in home economics, a skill that shaped the rest of her life. Her college studies included home management, family life, extension service research, and the sciences.[6]

Maltby's undergraduate training was complemented by a year of graduate work at Iowa State College. She took advantage of the school's national reputation as a leader in equipment studies and concentrated on "the principles of engineering" as applied to the "selection, care, use, [and] design" of housewares. Maltby devoted many classroom projects to glassware analysis, seeking to determine how Pyrex Ovenware could be transformed from a "gift item and a novelty" into a "staple product," from what she later called a "class" product to a "mass" product.[7] At Iowa, Maltby began honing her knowledge of glassware, an expertise that distinguished her from other equipment specialists and made her particularly marketable to Corning Glass Works.

---

6. Winifred Maltby Nixon (Lucy Maltby's sister), interview by author, September 1, 1993, Hammondsport, N.Y., tape recording, author's collection.

7. Delores Ferrante and Charles Ferrante v. City Stores Company, Inc. and Corning Glass Works, Trial Testimony of Lucy M. Maltby, Painted Post, N.Y., December 7, 1979, pp. 1–12, Maltby Files, CIDARM.

Maltby had been schooled in a tradition of home economics that combined conventional notions of femininity with a desire to resolve pressing social problems. Drawing on a fundamentally environmentalist philosophy, early twentieth-century home economists aspired, in Van Rensselaer's words, "to standardize and professionalize the home" to ensure the propagation of "good citizenship."[8] Second-generation home economists like Maltby modified this philosophy to suit the needs of their times. As highly educated women excluded from male middle-class occupations, home economists who embarked on careers in the 1920s continued the tradition established by their teachers, building "feminized" niches within professional culture. They became authorities in their own right, experts on subjects that were explicitly "womanly," that is, on anything and everything remotely connected to the home and hearth: cooking, nutrition, furniture, and appliances.[9]

Increasingly home economists who came of age after the Great War sought employment in American business. Corporate home economists evolved a cohesive group identity based on their common experiences as educators, scientists, and "mediators," or "diplomats in the consumer marketplace." To secure positions, these women espoused a separate-but-equal tactic, convincing male managers that they could make unique contributions to manufacturing firms by bringing the "woman's point-of-view" to product testing and customer service. From the male executive's perspective, home economics was a good investment, an inexpensive way to improve a company's link to the market and to female consumers.[10]

Careers in household equipment firms such as Corning Glass Works could provide home economists with opportunities for creative development not available in teaching, administration, or extension work. In firms that made consumer goods, women might collaborate in product innovation.[11] Household equipment careers, hence, may have appealed to women who had strong faith in the power of material things. In shaping key household tools, equipment specialists could physically imbue culture with their beliefs, interjecting their values into homes through ordinary tangible effects. Through product development activities, these home economists

8. Martha Van Rensselaer, "President's Address," *Journal of Home Economics* 7 (November 1915): 464 (hereafter *JHE*).

9. Margaret Rossiter, *Women Scientists in America: Struggles and Strategies to 1940* (Baltimore: Johns Hopkins University Press, 1982), pp. 51–72, 120–21, 258–59, 313–16.

10. Carolyn Manning Goldstein, "Mediating Consumption: Home Economists and American Consumers, 1900–1940" (Ph.D. dissertation, University of Delaware, 1994), pp. 233–34.

11. Institute of Women's Professional Relations, *Business Opportunities for the Home Economist: New Jobs in Consumer Service*, ed. Annie Louise MacLeod (New York: McGraw-Hill, 1938), pp. 105–28.

could reach their profession's ultimate objective, that is, influencing "the direct effects of environment" on character.[12]

Maltby's vision for a home economics department that would advance product development gave decision makers at Corning a new confidence in the potential of their consumer goods. If the glassworks was serious about housewares, Maltby argued, the firm must be serious about home economics. Maltby pressed Corning executives to allow her to conduct market research, test and develop products, and promote consumer lines.[13] Maltby's entreaty finally convinced Corning's managers that household science could benefit their corporation. In July 1929, she was hired to establish the Home Economics Department under the auspices of James L. Peden, the sales manager in charge of Pyrex products.

Maltby's hiring was not the first time that the "feminine perspective" had been harnessed for the benefit of product innovation at Corning Glass Works. The inspiration for Pyrex-brand Ovenware in part came from Bessie Littleton, whose husband was a Corning physicist. In July 1913, Littleton became aggravated when her Guernsey-brand earthenware casserole fractured after its second use. She implored her spouse, Jesse T. Littleton, to bring home a substitute from the glassworks; he returned the next day with the bottom of a sawed-off battery jar made from Corning's borosilicate glass, a heat-resistant formula created for making stronger railway products, including lantern globes and battery containers. Bessie Littleton baked a sponge cake in the jar, noting the unusual uniformity and easy removal of her dessert. Over the next month, she cooked in various makeshift kitchen containers, all made from Corning's heat-resistant glass. When Littleton discontinued her investigations because of a family illness, Corning researchers contacted nationally renowned domestic science consultants Sarah Tyson Rorer and Mildred Maddocks with queries about the practicality of glass baking ware. Rorer subjected trial utensils to rigorous tests and finally succeeded in making a delicious Baked Alaska. Bessie Littleton's culinary victories, confirmed by Rorer and Maddocks, led her physicist husband and other Corning managers, who had been contemplating a venture into consumer products for several years, to believe that cooking and baking could be made more efficient with heat-resistant glass products.[14] Corning

12. Eva W. White, "The Home and Social Efficiency," *JHE* 6 (April 1913): 125.

13. Wirth, "Three Decades Teach Her Consumer Needs," *Milwaukee Journal*, January 14, 1965, p. 16, Maltby Files, CIDARM.

14. [Jesse T. Littleton], "Report on the History of the First Pyrex Baking Dish," [ca. November 1917]; Catherine D. Mack, "Informal Notes Taken from Dr. Sullivan about the History of Pyrex Baking Ware," n.d.; Eugene Cornelius Sullivan, Corning Glass Works, to Vernon M. Dorsey, Washington, D.C., July 29, 1919; Otto W. Hilbert to Amory Houghton Jr. et al., "Baking

scientists continued to experiment with glass bakeware, receiving patents in 1919.[15]

From its inception Pyrex household glass embodied attributes that home economists considered indispensable to so-called good homes and, in turn, were requisite to progressive visions of social perfection. The new bakeware was not only sturdy; it was nearly unbreakable, eradicating replacement nuisances and costs during the age of what some contemporaries termed the servant problem. Unlike earthenware counterparts that cracked, providing "footholds for dangerous organisms, some of the most virulent type," Pyrex bakeware was noncorrosive and hence toxin-free. Food did not "adhere tenaciously" to its "perfectly smooth" surface, enabling easy cleaning and the nonretention of food odors or flavors. These attributes particularly made Pyrex a white middle-class product that appealed directly to phobias about germs and dirt and, more subtly, to a dislike of strong sensory stimulation associated with heavy or spicy foods, including African American, eastern European, and southern European cookery. Finally, much about Pyrex spoke to efficiency. This glassware was not only virtually indestructible and clean, but unlike earthenware, porcelain, or enameled dishes, Pyrex-brand baking ware, according to Corning scientists, absorbed rather than reflected oven heat waves, resulting in either increased cooking speed or decreased heating requirements. Pyrex Ovenware, thus, had been born in serendipitous circumstances, midwived by the combined efforts of a housewife, domestic science consultants, and Corning's researchers in physics and chemistry.[16]

To sell their wonder glass, Corning executives capitalized on the promises that chemistry, physics, and engineering held for early twentieth-century Americans. Corning's advertisements for Pyrex maximized middle-class women's concerns with scientific housekeeping while overlooking their roles in creating the product. Corning styled Pyrex as a cooking utensil that epitomized the essence of scientific culture. One advertisement announced that "a new material had come into the world" and professed henceforth that with Pyrex Ovenware, "progress" could be made in the home through baking.[17] Pyrex supposedly could eradicate "the drudgery of scouring and scrubbing, the fruitless and endless efforts

---

Ware," January 12, 1968, with typescript, "Notes Written by Dr. Sullivan 11-6-57"; Otto W. Hilbert to Amory Houghton Jr. et al., September 11, 1974, in Historical Memo Notebook 13: "Pyrex," CIDARM; "The Battery Jar That Built a Business: The Story of Pyrex Ovenware and Flameware," *Corning Glass Works Gaffer* 4 (July 1946): 3–18, CIDARM. For a fuller analysis of the development of Pyrex, see Blaszczyk, "Imagining Consumers," chap. 7.

15. U.S. Patent 1,304,622; U.S. Patent 1,304,623.

16. U.S. Patent 1,304,622.

17. "A New Material" advertisement, clipping from *National Geographic* (1916), ARV-7: Consumer Products Division, Folder: "Consumer Price Lists Prior to 1920," CIDARM.

to clean things which seem to resist all cleaning!"[18] When interpreted by journalists, Pyrex assumed a far more masculine image, remote from the kitchens of Bessie Littleton, Sarah Tyson Rorer, and Mildred Maddocks. One *Scientific American* critic paid homage to the glassware's supposed laboratory birth; Pyrex, the magazine boasted, had been "produced solely by the ingenuity of the chemist."[19]

The creation of Pyrex Ovenware and the recreation of the story of its genesis marked the inauguration of Corning Glass Works as a manufacturer of consumer goods. But why did sales of the new wonder glass flounder during the 1920s? To explore and resolve this problem, Corning managers first turned to experts at the J. Walter Thompson Company, one of the nation's leading advertising agencies. After three years of forceful national advertising, Thompson executives concluded in 1929 that Pyrex Ovenware was not selling because the price was too high. A Pyrex pie plate, for example, cost ninety cents whereas a comparable metal pan could be bought for "anywhere from fifteen cents to forty cents." People accustomed to cooking in aluminum, tin, and other metal containers still considered Pyrex an expensive luxury more appropriate as a bridal gift than as a domestic necessity.[20]

In addition to price, account representatives at Thompson acknowledged that consumers perceived two other basic problems with Pyrex Ovenware. Market surveys indicated that women were frustrated when the miracle glass actually broke; women who opened their ovens to discover "glass and potatoes splattered all over" said "thumbs down on Pyrex." Further, people thought that Ovenware designs were monotonous; they were bored with the "the same old thing year after year." Price, style, and durability all mattered to consumers. The solution to declining sales of Pyrex thus lay in lower prices and improved product design.[21]

Stagnant Ovenware sales, combined with the criticisms of advertising consultants, important technical developments, and several other factors, persuaded executives at Corning Glass Works that the company could compete in the housewares field only by adapting radically new tactics. Corning executives, building on suggestions from the Thompson agency, developed a comprehensive approach to consumer products that eventually fused market research, price reductions, technological innovation, and

18. "Bake in Glass" advertisement, clipping from *Good Housekeeping,* October 1915, p. 123, Jerry E. Wright Files, CIDARM.

19. "Glass for Cooking Utensils," *Scientific American* 117 (August 18, 1917): 113.

20. George D. Selden, "Account History: Corning Glass Works," December 14, 1925, and Minutes of Account Representatives' Meetings, July 23, 1929, TA.

21. Minutes of Account Representatives' Meetings, July 23, 1929, TA.

public relations. Lucy Maltby's Home Economics Department was a critical component of this new corporate strategy.[22]

Like other business home economists, Maltby often acknowledged that her department served as an intermediary between manufacturer and consumer. In fact, she described herself as a professional liaison to consumers.[23] As a corporate actor, she directed her department in orchestrating consumption, in helping Corning to "sell more Pyrex dishes." But as a consumer advocate, she sought to improve people's lives by creating utensils and recipes that lessened domestic chores, thereby realizing scientific notions of good housekeeping.[24]

To implement her twofold objective, Maltby gradually organized her department at Corning around three functions: Consumer Service, the Test Kitchen, and Field Service. Although the three divisions were interrelated, their functions became increasingly specialized over several decades. From 1929 to 1931, Maltby's department consisted of a small Consumer Service office centrally located in Corning's executive suites. In 1931, the Test Kitchen was established in the same office building. In 1944, the Home Economics Field Service, staffed by four to nine representatives, was added to the department.

In Corning's expert-oriented environment, Maltby toiled to establish and to maintain the Home Economics Department at a level of respectability and accountability that was unequivocally expected of scientific authorities. To safeguard the activities of her division and ensure the quality of its projects, Maltby hired highly educated home economists for her staff. Most had college degrees. Some, such as June Packard and Helen Martin, brought master's-level training to the Test Kitchen.[25] Lilla Cortright, who had earned a graduate degree at Cornell in 1943, worked in Corning's Test Kitchen off and on for almost two decades while she taught at Mansfield State Teachers College and pursued her doctorate at Pennsylvania State University.[26]

22. For more on the new Pyrex policy, see Blaszczyk, "Imagining Consumers," chaps. 7–9.

23. Lucy M. Maltby, interview, n.d., transcript, Maltby Files, CIDARM.

24. Maltby, interview, n.d.; Maltby, "Duties of the Home Economics Department," November 6, 1947, Maltby Files, CIDARM.

25. June Packard, interview by author, October 8, 1992, Corning, N.Y.; Helen Martin, interview by author, October 8, 1992, Corning, N.Y.

26. Lilla Cortright (later Lilla Cortright Halchin) first worked for the Corning Glass Works Home Economics Department in the summer of 1945 and left to accept a position at Mansfield State Teachers College for the academic year 1945–46. Between June 1946 and the summer of 1949, Cortright was back at Corning, where she supervised Test Kitchen operations; from the fall of 1949 to 1953, she was a doctoral student at Pennsylvania State University; from 1955 to 1964, she worked part-time in the Test Kitchen. Halchin received her Ph.D. in 1965 and devoted the rest of her career to teaching at Mansfield, where she eventually became head of the Home Economics Department (Halchin, interview by author, October 7, 1992, Mansfield, Pa.; Halchin to author, December 2, 1993).

In the thirty-six years of Maltby's directorship, these women and others like them applied training in science, nutrition, and human development to their work on Corning's consumer products.

When Maltby set up her Consumer Service office in the company's main administrative building in 1929, she may have been disconcerted by the amount of mail that poured into the company each week. But she soon turned this quagmire into a corporate asset. From the heap of incoming correspondence, Maltby added to her knowledge about the desires of women who purchased Pyrex baking ware. Hence letters were a vital tool for understanding the market. From the tedious, time-consuming task of responding to complaints, Maltby learned that consumers wanted two things: better instructions on using Pyrex Ovenware and more versatile glassware.[27]

To respond to these needs, Maltby in 1931 established her engineering laboratory: the Test Kitchen. Modeled after those at universities and other corporations, Corning's Test Kitchen reflected and reinforced the ethos of efficiency that characterized contemporary home economics and Maltby's departmental objectives. One corner was dominated by a panel of thermocouples, instruments used to measure oven temperatures accurately. The kitchen was equipped with an array of stoves and refrigerators; some old, some new; gas, electric, wood. During the 1940s, Test Kitchen staff donned antiseptic uniforms and white shoes; this pristine garb, also worn by home economics teachers, betokened the wearer's professional affiliation.[28] The spotless floor and enameled sinks glistened, shouting "cleanliness" and "science" to out-of-town buyers who visited the kitchen before or after negotiating purchases in the nearby sales offices. But the Test Kitchen was more than a showroom for the trappings of home economics; it reflected Maltby's empathy for consumers' diverse needs while testifying to her agenda as a corporate expert.

The Test Kitchen became a center of consumer product innovation at Corning Glass Works. Although Maltby never worked there, she guided the kitchen's mission of assisting new product development and facilitating product improvement. All prototypes of cooking utensils were tested on the kitchen's appliances before going into production. Models of potential lines were compared with competitors' products. When Corning was developing a double boiler, for example, the Test Kitchen was stocked with as many comparable "designs and makes as could be found." Fourteen double boilers—some aluminum, some enameled metal, some glass—were scrutinized by home economists who in turn informed designers about their merits.[29] Necessity thus dictated that Test Kitchen personnel comprehend the

27. Maltby interview, n.d.
28. Halchin to author, December 2, 1993.
29. "'Cooking Up' a Double Boiler," reprint from *Corning Glassmaker* (April–May 1953), Maltby Files, CIDARM.

languages and concepts of design, physics, photography, and engineering to communicate consumers' needs to their male colleagues. The Test Kitchen was, therefore, not simply a place for baking brownies. It was a common ground, a space where Corning professionals, both men and women, met—both literally and figuratively—to negotiate product design and to study product performance.

Although the Test Kitchen staff acted as mediators in product development, they also were self-motivated agents who exercised their scientific expertise and who, like the women Pyrex pioneers in the 1910s, brought practical skills to bear on product innovation. The products of the Test Kitchen—glassware, recipes, and publicity photographs—were born of a corporate culture that valued science, utility, economy, and versatility. Each of these items was infused with the qualities that Maltby and her colleagues at Corning and in the home economics profession believed were essential to modern life. Item after item illustrates Maltby's dual concerns as a corporate actor and consumer advocate.

Among the first consumer lines to benefit from the input of Maltby's Test Kitchen were Pyrex-brand cake dishes. Soon after her arrival, Maltby learned that consumers had many complaints about these baking utensils. Because these pans lacked handles, people accidently stuck their fingers into cake batter when loading ovens. The 9 1/2" diameter made it impossible to set pans side by side in modern eighteen-inch stoves; the volume did not accommodate new recipes for "respectably thick" or "scrumptiously high" two-layer cakes; and, finally, the dish was considered unsightly and hence inappropriate for increasingly popular oven-to-table use.[30] Again and again, Maltby and her staff recommended that the company modify Pyrex shapes to meet consumers' changing expectations.[31]

In the late 1930s and World War II, several factors enhanced the status of the Home Economics Department in the eyes of other experts in the company. Maltby's fruitful work on Pyrex cake dishes was one of her first accomplishments acknowledged by management. She also played a pivotal role in Corning's diversification into commercial dinnerware during the war.[32] Networking among home economists employed as government procurement officers, she secured substantial orders for glass tableware used in civilian and military cafeterias. Concurrently, she advanced her credi-

30. Maltby to F. C. Stebbins, "#221 Round Cake Dish," April 3, 1953; Maltby to T. H. Truslow, "Cake Dish Sales," April 8, 1957; "Duties of the Home Economics Department," November 6, 1947, pp. 16–19, Maltby Files, CIDARM; "Where Mrs. Homemaker Is Never Forgotten: Consumer Products Division's Proving Grounds for Corning Glassware," *Corning Glass Works Gaffer* 4 (October 1946): 5–6; Halchin interview.

31. "The Battery Jar That Built a Business," pp. 6, 18; "Where Mrs. Homemaker Is Never Forgotten," pp. 5–6.

32. Esther K. McMurrary to Maltby, February 7, 1944, Maltby Files, CIDARM.

bility by earning a Ph.D. in home economics education from Syracuse University.[33] These factors, combined with a major corporate reorganization along divisional lines, enabled Maltby to convince her superiors to expand their home economics program. By 1945, Maltby was directing an enlarged Home Economics Department in Corning's new Consumer Products Division.

After World War II, the Test Kitchen continued to contribute to consumer product development. Maltby routinely suggested new or improved products to her superiors.[34] Following her example, Test Kitchen home economists assumed active roles in numerous development and improvement projects. Lilla Cortright, for example, was instrumental in creating a set of stacking refrigerator dishes. In Cortright's account, she worked alone in the kitchen, routinely asking other Corning home economists for opinions and including their recommendations in the specifications she prepared for designers.[35] Once the refrigerator dishes or any product became part of the Pyrex line, Test Kitchen home economists monitored sales figures. When sales slumped, they suggested design modifications that made the product compatible with new dining habits or interior decorating fashions.[36]

Corning's stacking refrigerator dishes more than met Maltby's home economics objectives, her strict standards for "functional qualities so scientifically considered that it will be possible to prove through time-and-motion studies that Pyrex dishes meet the needs of the American homemaker."[37] Like railway signal ware, refrigerator dishes were the results of scientific research, but the Home Economics Department's contributions to product innovation were obscured in the company's published accounts. Maltby's assistants were portrayed as little more than errand girls who "go overtown, get a pound of butter, and make the dish fit."[38] This corporate myth differs from Cortright's account and raises questions about the authenticity of the official tale.

Test Kitchen staff cooperated with corporate experts in design, sales, advertising, and photography to package products effectively. Designed to kindle appetites, Pyrex publicity photographs epitomized the dilemma of business home economists who tried to balance their responsibilities to

33. Lucy Maltby, "Suggested Place and Extent of Nutrition Education in the Public Schools in Grade I through XII" (Ph.D. dissertation, Syracuse University, 1945).

34. Maltby to John Carter, "Your Suggestions Regarding a Five-Year Plan," December 18, 1953; Maltby to T. H. Truslow and R. Lee Waterman, "Consumer Products Line," October 7, 1955; T. H. Truslow, "Consumer Products Division—New Products Program," November 2, 1955, Maltby Files, CIDARM.

35. Halchin interview; Halchin to author, December 2, 1993.

36. June Packard, "Test Kitchen," [April 1955], Maltby Files, CIDARM.

37. Maltby to J. B. Ward, "Pyrex Housewares—Design Requirements," December 29, 1944, Maltby Files, CIDARM.

38. "Something New Has Been Added," Corning Glass Works Gaffer 5 (October 1947): 4.

employers with their commitments to American consumers. Unlike Pyrex itself, a product that actually fulfilled its utilitarian promises once in the home, portraits of pseudo-food and pseudo-meals attempted to stimulate desires for something that was actually unreal.[39] Corning's home economists were, in fact, deft masters of illusion who travailed under hot studio lights to create luscious likenesses of ideal Pyrex meals. Cheese soufflés and mouth-watering apple pies owed their robust shapes to the theatrical ingenuity of Test Kitchen home economists, who stuffed bundles of fluffy paper towels underneath pastry shells or crusts to prevent weary baked goods from sagging under sweltering spotlights.[40] Perfectly cut wedges of pie, miraculously crumb-free plates, transparent and spotless Pyrex dishes were the work of diligent home economists, armed with rags and ammonia, determined to put the best foot of the corporation forward and to sell more Pyrex glassware.

Ephemera—recipe cards, cookbooks, product labels—functioned as home economists' educational channels for teaching consumers the principles of scientific housekeeping. In *Pyrex Prize Recipes*, published in 1953, Corning's home economists emphasized the economy, versatility, and reliability of Pyrex. Through photographs, Maltby's staff suggested multiple uses for various shapes from percolators to teapots to refrigerator dishes. A coffeepot was not simply for brewing coffee but could be used as an asparagus cooker or a soup tureen.[41]

On another level, recipe cards and cookbooks functioned as professional signposts for Corning's home economists.[42] They were channels through which Corning women could demonstrate their knowledge of food science to their colleagues in the company. Recipes not only had to be chemically sound and genuinely appetizing, but they had to fit into Pyrex dishes, including new products designed for the postwar market. Cortright, for example, spent several weeks on ninety-six gingerbread formulas until she calibrated a delectable dessert that fit into Corning's new square cake dish. She drew on her knowledge of food chemistry, standard measurements, and packaged foodstuffs to create recipes that would be successful with unusual combinations of ingredients because of the postwar scarcity of certain food products, including fats and sugars.[43]

39. Margaret Lapp, interview by author, October 7, 1992, Horseheads, N.Y., tape recording, author's collection.

40. Halchin interview.

41. Corning Glass Works, *Pyrex Prize Recipes* (New York: Greystone Press, 1953), p. 13.

42. For a discussion of experts' tools and power relations, see Steven Lubar, "Representation and Power," *Technology and Culture* 36S (April 1995): S54–S81. Conference of the Society of the History of Technology, Madison, Wisc., October 1991.

43. Halchin interview; Halchin to author, December 2, 1993.

Although these home economics activities testified to professional knowledge valuable to Corning Glass Works, they epitomized tasks culturally defined as "women's work." The manipulation of foodstuffs could buttress cultural stereotypes about femininity, just as experimenting with miniature furnaces might bolster notions of masculinity. At Corning, however, both male and female professionals routinely deviated from culturally sanctioned gender roles as they strove to bring the firm's consumer product lines to perfection. Corning's male scientists, had patented more than a material; they had patented a baking dish. Corning salesmen also transgressed established gender roles as they tried to learn about the uses of Pyrex-brand glass dishes. In a specially designed Test Kitchen course, these men slipped on ruffled aprons to master Pyrex cookery. Under the direction of home economists, they conducted experiments in boiling water and baking casseroles that demonstrated the relative heat efficiency of glass and metal utensils.[44] To better understand the versatility and practicality of Pyrex, they served meals and cleaned dishes with their "own little . . . hot hands."[45] The training program was designed by Corning's home economists to familiarize men with feminized household tasks, know-how they subsequently used in the marketplace to sell more glassware. At the same time, the scientific components of the Test Kitchen course served to establish the legitimacy of Corning's Home Economics Department in the eyes of male managers.

Anticipating the tremendous potential of the postwar market, Maltby enlarged the scope of the Home Economics Department by adding a group of field service representatives in 1944. Taking advantage of air travel and the new mass medium, television, these women strove to place Corning's products, made ever cheaper and more diverse through technological innovation, before a wider audience. During the postwar period, Corning glassware finally became a mass-market product. While the mail room was her lifeline to consumers and the Test Kitchen her laboratory, Maltby's voice—her vehicle for transmitting the ideology of efficiency—was her staff of field service representatives.

Maltby herself was a champion networker who repeatedly called on the know-how of distant colleagues during her career at Corning. Educational and professional affiliations provided Maltby with contacts in food and appliance companies, public utilities, food service operations, and women's magazines. In many instances, she simply telephoned her colleagues for advice. In other cases, she spoke with home economists at professional conferences or at trade shows, such as the annual housewares

---

44. Halchin to author, December 2, 1993.
45. "Where Mrs. Homemaker Is Never Forgotten," p. 3.

exhibition in Chicago.[46] Some women supplemented Maltby's knowledge of culinary trends, while others helped her comprehend consumers' buying habits. Maltby's colleagues at the Wheat Flour Institute, Kraft Foods Company, the Poultry and Egg National Board, and General Foods Corporation edited recipes for her only commercial book, *It's Fun to Cook*.[47] Other women cooperated in many of Maltby's product development projects. Dietitians, restaurant managers, editors, and nutritionists all contributed to a study on household and institutional tableware that Maltby wrote for Corning in 1953.[48] Home economists at People's Gas Light and Coke (Chicago), the Admiral Corporation, and Sears, Roebuck and Company confirmed Maltby's impression that range-top cooking was surpassing baking in popularity. Feedback from these women led her to suggest improvements to Corning's faltering Top-of-Stove ware in the 1950s.[49] Maltby also used her professional connections to garner publicity for her corporation. She recognized the value of contacts like Reba Staggs, home economics director for the National Live Stock and Meat Board in Chicago. Maltby provided Staggs with glassware used by the Meat Board's traveling home economists in cooking demonstrations throughout the country. When these courses were over, the Meat Board donated the Pyrex cooking-school utensils to local public utilities and school districts, a move that yielded more exposure for Corning products.[50]

Beginning in 1944, a group of four to nine graduate home economists stationed in remote sales territories helped to shape markets for Pyrex glassware through public appearances and professional networking.[51] In some respects, the jobs of Corning's traveling field representatives followed well-

46. Lucy E. N. Walbridge, interview with author, September 1, 1993, Hammondsport, N.Y., tape recording, author's collection. Walbridge, Lucy Maltby's niece, worked part-time in Corning's Home Economics Department as a student and routinely accompanied her aunt to trade shows, conferences, and department stores.

47. Lucy Maltby, *It's Fun to Cook* (Philadelphia: John C. Winston, 1938). Correspondence with other business home economists includes Clara Gebhard Snyder, Director, Wheat Flour Institute, Chicago, to Maltby, February 20, 1948; Marye Dahnke, Director, Consumer Service Department, Kraft Foods Company, Chicago, to Maltby, February 26, 1948; Kathryn Bele Niles, Home Economics Director, Poultry and Egg National Board, Chicago, to Maltby, February 9, 1948; Ellen-Ann Dunham, Manager, Consumer Service Department, General Foods Corporation, New York, to Maltby, May 20, 1948, Maltby Family Papers, Corning, N.Y.

48. Maltby to Messrs. Peirson and Trumpane, "Progress Report on Tableware," February 15, 1944, Maltby Files, CIDARM.

49. Maltby to John Carter, "Suggestions Regarding Future Planning," December 30, 1953, Maltby Files, CIDARM.

50. Reba Staggs, Director, Department of Home Economics, National Live Stock and Meat Board, Chicago, to Maltby, March 12, 1948, Maltby Family Papers; Maltby to J. H. Bierer, "Work of the CGW Home Economics Department," August 10, 1961, Maltby Files, CIDARM.

51. Ferrante and Ferrante v. City Stores and Corning Glass Works, Testimony of Lucy M. Maltby, Painted Post, N.Y., December 7, 1979, p. 12; Maltby to J. H. Bierer, "Work of the CGW Home Economics Department," August 10, 1961; Maltby, "Duties of the Home Economics De-

established models developed in the interwar period by agricultural extension service workers and by spokeswomen for utilities, food companies, and
other consumer products industries. Like home economists who demonstrated newly developed electric ranges during the early 1920s, Corning's
post–World War II field representatives advised consumers about household
technology on behalf of their corporation. But unlike demonstrators, the
Corning women did not entertain audiences with cooking lessons. Instead,
they functioned as surrogate salespeople and as market researchers.

In Maltby's words, the foremost responsibility of a Corning field representative was to create a "feeling-of-need" for Pyrex products among consumers,
retailers, and other home economists. In this way, the jobs of traveling home
economists in part were designed to complement and supplement the work
of salesmen in the Advertising and Sales Promotion Department of the Consumer Products Division. Although they reported to Maltby, field representatives planned their itineraries based on input from district sales managers
who could pinpoint regions, towns, or stores with poor sales.[52]

The career of Ann Mikell illustrates the roles played by Corning's traveling
home economists in stimulating sales. A home economist from Mississippi
Southern College in Hattiesburg, Mikell worked for six years as a wartime food
management specialist for the United States Department of Agriculture and
for seven years as home economist for the Baltimore-Washington branch of the
Frigidaire division of General Motors before becoming a Corning field representative in 1953. To stimulate a "feeling-of-need" for Pyrex glassware among
consumers in her midwestern and southwestern territory, Ann Mikell logged
in forty-five thousand air miles annually between 1953 and 1959.[53] She held
Pyrex seminars at retail stores and public utility companies, lectured to school
groups, gave appliance companies samples of glassware, appeared on
women's television and radio programs, and distributed publicity photographs to magazine editors.[54] Through Mikell's work, Pyrex glassware appeared on women's TV shows from Topeka, Kansas, to Forth Worth, Texas.[55]

While Mikell and other field representatives strove to stimulate Pyrex
sales, they also functioned "as the eyes and ears" of Corning's Consumer

partment," November 6, 1947; "They Spread the Pyrex Ware Story," reprint from *Corning Glassmaker,* June–July 1953, Maltby Files, CIDARM.

52. Maltby, "Duties of the Home Economics Department."

53. Sarah Enochs, "Tested Recipes from Experts Are a Special Treat," *State Times* (Jackson,
Miss.), September 20, 1956; "If You Like to Travel, Try This Job," *Casper-Morning Star* (Casper,
Wyo.), September 23, 1959, Ann Mikell Files, CIDARM.

54. "They Spread the Pyrex Ware Story."

55. Margaret K. McDonald, Director of Home Economics, "What's Cooking" Show, WBAP-
TV, Fort Worth, Tex., to Mikell, February 9, 1954; Still photograph, "The Margaret McDonald
Show," WBAP-TV, Forth Worth, Tex., March 1956, with Mikell, McDonald, and Corning product on set; Still photograph, "Woman's World" Show, WIBW-TV, Topeka, Kan., June 15, 1955,
with Mikell, Dottie Page, and Corning product on set, in Mikell Files, CIDARM.

Products Division. From their face-to-face contact with retailers, consumers, and other home economists, Maltby's field representatives garnered reactions to old and new products. They also monitored changing consumer preferences for home furnishings, appliances, and food products, reporting the results of their observations to Corning's managers, engineers, salesmen, and designers in Consumer Products.[56]

The public relations and market research activities of Corning's surrogate salespeople reflected Maltby's vision of what home economics could do for Corning in the postwar era. Through their actions and physical appearances, women like Mikell reiterated and embodied the theme that Corning glassware was a sanitary, time-saving product capable of helping to "build a higher standard of living for mankind."[57] Judging from her immaculate image and feminized occupation, Mikell could be interpreted as the personification of the "feminine mystique." In reality, Mikell's impeccable appearance, combined with her college education, technical expertise, shrewd sales techniques, and busy schedule, testified to her professional allegiance to one of the nation's leading science-oriented corporations. Mikell reported that she was "constantly on the go."[58] Corning's traveling home economists had little time for household chores; Mikell rarely prepared her own meals, and she certainly never cooked in public. Her appearance and her actions spoke not to conservative notions of domesticity but to what was new about Corning Glass Works in the postwar period.

At the end of her thirty-six-year career at Corning Glass Works (1929–65), Lucy Maltby had kept the promises she had made to Corning executives in 1929. Her Home Economics Department functioned as the company's liaison to consumers, bringing the firm information about people's needs and desires in household glassware. More important, Maltby and her staff actively participated in evaluating those needs, in creating new lines, and in improving existing products to meet consumer demand. Corning's home economists were responsible for making sure that Mrs. Homemaker was never forgotten.

When she arrived at Corning, Maltby was cautious. Like other business home economists, she applied her education and experience to bettering Pyrex Ovenware shapes and to writing recipes. But by the 1940s, her Test Kitchen staff routinely conducted research on new items, tackling tasks the glass industry traditionally assigned to men. After World War II, Maltby's

56. Mary Lou Welschmeyer to Mary N. Alexander, March 19, 1964; Welschmeyer to G. L. Williams, October 6, 1964, ARV-7: Records of the Consumer Products Division, Box 17, Folder: "CERCOR Broiler Grill Files," CIDARM.

57. "Foods Go from Freezer Directly into the Oven," *Wichita Beacon* (Wichita, Kan.), January 31, 1954, Mikell Files, CIDARM.

58. "Visiting Home Economist Logs 75,000 Miles Yearly," *Arizona Republic* (Phoenix), March 9, 1963, in Mikell Files, CIDARM.

field representatives acted as salespeople, hazarding into another male realm. At the same time, Corning men often ventured into women's sphere to work in or with the Test Kitchen.

Corning's corporate culture permitted its experts to transgress gender boundaries so that the firm could better serve its markets. A mixture of culturally defined male and female skills was required to create and perfect glassware that was both highly scientific and highly domestic. These excursions were temporary and therefore not fundamentally threatening to Corning's corporate culture. For Corning salesmen, wearing aprons to whip up cake mixes with electric beaters seemed like fun. For Maltby, a career at Corning Glass Works provided the opportunity to realize the idealistic, pragmatic goals of professional home economics while living in her hometown. What Maltby gained in her personal life, she lost in her company salary. In comparison to male department heads, Maltby, like the members of her staff, was poorly paid.[59]

As Corning's home economists negotiated the corporate order, venturing into fields such as engineering, design, and sales, they encountered both resistance and cooperation from adjunct departments. The mixed reactions of men in the design department are cases in point. Some industrial designers marginalized the women's work. Paul V. Gardner claimed that Maltby simply operated the Test Kitchen and commented on the utility of his designs.[60] Others acknowledged Maltby as an unavoidable link in a chain but tried to short-circuit her work, repeatedly asking for information without reciprocating when the Test Kitchen requested data from the design department.[61] Still others acknowledged the centrality of Maltby and her team of home economists. Jerry E. Wright maintained that they "brought authenticity to the design process."[62]

Lucy Maltby spent her life in a feminine occupation, concurrently promoting the interests of consumers and her firm. At Corning Maltby wore the hat of an engineer, transgressing gender boundaries to work side by side with male employees—engineers, physicists, chemists, designers, salesmen, managers—who solicited her expertise on traditionally masculine subjects. Seeking Maltby's opinion on color, shape, size, material, and form became ritualistic among Corning's designers. The query "What does Lucy

59. Nixon interview. According to Nixon, Maltby's annual salary at her retirement in 1965 was $15,000–$16,000, and this figure was low in comparison to the salaries of male department heads at the company. Unfortunately, no payroll records survive in CIDARM.

60. Paul V. Gardner, Washington, D.C., telephone conversation with author, October 29, 1992.

61. Maltby to F. C. Stebbins, "Comments on Sketches of Proposed Flameware Designs," December 17, 1951; Maltby to Joseph S. Knapp, "Casserole Set, Drawings K-5321-C2, K-5322-C2, Proposed Nesting Casseroles—1, 1/2, 2 Quart Sizes," September 14, 1953, Maltby Files, CIDARM.

62. Jerry E. Wright, interview with author, October 5, 1992, Corning, N.Y., tape recording, author's collection.

think?" uttered by harried merchandising staff came to symbolize her influence in consumer product development. Maltby's legacy, like that of Lilla Cortright and Ann Mikell, is the sum of the many small changes she wrought on Corning's consumer products in more than three decades. Maltby recognized that success "depends to a considerable extent . . . on attention to small details."[63] Fittingly, more than a decade after her retirement, Lucy Maltby was a legend at Corning Glass Works, a woman credited with introducing "the consumer to Corning and Corning to the consumer."[64]

63. Maltby to T. H. Truslow and R. Lee Waterman, October 7, 1955, "Consumer Products Line," p. 1, Maltby Files, CIDARM.

64. On Maltby's role in bringing the consumer to Corning, see Thomas C. O'Brien, Assistant Counsel, Legal Department, Corning Glass Works, Corning, N.Y., to Lucy M. Maltby, Corning, N.Y., April 9, 1980, Maltby Family Papers, Corning, N.Y. CEO James R. Houghton acknowledged Maltby's contributions to Corning and consumers at her death in 1984. He wrote: "She helped to break new ground in the field of corporate responsibility to the consumer. The reputation that Corning products enjoy today in the consumer housewares market is due in no small part to Lucy Maltby's unswerving adherence to integrity." See Corning Glass Works, "Headlines in a Hurry," December 11, 1984, Maltby Files, CIDARM.

REMINISCENCES | *Hazel Reed*

HAZEL REED graduated from Cornell University's College of Home Economics in 1930 and worked as an extension agent in New York State before returning to Cornell in extension administration in 1949. She recalls her sense of accomplishment in helping families get along during the Depression and World War II.

I'm a New York State product. I was born, educated, have worked all my career, and have spent all my retirement years in New York State. Why did I choose home economics? I don't really know. I went to a very small school in which high school and grade school were all in one building. We had only the essential subjects. We didn't have homemaking in high school. We didn't have art or music or a guidance counselor. So I didn't know what college might hold for me. The year I graduated from high school there were ten of us in the senior class, and that was a big class. Usually, one person might go to college. Two or three would go to normal school, which was a two-year school at that time. Some would take nursing, and others would take whatever local jobs were available. Only a few went on for advanced education. There was no great competition to excel. Our only guidance and encouragement came from the teachers, principal, and our parents.

My senior year a young married couple moved to Savannah, my hometown. They were both graduates of Cornell. The wife was a home economics major, and when she learned I was interested in going to college, she immediately said, "Why don't you take home economics? I'll take you down to Cornell, show you the campus, and introduce you to Miss Flora Rose." She did, and that was my introduction and it sold me. I decided on home economics as a career.

I had had such limited opportunity in high school that I was overwhelmed my first year at Cornell with chemistry and lectures and laboratories and all the subjects I had to take. But I survived and did quite well. I took home economics and liked every phase of it. I couldn't decide what to specialize in. I thought probably I would teach when I finished so I took the general course, the required education courses for teaching, and all my electives in home economics.

When I graduated from Cornell in 1930, jobs were scarce. It was only a year after the stock market crash. Some of my classmates had not been able to come back for senior year. Those of us who did weren't sure we were going to get jobs. I was one of the lucky ones and had two offers. I selected the position as homemaking teacher in Oswego, New York, which was a very good job for that time. It was a fairly new school with a very well-equipped homemaking department and a cafeteria that the two homemaking teachers were expected to operate. I accepted that job at $1,500 a year. When I arrived on the job in September, I learned that because of the economic conditions all of the teachers in the Oswego schools were being asked to give back 5 percent of their salary. This was the Depression! But I had a job and that was wonderful.

In 1937, after seven years, I decided to go into Cooperative Extension. My first job there paid $1,800, which was no more than I had been receiving as a teacher because extension was an eleven-month job with one month vacation, compared with high school teaching, which gave me more time off. In both jobs, I sensed early on the need to understand the people I was going to teach. Homemaking teachers at that time were required to make home visits. That experience was a real eye-opener to me because the little village in which I grew up had a very homogeneous population of rural, farm people. I was not acquainted with a city population with ethnic groups and factories that had been very hard hit by the crash. I quickly learned why the youngsters didn't have money to buy good materials to make a dress or why they didn't have money to do some of their home projects such as extra cooking or refinishing furniture or making pillows to fix up their bedrooms. Their parents were afraid they wouldn't do it well and that the money would be wasted and there was no money to waste. It has always been part of the extension philosophy to start where people are and teach them skills to improve their situation. So getting acquainted with people—understanding their living situations and trying to adapt a program that would help them—was a major consideration and challenge to me.

I worked in extension for more than thirty years, twelve of them at the county level working with homemakers in three different counties, two of them rural and the last one in Syracuse working with city people. And I worked eighteen years at Cornell in extension administration. I think the most satisfying years of my career were the twelve years that I worked directly with people. I liked to be close to the people who were benefiting from home economics. You could see their struggles and sometimes their successes. In 1937 we were coming out of the Depression, but people had a big backlog of needs. They hadn't had money for seven or eight years. They had made over and made do and used up everything. It was very interesting to see, as they began to get a little bit of discretionary money, how they would use it and to help them use it well. Some did a good job applying the skills and knowledge they had acquired. Extension apparently meant a great deal to them. One homemaker invited me in to see her living room. Everything in it, from the hooked rug on the floor to the lamp shades and draperies, she had made herself as a result of extension teaching. Everything went well together and it was colorful and homelike. She was so proud of it! The family appreciated it, too, and you knew that what you had taught was used not only by the homemaker herself but enjoyed by the whole family.

The Depression obviously had a great effect on the content of the extension program. The emphasis was largely on skills because women had time but little money. They enjoyed getting together and making things for themselves and for their homes. They had time to do things, and if you taught them how, they could go to the attic and find something to make over and make do. It was amazing what came out of those attics.

As we moved out of the Depression and into World War II, it was mostly more of the same. During the war, we as extension agents did all the things that home economists did everywhere. We served on nutrition committees and defense committees designed to help evacuation centers, and we did research on our teaching program.

As more women went to work outside the home, this affected the times and places of our meetings. Many were held at night and in public meeting places. We were concerned about the children and how they would manage without an adult at home during the day—concerned, too, that extension meetings would take mothers away from home and children even more. We began to use other ways to get information to homemakers such as newsletters and radio programs.

As homemakers had more money to spend, extension programs became more consumer oriented. Projects had less emphasis on "how to" and more about how to buy, what qualities to look for. Was it better to make or buy or make over, considering the time factor? We also taught more about saving time, nutrition, and care of family and children.

Participation in extension grew rapidly throughout the state during and following World War II. To meet the demands, many local leaders were recruited and trained to do the teaching. That proved to be a very worthwhile effort. Local leaders had more time available than staff did for teaching and were more attuned to local needs. As they gained experience, they became more self-confident and more aware of community needs. They soon found themselves concerned with the problems related to families. They often became advocates for better school lunches, child care centers, recreation programs, and other areas requiring community action.

In 1949 I came to Cornell as a member of the extension administrative staff responsible with others for the home economics extension program throughout the state. From 1949 to 1967, when I retired, extension programs continued to change as the economic, social, and cultural conditions changed, but the fundamental purpose of extending research-based knowledge in home economics as it related to families and to the people of the state has never changed. This has always involved working very closely with college departments in program development.

As new technology became available, methods of extending programs changed. I remember well the first efforts of the Textile and Clothing Department to teach how to make a dress on radio and later on TV—the accompanying printed directions and drawings—and the organization necessary in counties to receive the program.

Over the years, first as a high school teacher, then as an extension agent in counties, and later as an extension administrator at Cornell, I have seen many changes in program emphasis and methods of delivery as we tried to meet the needs of individuals and families in an ever-changing world. Home economics has stood the test of time. The years 1930 to 1967 were challenging ones for home economists.

A home demonstration agent from the Alabama Department of Agriculture lectures to a group of African American women about sanitary procedures. *Helping Negroes to Become Better Farmers and Homemakers*, 1921.

Home Economics, Race, Class, and Ethnicity

Pioneer home economists were white, middle class, and among the educated elite. The majority of women in the home economics movement held college degrees at a time when only 3 percent of women graduated from college. Not surprisingly, they often replicated the values and prejudices of their class. They shared with other reformers of the era an ethnocentrism that uncritically promoted the superiority of ideas and ideals of white, middle-class culture. Yet their cultural conservatism needs to be understood in the context of a society in which their ideas were rightly labeled "progressive." Social Darwinism, the reigning orthodoxy, condemned any efforts to improve the lot of the poor, justifying laissez-faire by evoking natural selection and "survival of the fittest." Progressive reformers, including early home economists, argued for the importance of environment over heredity and encouraged social activism to ameliorate the worst consequences of urban industrialism. The substandard living conditions of new immigrants in cities like New York and Boston stimulated them to take action.

Some historians dealing with home economics have adopted a social control model which emphasizes the attempt by the middle class to impose its values and practices on the immigrant poor in the name of Americanization and reform. One problem with the social control model, however, is that it demonizes reformers for attitudes pervasive in the culture. At the same time, it ignores the agency of the oppressed and tends to privilege class over gender. As Carmen Harris's chapter eloquently shows, African American home demonstration agents in South Carolina managed to subvert the social control strategies of whites and worked to empower their people. The reminiscences of Genevieve J. Wheeler Thomas, an African American home economics educator, underscore Harris's point.

Without subscribing to the social control model, Joan Brumberg points to the normative and prescriptive standards home economists used in defining the good life in a photo essay drawn from educational films from the 1920s to the 1950s. The negative racial and gender stereotypes she discovers, though by no means limited to home economists, nevertheless underscore the dangers of unreflective enculturation.

9 Defining the Profession and the Good Life: Home Economics on Film

JOAN JACOBS BRUMBERG

Film is an important vehicle for interpreting life in the twentieth century, but it is also a powerful didactic tool, which the home economics profession understood before most professional groups. By the second decade of the twentieth century, home economists were using moving images and simple narrative stories to convince Americans of the transformative power and value of their work, particularly in rural areas.[1] Home economists used film not only to teach specific skills such as how to make a hat or a rug or rewire a lamp but also to advance their larger professional role and their claims to expertise in a society where other feminized service professions such as teaching, nursing, and social work already had established claims.[2]

I am indebted to the New York State College of Human Ecology at Cornell University for the funds that supported this film research and to James Novack for his technical support in making it possible to show them.

1. Home economists were leaders in the use of film because of their close association with the Department of Agriculture, which began to use photography and film very early for instructing people in scientific agriculture. I drew this information from a conversation with Mary Sommers, a Yale Ph.D. candidate, whose work on the history of the Department of Agriculture brought her to Cornell to use the collections of the New York State College of Home Economics.

2. My idea of "feminized service professions" as the basis of the modern social order is drawn from Joan Jacobs Brumberg and Nancy Tomes, "Women in the Professions: A Research Agenda for American Historians," *Reviews in American History* 10 (1982): 275–96. Teachers, nurses, and social workers did not generally employ film the same way home economists did, perhaps because their role was not as ambiguous and people were more familiar with what a nurse, teacher, or social worker did. Progressive era medicine, however, used film to spread information about health issues that were related to the concerns of home economists; see Martin Pernick, "Thomas Edison's Tuberculosis Films: Mass Media and Health Propaganda," *Hastings Center Report* 8 (June 1978): 21–27.

In my search for the cinematic record of home economics, I ultimately made only a small dent in the vast number of films about the field that exist in public and private archives. Yet even the small number of films that I surveyed reveal a great deal about the emergence of home economics and its subsequent institutionalization both as a field of study and as a profession for women.[3] All of the films I discuss were designed to instruct the audience about the basic value of home economics as a field of endeavor. And each used the particular persuasive techniques of its time to sell the importance of the field and its impact on human lives.

The earliest films—*The Happier Way* (1920) and *Helping Negroes to Become Better Farmers and Homemakers* (1921)—underscore the relationship of home economics to agricultural reform.[4] Both are silent films produced by the United States Department of Agriculture, in Minnesota and Alabama respectively. Both rely on a narrative of improvement and amelioration told in short story fragments that accompany carefully staged dramatic episodes. In both films, the home demonstration agent is an agent of middle-class transformation and the ultimate "deliverer" of troubled and deprived families. The first film centers on the plight of farm women; the second on the situation of rural African Americans.

The Minnesota film introduces the town of "Pleasantview," a generic farm community where everyone works hard. Yet the men who are keen on labor-saving machinery such as tractors remain inattentive to the needs of their overworked wives and daughters. In this way, the film acknowledges that there are gender conflicts on the family farm and that women's work was often forgotten in the rush to embrace new technologies. This admission was not surprising at a time when many rural daughters were leaving family farms precisely because the work was so hard and the boredom unbearable. In New York State, both the Country Life Movement associated with Liberty Hyde Bailey and Martha Van Rensselaer's call to "save steps" were responses to this problem of youthful rural exodus.[5]

3. I have not included here a vast number of educational films that were geared to making a product. There are films about home economics in the National Archives in Washington as well as the Archive of Factual Film at Iowa State University. I suspect that private archives of certain food industries such as General Mills and General Foods also have relevant films as do the archives of state Cooperative Extension services.

4. Both of these films are in the collection of the National Archives in Washington.

5. See Liberty Hyde Bailey, *The Country Life Movement in the United States* (New York: Macmillan, 1911); William Bowers, *The Country Life Movement in America, 1900–1920* (Port Washington: Kennekat Press 1974); on Martha Van Rensselaer and the Farmers' Wives Reading Course, see New York State College of Home Economics Records 23/2/749, Division of Rare and Manuscripts Collection, Cornell University Library, as well as Flora Rose et al., *A Growing College: Home Economics at Cornell University* (Ithaca: New York State College of Human Ecology, Cornell University, 1969).

The unending toil of farm women provides the justification for the intervention of the home demonstration agent, who is portrayed as the bearer of a new gospel of scientific redemption that will transform their domestic lives. To make this point persuasively, the film uses many of the familiar dramatic conventions of the early twentieth century. For example, "Louisa," a dutiful farm wife and mother, gives out from overwork and is near death. This threat to her life raises the prospect of the worst of all scenarios: a home without a mother. Ultimately, the farm wife (and family) are saved when the home demonstration agent arrives with labor-saving devices for the kitchen. In this way, the home demonstration agent leads the American farm family into the modern age.

Along with its message about the transformative power of home economics, *Helping Negroes to Become Better Farmers and Home Makers* exemplifies the deep racism that characterized American life in the 1920s. (The film was made under the auspices of the Department of Agriculture by filmmakers in Alabama.) By saying that this film is a racist document, I do not mean to suggest that home economists were any worse or better than the larger society. This was an era of intense racial hostility in the South, and many Americans, North and South, believed in the inferiority of "colored people." The film provides a white conception of African American home and community life and is replete with the very worst conventions and stereotypes about black people. On at least three occasions, the narrative is interrupted to present images of African Americans eating watermelons or breaking "spontaneously" into jig dancing.

Without apology, the film provides us with a view of the social structure of the Jim Crow South: white landlords, black sharecroppers, and segregation in public schools and within the extension field, as Carmen Harris has shown.[6] The story focuses on the family of Rube Collins, an African American farmer, who does not own his own land and who needs approval from the white boss to try new innovations. (The nickname Rube—for Reuben— may be an intentional play on the idea that a "rube" is someone who is uninformed and unsophisticated.) But Rube Collins's life—and the life of his entire community—is transformed in the film by the work of a male African American demonstration agent trained at Booker T. Washington's Tuskeegee Institute, the school that was widely regarded as the showpiece of black educational efforts in this era.

Although the Alabama film never questions the ideology of race and power in the South, it does put an emphasis on instruction of blacks by blacks. We see African American men become professionals (this change in

6. Carmen Harris, "Grace under Pressure: The Black Home Extension Service in South Carolina, 1919–1966," in this volume.

status is indicated by new clothes as well as a solemn demeanor), and we are also shown black women who are active and useful home demonstration agents. The division of labor is always conventional, however: black women equipped with information about nutrition, food preparation, and health care talk to groups of black mothers and children; male agents talk to men about land use, crops, and machinery. Throughout, African Americans are shown using new technologies to improve their health and homes as well as farms and schools.

Home economists of both races disseminated scientific information about cleanliness and germs much in the way that Nancy Tomes has described it in an earlier essay.[7] In publications and in this film, the early twentieth-century home economist made washing and dusting major preoccupations in the "curriculum." When racist ideology was combined with "germ theory," special emphasis was placed on changing the personal hygiene practices and decorum of African Americans, who were assumed to be deficient in this domain. We first see the Collins household in disarray and dirt. After the arrival of extension agents, Rube's family life improves because of fly paper, shoe shining, and table setting—all signs of respectability in the view of the middle-class, white filmmakers.

The home demonstration agent still figures prominently over two decades later in *Teen Togs*, a film with sound produced by the Georgia Agricultural Extension Service. In this 1943 film, the agent helps adolescent girls cope with normal social anxieties and wartime scarcity. But the agent is never seen, and her voice and ideas serve as a kind of "angel adviser." The fact that the entire narrative was written in verse makes it hard to take this film seriously but, at the time, poetry was assumed to be an engaging technique that would capture the attention of an adolescent audience.

Teen Togs incorporates mid-century notions of normative adolescent development, particularly the idea that teenage girls are always concerned about their appearance.[8] The film articulates the concept of a wardrobe and the idea that girls must plan ahead to achieve an appropriate one. The narrative story is simple: a farm girl of seventeen or eighteen is invited by her older sister for a weekend at the state university. This invitation is exciting, but it also causes some concern. What clothes should she take on her first foray into the collegiate world? She turns to the home demonstration agent to relieve her anxiety and to help plan and create a suitable wardrobe.

The messages in *Teen Togs* are obvious: there are right and wrong clothes; the right clothes contribute to a girl's social success; a smart wardrobe is

7. Nancy J. Tomes, "Spreading the Germ Theory: Sanitary Science and Home Economics, 1880–1930," in this volume.

8. See advice books such as Betty Betz, *Your Manners Are Showing: A Handbook of Teenage Know-How* (New York: Grassit and Dunlap 1946) and, of course, *Seventeen*. This film is in the Archives of Factual Film at Iowa State University.

within any girl's reach if she approaches the problem in a rational manner. Although the film is laden with middle-class assumptions about what is appropriate and tasteful, the filmmakers try to sell the idea that clothing is an essentially democratic vehicle for social mobility among girls. Any girl who can sew for herself can go to college without embarrassment, the film suggests. Films such as *Teen Togs* raise important questions about the role of home economists in paving women's path into the consumer society: What role did home economics education play in the critical transition to store-bought clothes? Did they try to stave it off? Did home economists ever question the values implicit in their articulation of standards of taste? Did they understand how so much attention to "good grooming" in girls linked their self-esteem to appearance and consumer purchases?

The larger value of home economics education was another selling point in the evolution of films about the field. *A College of Home Economics,* produced by the Department of State in 1947–48 for use by the United States Information Agency, was part of the "Voice of America" program. This film, which was expensive and technically sophisticated for its day, was essentially a propaganda piece and part of the Cold War arsenal used to sell the American way of life. The film was narrated by Ralph Bellamy and eventually translated into twenty-six different languages and shown in fifty two different countries. The suggestion was that the New York State College of Home Economics at Cornell University was a model that could be followed abroad.[9]

The State Department's conception of the film and its ideas about how to portray the College of Home Economics caused some difficulty at Cornell, where it was filmed. In Ithaca, Dean Elizabeth Vincent set up a committee of selected faculty representatives from each department within the college to work with Hamilton MacFadden, chief of motion pictures at the Department of State in Washington. The correspondence reveals that there was some tension over what would be shown. Dean Vincent clearly wanted the film to locate Cornell's College of Home Economics within the larger university so that it would not appear to be simply another vocational school for women. Like many home economists of her day, she wanted to position

9. Cornell was probably chosen over other colleges of home economics for a combination of reasons: it was the only Ivy League university in America with such a college; it provided scenic locations; the school was very well-known and respected; and Eleanor Roosevelt had a long association with it. See Box 25, Folders 3–35, New York State College of Home Economics Records, Division of Rare and Manuscript Collections, Cornell University Library. I am indebted to my undergraduate students for uncovering correspondence about this film in a related research project for a course that I teach on the history of women in the professions. Eventually, I was able to locate it at the National Archives. Cornell had no copies because it was not intended for domestic audiences. Thus it "premiered" in Ithaca at the 1991 conference "More Than Glorified Housekeeping: Rethinking Home Economics in the Twentieth Century."

her field within the larger arena of higher education and professional life in the United States.

Because the State Department's goal was to offset Communist claims about the United States, the film offered a running commentary on the meaning of democracy, which was defined in a number of different and all-inclusive ways, including "the opportunity to function in a group." Mac-Fadden was well aware of the charge that the United States was a racist society so he deliberately wanted to plant minority and foreign students to give the College of Home Economics, and the American university, a more international look. Dean Vincent objected to this strategy because she did not want to present an unrealistic portrait of the racial composition of the college. She wrote MacFadden: "There should not be a preponderance of Hindu, Chinese and Negro students since they represent a very small part of our student group. We agree that they should be present, however." Vincent was sensitive enough to racial issues to veto a dormitory scene that showed Chinese women students washing the hair of another student because it suggested servitude. "Such service should be done by an American girl in the movie," she wrote.

Elizabeth Vincent was obviously more concerned about the professional image of home economics as a field than she was about giving a multicultural face to the student body. Most of all, she wanted the film to emphasize the multiple hats of the home economist, and she gave only secondary attention to MacFadden's primary goal: to use home economics at Cornell to sell the American way of life. In the end, she won. Although the film does explain that most home economics graduates go on to be wives and mothers, in the opening sequence, done in dramatic "Pathe newsreel" style, the audience is taken to New York City to Rockefeller Center to meet a home economist who is an associate editor at the *Ladies Home Journal*. That woman then travels to her alma mater in Ithaca to meet with other home economists: one is a director of education for a radio network and another is the director of the Test Kitchen for Corning Glass.

What was the ultimate message of this widely seen and influential film? After the opening sequence that shows home economists in their work, the daily lives of five "coeds" who are studying home economics are described. The film provided an interesting but elaborately staged visual record of female student life in an era when most of the undergraduate women at Cornell were still located in the New York State College of Home Economics. In the film, home economics education at Cornell University is used to symbolize the best of American life: advanced education for women, religious freedom, democratic decision making, progressive science, intelligent consumerism, and even companionate marriages. Women educated in the United States in home economics were enlightened, treated well, and trained for their traditional roles as wives and mothers as well as new careers related to improving their families and communities. In a final scene, the most attractive of the focal coeds is seen standing in profile on one of the university's characteristic suspension bridges. As the wind dramatically blows her hair, she looks optimistically to the future while the familiar strains of the Cornell alma mater play in the background.

Why Study Home Economics? (1955) was a persuasive film aimed at American high school girls rather than women abroad. Made by Young America Films (Centron), the film was part of a series on careers for adolescents.[10] It begins with two wholesome adolescents planning their high school program; one suggests that home economics may be a silly thing to study. "What can I learn in home economics that I cannot learn at home?" she asks, essentially reframing the old question about the value of systematic study of things alleged to be "natural" among women. In the conservative 1950s, when marriage, domesticity, and motherhood appeared to have such wide appeal, it is interesting that home economists admitted that this debate existed within the culture of teenage girls.[11]

Why Study Home Economics? goes on to provide a reenactment of a counseling session in which a school guidance counselor discusses the personal and occupational potential of home economics education with the girl, who is less skeptical and more curious. At the close of the film, the advisee has been convinced by the counselor's words, and she confidently tells the audience that home economics *is* worth studying because it will help her whether or not she becomes a wife and mother. The film suggests that the profession felt the need to promote its image among a generation of post–World War II teens who were beginning to question single-sex educational environments such as the home economics classroom or college. In the simple dialogue between two girls, the story foreshadowed the waning appeal of a field that had once attracted large numbers because it was the best way to justify collegiate education for women.

The films discussed here are relics of a different era when home economists were so optimistic about science and confident of their ability to improve the quality of life that they sought to sell themselves and their work to the American people. All indications are that they used film more consistently and aggressively than teachers, social workers, or even nurses. Film was part of the instructional arsenal and also a way to show the world what a home economist looked like and what she did.

---

10. This film is in the collection of the Archive of Factual Film, Iowa State University.

11. On the 1950s, see Elaine Tyler May, *Homeward Bound: American Families in the Cold War Era* (New York: Basic Books, 1988), and chapter 9 in Stephen Mintz and Susan Kellogg, *A Social History of American Family Life* (New York: Free Press, 1989).

By the 1960s and 1970s, home economics education was very much in question because a wide variety of social and cultural forces were transforming the family and work roles of American women. Because its single-sex nature seemed anachronistic (or even illegal), many schools dropped the home economics requirement or the entire program. Educators in the field were sometimes forced to defend themselves against charges that they were reactionaries and unsympathetic to modern feminism.[12]

Unfortunately, I am not able to conclude this brief film history with a good example of a home economics film that emerged out of this recent, painful stage of the profession's history. Are there films that make a deliberate pitch to recruit males into home economics classes? Or films that posit the relevance of a revitalized home economics curriculum to the world of contemporary families and social problems? My suspicion is that home economists have developed somewhat different strategies in the past two decades because of their heightened self-consciousness about their traditional image as well as changes in the expectations of audiences. In the 1990s, didactic films must appear to be anything but instructional or purposeful. Yet we should not discount the possibility that contemporary home economists could use the new televisual environment to help clarify their professional role or encourage national dialogue about the ways in which American homes and families have changed. If home economists decide to provide intellectual leadership in this discussion, it could add immeasurably to the prestige of a profession that has been too long forgotten and misunderstood.

12. See, for example, Dena Attar, *Wasting Girls' Time: The History and Politics of Home Economics* (London: Virago, 1990).

A farm woman's life includes backbreaking labor. (*The Happier Way*, 1920)

Without mother, the men must do the laundry. (*The Happier Way*, 1920)

After the demonstration agent does his work, Louisa has an efficient kitchen. (*The Happier Way*, 1920)

The Department of Agriculture sends a Tuskeegee graduate to help African American farmers. (*Helping Negroes to Become Better Farmers and Homemakers*, 1921)

Posters advertise the possibility of learning scientific agriculture at different locations. (*Helping Negroes to Become Better Farmers and Homemakers*, 1921)

An African American demonstration agent shows women home health care and nutrition techniques. (*Helping Negroes to Become Better Farmers and Homemakers*, 1921)

Black women portrayed stereotypically as celebrating improvements by eating watermelon. (*Helping Negroes to Become Better Farmers and Homemakers*, 1921)

A girl must be in style even when feeding chickens on the farm. (*Teen Togs*, 1943. Photo courtesy The University of Georgia Cooperative Extension Service)

High school friends are always interested in a developing wardrobe. (*Teen Togs*, 1943. Photo courtesy The University of Georgia Cooperative Extension Service)

Students of home design need to measure the dimensions of a table against the physical needs of a home-maker. (*A College of Home Economics*, 1947–48)

A student learns to select produce for value and asethetics. (*A College of Home Economics*, 1947–48)

Home economists could take their food preparation and cooking skills to television. (*Why Study Home Economics?* 1955. From Collection of Archives at Factual Film, Iowa State University.)

10   Grace under Pressure: The Black Home Extension Service in South Carolina, 1919–1966

CARMEN HARRIS

The history of home demonstration work in the southern United States, like the history of all the region's institutions, is a story of legal segregation and disparate treatment for blacks. This essay is a case study of the black women who worked as home demonstration agents in South Carolina between 1919 and 1966. These agents achieved success practicing their profession despite a system of oppression under which white South Carolinians attempted to use black home agents as part of their social control mechanisms. The agents, through their approach to their work, managed to empower themselves and the rural blacks they served.

Three South Carolina colleges play a role in this story. In 1890 Clemson Agricultural College was founded and replaced South Carolina College as the land-grant institution for the state. The school operated in a military style and accepted only white men. Winthrop College, a private normal institute established in 1886 for white women, became Clemson's sister land-grant institution in 1890. In 1895 the South Carolina General Assembly voted to establish the Colored, Normal, Industrial, Agricultural and Mechanical College as a coeducational college for black men and women. Although all three schools had land-grant status, the General Assembly designated Clemson College as the institution to receive all federal monies derived from land-grant legislation.[1]

I am deeply indebted to Stephen Lowe for his criticisms of this essay and to Adraine Jackson of Clemson University Special Collections in Clemson, South Carolina.

1. Various institutions served as South Carolina's land-grant college between 1865 and 1890. For a discussion of the history of the state's agricultural colleges, see Carmen Harris, "Blacks in Agricultural Extension in South Carolina" (M.A. thesis, Clemson University, 1990), pp. 11–15;

In 1904 agricultural extension work with white men and boys began in the South. The United States Department of Agriculture appointed Seaman A. Knapp, a former agriculture professor and president of Iowa State College, to direct a program to encourage diversified farming in southern states where the boll weevil threatened the already weakened cotton crop economy. By 1906 the work with white men and boys was well under way. At that time Knapp, with some reluctance and under pressure from the federal government and the philanthropists who paid for extension work, instituted extension work with black men.[2]

In 1907 J. Phil Campbell, a Georgian whom Knapp had appointed as the first extension agent in South Carolina, brought up the idea of employing women as home economics agents to do extension work with women and girls. Knapp agreed to begin club work with girls, but after two years such work was still in the planning stage. Local women, not federal officials, took the initiative in establishing girls' club work in their states. Marie Cromer, a schoolteacher from Aiken, South Carolina, established the first tomato club for girls in the United States. Cromer taught the girls how to raise and can tomatoes for home use and for sale. Knapp received the news of the club's accomplishments favorably and appointed Cromer a girls' club agent in 1910. Nevertheless, he refused to authorize broader extension work with women, appointing only girls' club agents before his death in 1911. By 1912, however, there were at least two white women agents in South Carolina whose title was home demonstration agent. There is no indication that these women did any work with black farm women.[3]

By 1914 two black South Carolinians advocated home demonstration work with women and girls. Mrs. Miller Earl promoted tomato clubs for black girls, and Ransom W. Westberry, one of the first black agricultural agents in South Carolina, suggested that work with black women and girls was essential to racial uplift. In a speech before black farm families in Anderson, South Carolina, in June 1914 he said: "No race of people can rise

---

Daniel Walker Hollis, *University of South Carolina*, vol. 2, *College to University* (Columbia: University of South Carolina Press, 1956), chap. 4; Yates Snowden, *History of South Carolina*, 5 vols. (New York: Lewis, 1920), 2:917–18; James F. Potts, *The History of South Carolina College* (Columbia, S.C.: R. L. Bryan, 1978), p. 2; Joel Schor, "The Black Presence in the U.S. Cooperative Extension Service to 1983: A Profile," author's manuscript, May 25, 1983, pp. 4–5.

In this essay the Colored, Normal, Industrial, Agricultural College is referred to as South Carolina State College or State College.

2. Schor, "Black Presence," p. 132.

3. Thomas W. Morgan, "The First Fifty Years of Smith-Lever," p. 7, n.d., typescript, Box 14, Agricultural Extension, Field Operations, Clemson University Special Collections, Strom Thurmond Institute, Clemson, S.C. (hereafter Clemson); Payroll roster, Box 4, South Carolina Records of the Federal Extension Service, Secretary of Agriculture, DC 1913–14, Record Group 33, National Archives; Oscar B. Martin, "The Beginning of Home Demonstration Work," p. 1, n.d., typescript, Box 31, Agricultural Extension, Administrative Files, Clemson.

above their women. They should be encouraged in their efforts to teach girls to raise tomatoes, and the next generation will understand the arts of farming better than we do. . . . I know of no other being who is more willing to learn new things than the females."[4] Yet neither Westberry nor Earl had the status or power to require state extension officials to begin work with black women and girls.

The Smith-Lever Act, passed in May 1914, mandated that cooperative agricultural extension work be conducted jointly by land-grant colleges and the United States Department of Agriculture. Unlike the 1890 Morrill Act, the Smith-Lever Act made no explicit provision for allocation of money for use by African Americans. It placed the control of extension work and of all extension monies with the college or colleges designated by each state's legislature. The South Carolina General Assembly designated Clemson College as the cooperating institution.[5]

Implementing Smith-Lever proved difficult in South Carolina. Most of the state's farmers were landless blacks, either tenants or sharecroppers. Yet Clemson College officials decided to end their black agricultural agent program because, they argued, it "would injure the work with a certain class of our white people." When they proceeded to give notice to the state's seven black agents, officials at the United States Department of Agriculture along with Robert S. Wilkinson, president of South Carolina State College, protested. Eventually, Secretary of Agriculture David Houston insisted on the retention of the black agents. Clemson officials relented but placed them under the direction of the "State Negro College [South Carolina State College] at Orangeburg."[6]

During the debate between federal and state officials about the termination of the black agricultural agents, the issue of the black women's role in

4. Schor, "Black Presence," pp. 138, 140.

5. U.S. House of Representatives, *Hearings, Report and Debate: Smith-Lever Act of 1914* (reproduced October 1959 by Virginia Agricultural Extension Service, Blackaburg, Va.), pp. 3063, 3146. See also Officers and Various Directors of the Chicago Branch of the National Association for the Advancement of Colored People to David A. Houston, Secretary of Agriculture, September 12, 1913, Records of the Secretary of Agriculture, General Correspondence, Negroes, 1909–23, Record Group 16, National Archives; Earl William Crosby, "Building the County Home: The Black County Agent System, 1906–1940" (Ph.D. dissertation, Miami University of Ohio, 1977), pp. 56–57; Russell Lord, *The Agrarian Revival: A Study of Agricultural Extension* (New York: American Association for Adult Education, 1939), pp. 92–94; Schor, "Black Presence," pp. 34–35; Bradford Knapp to W. M. Riggs, President of Clemson Agricultural College, December 22, 1914, Riggs to Knapp, January 6, 1915 and Knapp to Riggs, January 27, 1915, Presidents' Papers, Riggs Series, Clemson.

6. W. W. Long to Walter M. Riggs, June 22, 1914, Riggs to Robert S. Wilkinson, July 27, 1914, Long to "All Agents," March 19, 1915, Riggs to Secy. D. F. Houston, April 5, 1915 (telegram), Houston to Riggs, April 5, 1915 (telegram), Presidents' Papers, Riggs Series, Clemson. These protests came as President Woodrow Wilson was eliminating blacks from the federal work force in Washington, D.C.

extension work came up. Bradford Knapp, who had succeeded his father as director of extension work in the South, wrote to Clemson president Walter M. Riggs:

> There are some things which the white County Agent and the white woman Home Economics Agent cannot do for the negroes . . . and that is when we come to touch on the negro home. The matter of moral, sanitary and economic conditions in negro homes under the Lever bill, is something which I would not want to tackle except with persons who could go into these homes. Therefore, in the home economics extension work for negroes, I should certainly use negro employees by putting a few to work and supervising them carefully.[7]

At the end of the first year after passage of Smith-Lever, federal and South Carolina officials had reached a deadlock. After being forced to retain black agents or risk federal action that would damage white extension work, Clemson officials kept the number of black agricultural agents at seven. Having preserved the jobs of the black agents, federal extension officials pushed no further. State College president Robert S. Wilkinson, who had fought hard to retain the black agricultural agents, turned his attention to home demonstration work.

Although Wilkinson was president of State College, the power in the institution lay in the hands of the Board of Trustees, which was all white. In 1915 the board authorized Wilkinson to enter into a cooperative agreement with Winthrop College for supervision of black women's work. The board allocated money to hire a black woman as home agent in Orangeburg County (where the school was located), but subsequent reports do not show that the position was ever filled.[8]

The confluence of several factors during World War I finally prompted extension officials to hire black women to work in the home demonstration service. With the coming of the war, many blacks left the South to fill jobs in northern industry, and many black men were drafted. Farming in the South remained labor-intensive. Not surprisingly, black flight alarmed southern white landlords and state officials. Editorials in black urban newspapers—urging migration—and by black and white southern leaders—urging whites to reform and blacks to stay where they were—agreed on only one point: blacks were not being treated fairly. White landlords and government offi-

---

7. Bradford Knapp to Walter M. Riggs, January 27, 1915, Presidents' Papers, Riggs Series, Clemson.

8. "Report of the President," in Colored Normal Industrial, Agricultural and Mechanical College of South Carolina (hereafter CNIAMC), *Annual Report of the Board of Trustees of the Colored Normal Industrial, Agricultural and Mechanical College of South Carolina* (Columbia, S.C.: Gonzales and Bryan, 1915), pp. 5, 11.

cials had little choice but to address the needs of black farm laborers if they wished to keep them on the farms.[9]

Since both Clemson and Winthrop extension officials knew that it was socially and politically impossible for white women to enter black homes and work with black clients, the only alternative was to engage black home demonstration agents. Thirteen black women became emergency home agents in 1919, although in official reports they were referred to as "assistants" in home demonstration. Christine N. South, state agent for home demonstration in South Carolina in 1919, described the agents as "sensible and practical women . . . all of them far above average in education" and remarked that "some of them were real leaders of their people."[10]

The home demonstration agents' work focused primarily on food production (winter gardens, canning, and bread making) and sanitation (prevention of malaria, typhoid, and tuberculosis). For the most part black South Carolinians received the program with enthusiasm, although some remained suspicious. "Ain't foolin' wid dat lady," said one woman, "first thing we all know we'll be canning in France." The agents proved their worth, and by 1920 black home extension work finally became a permanent part of the South Carolina extension service; however, once the emergency appropriation ended, the length of their employment was cut to terms of only two and a half months. That summer fourteen black women went to State College, where Winthrop College home economics supervisors and staff from the tuberculosis association and state health department trained them.[11]

One reason why extension officials decided to continue to employ black home agents after the war emergency was their concern about the spread of infectious disease, stimulated by the deadly influenza epidemic of 1918 and the widespread incidence of communicable diseases among rural blacks. The goals of the program toward eradicating these diseases among blacks meshed well with Christine South's goals for white women's extension work. In her 1920 report, South noted the increased contact between the white farm home and the "outside world." "If the laundress has tuberculosis or lives in a house laden with tubercular germs," she wrote, "the disease invades the [white] home." Although she cited this example to illustrate the importance of extension work among white women, it certainly

9. *What the Agricultural Extension Service Is Doing for South Carolina, Annual Report for 1920* (Clemson College, S.C.: Clemson College, 1921), p. 96; "Report of the President," CNIAMC (1912), p. 9; (1913) p. 16; (1914) p. 10; (1915) p. 5; David B. Johnson to Bradford Knapp, June 6, 1918, Records of the Federal Extension Service, Box 35, RG 33, Misc. S.C., 1917–18; Schor, "Black Presence," pp. 39, 41.

10. *What the Agricultural Extension Service Is Doing for South Carolina,* p. 92.

11. Ibid., pp. 92–93.

underscored the necessity of work with black women as well because many of them worked as laundresses and other domestics for white families.[12]

Concern for black migration did not end with the armistice. A federal report on cooperative extension written in 1923 noted that blacks who remained impoverished migrated North at higher rates than blacks who owned their homes and practiced diversified agriculture.[13] The black extension program emphasized subsistence—not independence—which suggests that at least from the perspective of white extension officials, the program had limited goals, which seemed reasonable to them given their low assessments of about black aspirations. Rather than develop individualistic, capitalist-oriented activities among black families, the program attempted to improve the peonage that characterized southern agriculture. If blacks were satisfied within the framework that existed, whites believed they would stay where they were and work contentedly without developing greater expectations.

Black state leaders who viewed black home agents as blacks first and as women second opposed the organizational structure of South Carolina's home demonstration service. Black women worked under the white women agents and through Winthrop College. In other states all black extension workers, men and women, worked under the supervision of the black land grant colleges. Robert Wilkinson complained in his 1921 president's report, "We have no part whatever in the Home economics work. This is carried on entirely by Winthrop College. Our students therefore have no incentive to improve themselves along this line."[14]

Later Mattie Mae Fitzgerald, a black woman, became state supervisor of Negro work with headquarters at South Carolina State College. Fitzgerald's appointment proved mostly cosmetic. The actual planning and coordination of black home demonstration work continued to come from Winthrop College. Wilkinson's presidential reports testify to the limited role State College played in home demonstration work, even after Fitzgerald's appointment. Although he gave detailed examples of the accomplishments of black agricultural agents, he virtually ignored the women's work. Nor was Fitzgerald's position as state supervisor of Negro

12. Ibid., pp. 78, 91–93; Mattie Mae Fitzgerald, "District Work: 2. Report of Negro District Agent," "Result of Home Demonstration Work in South Carolina, December 1922," pp. 1, 3–4, Box 2, Agricultural Extension, Field Operations, Clemson; Dora E. Boston, "Annual Narrative Report of State Supervisor of Colored Home Demonstration Work, 1923," p. 12, Box 2, Agricultural Extension, Field Operations, Clemson.

13. *Cooperative Extension Work in Agriculture and Home Economics, 1923* (Washington, D.C.: U.S. Government Printing Office, 1924), p. 57.

14. Wayman Johnson, "History, Growth and Transition of 4-H among Negroes in South Carolina," p. 19, n.d., Reference and Serials Center, Miller F. Whittaker Library, South Carolina State College Orangeburg, S.C. "Report of the President," CNIAMC (1921), p. 12.

work acknowledged by white extension officials, who refused to use her title, referring to her and to Dora Boston, who succeeded her in August 1923, as Negro "District" agent.[15]

The home demonstration program for white women in South Carolina grew slowly but progressively after the passage of Smith-Lever until by 1931 each of the state's forty-six counties boasted a white agent. In contrast, work among black women experienced restricted growth because of the limited financial resources white administrators allocated to the black program. In 1923 the length of the work year for black home extension agents increased from three and one-half to eleven months, but the number of agents declined proportionately. Whereas in 1922 thirteen agents under Fitzgerald worked an aggregate of forty-nine months, the following year only three agents and the supervisor worked an aggregate of forty-four months. Two more agents were added in 1924, not because of an increase in funds but because local officials in Charleston, Marion, and Richland counties valued the services of their agents enough to pay them, thus freeing funds used to hire two more agents.[16]

After 1923 South Carolina's black extension program increasingly emphasized practical aspects, which made it distinctive from the white women's program. Not surprisingly, programs that required little if any capital outlay proved the most successful among the state's black farm women. Food production and conservation constituted the most popular part of the extension program. In 1922 black home agents reported that more than seven thousand women were involved in home and winter garden demonstrations and estimated that the canned fruits and vegetables produced by these women were valued in excess of $79,000. Statistics for 1924, 1925, and 1929 show that club members canned nearly 46,000 quarts of fruits and vegetables, made almost 1,400 quarts of fruit juices, 4,200 quarts of jelly and preserves, and 2,800 quarts of pickles, and dried over 37,000 pounds of fruits and vegetables. Agents encouraged farm women who participated in extension programs to use more dairy products and worked to incorporate milk into the diets of rural schoolchildren. Some progress was made in home improvements, but because money was so scarce most improvements simply involved more efficient re-

15. Johnson, "History, Growth and Transition," p. 19; Fitzgerald, "District Work"; Boston, "Annual Narrative Report, 1923"; Boston, "1924 Narrative Summary"; Dora E. Boston, "Report of Dora E. Boston, State Supervisor of Colored Demonstration Agents, 1925," Ser. 33, Folder 190, Home Demonstration Reports, Clemson.

16. Fitzgerald, "District Work," pp. 1, 3–4; *What the Agricultural Extension Service Is Doing for South Carolina*, pp. 91–93; Boston, "1924 Narrative Summary," pp. 9–12; Boston, "Report of Dora E. Boston, 1925," pp. 20, 22–23, 25, 27–28; "Report of the President," CNIAMC (1929), pp. 28–29.

arrangements of furniture. Some piecemeal repairs were made to homes by recycling wood from dilapidated outbuildings.[17]

Sanitation and hygiene continued to be important aspects of the black extension program. Activities to prevent disease, were, for the most part, well received. Agents supervised the cleaning and oiling of ditches to eradicate mosquitoes and showed their clients how to make garbage containers. Agent Connie Jones reported that she distributed disinfectant. White state officials assisted the agents in their efforts to fight disease. While Dora Boston served as agent in Colleton County in 1922, she referred several clients to the county's health nurse for treatment. Local authorities helped her establish a two-day clinic. The state tuberculosis association sent two speakers to the clinic, and one of its nurses attended meetings with Boston to make speeches on tuberculosis prevention. In 1924 the Richland County agent obtained free medical treatment for her clients.[18]

Working to improve rural blacks' health was not always an easy task because some had become resigned to their fate. Dora Boston recalled that when she approached a man about cleaning a ditch to prevent malarial mosquitoes from breeding, he remarked, "I've had this fever for years and most people around here have it. I'll just have to work before it comes on because I am not much good afterwards." His, however, was not the general response. During Health Week in 1924 participants cleaned yards, livestock pens, and homes, and more than 430 schoolchildren wrote and read papers on health.[19]

Developing a community ethos among rural blacks proved crucial for the success of home extension work. In her 1922 report, Fitzgerald noted the popularity of club activities among both women and girls. She said they enjoyed giving "club yells" and singing "club songs." Agents gave club members instructions in parliamentary procedures, and the clubs elected their own officers. The report noted the "zeal and great willingness" of women club members, which "demonstrat[ed] the fact that the one great necessity is leaders." Club leaders kept the interest in extension alive by holding meetings and doing demonstrations while the agent was working in another part of the county. Agents organized community-based contests through which members "unconsciously . . . learn[ed] the necessity of a community

17. Fitzgerald, "District Work," pp. 1, 3–4; *What the Agricultural Extension Service Is Doing for South Carolina,* pp. 91–93; Boston, "1924 Narrative Summary," pp. 9–12; Boston, "Report of Dora E. Boston, 1925," pp. 20, 22–23, 25, 27–28; "Report of the President," CNIAMC (1929), pp. 28–29.

18. *What the Agricultural Extension Service Is Doing for South Carolina,* p. 93; Fitzgerald, "District Work," p. 3; Boston, "Annual Narrative Report, 1923," p. 6; Boston, "1924 Narrative Summary," pp. 10, 12; "Report of the President," CNIAMC (1929), p. 29.

19. Boston, "Annual Narrative Report, 1923," p. 6; Boston, "1924 Narrative Summary," p. 10; "Report of the President," CNIAMC (1929), p. 29.

center" and to interest people in the extension program. In 1924 agents established sixty-five clubs and created the Head to Foot Club to improve personal appearance. Dora Boston insisted that emphasis on appearance helped in forming "the habit of cleanliness," and in this way "homes would be affected." Agents taught club members how to wash and comb their hair, how to care for their skin and teeth, how to make clothes (including underwear), and how to dress properly. Club members made 2,978 pieces of underwear and more than 2,600 dresses and coats. Boston also noted that the Richland County agent held "two community fairs and two meetings which she called popular days" to bring half of the county together. County fairs provided another way of reaching rural blacks. Speakers on public health attended the fairs to provide information on health issues. At these fairs black clubsters would show off the products of their labor. Canned foods and fresh produce were displayed in abundance. Many blacks initially suspicious of extension work became converts when they attended these fairs. The early reports also suggest that black extension agents were becoming integrated with other community leaders. Local churches served as gathering places for large meetings. In 1923 Boston reported that she secured the cooperation of teachers and preachers whenever she began to develop community projects.[20]

In his report to the state General Assembly in 1924, Robert S. Wilkinson noted the effect of black extension work in South Carolina. "The Negro work," he wrote, "is an influence in the right direction in the matter of Negro migration to Northern industrial centers." Dora Boston echoed his sentiment. She noted that agents had demonstrated how community cohesion "stabiliz[ed] rural life." She pointed with pride to the way homes and outbuildings had been painted or whitewashed, family nutrition and clothing had improved, and family incomes had increased. "The homes are more comfortable and women have broader visions, a greater income, better living and community conditions, . . . and a rural society that will produce satisfaction," she wrote. "Home Demonstration workers have as an aim an efficient, satisfied rural State and are working toward that goal."[21]

These successes seem all the more remarkable when one considers the obstacles created by black poverty and white bigotry. White extension officials believed that the lion's share of funds spent on extension work should go to white extension programs because whites provided most of the tax dollars. As a result, the black extension program remained understaffed and underfunded. Dora Boston wrote that black home agents "may be compared

20. Fitzgerald, "District Work," pp. 2, 4; Boston, "1924 Narrative Summary," pp. 2–3, 9–12; Boston, "Report of Dora E. Boston, 1925," pp. 20, 22–23, 25, 27–28; "Report of the President," CNIAMC (1929), pp. 28–29.

21. Boston, "Annual Narrative Report, 1923," p. 2; "Report of the President," CNIAMC (1924), p. 28; (1929), p. 29; Boston, "1924 Narrative Summary," pp. 12–13.

to a farmer without farm implements; they have no equipment"—no pressure cookers for canning, no projectors to show motion pictures. When black agents were lucky enough to have offices, they were often located in their own homes or provided by black businesses. Most had no office furniture, and none had clerical help.[22]

Despite their limited numbers, the agents' message got through. Boston had a professional vision for black home agents. She recommended that agents be given furloughs to attend summer school because "paramount preparation makes one fit for service." Of the home agent program itself she wrote, "Although the negro work is still in its experimental stage, good work has been done and it has a bright and promising future. The agents are making their way by adapting their work to the actual needs of the community."[23] Despite these successes, Clemson officials did not increase their commitment to the black home extension service. The number of black home agents did not increase as extension funds, by law, increased each year. The actions Clemson extension officials took in 1928 offer an example of how they attempted to keep the number of black agents as low as possible.

The Capper-Ketcham Act of 1928 provided funds to all states to enlarge their extension programs. The act required that 80 percent of the funds distributed to a state be spent to hire new agents. The remaining 20 percent was to go for Negro work. At first, South Carolina's director of extension, William W. Long, ignored the act's provisions. He set aside 75 percent of the money for white men's work and hired three white home agents out of the 25 percent he put aside for white women's work. When federal officials objected that he had shortchanged both women and blacks, he attempted to circumvent the law by transferring the black women's headquarters from Winthrop College to South Carolina State and replacing the Smith-Lever funds appropriated for their salaries with Capper-Ketcham funds. He insisted that by giving State College $2,500 (half of the first-year Capper-Ketcham appropriation) he had carried out "the principle of the law." Federal officials disagreed, observing that "changing the supervision from Winthrop to the negro college does not make it a new piece of work." In 1929 Long belatedly agreed to hire three new black women agents, bringing the total to eight, compared to thirty-eight white women agents.[24]

State College's new role in supervising black women agents no doubt pleased President Wilkinson, who included a section on the women in his

22. Boston, "1924 Narrative Summary," pp. 5–6, 11, 13–14.

23. Ibid.

24. W. W. Long to C. B. Smith, July 28, 1928; Smith to Long, August 1, 1928, Long to J. A. Evans, August 29, 1928 (telegram); Evans to Long August 30, 1928 (telegram); Evans to Long, August 30, 1928; Long to Evans, August 30, 1928 (telegram); Evans to Long, August 31, 1928; Long to Smith, May 3, 1929, all in Box 187, Records of the Federal Extension Service, Director, S.C., 1928–29, Record Group 33, National Archives.

1928 report and praised their "outstanding accomplishments." Thanks to Long's duplicity, State College finally gained official control over all black extension work, although for some time Winthrop College continued to play the role of silent partner in administering black women's work. But Winthrop's role diminished as personnel changes in the black home extension service brought a woman with professional acumen to the helm of the black women's program.

In 1930, when Dora Boston married Harry Daniels, the state supervisor for Negro men's work, extension officials fired her from the service. Wilkinson selected Marian B. Paul, whose husband was not in extension work, to succeed Boston as the state supervisor of Negro home demonstration work. Paul, a home economics graduate of Pennsylvania State College, had worked in the service as an emergency agent in 1920–22. Marian Paul would bring to fruition the aspirations Dora Boston had spelled out for women's home demonstration work. Paul presided over the flowering of the black home extension service. During her thirty years as the leader of the program, she guided the development of a professional extension force and the creation of a professional ethos for black home extension workers.

When Paul became the state supervisor, there were eight agents in the field. The staff had not grown since the increase mandated by Capper-Ketcham in 1929. The Depression brought calls for cutbacks. In January 1931 a bill to eliminate all home demonstration work failed in the General Assembly. Nevertheless, Greenville County's legislative delegation discontinued the funding for its black home agent. Marian Paul, Lonnie I. Landrum (the white state supervisor for home economics work), and President Wilkinson worked together to keep the agent on the job. Although they could not convince state authorities to continue funding the position, they were able to keep the agent working for another five and a half months by reallocating some of their own funds. Blacks in Greenville County also pledged money for her salary and raised $300 through personal donations and fund-raising. Through their own efforts, they were able to retain the services of their agent for another three and a half months. In 1932 extension officials reduced the seven remaining agents' work year to eleven months.[25]

Under Paul's leadership the number of black agents grew by fits and starts between 1933 (the year that black women began working year-round) and 1961 (see Table 10.1). Ironically, the only time during the period that each county had a black home agent was in 1933–34, during the depths of the Depression, when emergency funds became available and women who qualified for relief were hired as agents. Early in World War II the number

25. "Report of the President," CNIAMC (1929), pp. 28–29; Marian B. Paul, "1932–33 Narrative Annual Report of Marian B. Paul," pp. 2–3, Box 12a, Agricultural Extension, Staff Development, Clemson.

TABLE 10.1. Census of black home demonstration agents in South Carolina, 1919–1961[a]

Year ending	Agents	Supervisors	Assistant supervisors	Assistant agents	4-H club agent	Specialists	Emergency agents
1919	13	0	0	0	0	0	0
1920	14	1	0	0	0	0	0
1922	13	1	0	0	0	0	0
1923	3	1	0	0	0	0	0
1924	5	1	0	0	0	0	0
1929[b]	8	1	0	0	0	0	0
1931[b]	8	1	0	0	0	0	0
1932	7	1	0	0	0	0	0
1933	7	1	0	0	0	0	0
1934	8	1	0	0	0	0	37[c]
1935	9	1	0	0	0	0	37[c]
1936	13	1	0	0	0	0	0
1937	14	1	0	0	0	0	0
1938	15	1	0	0	0	0	0
1939	15	1	0	0	0	0	0
1940	16	1	0	0	0	0	0
1941	18	1	0	0	0	0	0
1944[b]	14	1	0	0	0	1	12
1945	20	1	0	0	0	1	16
1946	26	1	1	0	0	0	0
1947	26	1	1	0	0	0	0
1948	28	1	1	0	0	0	0
1949	29	1	1	0	0	0	0
1950	29	1	1	0	0	0	0
1951	29	1	1	0	0	0	0
1952	30	1	1	1	0	0	0
1954[b]	32	1	2	4	0	0	0
1955	33	1	2	4	0	0	0
1956	33	1	1	6	1	0	0
1957	33	1	1	6	1	0	0
1958	33	1	1	6	1	0	0
1959	31	1	1	4	1	0	0
1960	33	1	0	2	1	0	0
1961	33	1	0	1	1	0	0

[a]In 1966 the black and white services integrated. Fifteen agents ranked as associate agents, nineteen as assistants in the new program. The supervisor's title was changed to assistant in home economics, and the 4-H Club leader's title was changed to assistant girls 4-H Club agent.

[b]Denotes break in annual sequence.

[c]The emergency agents worked for eighteen months, probably all of 1934 and though June of 1935.

of agents doubled to thirty-four, but in 1943 extension officials reduced the force. Throughout the 1950s and 1960s the number of county agents never reached forty, while the number of assistant county agents fluctuated between two and six. In contrast, the permanent staff of the white women's program grew steadily. In 1923 thirty-eight white home demonstration agents worked in South Carolina, and by 1931 there were forty-six—one for each county. Over time, more counties also hired assistant white home agents.[26]

Paul constantly pressed for more black agents. Much of her time was spent lobbying state leaders for more funds and pressuring counties to provide funds to help pay agents' salaries. She personally visited the General Assembly to ask white legislators to vote appropriations for their counties. She detailed the countless additional visits she made to legislators' homes and places of business. Although her efforts were not always successful, Paul persevered.

Over time her lobbying paid off and she was able to secure funds from every county in which there was an agent (thirty-eight of forty-six in the state). As agents proved their mettle and as social and economic policies changed, more and more counties made appropriations for extension work. By the 1940s Paul had more pledges for county funds than Clemson officials were willing to match with federal and state Smith-Lever funds.[27]

Procuring money for extension work was only one of Paul's duties. As supervisor, she visited the agents monthly to evaluate their work and to help them in planning their programs and with record-keeping. In her second annual report Paul noted that she held the positions of "Supervisor, specialist, 4-H leader, and county Home Agent." In this last capacity Paul conducted extension work in three counties that had no agent and organized six clubs in an effort to demonstrate to tightfisted officials the need to fund agents in those counties. By 1935 Paul no longer did county work, but she continued to assist the agents in their fieldwork.[28] Over the years her job did not become easier, but it became more diverse.

As an administrator, Paul devoted a large percentage of her time to attending meetings of black farm councils and other county-wide meetings.

26. *A Year of Progress: Annual Report of the Extension Service for 1925* (Clemson College, S.C.: Clemson Agricultural College, 1925), p. 37; William W. Long, "Program of Extension Work, South Carolina, 1931," p. 2, Box 2, Agricultural Administration, Staff Development, Clemson; Marian B. Paul, "Plan of Work, 1945," p. 2, Box 9, Agricultural Extension, Field Operations, Clemson; Marian B. Paul, "Home Demonstration Plan of Work for Negroes, 1946," p. 2, Box 35, Ibid. See Table 10.1.

27. Marian B. Paul, "South Carolina Annual Narrative Report, 1948," p. 5, Box 70, Agricultural Extension, Field Operations, Clemson, and Marion B. Paul, "Annual Report of Cooperative Extension Work in South Carolina, 1936, Negro Home Demonstration Division," p. 6, Box 8, ibid.

28. Paul, "1932–33 Narrative Annual Report of Marian B. Paul," p. 7.

During the Depression, she was called on continually to help blacks find jobs and to recommend blacks for positions in the Youth Administration and for Works Progress Administration programs. State health officials, social workers, bureau chiefs, and state New Deal officials enlisted her aid in providing services to black clients. Charities also sought her assistance in soliciting black participation in fund-raising drives.[29]

To free herself for the many duties required of her, Paul worked to change the top-down planning that had characterized extension work in the 1920s and to grant agents greater autonomy. Because she expected them to be able to act independently, Paul insisted that all agents hired after 1930 hold a college degree. In 1930 State College had begun to grant bachelor's degrees, and Paul, with an office on the campus, actively recruited graduates. These young women were usually South Carolina natives familiar with local conditions and racial mores. Paul also preferred that they have teaching experience and own an automobile, a tall order for recent college graduates anywhere, but especially for black women in the rural South during the Depression.[30]

Paul constantly emphasized the importance of education for extension work. She encouraged agents who lacked degrees to attend State College, where the Department of Home Economics provided short courses during the summer. And she urged her agents to pursue postgraduate education, even though racial segregation meant they had to do so outside the South. Paul herself attended summer schools at Columbia and Cornell universities. Several other agents attended Cornell, Iowa State, and other eastern and midwestern land-grant colleges. Beginning in 1930, black agents received training through Rosenwald Summer Schools. That year the Rosenwald Fund, endowed by Sears, Roebuck executive and philanthropist Julius Rosenwald, began funding regional summer institutes for black extension workers. State College in South Carolina was among three regional sites selected for the inaugural conferences.[31]

Paul looked for women who "possess[ed] culture, skill, training, experience, tact, a pleasing personality, and physical soundness." Given the high status home agents enjoyed within the black community, it is not surpris-

29. Marian B. Paul, "Annual Report, Negro Home Demonstration Work, 1937," pp. 19–20, Box 8, Agricultural Extension, Field Operations, Clemson.

30. Ibid., p. 4; Paul, "South Carolina Annual Narrative Report, 1948," p. 5.

31. Prairie View A&M in Texas, Hampton Institute in Virginia, and State College were the three sites selected. See Paul, "1932–33 Narrative Annual Report of Marian B. Paul," pp. 5, 14; Marian B. Paul, "Annual Narrative Report of State Supervisor of Negro Home Demonstration Work, 1937–8," p. 20, Box 9, Agricultural Extension, Field Operations, Clemson; Marian B. Paul, "South Carolina Narrative Annual Report, 1938–39 of [State of] South Carolina," p. 19, Box 11, ibid.; Marian B. Paul, "South Carolina Narrative Report, 1946," p. 4, Box 35, ibid.

ing that Paul desired these traits. The agent took her place among black leaders in the county where she worked. To do so successfully, she had to gain the confidence of other black leaders and of white leaders as well. Agents worked closely with black teachers and clergy and often used black churches as forums to promote extension programs. The support of white leadership was also crucial. Paul's agents forged links with white organizations such as the Red Cross, with local nurses and health organizations to get services for their clients, and with white women's farm councils to press for the hiring of more black agents. Landlords who saw the benefits of the program for their own sharecroppers or those of their neighbors often took the lead in getting their tenants interested in the program.[32]

Despite the high standards, the hard work, and salaries that were too low even with county supplements, Paul successfully recruited top-notch agents, and she gave them great latitude in their work. Her agents made their own contacts with community leaders and constructed their own individualized programs of work. Paul encouraged them to tailor their programs to the needs of the people they served. The agents took a demographic survey of the county, which included population counts, patterns of farm ownership, health and sanitary conditions, cash crops produced, home industries and marketing possibilities, and the number of families already following some improved practices.[33] Armed with these facts, they then developed programs uniquely suited to the needs of the communities they served. No wonder the agents were held in such high esteem by their clients. In her 1932 report Paul noted, "The Home Demonstration Agent is looked upon by the County as a sort of 'Fairy God Mother' or 'Magician.' She is often called upon to do the impossible, such as to prescribe for those who are ill, to patch up family quarrels, to find employment for the idle, to aid in building churches and school houses—and . . . to bury the dead. . . . [I]t shows that the Agent has gained the confidence and love of her people and her County."[34]

The general enthusiasm with which blacks greeted home extension work demonstrated its importance to whites as a possible means of controlling their agrarian work force. The "Live-at-Home" program sounded the keynote in their efforts. The name formalized a program in existence and largely unchanged between 1919 and the 1930s. Aptly titled, Live-at-Home worked to raise the standard of living among the rural poor and not coincidentally to slow migration to the North. The program targeted very poor

32. Paul, "Annual Report, Negro Home Demonstration Work, 1937," p. 4; Paul, "South Carolina Annual Narrative Report, 1948," p. 5; Paul, "1932–33 Narrative Annual Report of Marian B. Paul," p. 6.

33. Paul, "Annual Narrative Report, 1937–8," pp. 25–26.

34. Paul, "1932–33 Narrative Annual Report of Marian B. Paul," p. 4.

whites and all blacks. Its goal, according to State Home Agent Lonnie I. Landrum, was to make "tenant families more self-sufficing." During the Depression, agents encouraged farmers to cultivate year-round gardens, keep a cow and other food-producing livestock, and can vegetables and fruit to prevent families from seeking government assistance. This work received enthusiastic white support. Since southern cash crops remained labor-intensive into the 1940s, whites encouraged the Live-at-Home program. Some landlords required their tenants to enroll in "plantation programs." More than 80 percent of those enrolled were black. White home demonstration agents in eight counties designed plantation programs to show "tenant families that in South Carolina it is possible for the low-income group of farmers to have balanced adequate diets, and better standards of living than they may now have." The agents never discussed for-profit work, such as marketing surplus food, unless tenants specifically requested it.[35]

In many ways the programs Paul and her agents carried out were similar to the plantation program or the Live-at-Home work. The general aims of South Carolina's extension program were "proper and sufficient food for every family," "appropriate and comfortable clothing," "sanitary and attractive houses," and "adequate cash income." The order in which Paul presented her objectives for black demonstration work suggests that her priorities differed from those of white administrators. Her objectives were to achieve higher standards of living for rural families, to help rural families become self-supporting and independent, to enable farm families to live at home, and to ensure the proper condition of the soil. She also listed goals far beyond those described for plantation work, which included keeping "all children in school"; promoting "economical management, rural libraries, home ownership, [and] better education," providing "marketing information and advantages," and "instilling frugality."[36]

The agents, like other black elites, were well aware of the linkage between racism and the economic deprivation of rural blacks. Paul's annual reports declare that whites intended blacks to be backward, turning back upon whites their own stereotypes of black inferiority. "The rural Negroes of South Carolina," she conceded, "for the most part are ignorant, timid, unambitious, uncultured and poor." Why? "*Ignorant* because of the deficient facilities of rural education, *timid* because of the brow-beating methods of his financial and intellectual superiors, *unambitious* because of his discouragements and discriminations, *uncultured* because of his lack of opportunity, his meager contacts and limited advantages, because of his

35. *Extension Work in South Carolina 1937: Review of Agricultural Progress* (Clemson, S.C.: Clemson Agricultural College, 1937), p. 104; *Extension Work in South Carolina 1938: Review of Agricultural Progress* (Clemson, S.C.: Clemson Agricultural College, 1938), pp. 128–29.
36. Paul, "Annual Report, Negro Home Demonstration Work 1937," pp. 11–12.

illiteracy, his economic inefficiency and his confined benefits.[37] She concluded, "The rural Negro is not shiftless" as was so often claimed in the "propaganda of those wishing to exploit him. . . . He has been, however, a victim of circumstances."[38]

When white southerners attempted to blame South Carolina's blacks for the state's lack of progress, Paul responded in a defensive salvo certainly reckless for her day:

> No. 1. The Negro is not the problem, but rather the problem is the white man's attitude toward him. . . . Some, due to ignorance and circumstances are held almost in peonage. The poor, inadequate school facilities, plus the landlord's attitude toward education are partly responsible for the illiteracy among Negroes. The great majority of the people with whom we work . . . are a people forgotten by many. Nevertheless, they are individual beings with hopes and longings. It is true that many of these people have accepted the dreary existence that seems to be the lot of the Negro sharecropper, perhaps because that seems to be the simplest and easiest solution to an almost useless struggle.[39]

Paul's reports also show that she and her agents encouraged resistance to the status quo. For example, she noted that many black children had misshapen feet caused by ill-fitting shoes, and she encouraged their parents to buy shoes only in stores that permitted them to try them on first, even though such a demand violated the standard practice of white merchants.[40]

When the United States entered World War II, Paul used the occasion to demonstrate the contradiction between fighting for foreign freedoms while blacks were denied freedom in America. "The Negro stands ready, as always, to serve his country," she wrote in 1941. "And the Negro Home Demonstration agents of South Carolina have pledged themselves to wage war against ignorance, hatred, poverty, and indolence." In her plan of work for 1945 Paul wrote that blacks "see a ray of hope for liberation from economic slavery, from tenancy, from ignorance—they have hope for the 'four freedoms.'"[41]

In the immediate postwar years Paul continued her outspoken push for a better life for South Carolina blacks. "Education, the recent war where many of our boys gave their lives, and the plea for democracy and world

37. Paul, "Annual Narrative Report, Negro Home Demonstration Work, 1937–8," p. 1.

38. Ibid.

39. Paul, "South Carolina Narrative Annual Report, 1938–39," p. 1.

40. Ibid., p. 101; Marian B. Paul, "South Carolina Narrative Annual Report, 1940–1941," p. 116, Box 7, Agricultural Extension, Field Operations, Clemson.

41. Marian B. Paul, "South Carolina Annual Narrative Report, 1939–1940, of Marian B. Paul," p. 1, Box 14, Agricultural Extension, Field Operations, Clemson; Paul, "Plan of Work, 1945," p. 2, Box 9, ibid.

peace, have made the Negro dissatisfied with the status quo," she declared in her 1948 annual report. "For eighty-two years," she wrote, "he [the Negro] has 'with crumbs from the table' patiently waited for a better opportunity, for justice, for citizenship. . . . Now, with recent court actions a new era is approaching."[42]

Times were changing. By 1949 the white primary had been successfully challenged in South Carolina and other southern states, and President Harry Truman had issued his executive order to desegregate the military. Yet these victories created a backlash. Paul noted that Clarendon County had discontinued its appropriation and forbidden the continuation of black extension work because the state senator representing that county was "annoyed by political trends."[43] In the face of the backlash, intensified by the rise of anticommunism and the McCarthy witch-hunts, Paul muted her criticisms. After 1949 her annual reports, once outspoken, became more cautious and circumspect. They provide examples, both distinct and subtle, of the increasing pressure brought to bear on southern black leadership as the South closed ranks in the face of pressure to desegregate.

During the early 1950s, Governor James F. Byrnes determined to stave off federal intervention by making separate but equal a reality. The state built new schools for black children. Black extension workers also benefited. For several years Paul had requested more administrative staff. In 1954 extension officials approved a position for a second assistant supervisor. Paul also tried to get a 4-H club leader for blacks, but rather than hire another person, extension officials changed the second assistant supervisor's title to Negro girls' 4-H leader. Some counties scrambled to hire black home agents. In 1954 Chesterfield and Clarendon counties paid the full salary of an agent even though no matching funds were available.[44] The fact that *Brown* v. *Board of Education* (of which *Briggs* v. *Elliott*, a case originating in Clarendon County, formed a part) was being deliberated by the Supreme Court probably influenced that county delegation's change in attitude.

In Paul's estimation, black demonstration agents' ultimate goal was to change rural blacks' behavior to encourage them "to assume responsibilities which will enlarge their capacities and fit them for worthwhile citizenship." Paul claimed that the agents exerted a strong influence on black leadership and on their clients as well. The respect the agents enjoyed in their communities, she suggested, made them models of conduct. "It is, therefore, [the agent's] duty to direct all of her clear thinking into channels for harmony, progress and for the well being of the nation. She must be alert

42. Marian B. Paul, "Plan of Work, 1948," pp. 7, 9–10, 13, Box 28, Agricultural Extension, Official Operations, Clemson.

43. Paul, "South Carolina Annual Narrative Report, 1948," p. 6.

44. Marian B. Paul, "Annual Narrative Report, Home Demonstration Work among Negroes in South Carolina, 1954," p. 6, Box 129, Agricultural Extension, Field Operations, Clemson.

to sense danger and tactful not to offend." This theme of controlling public sentiment appears consistently in Paul's annual reports. Some clients perhaps perceived the agent's work as social control. Paul wrote that agents "must not become discouraged when [rural blacks] doubted their sincerity and leadership."[45] It is also evident from her narratives that she believed black South Carolinians should be accorded more equality in society. She wrote of the importance of teaching blacks to learn to "respect the rights, privileges, and properties of others," but she also suggested the importance of providing equality to all citizens. The home agent's task was to help blacks understand "county, state national and international affairs" so that they, and the United States, could take their place in the new order.[46]

As the southern social system came under greater attack during the mid-1950s, extension officials retaliated by reducing the autonomy of black extension workers. After 1954 Paul no longer went to county legislative delegations to request appropriations for agents. Rather, she met with white supervisors to discuss the merits of each funding request. Those deemed acceptable were sent on to Clemson, where the Board of Trustees reviewed them. After that review, the state director submitted all approved requests to the legislature. Paul's status had been reduced to the equivalent of a white district agent, the same as Fitzgerald's and Boston's status in the early 1920s. Until 1954 Paul had visited legislators to solicit funds for black home extension work as part of her job. In later reports she noted that if she felt it necessary to make a personal appeal, she was "granted that privilege." Paul continued to eschew overt political rhetoric. She wrote that her task was to convince county delegations that blacks "considered the economic problem #1."[47]

45. Marian B. Paul, "South Carolina Annual Narrative Report, 1949," pp. 5, 24, 41, Box 158, Agricultural Extension, Field Operations, Clemson; Marian B. Paul, "Annual Report, County Home Demonstration Work, State of South Carolina, 1951," pp. 20, 32, 46, Box 17B, ibid.; Marian B. Paul, "Annual Report, County Home Demonstration Work, State of South Carolina, 1952," p. 37, Box P56, ibid.; Marian B. Paul, "Annual Narrative Report, Home Demonstration Work among Negroes in South Carolina, 1955," p. 40, Box 93, ibid.; Marian B. Paul, "Annual Report, Cooperative Extension Work, South Carolina, 1957, Home Demonstration Division, Negro Home Demonstration Work Project," p. 7, Box 101, Agricultural Extension, Field Operations, Clemson. Paul also stressed the need for racial harmony and cooperation between black and white extension agents. She repeatedly mentioned the lack of tension in the working relationships between white and black officials. Indeed, in one report she wrote that the black and white agents shared "bonds of friendship and mutual understanding . . . which, I dare say [are] nct excelled elsewhere in the United States of America" (Paul, "Annual Narrative Report, Home Demonstration Work among Negroes in South Carolina, 1955," p. 17).

46. Paul, "South Carolina Annual Narrative Report, 1949," p. 17; Paul, "Annual Report, County Home Demonstration Work, 1951," p. 46; Paul, "Annual Narrative Report, Home Demonstration Work among Negroes in South Carolina, 1955," p. 40.

47. Paul, "Annual Narrative Report, Home Demonstration Work among Negroes in South Carolina, 1954," p. 5; Paul, "Annual Report, Cooperative Extension Work, 1957, Negro Home

By 1957 Clemson officials had completely implemented central planning at the county level. The white agricultural agent became the supervisor of all other agents in the county. Administrative requests from black home agents had to be approved by both the white home agent and the white agricultural agent. Paul wrote that this new system brought about more uniformity in delivering extension services, but at the same time it tended to "crush initiative" among black agents.[48] Extension professionals, like members of other government-dependent black professional classes, increasingly came under the scrutiny of white officials. These new restrictions must have been bitter for Paul to swallow. By 1959, sixty-three-year-old Marian Paul had had enough. She retired, stating that she had "worked long enough and wished to have peace and quiet."[49]

Two women who began work in the extension service in the late 1940s and early 1950s carried on the struggle for black rights within the extension program. Sara Aiken, who came into the extension service immediately after she received her B.S. in home economics from South Carolina State College in 1947, had worked in Darlington County for seven years before accepting a position at State College as assistant state supervisor in 1954. In 1955 she became Negro girls' 4-H leader. Aiken did some postgraduate work, including summer study at Cornell University. In 1960 Aiken, by then Sara Waymer, succeeded Marian Paul as state supervisor of Negro work. Altamese B. Pough began work immediately after graduating from State College in 1951. She worked in Berkeley County until 1954, when she left extension work to have a child. She returned to work in 1956 in Colleton County and later transferred to Berkeley County, where she remained until she was named state 4-H agent for girls in late 1961.[50]

By the 1960s significant changes had occurred in the lives of rural blacks. Mechanization, begun in the mid-1940s, transformed black farm life. Mechanical cotton pickers alleviated whites' needs for manual laborers. Blacks became expendable. Waymer noted that the home agent of the 1960s had to consider the changing trends that affected blacks' lives in designing a program. The ills of the early part of the century had by no means been completely eradicated. But the average client of the 1960s was a "middle-class" farm wife who worked off the farm to supplement the family's income. Although some of the drudgery of farm life had been eliminated, blacks still

Demonstration Work Project," p. 19; Marian B. Paul, "Annual Narrative Report, Extension Work among Negroes in South Carolina," 1956, p. 2.

48. Paul, "Annual Cooperative Extension Work, 1957, Negro Home Demonstration Work Project," p. 19.

49. Marian B. Paul, Resignation form, November 10, 1959; Marian B. Paul to G. H. Bonnette, Administrative Assistant, December 18, 1959, Clemson.

50. Interview with Rosa Odum, Altamese B. Pough, and Sara A. Waymer, retired home demonstration agents, Orangeburg, South Carolina, July 1988, pp. 2–3.

struggled against the same kinds of oppression that had existed since Reconstruction. It remained the task of the agent of the 1960s, wrote Waymer, to "enlighten our people from economic, educational and social bondage."[51]

By 1960 the route to enlightenment was political. Extension officials, like other black state civil service employees in the South, found themselves in a precarious position. Any person who openly advocated or participated in civil rights protests would, in all probability, lose his or her job. In the 1950s, Clemson officials inaugurated a policy prohibiting agents from becoming involved in political organizations. Black agents had to sign a letter stating whether they belonged to the National Association for the Advancement of Colored People (NAACP). The wise agent was not a member. According to Pough, extension officials insisted the NAACP was "subversive" and "communist-inspired." She believed that these McCarthy-era charges prevented black extension agents from participating in the organization's civil rights activities.[52]

The 1960s proved a difficult time for home extension workers, especially those on the front lines of integration like Waymer and Pough. The NAACP had not only challenged the separate school system in South Carolina in the *Briggs* case, but its Legal Defense Fund lawyers had also challenged the unequal salaries of black teachers and included black extension agents in that challenge. By the 1960s the NAACP used legal means to force the extension service to open its files. As the disparities of the segregated system came under further attack, southern state directors coordinated resistance efforts. At their 1961 meeting the directors discussed the pressure the NAACP was putting on the administration of President John Kennedy to integrate extension work. South Carolina extension officials hurried to upgrade facilities and training in an attempt to avoid integration. They even removed the word "Negro," which black agents had been required to include in their titles since the 1920s.[53]

In South Carolina the transition to integration was not easy, even though Clemson had managed to integrate the student body without violence in 1963. Pough recalled that at a staff meeting George Nutt, the director of extension work, had told her "there's nothing in the law that says you have to have black extension workers." She responded, "That may not be, but

51. Sara A. Waymer, "Annual Cooperative Extension Work, South Carolina, 1960, Home Demonstration Division, Negro Home Demonstration Work Project," p. 8, Box 31, Agricultural Extension, Field Operations, Clemson.

52. Interview with Rosa Odum et al., pp. 35–36; *Clemson University Extension Service: Some Notes and Statistics Relating to Negro Participation* (Frogmore, S.C.: Penn Community Services, 1967), p. 12.

53. Interview with Rosa Odum et al., pp. 35–36; "Southern Directors, Minutes of Meetings, September 11–13, 1961," pp. 7–8, Box 4, Agricultural Extension, Field Operations, Southern Directors, Clemson.

inasmuch as you have them you have to do something about them." After the Civil Rights Act passed in 1964 and it became evident that the extension program had to integrate, Nutt called the white agents to Clemson College and told them about the law. But integration did not follow immediately. When Clemson president Robert C. Edwards found out that integration had not occurred, he made extension officials summon all agents—black and white—to Clemson on a Sunday to explain the integration process. Edwards even attended the meeting at which the extension officials explained the changes.[54]

Waymer and Pough made the "historic" move to Clemson when extension was integrated, both at great personal cost. Waymer brought her six-year-old daughter, but her husband remained in Orangeburg. Pough left her daughter in the care of a housekeeper. Waymer recalled that she and Harvey Gantt, who had sued the school for admission and successfully matriculated in 1963, were the first blacks on campus. "As I look back on it now, I was a pioneer," she said. After two years Waymer returned to Orangeburg, where she continued to work for the extension service until she retired in 1978. Pough went to Clemson in 1966 and resigned from the service after one year. She returned to Orangeburg to raise her daughter. She later recalled, "I thought about it [moving 130 miles to Clemson] long and hard because I did have a child. But I felt like, in a way, that I was sort of obligated to go for many reasons. . . . I wanted to see firsthand what it would be like."[55]

Whites punished blacks—sometimes intentionally, sometimes unconsciously—for seeking full participation in the extension program. Both Waymer and Pough experienced subtle discrimination at Clemson. Pough recalled that when she spoke to whites she met in the halls or in the lounge, on numerous occasions they would open their mouths to speak but nothing came out. Pough felt "sorry" for the whites; "I guess they really hated themselves for not being able to relate." There was also discrimination in the job assignments that Waymer and Pough were given at Clemson. Their assignments, according to Pough, were "simple things." They spent a great deal of their time judging contests.[56]

White officials used integration as an excuse to demote and dismiss black agents. Extension officials had already begun to decrease the number of black agents by 1959. In that year Clemson administrators cut four positions from the black home demonstration service. After Marian Paul retired, they eliminated the position of assistant state supervisor, as well as two agent and one assistant agent positions. Extension officials justified the cuts by pointing out that the black farm population had declined and arguing that

54. Interview with Rosa Odum et al., pp. 7–8, 53.
55. Ibid., pp. 2–3, 5, 51.
56. Ibid., pp. 12, 52.

"because their work is restricted to Negro farm families, in some counties their work-load may become too small to justify them."[57]

By late 1961 extension officials devised a new organizational chart that reinforced the racial hierarchy. At the administrative level Waymer's title became assistant in home economics and Pough's title changed to assistant girls 4-H club agent. The changes followed the same pattern at the county level. In every county, regardless of the black agent's years of experience and training, a white home agent became the senior or supervisory home economics agent. In seventeen counties black assistant or associate agents had more experience than their white supervisors. Thirteen white women who were appointed supervisory home agents had between zero and four years' experience. Blacks were designated "associate or assistant" depending on the number of years in the service and received a salary $700 lower than that of white agents with the same title. Table 10.2 shows some of the more egregious examples of the disparity between the years of experience of the black agents and those of their white supervisors. Twenty-five of the thirty-four black agents had more experience than their white counterparts, yet not one was appointed the head agent in her county.[58]

Passage of the Civil Rights Act of 1964 gave the agents an effective weapon with which to defend their rights. By 1966 both Pough and Waymer

TABLE 10.2. Comparison of the years of work experience of supervising agents and their subordinates

County	Supervising agent (white)	Assistant or associate agent (black)
County 3	8	21
County 33	2	16
County 15	4	9
County 18	4	18
County 26	3	17
County 27	1	20
County 29	2	23
County 35	4	30

57. "Organization of the Clemson College Extension Service in Districts and Counties of South Carolina," ca. 1962, pp. 2, 6, Box 3, Agricultural Extension, Field Operations, J. K. Williams, "Report on Extension Work, 1960," pp. 6–7, Box 2, ibid.; George B. Nutt to Robert C. Edwards, December 27, 1961, Box 1, ibid.

58. Clemson University officials attempted to legitimate these disparities by employing a rating system instituted in 1962. The 0–4 ranking system (four being the highest) supposedly provided merit raises to university employees. While nearly 87 percent of all agents got a rating of 3 or 4 (65.6 percent and 21 percent respectively) only 46 percent of black agents got that rating (45 percent and 1.4 percent respectively). Nearly half, 48 percent, of the black agents received a rating of 2 while only 13.4 percent of white agents received that rating. No white agent received a rating below 2 but three black agents received a 1 and one agent a 0 rating. The rating

had tested the effectiveness of the new law. At a state extension meeting held at the Wade Hampton Hotel in Columbia, a waitress refused to serve Pough. After talking it over with her husband, she wrote to the hotel manager and sent copies to Nutt, President Edwards at Clemson, and her other immediate supervisors. In her letter she threatened to sue the hotel for punitive damages. Nutt responded by trying to intimidate her, but Pough recalled, "I didn't back down not one iota from the director." Nutt talked to the management at the hotel, and Pough received a profuse letter of apology. Nevertheless, she recalled the episode as a "humiliating experience." "I guess you learn to be thick-skinned," she concluded. "I knew it was a new experience for them. . . . I usually tried to be tolerant."[59]

Sara Waymer became a "watchdog" for civil rights violations out of personal conviction and at some professional risk. "I had a strong feeling that 'right is right,' I hoped that if we pointed out that a black agent was being treated unfairly that the federal authorities would back us up." When she went to work at Clemson, Waymer often found that the extension program operated contrary to federal law. But although she and Pough pointed out violations of the law, extension officials responded that they would continue their programs until they were legally challenged.[60]

Before Waymer left State College to move to Clemson in 1965, she began a log of the adjustments Clemson officials would need to implement to comply with the Civil Rights Act of 1964. She kept the log during the two years she worked at Clemson. The list covered all aspects of the extension program. Waymer's notations indicate that extension officials not only failed to make equal opportunity a reality, but that some of the overt vestiges of racial segregation, such as separate entrances for blacks and whites, also remained in place.[61]

Waymer trusted in federal authorities to support her and push for integration. In September 1966 she complained to the Justice Department about an agent who was being treated poorly in one lower-state county. Federal officials came to South Carolina to interview the agent's clients and spent two weeks in the state before Clemson officials became aware that an investigation was under way. When the investigators came to Clemson, they interviewed Pough, who had worked with the agent at one time during the

system may also explain the disparity between black and white salaries despite the adjustments made in the 1950s. See *Clemson University Extension Service*, p. 12.

59. Interview with Rosa Odum et al., pp. 13–16.

60. Ibid., p. 17; telephone conversation with Sara Waymer, May 24, 1993.

61. Interview with Rosa Odum et al., pp. 6–7; "Checklist of Adjustments by Clemson University Extension Service to Comply with Civil Rights Law of 1964," December 30, 1964 (copy marked by Sara Waymer in the author's possession).

1950s. The complaint succeeded, and the agent enjoyed a long career in the extension service. That a black agent could successfully protest unfair treatment marked a "revolution in extension [work]," according to Pough.[62]

Integration, however, did not always work to the benefit of black extension. When she retired in 1959, Marian Paul said that her only regret was that she had not succeeded in having an agent appointed to every county. Her dream was never fulfilled. Indeed postintegration policies worked to erase many vestiges of black institution-building. Some of the projects and organizations that represented decades of labor for black home demonstration were absorbed; most were eliminated. The camps that black home and agricultural agents personally constructed and paid for were turned over to counties for their use or fell into decay. When asked if the fight for integration was worth it, Pough responded: "That all depends on how you look at it. I'll have to say it like that because there are some things that were worthwhile that went out of existence—were not continued and yet other things came in. . . . It all depends on how you look at it. But I think, oh I would think overall, that it was more beneficial."[63]

The black home extension program left many legacies. The agents encouraged 4-H club members, boys and girls, to attend college. Agents established a 4-H student loan program through which club members could borrow money to attend State College. Agent Cammie F. Clagett of Spartanburg County influenced several of her students to attend the college. Pough took State College students into her home, where they worked for their upkeep when they could not afford to live on campus. Many of these 4-H club members went on to hold professional positions in a variety of fields. Club elections, in use since the early 1920s, familiarized blacks with the democratic process and developed leadership skills. Pough noted that as a result of politicking for statewide offices, club members learned lessons that helped them as they moved into government.[64]

These activities and lessons were not the expected outcomes of the Live-at-Home program. Despite the efforts of whites to keep blacks in an economically subordinate position and outside the political arena, agents helped their clients to challenge and not just to survive the system. Waymer recognized that agents were more than just extension workers. "We were leaders in the community. And we did as much on Sunday as on Monday." When state officials forbade agents to organize politically or push openly for integration, they acquiesced, but through the grass-roots leaders they had trained, they encouraged others to carry on the fight. Although they

62. Interview with Rosa Odum et al., pp. 11–12.
63. Ibid., pp. 55–61.
64. Ibid., pp. 40–44.

stood in the shadows of pro-integration leadership, black agents had prepared the troops for battle. Indeed, one might argue that the program ultimately succeeded in its own demise. Although integration by no means
signified full citizenship, Paul's declaration that "an enlightened people
could save themselves" had certainly been demonstrated.

REMINISCENCES | *Genevieve J. Wheeler Thomas*

GENEVIEVE J. WHEELER THOMAS graduated in home economics from Spelman College in Atlanta, Georgia, in 1936. In the midst of the Depression she went to work in home economics education. Thomas recounts her experiences in the communities she served in Georgia and Florida and the accomplishments and frustrations of her later career at Florida A&M, where she served as dean of home economics.

I grew up in an urban area—Atlanta, Georgia—the "Gateway to the South." I received my high school education on the campus of Spelman College. In 1931 the high school was no longer Spelman High School. There are five colleges in Atlanta, and they formed a consortium, the Atlanta University System. Spelman High School became Atlanta University Laboratory High School, and that was where my high school education was completed.

I cannot remember my high school home economics experience as being exciting. Of course, it was cooking and sewing. I remember that I did think that the foods teacher was competent and she provided many worthwhile experiences. She was personable, and I liked her very much. But the clothing teacher left much to be desired. I remember making a dress that I was never able to wear. It was a miserable failure. My mother was horrified that I could not coordinate my feet and hands on a treadle machine since I came from a family of tailors and seamstresses. My great-grandparents and grandparents earned their livelihoods as tailors and seamstresses. My mother was a teacher. I was not living up to the image expected. The Singer Sewing Machine Company sponsored a weekly sewing class, and my mother enrolled me with the promise that she would buy me an electric machine if I would learn to sew.

After completing high school, I enrolled in Spelman College. My high school and college life was spent on this campus. The college girls would tell you, "If you're going to major in anything, major in home economics because that's where the jobs are and that's where you get the most money." This was in the 1930s, and we were just emerging from the Depression as I entered college. So it was economics that directed me into choosing home economics. What options did we have? A black woman could either become a secretary, a nurse, or a teacher. My option was teaching. I was not interested in elementary school teaching. I didn't want to teach English or foreign languages, and I was a poor math student. Because the demand for home economics teachers was great and my knowledge and competencies in this area were good, home economics became my career choice.

Spelman had an excellent home economics department, a beautiful, well-equipped building and very competent teachers. The teachers were graduates of some of the most prestigious universities and colleges of home economics in the United States. Spelman College is a small liberal arts college for colored women that was founded by two New England women. We always had an integrated faculty. I never felt that I was in a women's ghetto. When all of the colleges became a part of the Atlanta University System, we had an exchange of teachers and students. Although I had no men teachers in home economics, I did have men teachers in such courses as psychology, sociology, economics, and physics. Men from Morehouse College, which is adjacent to Spelman, were allowed to come over and take classes with us, and when we were seniors we were allowed to take courses at Morehouse. We did not feel as if we were just women all by ourselves.

My college life was very, very exciting and rewarding. Our home economics department was highly respected. The teachers instilled in us a sense of social responsibility and imbued us with the idea of life for service. Also, at this time, no matter what your major was, you got a teacher's certificate so you had something to fall back on.

When I graduated, I received many offers to teach in small Georgia towns and wouldn't accept any of them because of their location in the state and the salaries offered. My mother finally said to me, "Now you know you have got to work so you'd better take one of these offers." Finally, I received an offer to teach home economics in a small Georgia town for $50 a month (this was the best salary offer). I thought, "Oh goodness, is this the best I am going to do?" Then, at the last minute (I always seemed to get my best jobs on Labor Day), I received a wire from a small Presbyterian junior college in Concord, North Carolina, offering me a job as dietitian. The salary was $75 a month and room and board. I had worked in the dining hall during my senior year, and the dietitians in charge thought I was pretty good so they had recommended me for the job at this little junior college. I worked there in 1936-37. At the end of that year, I knew that dietetics was not for me. When I went to bed at night, I'd dream about loaves of bread and sides of beef that would be delivered in the early morning from Charlotte. The job was confining and limiting. I had no assistance other than students and two cooks. At the end of the year, I quit.

I have been lucky to have people give me pretty good advice. On the advice of the dean of women at Barber-Scotia I went to Teachers College, Columbia University, and began graduate work in 1937. In the fall, I got a high school job in Marietta, Georgia. I loved it. Working with high school students was a joy. It gave me an opportunity to go into the homes of students and really learn about families. But Marietta was just north of Atlanta and not rural; I knew nothing about that kind of life. Each summer, I would go back to Columbia to work on my master's degree. I taught in Marietta for three and one-half years. The last half year I took a leave to finish graduate work. I received an offer to go to Florida A&M College in Tallahassee in the position of resident teacher-trainer in home economics. I think they are now called teacher-educators. This was my first experience with a land-grant college and with agriculture and rural life. Though Tallahassee is not rural, teacher-trainers in agriculture and home economics were required by the U.S. Office of Education to work with rural families. This was my introduction to the extension program. Each summer between the close of the regular college term and the summer session, while all other teachers were getting a break, I had to stay on campus and work with the 4-H club program. I learned a lot about extension.

I think the high point of my career was when I was a teacher-trainer. It was rewarding to watch young people grow and develop into good teachers. Part of my job was to go around the state and follow up on first-year teachers. Also, at times I traveled with the itinerant teacher-trainer to visit in-service teachers. I can recall one time during the war years when I went into a high school home economics class in Ocala, Florida. I had taught all of these young student teachers about what they could do in certain situations. On this particular day, when I walked into the classroom, the teacher said, "Oh, I am so glad you came because I want you to tell me, what do I do with all of these?" She had so many students in her class that they were sitting in the windows. She didn't know what to do. It was encouraging to see teachers so enthusiastic about teaching despite handicaps and about going into homes and learning how families lived. Families were anxious to learn more about how to rear their children and feed their families. It was a wonderful experience. I went to A&M in 1941, at the beginning of World War II. During the war years, we did everything. We made furniture out of baskets and orange crates. We taught Red Cross nursing courses. We helped families learn how to plant gardens so they might feed themselves. During this period in our department the enrollment soared because men had gone off to war and were sending money back so that their sisters could attend college. We had a bumper crop of home economics students.

The second high point of my career came when I was named dean. First I was acting dean, then dean of the Home Economics Division. It was the worst of years; it was the best of years. The worst was that we didn't have much money to operate on. Our physical facilities were limited and inadequate for the large enrollment. But the good part was that the students were so enthusiastic about learning and becoming good home economists. We had an excellent, well-trained faculty who wanted a good program. Fortunately, the president of the college was married to a home economist so he was in tune with our needs and goals and we were able to get a little more money for needed equipment.

We still were in the same old white frame building, but some much needed renovations were made. One of my first goals was to get some good equipment. This we did on some consignment programs offered by manufacturers. Then the next challenge was to revise and improve the curriculum. We had only one curriculum—home economics education. We required our students to take general chemistry, organic chemistry, biology, bacteriology, anatomy, physiology, and physics. What was left to teach in home economics after all that? We were top-heavy in science. We eliminated some of the science so as to add more home economics courses, family-oriented courses, and free electives. Then, we developed the curriculum—clothing and textiles, foods and nutrition, and institutional management. This was indeed a great challenge and it was a joy to see goals come to fruition.

In the 1950s we became Florida A&M University and the autonomy of home economics ended. To get a new building, the legislature decreed that agriculture and home economics be combined. We became the School of Agriculture and Home Economics. Titles were changed. The man who had been dean of agriculture became dean of the school, and I became director of the Division of Home Economics. Later, I was head of the Department of Home Economics. But the wonderful part of the change was that we were getting a new building. Finally, we had all the classrooms, laboratories, and equipment needed for a really good program. All of my energies went into research and planning for this new facility. It was a beautiful, well-equipped, and furnished building. A year after its completion, I left administration and went back to full-time teaching. In 1975 the person heading home economics took a leave, and I was drafted into the position of interim director. But by this time I had just about had it. In the late 1960s and early 1970s enrollment was at an all time low. Students had more career options. In 1977 I retired.

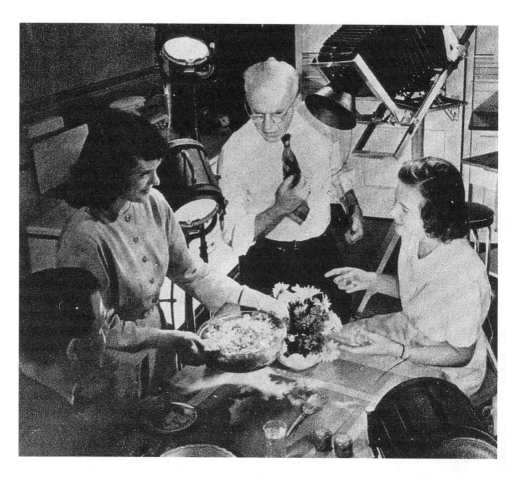

Test kitchen home economists preparing ideal Pyrex meals for photography. "Where Mrs. Homemaker Is Never Forgotten: Consumer Products Division's Proving Ground for Corning Glassware," *Corning Glass Works Gaffer* 4 (October 1946): 3, courtesy of the Corning, Incorporated, Department of Archives and Records Management, Corning, New York.

Who Speaks for the Consumer? Home Economics and Business

In 1924 the American Home Economics Association created a special section called Home Economics in Business. During the 1920s a significant number of home economists entered business and industry in consumer relations, marketing, product development, testing, and demonstration. Acting as liaisons between the company and the consumer, they faced the dilemma of serving two constituencies. As home economics professionals they tried to resolve the tension by emphasizing education over selling—educating companies to the needs of women consumers and educating women in the use of the latest household technologies.

Ronald Kline styles home economists as "agents of modernity," referring specifically to the women who worked to introduce rural electricity. Like most Americans in the period between the world wars, they uncritically accepted technology as a boon. Certainly many farm women welcomed the electricity that powered water pumps that put an end to hauling and radios that helped to end isolation. As Kline points out, however, utility companies and cooperatives, eager to sell more and more electricity, used home economists to convince farm families to purchase expensive and sometimes unnecessary appliances.

Certainly many businesses, like the utility companies, saw the role of home economists as nothing more than "Selling Mrs. Consumer." Christine Frederick, an early spokesperson for scientific management, published a best-seller with that title in 1929. Home economics, which expanded into business and industry at the same time as the rise of public relations, modern advertising, and marketing, risked having its mission confused and conflated with theirs.

Gender stereotypes also led to confusion over who actually was a home economist. Businesses, quick to realize that it paid to have links with the consumer, often assumed that any woman could act as a home economist. Christine Frederick was widely cited as a home economist although she had no formal training in the field. Some businesses established so-called home economics departments staffed by women with no training in home economics. The AHEA compounded the problem. Unlike other professional organizations such as the American Dietetics Association, which set standards and demanded specific professional qualifications including college preparation for membership, the AHEA welcomed all comers into its ranks. Women who worked in business but had no training in home economics could claim professional affiliation. Trained home economists, for their part, yielded to the temptation to sell themselves to business for their supposed ability to "Sell Mrs. Consumer." In this setting it is not surprising that home economists drew criticism as being little more than company flacks.

As Lisa Mae Robinson points out, however, Mary Engle Pennington fought a losing battle with her employer, the National Association of Ice Industries, to improve the ice refrigerator. Her career was motivated by a commitment to safe food storage, not increased refrigerator sales. Carolyn Goldstein styles home economists as "diplomats in the marketplace" who tried hard to preserve the distinction between selling and educating.

Satenig St.Marie, a home economist who succeeded in business, becoming a vice-president with JCPenney Company, recalls in her reminiscences how she brought her home economics training to bear in consumer relations.

11 Agents of Modernity: Home Economists and Rural Electrification, 1925–1950

RONALD R. KLINE

A popular view of the social importance of rural electrification in the Great Depression is shown by a scissors picture published in *Survey* magazine in 1932 (see Figure 11.1). The top panel depicts the hardships of life on the farm before electricity. On the left, an anemic-looking cow gives milk to a farmer, hunched over by the drudgery of his daily toil. A chicken and rooster listlessly stare at the meager production of one egg. In the house, lit by a kerosene lamp, a tired farmwife scrubs clothes near a hot, menacing stove, while her little boy and his dog demand attention. In the second panel, these actors pull back in fear and apprehension as the kilowatts come into their life.

The third panel shows life with electricity. The cow now dances with joy, hooked up to a milking machine in a well-lit barn; the rooster and hen proudly lead a parade of eggs the hen has produced. In the brightly lit home, electricity pumps water, cooks a meal, toasts bread, and makes coffee, while a contented washing machine burps soap bubbles. Where are all the people and the dog? They are in the bottom panel, relaxing in rocking chairs, cooled by electric fans. Subtle signs of urbanization are evident. The boy is now a little scholar with glasses, and the wife is fashionably attired and reads the paper. The farmer snores in luxurious comfort.[1]

I would like to thank Kathleen Babbitt, Chris London, Margaret Rossiter, and the editors of this volume for their helpful suggestions on earlier drafts of this essay, Gould Colman for his research assistance in the Cornell University Archives, archivists at the Franklin D. Roosevelt Library and the National Archives, and Joan Brumberg for encouraging me to pursue this topic.

1. Morris L. Cooke, "Light and Power: Planning the Electrical Future," *Survey* 67 (1932): 608–9. Martha Bruere and her husband, Robert, had published a prewar series of articles on

Figure 11.1. "Current comes to the farm. 1. The not-so-good old days. 2. The K. W. H.'s are coming! 3. The well equipped farm. 4. More power to their elbow." *Survey* 67 (1932) : 608–9, copyright 1932 by Survey Associates, Inc., New York.

The drawing, of course, presents an extreme and distorted view. The evidence we have indicates that farm life for most people was not that bad before electricity and not utopian afterward. What the drawing does show is a widespread, progressive view of electricity, an ideology shared by such diverse groups as prominent farm women, novelists, industrial leaders, and politicians on the Left and the Right. They—and, presumably, the public— saw electricity as a modernizing force that would clean up the cities, improve the home, make rural life more satisfying, and decentralize industry by enabling factories to be located away from major urban centers.[2]

Supporting this utopian vision was the Country Life movement, which began with the influential Country Life Commission called by President Theodore Roosevelt in 1908. Led by Liberty Hyde Bailey, director of the College of Agriculture at Cornell University, and other agrarian reformers, the movement's ideal of using expert knowledge to raise the rural standard of living was incorporated into the Smith-Lever Act of 1914, which established the present system of county agricultural and home demonstration agents. In many articles, books, and conferences, Country Lifers in academia, government, and industry called for the rural adoption of such urbanizing inventions as good roads, running water, and electricity to improve the life of farm men and, especially, farm women and thus halt the worrisome migration from country to city.[3]

In this essay I discuss an important group of people left out of the scissors picture: the large number of home economists who worked in a vast network of manufacturers, utility companies, state colleges, government agencies, and farm cooperatives to electrify rural America. Similar to the "corporate-rural network" described by historian Olivier Zunz for the railroad, reaper, automobile, and sewing machine, the rural electrification network was a complex web in which no one group prevailed, but all served a common goal in the end.[4] Zunz's networks included rural agents who mediated between their distant employers and local customers; the analo-

---

their survey of rural conditions, "The Revolt of the Farmer's Wife," *Harper's Bazaar*, November 1912 to May 1913.

2. See James W. Carey and John J. Quirk, "The Mythos of the Electronic Revolution," *American Scholar* 39 (1970): 219–41, 395–424; Thomas P. Hughes, "The Industrial Revolution that Never Came," *American Heritage of Invention and Technology* 3 (Winter 1988): 58–64; Ronald Kline, *Steinmetz: Engineer and Socialist* (Baltimore: Johns Hopkins University Press, 1992), pp. 252–61; and *Rural Electrification News*, September 1935, p. 20.

3. *Report of the Commission on Country Life*, introduction by Theodore Roosevelt (New York, 1971), esp. pp. 103–6; William L. Bowers, *The Country Life Movement in America, 1900–1920* (Port Washington, N.Y.: Kennikat Press, 1974); and David B. Danbom, *The Resisted Revolution: Urban America and the Industrialization of Agriculture, 1900–1930* (Ames: Iowa State University Press, 1979), pp. 25–47, 62–63.

4. Olivier Zunz, *Making America Corporate, 1870–1920* (Chicago: University of Chicago Press, 1990), chap. 6.

gous group in rural electrification consisted of home demonstration agents in the U.S. Department of Agriculture Extension Service and other home economists who worked for utility companies and federal agencies. These professionals served as "agents of modernity," literally and figuratively. They acted on their belief in the progressive ideology of electricity as they helped transfer this technology from an urban to a rural culture. Yet in the process of "educating" their clients—of persuading them to sign up for electricity and buy more appliances once they were hooked up to the network—home economists faced dilemmas about a presumably neutral professional promoting a specific technology and the puzzling fact that many farm people resisted their efforts.

In examining the role of home economists in the crucial early years of the rural electrification program, we should recall that the pace of electrification in the United States was not rapid. It was not until 1925, nearly a half-century after Thomas Edison and his co-workers built their first commercial central station, that more than one-half of U.S. homes had electricity (1921 for urban dwellings). According to historian David Nye, "utilities and electric corporations were slow to exploit the domestic market because they saw greater profits elsewhere," namely in street lighting, streetcars, and factories.[5] It is not surprising, then, that they were even slower to develop the rural market, which had a much lower population density and less disposable income than urban areas.

In 1923 the industry established the national Committee on the Relation of Electricity to Agriculture (CREA) to study the matter. Consisting of representatives from agricultural colleges, manufacturers, farm organizations, and other groups, the CREA discovered many rural uses for electricity in several state projects. Yet only 10 percent of American farms had central-station electricity by 1935, a figure that masked the wide variation by region: from 1 percent to 8 percent in the South to over 50 percent in western states such as California that were dependent on irrigation for their agriculture.[6] Matters did not improve until President Franklin Roosevelt established the Tennessee Valley Authority (TVA) in 1933, which built and operated a massive flood-control and hydroelectric project, and the Rural Electrification Administration (REA) two years later. Headed by the progressive reformer and engineer Morris Cooke, the REA's threat to provide public power stimulated utilities to build rural lines, and it ran a successful program of loaning money at favorable terms to rural cooperatives. Under close REA supervision, hundreds of

---

5. U.S. Bureau of the Census, *The Statistical History of the United States from Colonial Times to the Present*, 2 vols., rev. ed. (Stamford, Conn.: Fairfield Publishers, 1965), 1:510; and David E. Nye, *Electrifying America: Social Meanings of a New Technology, 1880–1940* (Cambridge: MIT Press, 1990), p. 277.

6. *Rural Electrification News*, March 1936, p. 16.

co-ops were formed to generate power or buy it wholesale from utilities, then distribute it on REA-designed lines the co-op had built to people who used REA loans to wire their houses and buy appliances. Upon becoming part of the U.S. Department of Agriculture in 1939, the REA and that agency's extension service became part of an extended network of public and private agencies that brought electricity to rural people.[7]

Home economists played a significant role in this network, just as they did in electrifying urban homes during the 1920s and 1930s. During these banner years for home economics, utility companies felt compelled to increase domestic sales of electricity to make more profitable daytime use of their plants. They thus hired home economists to conduct demonstrations of electrical appliances, run classes on electric cooking, make home visits to customers, and so forth. Electrical manufacturers such as General Electric and Westinghouse also hired home economists to give advice on the design and marketing of appliances.[8]

The growing demand for home economists in this new field can be seen in the career of Eloise Davison. A professor of home economics at Iowa State College, she became, in 1925, the first representative of the American Home Economics Association to the CREA. While at Iowa, she studied the use of household appliances on a CREA project and taught a course for home economists employed by electrical manufacturers and utility companies. She then joined the powerful trade group the National Electric Light Association (NELA) in 1928, the same year the NELA recommended that its member utilities hire home economists to help develop the domestic market. She left the NELA to become a consultant in New York City, then switched to government work in 1935 and started an educational program for the Electric Home and Farm Authority (EHFA), an appliance-purchasing agency set up in the TVA area. Although her career is undoubtedly atypical in the number of varied and high positions she held, it does illustrate the range of jobs open to home economists in the electrical field.[9]

7. D. Clayton Brown, *Electricity for Rural America: The Fight for the REA* (Westport, Conn.: Greenwood Press, 1980); and Philip J. Funigiello, *Toward a National Power Policy: The New Deal and the Electric Utility Industry, 1933–1941* (Pittsburgh: University of Pittsburgh Press, 1973).

8. Nye, *Electrifying America,* pp. 238–39, 254–59, 268–77, 386. On the growth of home economics in this period, see Barbara Ehrenreich and Deirdre English, *For Her Own Good: 150 Years of the Experts' Advice to Women* (New York: Doubleday, 1978), chap. 5; and Margaret W. Rossiter, *Women Scientists in America: Struggles and Strategies to 1940* (Baltimore: Johns Hopkins University Press, 1982), pp. 200–201, 258–59.

9. Eloise Davison, "Electricity and the Farm Home," *Journal of Home Economics* 18 (April 1926): 215–16; Davison, "Iowa's Rural Community for Electrical Development," *CREA Bulletin,* May 12, 1926, p. 3; Davison, "Electrical Equipment Short Course," *CREA Bulletin,* June 15, 1927, p. 7; Louise Stanley, "Home Economics and Rural Electrification," *Journal of Home Economics* 28 (October 1936): 559–60; and Iona R. Logie, ed., *Careers in the Making,* 2d ed. (New York: Harper & Brothers, 1942), pp. 145–51.

Ironically, the REA, whose public-power supporters had severely criticized the privately owned utilities for their corrupt financial practices, adopted many of the sales strategies of its opponents. Like its foes, the REA came to understand the importance of using home economists to develop the domestic market because it realized that co-ops would not be able to pay off their loans if farmers purchased only "lights," irons, and radios, which they tended to do. The REA then emulated the utilities and embarked on an extensive load-building campaign in 1937 to sell appliances. A new Utilization Division, headed by George Munger from the EHFA, hired a well-trained field staff of agricultural engineers and home economists, most of whom had been county extension agents. Chief home economist Clara Nale, for example, came from the TVA after a stint with the Alabama extension service. Nale was so successful in her recruiting that the USDA's Bureau of Home Economics complained in 1939 that she had hired nearly all of the nation's home economists who had extension experience and technical training in electrical household equipment.[10] In their work for the REA, the former agents used the traditional methods of extension (bulletins, pamphlets, film strips, skits, and demonstrations, including exhibition farms and kitchen parties) but usually worked with large groups because only seventeen home economists covered the entire country at the peak of the prewar program.[11]

A major promotional effort was the REA's Farm Equipment Tour, a popular traveling exhibition of appliances displayed under huge circus tents. Crowds ranging from under a thousand to ten times that number watched manufacturers' representatives operate such interesting devices as a rotating drum with rubber "fingers" that plucked chickens. REA home economists gave lighting, cooking, and housecleaning demonstrations and ran the lucrative lunch tent, much as their colleagues did at county and state fairs. The leaders of the REA forged close ties with manufacturers and dealers, who exhibited their equipment on the tour, so as to sell enough elec-

10. REA, *Annual Report, 1937*, pp. 70–71; John Carmody to Glenn W. Pherigo, April 23, 1937, John M. Carmody Papers, Franklin D. Roosevelt Library, Hyde Park, N.Y. (hereafter JMC); Carmody to Morris Cooke, June 28, 1937, Box 147, Morris L. Cooke Papers, Franklin D. Roosevelt Library, Hyde Park, N.Y., *Rural Electrification News;* February 1938, pp. 5–6; Clara O. Nale, "Home Economics in the Field of Rural Electrification," *Journal of Home Economics* 30 (April 1938): 223–25, biographical information on p. 288; and an address by Lenore Sater in "Rural Electrification Administration Annual Administrative Conference of Staff and Field Personnel," January 9–13, 1939, p. 581, Box 91, JMC.

11. "Utilization Division Field Staff," November 1, 1939, Entry 17, Box 4, Records of the Rural Electrification Administration, Record Group 221, National Archives (hereafter RREA). The kitchen parties had an air of "keeping up with the Joneses." See *Rural Electrification News,* July 1938, pp. 20–21, and December 1939, pp. 3–5.

trical appliances to make the co-ops profitable.[12] Events inaugurating an electric line had a similar function, and REA home economists created skits and pole-raising ceremonies to sell the progressive virtues of electricity at these affairs.[13]

Much of their promotional material employed gender-related schemes aimed at farm men, who usually controlled the purse strings. The ploy of having prominent men in the community, including the head of the co-op, don aprons and do the cooking at an REA annual meeting was a popular attraction. The message was that cooking with electricity was so easy that even a man could do it.[14] In another event, supported by the REA, the journal *Prairie Farmer* sponsored a Men Folks' Washday in Wisconsin in 1937. The assumption was that once farm men experienced the backbreaking work of hauling water and scrubbing clothes by hand, they would buy their spouses an electric washing machine.[15] Several cartoons that appeared in the *Rural Electrification News* and were made available to publishers reflected the perceived rural system of patriarchy and gave credit to the husband for buying the "tired farm wife" such labor-saving devices as water pumps, electric ranges, washing machines, and vacuum cleaners. In only one of the twelve cartoons published from 1938 to 1939 did a woman have the idea to electrify her house and that was to provide running water for her husband's bath so that he would no longer slip and fall out of a tub on a soapy kitchen floor.[16] In fact, women may have had more power over these purchases than these cartoons implied.

The REA received some help from home demonstration agents in the extension service, many of whom had cooperated with the agency before it merged with the USDA in 1939. Farm and home agents helped organize co-ops in thirty-four states by 1940.[17] REA home economists trained extension agents, and the director of the extension service encouraged the two groups to work together. Although many agents were hired in this period to handle the New Deal agricultural programs, more help was needed because of the big jump in rural electrification. The number of families installing electricity per home agent, for example, rose from five in 1930 to

12. REA, *Annual Report, 1939*, pp. 76–80; *Rural Electrification News*, December 1938, pp. 3–6; October 1939, pp. 6–8; January 1940, p. 16; June 1940, pp. 7–9; "1939 Farm Equipment Tour Itinerary—Revised," November 21, 1939; D. W. Teare to Oscar Meier, March 13, 1941, and Teare to C. A. Winder, August 25, 1941, Entry 76, Box 2, RREA.

13. *Rural Electrification News*, November 1938, pp. 3–13, 18–19, 29.

14. *Rural Electrification News*, August 1939, cover.

15. See, for example, *Rural Electrification News*, July 1937, pp. 7–8.

16. See the back pages of *Rural Electrification News*, October 1938, January, February, May, and July 1939 (bath scene).

17. Harold H. Beaty, "Summary of Letters from Extension Service Directors," November 4, 1940, Entry 76, Box 3, RREA.

seventy in 1940.[18] After the merger, Clara Nale worked with the Bureau of Home Economics to develop educational film strips, even though she thought the bureau was focused too much on long-term research and was "under the direction of people who are too far removed from the field of rural electrification and its attendant problems to be of much help in a program that is as new and widespread as REA is." Milburn L. Wilson, the new director of the extension service, praised REA's annual reports and sent them to all state directors. Wilson also supported the appointment of former county agent Oscar Meier as the liaison between REA and the extension service in 1940.[19]

As head of REA's Cooperatives' Education Section (which took over the functions of the Utilization Division), Meier attended to the problems of poor farmers by promoting self-help wiring programs and criticizing REA personnel for concentrating on the upper two-thirds of farmers traditionally served by the Farm Bureau and the extension service. He worked with 4-H clubs, encouraged REA field staff to cooperate with county agents, and persuaded the extension service to hire state rural electrification specialists. In the spring of 1941, he moved six field home economists to his Washington office to develop programs in the areas of lighting, kitchen design, laundry equipment, school electrification, 4-H clubs, and the Farm Tour.[20] The entry of the United States into World War II in December 1941 halted most of REA's efforts. Meier joined the War Production Board, Oneta Liter and two other home economists were loaned to the Bureau of Home Economics to do research on food conservation, and the Farm Tour was canceled because of the lack of rubber tires for its trucks. REA's educational plans were put on hold until it started building rural lines in earnest after the war. The agency then encouraged co-ops to hire home economists, which many did during the postwar consumer boom.[21]

18. *Rural Electrification News,* November 1936, p. 30; December 1936, pp. 22–23; Florence L. Hall, *Report of Home Demonstration Work, 1937,* USDA Extension Service Circular 294, November 1938, p. 2; C. W. Warburton, *Aims and Objectives of Home Demonstration Work,* USDA Extension Service Circular 265, June 1937; address by Warburton in "REA Annual Conference, 1939," pp. 547–59; Gladys Gallup and Florence L. Hall, *Progress in Home Demonstration Work,* USDA Extension Circular 319, February 1940; and Gallup, "The Effectiveness of the Home Demonstration Program of the Cooperative Extension Service of the United States Department of Agriculture in Reaching Rural People and in Meeting Their Needs" (Ph.D. dissertation, George Washington University, 1943), p. 133.

19. Oscar Meier to Clara Nale, et al., September 20, 1940; M. L. Wilson to All Extension Directors, April 16 and July 1, 1940, Entry 17, Box 4, RREA; and Nale to C. A. Winder, December 16, 1940, Entry 76, Box 1, RREA.

20. Oscar Meier to Robert Craig, June 5, 1940; Meier to George Munger, July 27, 1940; Meier to M. L. Ramsay, August 14 and September 19, 1940; Meier, "Social Aims of the Electrification Program, National Standpoint," November 16, 1940; Meier to C. A. Winder, February 18, 1941, Entry 17, Box 4, RREA; and Meier to Winder, December 6, 1940 and January 18, 1941, Entry 76, Box 3, RREA.

21. Oscar Meier to M. M. Samuels, January 13, 1942; Meier to C. A. Winder, February 2, 1942, Entry 76, Box 1, RREA; Meier to Harry Slattery, February 24, 1942, Entry 17, Box 4, RREA;

Although the REA and the extension service cooperated on many fronts, it was an uneasy partnership before the war. Extension directors complained that REA field representatives did not always work with county agents, and the REA noted that many agents neglected the co-ops after they helped organize them. One factor was the "inexperience of home demonstration agents with electric household equipment," an endemic problem in the profession. Some agents were also criticized by their superiors for helping to organize co-ops.[22] That sentiment was particularly strong in New York, where that state's Public Service Commission, the Empire State Gas and Electric Association (a utility group), Cornell University's colleges of agriculture and home economics, and farm organizations cooperated to run their own rural electrification program and minimize REA's influence in the state. The leaders of these groups, for a variety of reasons, shared an ideological opposition to the long-term central planning aspects of many New Deal agencies, which they considered to be economically unsound and insidious forms of government control. The REA loaned a substantial amount of money to the New York State Electric and Gas Corporation for rural line extensions, then established six co-ops in the early 1940s, after it became dissatisfied with the utility company's rural programs.[23]

Located at public nodes between the producer and the consumer in this network, home economists faced a dilemma. Although their profession stressed adult education, manufacturers, utilities, and the REA hired them to "educate" rural folk to use more electricity, resulting in a divided loyalty between professional ideals and business demands similar to that described by historian Edwin Layton for salaried engineers in this period. Like other occupations that were professionalizing at the turn of the century, engineering established professional societies, journals, and educational programs that emulated the ideals and structure of the older professions and the physical sciences. Civil engineers had been largely self-employed, as were the prototypical professionals, doctors, and lawyers. But most engi-

REA, *Annual Report, 1942*, p. 6; REA, *Annual Report, 1945*, pp. 12, 18; *Journal of Home Economics* 38 (April 1946): 230; REA, *Annual Report, 1950*, pp. 39–40; and REA, *Annual Report 1951*, pp. 41–42.

22. Beaty, "Summary of Letters"; and Udo Rall, "The REA Program and the Extension Service," June 3, 1941, quotation on p. 4, Entry 76, Box 1, RREA.

23. Lincoln Kelsey to Specialists and Others in the Colleges of Agriculture and Home Economics, April 3, 1936, College of Home Economics Papers, Division of Rare Books and Manuscript Collections, Cornell University Library (hereafter CHE); *Rural Electrification News*, July 1936, pp. 16–18; Kelsey to L. R. Simons, July 27, 1936, Carl E. Ladd Papers, Division of Rare Books and Manuscript Collections, Cornell University Library, Box 11; J. P. Schaenzer, "Coordinated Rural Electrification Activities in the State of New York," *CREA Newsletter*, June 1938, pp. 4–11; Harry Slattery to David Smith, August 8, 1940, Box 25, Slattery Files, RREA; *Rural Electrification News*, September 1943, p. 14; and Gould P. Colman, *Education and Agriculture: A History of the New York State College of Agriculture at Cornell University* (Ithaca: Cornell University Press, 1963), pp. 414–28.

neers in the early twentieth century, especially mechanical and electrical engineers, tended to work for large companies, where employers often pressured them to violate the norms of their profession such as keeping research results secret and giving expert opinions in favor of the employer's product.[24] As salaried professionals, home economists faced similar problems when they began to work for electrical manufacturers, utilities, and government agencies in the 1920s.

A member of Meier's staff noted this predicament in 1941: "County agents, being educators, have been alienated by REA co-op's disregard of the educational approach in favor of a commercialized selling and load building program with a close dealer tie-up."[25] Although increased rural electrification was also a goal of the extension service,[26] many of its home economists followed a time-honored tradition in their field and discussed the relative merits of several types of household appliances. An Alabama agent, for example, suggested how consumers could make technical and economic comparisons between gas, kerosene, and electric refrigerators. Home economists also were aware that many of their clients had less cash income than city folk. A Tennessee agent declared in 1936 that "much poor lighting is due to lack of forethought and care rather than a lack of electricity." Louise Peet, a specialist in household appliances and professor of home economics at Iowa State University, wrote an article in 1944 on how to improve kerosene and gas-mantle lamps because a "large percentage of farm homes are still dependent on liquid fuels for light."[27]

Home economists at Cornell faced a particularly difficult situation because of the close association between utility companies and the university. Seeing rural electrification as a means to carry out the goals of the Country Life movement and to strengthen its expertise in household technology, the Cornell home economics department encouraged Professor Florence Wright and her colleagues to develop the new field as they would any other, by teaching classes, writing pamphlets, and training extension agents. They also conducted statewide electrification meetings in conjunction with the home service directors from utility companies from 1936 to 1939. Wright, who served on the university committee that coordinated the rural electrification program in the state, was fully aware of potential conflicts of inter-

24. See Claire Gilbert, "The Development of Selected Aspects of Home Demonstration Work in the United States" (Ph.D. dissertation, Cornell University, 1958); and Edwin T. Layton, Jr., "Science, Business, and American Engineering," in *The Engineers and the Social System,* ed. Robert E. Perrucci and Joel E. Gerstl (New York, 1969), pp. 51–72.

25. Rall, "The REA Program and the Extension Service," p. 3.

26. Gilbert, "Development of Selected Aspects of Home Demonstration Work," p. 131.

27. Nell Pickens, "Farm Home Refrigeration," *Progressive Farmer,* June 1935, p. 24; Lillian L. Keller, "Farm Home Lights," *Progressive Farmer,* December 1936, p. 48; Louise J. Peet and Ruth Pratt Koch, "Lighting the Home with Liquid Fuels," *Journal of Home Economics* 36 (June 1944): 354.

est and sought to avoid them. In a 1936 paper read before the American Society of Agricultural Engineers, she said that she always made it clear to utility company home economists "that when working on a program with us they must keep entirely on an educational basis."[28]

How did rural people respond to the electrification program? Although the data are fragmentary, the broad outlines of their response are clear. First, there seems to have been a large demand for electricity among rural people. An Iowa man wrote the REA in 1936, "We farmers in Cedar County want and need electricity. Electricity is something I have been dreaming of for a long time." An Indiana woman was overheard to exclaim at an REA meeting in 1935, "Daddy had better sign up or things are going to get hot around here . . . This is one time when he is going to make up his mind in a hurry." That same year, the REA published excerpts of "hundreds of letters" from farm women who wanted electricity.[29] Because women were the primary users of electricity on the farm before the war, the REA created a joint membership policy for husband and wife, and its home economists encouraged women to participate in the organization. Women served on the boards of several co-ops, and two co-ops in Illinois and Louisiana elected women presidents before the war.[30]

Yet many farm men resisted the new technology, just as the previous generation had opposed the noisy and dangerous automobile at the turn of the century.[31] Although thousands flocked to the Farm Tour, hundreds did not trust a New Deal agency, did not join a co-op for fear of losing their farms if the co-op failed, did not give a right-of-way across their fields because it would interfere with the plowing, and did not sign up and pay the $5 to $10 membership fee because of financial reasons, fear of electricity, and other reasons. Many signed under pressure from their neighbors or spouse and

28. Lincoln Kelsey to Extension Staff Members, April 15, 1936, Box 35, CHE; Florence E. Wright, "Rural Home Lighting Problems," paper presented to the American Society of Agricultural Engineers, October 15–17, 1936, copy in New York State College of Home Economics, *Annual Report, 1936*, part 2, quotation on p. 2; and Ruth B. Comstock, "A College and a Utility Cooperate on Home Lighting," *Electrical Merchandising*, December 1939, pp. 14–15, 44.

29. Elwood P. Hain to Boyd Fisher, n.d. [ca. April 12, 1936], Entry 3, Reel 23, RREA; and *Rural Electrification News*, October 1935, pp. 16–18, 25 (quotation).

30. C. A. Winder to All REA Cooperatives, March 8, 1940, Entry 88, Box 10, RREA; *Rural Electrification News*, October 1939, p. 19; remarks by Clara Nale in "REA Annual Conference, 1939," p. 629; and Gary A. Donaldson, "A History of Louisiana's Rural Electric Cooperatives, 1937–1983" (Ph.D. dissertation, Louisiana State University 1983), p. 128. For examples of other women on co-op boards, see Harold Severson, *Architects of Rural Progress* (Springfield: Association of Illinois Electric Cooperatives, ca. 1965), p. 139; Kenneth E. Merrill, *Kansas Rural Electric Cooperatives: Twenty Years with the REA* (Lawrence, Kan.: Center for Research in Business, University of Kansas, 1960), pp. 140, 144, 147, 170–71; and Delaware County (N.Y.) Electric Cooperative, Board of Trustees Minutes, December 6, 1943, Entry 77, Box 94, RREA.

31. See Reynold M. Wik, *Henry Ford and Grass-Roots America* (Ann Arbor: University of Michigan Press, 1972), pp. 15–17; and Michael Berger, *The Devil Wagon in God's Country: The Automobile and Social Change in Rural America, 1893–1929* (Hamden, Conn.: Archon Books, 1979), pp. 16–28.

installed only lights.[32] A brightly lit farmhouse (along with the previous urbanizing inventions of the telephone, automobile, and radio) showed that its owners were not the hicks city people joked about when they made fun of primitive life in the country.[33]

An indication of the rural response to the new technology is given by surveys of newly electrified farms on REA lines (see Table 11.1). The data re-

TABLE 11.1. Appliance ownership of newly electrified
REA farms, in percent

	1938	1939	1940	1941
Radio	86	82	88	90
Iron	81	84	84	85
Washing machine	47	59	55	55
Refrigerator	26	32	33	42
Toaster	24	31	29	32
Vacuum cleaner	16	21	21	21
Hot plate	12	19	15	15
Coffee maker	6.0	6.3	7.9	8.9
Water closet	—	6.4	6.2	6.3
Range	5.0	3.1	4.2	4.4
Water pump	17	19	15	18
Motors < 1 horsepower	9.0	18	15	15
Cream separator	5.0	14	7.5	8.2
Chicken brooder	1.0	3.2	4.2	6.7
Milking machine	2.0	3.8	2.1	2.6

Sources: Rural Electrification News, July 1938, pp. 4–10; January 1940, pp. 6–8; October 1940, pp. 10–11; and J. Stewart Wilson to Robert Craig et al., August 8, 1941, entry 17, box 4, RREA.

Notes: Figures are rounded to two significant places. The number of projects in each survey varied from 46 (1938) to 123 (1939), the average length of service from 8.4 months (1938) to 19.3 months (1941), the number of customers responding from 17,100 (1938) to 70,893 (1941), and the percentage responding from 63.5 (1938) to 68.8 (1939).

32. See, for example, William Nivison to John Carmody, November 5, 1937, Victoria Harris to Carmody, November 6, 1937, Thelma Wilson to Carmody, November 7, 1937, Mary Taylor to Carmody, November 8, 1937, Box 84, JMC; E. F. Chestnut, "Rural Electrification in Arkansas, 1935–1940: The Formative Years," *Arkansas Historical Quarterly* 46 (1987): 215–60; Harold Severson, *Corn Belt: A Pioneer in Cooperative Power Production* (Humboldt, Iowa: Corn Belt Power Cooperative, 1972), pp. 39, 85, 119, 130, 136; Severson, *Determination Turned on the Power: A History of the Eastern Iowa Light and Power Company* (N.d.: N.p., 1964), pp. 16–17, 24–28, 32; D. Jerome Tweton, *The New Deal at the Grass Roots: Programs for the People in Otter Tail County, Minnesota* (St. Paul: Minnesota Historical Society Press, 1988), chap. 9; Robert A. Caro, *The Years of Lyndon Johnson*, vol. 1 (New York: Random House, 1982), chap. 28; and Lemont K. Richardson, *Wisconsin REA: The Struggle to Extend Electricity to Rural Wisconsin, 1935–1955* (Madison: University of Wisconsin Experiment Station, 1961), pp. 44–47. On wanting mainly

veal a remarkable consistency in which appliances were first purchased from 1938 to 1941. (Since the order is not based simply on price, the list also gives an idea of which appliances were valued on the farm.) Despite increased farm income in this period and the best efforts of REA agents, new co-op members bought mainly radios, irons, and washing machines. These were familiar appliances that prosperous farmers had run on either batteries or gasoline before they had electricity. The woman got the better end of the bargain than her spouse because there was little electrical equipment for the barn. Other items that had more of an urban aura such as vacuum cleaners and coffee makers were seen as "foolish luxuries."[34] Table 11.2 illustrates this urban-rural contrast. The percentage of new REA customers buying radios, irons, washing machines, and hot plates in 1940 was comparable to the national figures for these goods. Yet rural people purchased

TABLE 11.2. National vs. REA ownership of selected appliances, in percent

	U.S. wired homes 1940	New REA customers 1940
Iron	95	84
Radio	81[a]	88
Washing machine	60	55
Refrigerator	56	33
Toaster	56	29
Vacuum cleaner	48	21
Coffee maker	33	7.9
Hot plate	17	15
Range	10	4.2

Sources: Electrical Merchandizing, January 1940, pp. 10, 14–15; and *Rural Electrification News*, October 1940, pp. 10–11.

Notes: Figures are rounded to two significant places. The number of wired homes in the United States was 22.7 million urban and rural non farm, plus 1.8 million farms. The number of new REA customers was 43,000.

[a]Pecentage of total households (wired and non wired), caculated from U.S. Bureau of Census, *Historical Statistics of the United States, Colonial Times to 1970* (1970; rpt. New York: Basic Books, 1976), Ser. A 320-349 (p. 42), and Ser. R 93-105 (p. 796).

"lights," see Dora B. Haines and Udo Rall, "The Place and Function of an REA Educational Program," October 4, 1939, Entry 76, Box 1, RREA.

33. See Don S. Kirschner, *City and Country: Rural Responses to Urbanization in the 1920s* (Westport, Conn.: Greenwood Press, 1970); and James H. Shideler, "Flappers and Philosophers and Farmers: Rural-Urban Tensions of the Twenties," *Agricultural History* 47 (1973): 283–99.

34. William Nivison to John Carmody, November 5, 1937, Box 84 (quotation), JMC.

fewer refrigerators, toasters, vacuum cleaners, and coffee makers. The expensive electric range was unpopular in town and on the farm.[35]

Radios were popular in the country because they relieved isolation; irons and washing machines made household work easier. Yet the effects of using these and other home appliances supports the thesis of historian Ruth Cowan in *More Work for Mother*. The so-called labor-saving devices for the home tended to save the work of men and boys more than women and did not reduce the amount of time spent on housework. Ironically, the "agents of modernity" thus helped transfer a technology that had many unintended effects on rural life. Clara Nale noted this phenomenon in 1937: "In using an electric range, the farm wife is greatly reducing the amount of work necessary for her husband in felling trees and sawing and splitting the logs, as well as eliminating work for herself." Yet Nale argued that this was a selling point, not a detriment to her clients, because she thought the range freed both sexes for other farmwork.[36]

Nale found that rural people were unpredictable. A survey of ten Ohio co-ops showed that 40 percent of families had purchased vacuum cleaners but only 17 percent had bought water systems, even though salespeople at equipment dealers and the REA offices seem to have pushed both appliances equally hard. Nale thought farm women should plan better. They should save their money for a labor-saving water pump rather than buy a vacuum cleaner when they had "comparatively few rugs."[37] The paternalism in Nale's plea was also evident when she wrote that "it is the privilege of home economists to study this program in all its broadest implications and to *interpret* its possibilities to the rural homemakers of America."[38]

By interpreting the artifacts of rural people for them in their best interests, home economists and agricultural engineers did not always endear themselves to a social group known for its pride and independence. Although rural people appreciated information on wiring the farmstead, selecting appliances, and repairing them, they probably resented the occasional humorous article in the *Rural Electrification News* on farmers'

35. See also Jane Busch, "Cooking Competition: Technology in the Domestic Market in the 1930s," *Technology and Culture* 24 (1983): 222–45; and Mark Rose, "Urban Environments and Technological Innovation: Energy Choices in Denver and Kansas City, 1900–1940." *Technology and Culture* 25 (1984): 503–39.

36. Reynold M. Wik, "The Radio in Rural America during the 1920s," *Agricultural History* 55 (1981): 339–50; Ruth Schwartz Cowan, *More Work for Mother: The Ironies of Household Technology from the Open Hearth to the Microwave* (New York: Basic Books, 1983); and Clara Nale, "Electric Aids for Farm Wife Make Her Self-Sufficient," *Rural Electrification News*, December 1937, p. 9.

37. Clara Nale, "Interesting Farm Women in Rural Electrification," paper presented to the American Society of Agricultural Engineers, June 22, 1939, p. 2, copy in USDA National Agricultural Library, Beltsville, Md.

38. Nale, "Home Economics in the Field of Rural Electrification," p. 225, emphasis added.

ignorance about electricity. Minnesota women politely watched REA's Victoria Harris cook a dinner for fifteen hungry harvest hands on an electric range in 1938, then kept their woodstoves, which warmed the kitchen on cold winter mornings.[39] Indiana women definitely disliked the attitude of REA's Enola Retherford, who gave them a "balling out" at the Farm Tour in 1941 if "they were noisy or had gotten up to leave" during her demonstration.[40] Extension workers did not fare much better. Iowa women tuned in to local women "neighboring" as radio homemakers more often than to broadcasts of expert advice from the college. A survey in the 1950s reported that a large number of farm women preferred to hear their home economics lessons from local leaders than from college-educated agents.[41]

Many of the difficulties encountered by home economists in electrifying rural America stemmed from the history and politics of their profession. As the emisaries of the Country Life movement to farm women, home economists—by virtue of this ideology and the resulting occupational structure—occupied a middle position between the city and the country, the producer and the consumer. As "agents of modernity" mediating the transfer of a supposedly "progressive" urbanizing technology to the countryside, home economists saw themselves primarily as interpreters of this new technology to farm women, rather than as sources of information on alternative household technologies. Consequently, they faced a professional dilemma regarding the promotion of electric appliances, were prone to paternalism, and felt the brunt of the urban-rural tensions rife in this period.

Although home economists and other professionals have experienced similar problems since the time of Ellen Richards, the plight of the generation who practiced in the interwar period was compounded because they saw themselves as agents of an inevitable social force, modernity, and its handmaid, consumer technology, made possible by electrification. Many of the unintended effects and social ills that we now associate with modern technology were either not recognized or were deemphasized before the war. Even the severe criticism of technological unemployment during the Great Depression by the technocracy movement and other groups failed to shake the pervasive belief in technological determinism and the overall social benefits of technology during this period.[42]

The urbanizing influences of World War II and the postwar years, when large numbers of farm youth were exposed to city life and wholesale

39. Victoria Harris, "A Harvest Dinner Convinced Them," *Rural Electrification News,* July 1938, pp. 17–19.

40. D. W. Teare to Oscar Meier, June 15, 1941, Entry 76, Box 2, RREA.

41. Gilbert, "Development of Selected Aspects of Home Demonstration Work," p. 161; and Jane Stern and Michael Stern, "Neighboring," *New Yorker,* April 15, 1991, pp. 78–93.

42. See William E. Akin, *Technocracy and the American Dream: The Technocrat Movement, 1900–1941* (Berkeley: University of California Press, 1977).

migration to the city and mass consumerism occurred, probably made the lot of home economists in rural electrification easier than that of their sisters before the war. They undoubtedly encountered much less resistance to electrification, which farm men and women now saw as a necessity rather than a luxury.[43] In the long run, reflective home economists and other reformers may have viewed modernity more skeptically by the 1960s. They may have looked back and seen that the homogenizing aspects of electrification and electronic mass media had, ironically, helped make farm life more attractive, in part, by urbanizing a rural culture so admired by the Country Lifers.

43. See John L. Shover, *First Majority—Last Minority: The Transformation of Rural Life in America* (DeKalb: Northern Illinois University Press, 1976); and Pete Daniel, "Going among Strangers: Southern Reactions to World War II," *Journal of American History* 77 (1990): 886–911.

12 Safeguarded by Your Refrigerator: Mary Engle Pennington's Struggle with the National Association of Ice Industries

LISA MAE ROBINSON

In the 1920s and 1930s, many home economists and female scientists found employment in the food and home products industry advising consumers, developing and promoting new products, and creating new markets. Mary Engle Pennington, a chemist and bacteriologist, found such a position in 1923 with the National Association of Ice Industries (NAII), the trade association of the ice manufacturing industry. The NAII hired Pennington as the director of its new Household Refrigeration Bureau to promote the use of home refrigerators cooled by ice and to head off the growing competition from electric refrigerators.[1]

An examination of Pennington's work with the Household Refrigeration Bureau illuminates the relationship between scientific authority, household technology, and gender relations. This essay will show how both female home economists and male ice industry managers successfully exploited assumptions about science and gender to further their respective aims. Industries employed female home economists because they believed that only women could successfully sell products to other women, namely to "Mrs. Consumer." Home economists accepted and promoted this gender

I would like to thank Rima Apple, Carolyn Goldstein, Julia Grant, Larry Holmes, Marty Pernick, Naomi Rogers, Carolyn Shapiro, Sarah Stage, Virginia Vincenti, and John Harley Warner for their comments on various drafts of this paper.

1. Margaret Rossiter, *Women Scientists in America: Struggles and Strategies to 1940* (Baltimore: Johns Hopkins University Press, 1982), pp. 258–59; Lisa M. Robinson, "The Electrochemical School of Edgar Fahs Smith" (Ph.D. dissertation, University of Pennsylvania, 1986), pp. 220–25; Barbara Sicherman and Carol Hurd Green, eds., *Notable American Women: The Modern Period* (Cambridge: Harvard University Press, 1980), pp. 532–34.

253

stereotype because it created new careers for women and, in the case of the ice industry, a place for female professionals in an otherwise solidly male industry. The home economists' message of scientific housekeeping attracted reform-minded women such as Mary Engle Pennington, who wanted to improve the health of all people by raising living standards and increasing hygiene in the home. In the end, all parties—manufacturers, home economists, and housewives—embraced the authority of science in their competition for dominion over the kitchen.[2]

In the early twentieth century, there were various forms of home refrigeration, including two types of "refrigerators," those cooled by blocks of ice and those cooled by mechanical means. Each form had its advantages and disadvantages, but no method demonstrated a clear technological superiority over all the others. In the 1920s and 1930s, the trade associations of the ice, electrical, and gas industries engaged in a fierce competition for customers, employing a variety of advertising techniques to encourage sales of their respective refrigerators. All three employed home economists to promote their products.

The ice manufacturing industry, in particular, faced the critical problem of an ever-growing surplus of ice. Ice companies had gradually adopted both steam- and electric-powered mechanical refrigeration technology since the 1890s, and most had stopped harvesting natural ice. Furthermore, the number of ice manufacturing plants had grown sharply. In 1900 there were 787 ice manufacturing plants, 1,320 in 1905, and 2,917 in 1907. Ice was manufactured by pouring distilled water into fifty-pound molds that were immersed in mechanically cooled brine. This manufactured ice was clear and free from impurities, unlike natural ice, because the freezing process forced any dirt and air into the center of the block, and it could be removed before the ice was sold. In 1905, over seven million tons of ice were produced. By 1910, five thousand ice plants were spread across the United States, making ice abundantly available all year long.[3]

In response to this overproduction, ice manufacturers tried to lower production costs by using more efficient machines and making and storing

2. The phrase "Mrs. Consumer" comes from Christine Frederick, *Selling Mrs. Consumer* (New York: Business Bourse, 1929).

3. Oscar Anderson, *Refrigeration in America* (Princeton: Princeton University Press, 1953), p. 125; Ruth Schwartz Cowan, *More Work for Mother: The Ironies of Household Technology from the Open Hearth to the Microwave* (New York: Basic Books, 1983), pp. 129–31; U.S. Congress, House of Representatives, *Food Investigation* (Washington, D.C.: U.S. Government Printing Office, 1918), pp. 17–18; U.S. Department of Commerce and Labor, Bureau of the Census, *Census of Manufactures: 1905, Slaughtering and Meat Packing, Manufactured Ice and Salt* (Washington, D.C.: U.S. Government Printing Office, 1907), pp. 54–55. See also Joseph C. Jones, Jr., *America's Icemen: An Illustrative History of the United States Natural Ice Industry, 1685–1925* (Humble, Tex.: Jobeco Books, 1984); Richard Osborn Cummings, *American Ice Harvests: A Historical Study on Technology, 1820–1918* (Berkeley: University of California Press, 1949).

more ice in cooler weather, when it was cheaper, and to improve the practices of ice delivery men, who were often accused of cheating customers and being dirty and impolite. The industry journal, *Ice and Refrigeration*, contained many articles and editorials discussing ways to reduce the costs and increase the profits of ice manufacturing. Icemen also courted a new market for their surplus—refrigerated boxcars. In 1905, more than eighty-five thousand railroad cars were equipped with bunkers, all of which needed to be supplied with ice. The use of refrigerated boxcars, particularly by meat-packers, expanded rapidly until 1917, when the Federal Trade Commission investigated the monopolistic practices of the "Big Five" meatpacking companies, which owned 91 percent of all refrigerated boxcars used to ship meat in the United States.[4]

In 1918, ice manufacturers again began to search for new markets. They formed a trade association, the National Association of Ice Industries, "to develop new fields of use for ice and persistently inform the public of their advantages." They concentrated on advertising the virtues of ice and found that manufactured ice's purity, as demonstrated by its clarity, was its strongest selling point. Although there were many calls within the association to develop the field of home refrigeration, the NAII took no direct action to promote use of ice in the home until 1923.[5]

In the 1910s and early 1920s, the ice industry had little to fear from electric home refrigeration. Ice refrigerators had several significant technological advantages, most important of which was their low cost. In 1923, the cheapest electric refrigerator cost $450, whereas an ice refrigerator could cost less than $30. The earliest electric refrigerators, such as the Kelvinator in 1912 and the Frigidaire in 1916, did not enjoy much initial success because they were expensive, contained flammable refrigerants, and were plagued with repair problems. Domestic scientists promoted the ice refrigerator for the "modern kitchen," along with the gas stove and incinerator, an electric light, and small electric appliances. Furthermore, such kitchens usually had only one electric outlet, which would have to be used for both lighting and the electric refrigerator. Few housewives cared to confront the difficult choice between illuminating their kitchens or running their electric refrigerators.[6]

4. U.S. Department of Commerce and Labor, *Census of Manufactures*, pp. 54–55; U.S. Congress, House, *Food Investigation*, pp. 17–18. The "Big Five" companies were Swift, Armour, Wilson, Cudahy, and Morris.

5. *Proceedings of the Thirteenth Annual Convention of the National Association of Ice Industries* (Chicago: NAII, 1930), frontispiece.

6. Cowan, *More Work for Mother*, pp. 122, 131–32; *Saturday Evening Post*, May 4, 1929, p. 111. For the "modern kitchen," see Martha L. Metcalf, *Student's Manual in Household Arts: Food and Cookery* (Indianapolis: Industrial Education Company, 1915).

By 1923, there were only twenty thousand electric refrigerators in the United States, and even as late as 1935 only 21 percent of the homes in an electrified city such as Muncie, Indiana, had electric or gas refrigerators. In the face of the electric refrigerator's technological disadvantages, electrical manufacturing companies concentrated on selling small home appliances such as toasters, irons, and vacuum cleaners, but they also worked diligently to improve the reliability of electric refrigerators while lowering their cost. Throughout the 1920s and 1930s, the technological gap between electric and ice refrigerators gradually closed, and the price of electric refrigerators dropped rapidly. By 1929 the cost of an electric refrigerator was $215, and by 1935 high-quality electric and ice refrigerators cost about the same to purchase and maintain.[7]

Not only was there fierce competition among the various refrigeration technologies, but the language used to describe these devices was also contested. In the 1910s, icebox manufacturers redesigned their product, which was a zinc-lined box resting on the floor holding both an ice block and food in the same compartment. The new "ice or iced *refrigerator*," as the manufacturers named it, was a cabinet up on legs, had two doors on the front, was divided into two compartments (one for ice and one for food), and was lined with porcelain. This unit was more convenient to use, kept food away from the melting ice, and improved air circulation within the refrigerator. But as electric refrigerators became more common, the word "refrigerator" came to mean any upright cabinet cooled by any available means, whether by blocks of ice or mechanical devices powered by electricity, gas, or oil. Although the electric industry was keen to maintain a distinction between its "refrigerator" and the ice industry's "icebox," the public initially made no such distinction. Furthermore, domestic science textbooks did not immediately incorporate mechanical refrigeration technology into their discussions of home appliances. These books were designed for use as texts in high schools and "for study groups of rural extension and other club women and in the housekeepers' courses given by schools and colleges," and they usually used the word "refrigerator" to mean only iced-cooled units.[8]

The semantic battle between the ice and electric industries for ownership of the word "refrigerator" escalated in the 1920s, even as sales of ice increased steadily. Icemen became increasingly defensive about the use of the term "icebox," which they felt made their product seem old-fash-

7. David Nye, *Electrifying America: Social Meanings of a New Technology* (Cambridge: MIT Press, 1990), pp. 20, 28, 275–76, 356, 382, 425 n.85.

8. Metcalf, *Student's Manual*, pp. 21–22; Mary E. Williams and Katharine Rolston Fisher, *Elements of the Theory and Practice of Cookery: A Textbook of Domestic Science for Use in Schools* (New York: Macmillan, 1916), 45–46; Lydia Ray Balderston, *Housewifery: A Manual and Text-Book of Practical Housekeeping* (Philadelphia: J. B. Lippincott, 1919), preface, 211–15, 269–71.

ioned. The real battleground, however, soon became the industry-sponsored educational and advertising literature for the general public, in which the NAII insisted that the word "refrigerator" refer only to ice-cooled units.

In 1923, the NAII finally focused on the need to promote the use of ice in the home. The icemen's interest was sparked by the growing problem of refrigeration in apartment buildings. Apartment building owners usually installed cheap, substandard ice refrigerators to save money, but tenants were then dissatisfied with the result—ice that melted quickly and had to be replaced often at the tenant's expense. In response, tenant groups lobbied, often successfully, for the installation of small, centralized mechanical refrigeration plants that could serve the entire building. The NAII believed that both conditions posed serious threats to the sale of household ice. Cheap ice refrigerators undermined the reputation of ice as a household refrigerant, and the use of central refrigeration units directly reduced the sale of household ice.[9]

In response to this problem of apartment refrigerators, the NAII's Committee on National Advertising and Publicity launched a vigorous campaign to increase the sale of household ice refrigerators and ice for the home market. The NAII raised money for these efforts from a voluntary levy on its members of one cent per ton of ice sold, from the sale of advertising material such as wagon emblems, and from the rental of a film, *How Would You Like to Be the Ice Man,* made by the association and designed to be shown to the public by ice manufacturers. The NAII hoped to use this extra money to increase the number of households owning ice refrigerators, get those households already owning ice refrigerators to buy larger ones (and therefore use more ice), counteract the promotion of mechanical refrigerators, and win back customers who had bought a mechanical refrigerator but had become dissatisfied with its operation.

The establishment of the Household Refrigeration Bureau in New York City marked the most important part of this sales campaign. The committee designed the bureau "to obtain practical and accurate information on the application of refrigeration principles and appliances in the home and to distribute that information to home economists, educational institutions and housekeepers throughout the country." The committee directed the bureau to "furnish data on which to base an appeal for all-the-year-round use of ice in the home," increase the popularity of ice and public confidence in the ice industry, and lend prestige to the association. To accomplish these goals, the NAII's directors allocated 17 percent of their total revenues for the

9. *Proceedings of the Sixth Annual Convention of the National Association of Ice Industries* (Chicago: NAII, 1923), pp. 160–61.

bureau's activities and hired Mary Engle Pennington as the first director for a yearly salary of $3,000. Her first task was to write a series of pamphlets on home refrigeration using ice.[10]

Before coming to the Household Refrigeration Bureau, Pennington had enjoyed a distinguished career at the U.S. Department of Agriculture as head of the Bureau of Chemistry's Food Research Laboratory. While there, she conducted extensive research on the effects of cold storage on poultry, eggs, fish, and shellfish and set hygiene standards for commercial poultry and egg processors. Her work was critical to the enforcement of the 1906 Pure Food and Drugs Act. Pennington advocated the creation of an unbroken "cold chain" stretching from the farmer to the consumer, but her work at the Food Research Laboratory concentrated on commercial poultry and egg processing.[11]

Pennington first came to the attention of the NAII when J. F. Nickerson, the editor of *Ice and Refrigeration*, met her in 1908. Nickerson, impressed with Pennington's knowledge of cold storage, recommended to the secretary of agriculture that she represent the United States at the First International Congress of Refrigeration in Paris. While at this conference, Pennington saw "the opportunity for enlarging the scope [of her work] and putting it in proper lines for real benefit to the consumer." Nickerson believed that there was no other person in the country who was more qualified to undertake a serious scientific study of household refrigeration.[12]

By 1919, Pennington was dissatisfied with the increasingly complicated relationship between the Bureau of Chemistry and the Food Research Laboratory and felt that the new bureau chief, Carl Alsberg, constantly thwarted her work by cutting her funding for original research. She left the federal government to work as a consultant for the American Balsa Company, a manufacturer of refrigerated boxcars. This company was also engaged in research, partly funded by the NAII, on the design of household ice refrigerators. In 1920, Pennington set herself up in New York as an independent refrigeration consultant. But she continued to believe that the cold chain remained incomplete, and therefore ineffective, as long as household refrigeration was not included. In 1923 she accepted the NAII's offer to head the Household Refrigeration Bureau, even though her yearly salary was about half her salary at the Food Research Laboratory, because she saw it as a way to continue preaching "the doctrine of continuous refrigeration" and "to

10. Ibid., pp. 155, 180.
11. Lisa M. Robinson, "Regulating What We Eat: Mary Engle Pennington and the Food Research Laboratory," *Agricultural History* 64 (1990): 142–53.
12. *Sixth Annual Convention*, pp. 181–82.

pass on in simple language the information now available on the use of low temperatures in the household."[13]

From 1923 until 1930 Pennington wrote thirteen pamphlets for the Household Refrigeration Bureau and set up an extensive distribution network among home economics teachers, home demonstration agents, welfare agencies, and women's clubs.[14] During the bureau's first year, Pennington sent out 96,870 pamphlets to approximately twenty thousand people. By the time Pennington left the bureau in 1931, the number of pamphlets distributed had grown to 1,250,398 and the mailing list contained thirty-five thousand names. Pennington intended her pamphlets to serve as texts in home economics courses in universities and high schools where she hoped they would contribute to "the betterment of daily living."[15] Pennington also hoped her pamphlets would educate housewives about the principles of scientific housekeeping. She believed that "the newer teaching of home economics" would "enable housekeepers to understand the behavior of perishable foods and the necessity of keeping them cold."[16] Pennington believed that education in scientific principles would enable the housewife to make more intelligent choices when selecting and using a refrigerator and take better care of the food stored there.

Pennington designed her pamphlets not simply to educate the housewife but also to sell a particular product, the *ice* refrigerator. Accordingly, she used basic home economics concepts such as economy, efficiency, nutrition, and, most important, hygiene, to make an emotional appeal to housewives to be vigilant in safeguarding the health of their families. In particular, Pennington invoked maternal anxiety over the health of children to make the case for buying and using ice refrigerators. She stressed the importance of having an adequate ice supply, writing, "When a baby's health hangs in the balance the intelligent mother will see to it that the ice supply

13. M. E. Pennington et al., *Storage Investigations, 1921–1922* (Canton, Pa.: Marble Laboratory, 1923); Pennington, *The Care of the Home Refrigerator* (Chicago: NAII, 1924), p. 1; Pennington, *Journeys with Refrigerated Foods: Eggs* (Chicago: NAII, 1928), p. 2; Pennington, *Food Wholesomeness, Food Economy, Food Quality* (Chicago: NAII, 1923), back cover.

14. Pennington's pamphlets, all published in Chicago by the NAII, were *Food Wholesomeness, Food Economy, Food Quality: Safeguarded by Your Refrigerator* (1923); *Ice Cream Making and Appliances in the Home* (1923, supplemented in 1928 by *Ice Cream Freezers* and revised and renamed in 1931 as *Desserts Frozen with Ice and Salt*); *Where to Place Food in the Household Refrigerator* (1924); *The Care of the Home Refrigerator* (1924); *The Care of the Child's Food in the Home* (1925); *Why We Refrigerate Foods* (1926); *The Romance of Ice* (1927); *Cold Is the Absence of Heat* (1927); *Journeys with Refrigerated Foods: Eggs* (1928); *How to Use a Good Refrigerator* (1929); *Home Refrigeration of Fresh Vegetables* (1929); *Buying a Refrigerator* (1930); *Journeys with Refrigerated Foods: Series 2—Fruits* (1930).

15. *Ice Cream Making*, frontispiece.

16. *Journeys: Eggs*, p. 8.

never runs too low." With such a serious responsibility, mothers could not afford to choose a refrigerator without the help of expert advice.[17]

The Household Refrigeration Bureau was only too happy to provide such advice. Seven of Pennington's thirteen pamphlets contained warnings about the health risks of inadequate refrigeration, which she backed up by scientific authority. Pennington cited scientific studies done by the Dairy Division of Cornell University to support her claim that only the most tightly constructed and heavily insulated (and therefore most expensive) ice refrigerators could adequately protect a family's food. Pennington counseled mothers not to fall prey to false economy by buying a cheap refrigerator but to buy the biggest and best insulated refrigerator, no matter what the cost, and to keep it well supplied with ice at all times. She also encouraged housewives to spend more money on ice by directing them to buy ice even in the winter, to place standing orders for ice, and to keep the ice compartment at least half full at all times rather than ordering ice when it ran low.[18]

The Household Refrigeration Bureau was not alone in promoting the virtues of its products by making claims for their health-preserving qualities. Many advertisements in the 1920s and 1930s, such as those for vacuum cleaners and washing machines, championed the appliances' ability to help the "conscientious mother" protect her family. Refrigerator advertising often focused on the mother's responsibility to protect her children's health, and pictures of smiling children were greatly in evidence. One such advertisement in the *Saturday Evening Post* in 1929 prominently displays a smiling baby and warns, "Don't risk Baby's health by skimping on ICE." The advertisements for both electric and ice refrigerators claimed unique abilities to keep food, and therefore children, safe. The ice industry claimed that the continual replenishment of moist cold air from the melting ice was essential for fresh, healthy food, while the electric industry stressed that its refrigerators were capable of maintaining lower temperatures. The Household Refrigeration Bureau's pamphlets made the case for ice by stressing its ability to add moisture to the air and to absorb unpleasant, and possibly dangerous, food odors.[19]

In such an emotional campaign, milk played a crucial role as both the symbol of maternal care and the actual food of most children. Pennington exhorted mothers to acquire knowledge of "what real 'cleanliness' means in the sense of keeping food 'germ free' or with a 'low bacteria count'" and

17. *Care of the Child's Food*, p. 12.
18. Ibid., pp. 4, 8.
19. Roger Miller, "*Selling Mrs. Consumer:* Advertising and the Creation of Suburban Sociospatial Relations, 1910–1930," *Antipode* 23 (1991): 263–301; *Food Wholesomeness*, p. 2; *Cold Is the Absence of Heat*, pp. 14–16; *Saturday Evening Post*, March 30, 1929, p. 187.

to "know how to use the home utensils and facilities in place of the laboratory apparatus that such 'cleanliness' may be a certainty and not a haphazard thing." Mothers needed expert advice because they had a special responsibility to safeguard their families' health by ensuring that "cleanliness prevails and cold is maintained." Pennington reminded the "intelligent mother" to "take such exemplary care of the milk after she gets it that no shadow of blame can attach to her should trouble arise."[20]

Pennington had long been interested in "the problem of obtaining milk clean from the cow and delivering it clean to the consumer." Before working for the federal government, she had worked for the Philadelphia Board of Health setting standards for the city's certified milk and persuading the Pennsylvania Railroad to provide refrigerated boxcars for transporting milk. Her successes with both projects brought her to the attention of Harvey W. Wiley, chief of the USDA's Bureau of Chemistry, who hired her to direct the Food Research Laboratory. Pennington opposed pasteurization because she believed that the process altered milk's taste, promoted the growth of bacteria when milk was kept at room temperature (a common practice), and provided the means by which unscrupulous dairy operators could salvage contaminated and spoiled milk.[21]

Pennington advocated buying certified, unpasteurized milk rather than "loose" milk from large containers which was measured out into the purchaser's receptacle. Such milk, she warned, was responsible for "thousands of deaths of tiny children annually" and "the heartbreak of the mothers who have borne them." In *The Care of the Child's Food in the Home*, Pennington highlighted the possible contamination of loose milk by drawing flies swarming around the open milk container. She warned mothers, "Dust is always loaded with germs which may cause diarrhoea, typhoid, tuberculosis or other disease." Other home economists also counseled women to "protect food from flies. Flies come from dirty places and may carry germs of typhoid fever or other diseases on their feet." Pennington recommended the ice refrigerator as the perfect place to store milk because not only did the refrigerator's low temperatures retard the growth of bacteria, but flies and dust were kept out. She also advocated keeping milk in glass bottles rather than in uncovered containers to protect it further from dirt and insects.[22]

Mothers had to be ever vigilant to avoid "serious illness or even the loss of your baby," risks underscored in *The Romance of Ice* by the drawing of a child attended by a doctor and nurse. To counter such risks, Pennington praised ice, the "guardian and caretaker" that could "protect our milk sup-

20. *Care of the Child's Food*, pp. 1–4.

21. Mary E. Pennington, "Bacterial Growth and Chemical Changes in Milk Kept at Low Temperatures," *Journal of Biological Chemistry* 4 (April 1908): 353–93.

22. *Care of the Child's Food*, pp. 2–8; Williams and Fisher, *Elements of the Theory and Practice of Cookery*, pp. 45–46.

ply." Even in a pamphlet designed primarily to explain the physics of refrigeration, she used the imagery of germs to encourage the purchase of the most expensive ice refrigerators. In *Cold Is the Absence of Heat* (Figure 12.1) Pennington depicted heat molecules as little bearded imps swarming all over the refrigerator. An expensive, well-insulated refrigerator kept the imps outside, but the poorly insulated one permitted hot germs to dance all over the food. Pennington reminded the reader that a good mother keeps food for her family, and especially for her children, only in a well-insulated, well-sealed ice refrigerator.[23]

Safeguarding family health not only involved keeping contamination and germs at bay; the housewife also had to make sure her family ate the "right" food. But the scientific community disagreed over what constituted healthy food. Chemists generally argued that the chemicals present in food solely determined its value for human nutrition, whereas bacteriologists, concerned about the presence of dangerous bacteria, generally stressed a food's fresh, attractive appearance as the sole indication of its value. Pennington, trained in both chemistry and bacteriology, attempted to bridge this disagreement by

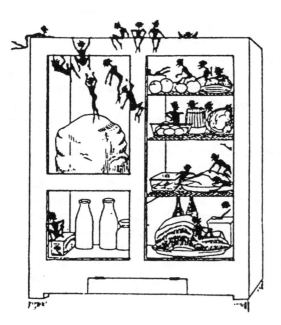

Figure 12.1 From M. E. Pennington's *Cold Is the Absence of Heat* (1927), Household Refrigeration Bureau Bulletin number 8, National Association of Ice Industries.

23. *Romance of Ice*, p. 13; *Cold Is the Absence of Heat*, pp. 1–20.

stressing the ability of ice to preserve both food's appearance and its chemical composition. Several of her pamphlets equated food's appearance with its nutritive value and advocated eating fresh vegetable salads and carrot and celery sticks stored in glass jars to obtain valuable vitamins. Pennington claimed that only the cold humidity of an ice refrigerator could keep fruits and vegetables crisp enough to be palatable and at the same time preserve vitamins. She also encouraged housewives to feed their families fresh meat as often as they could afford it to obtain sufficient protein in the family diet. She pointed out that meat usually dried out quickly in the dry air of the mechanical refrigerator because it was usually wrapped only in brown butcher's paper. She believed that any deterioration in appearance, whether because of slime or a hard, dry exterior, indicated a decline in the meat's value as a food.[24]

Pennington also tried to teach women that the proper use of an ice refrigerator could help them run their households more economically and efficiently. She praised the high humidity found in ice refrigerators for keeping food from drying out, thereby preventing food waste and saving money in the household budget. Pennington also explained that increased insulation enabled ice refrigerators to use ice more efficiently, making them more economical to own in the long run in spite of their initial higher purchase cost. "The housewife who encourages the building of better refrigerators," she insisted, "is doing her bit for progress."[25]

Pennington designed most of the Household Refrigeration Bureau's pamphlets to educate housewives about the scientific principles underlying refrigeration and to demonstrate the superiority of ice as a refrigerant, but *Ice Cream Making and Appliances in the Home* had a very different message. This pamphlet, which was the one most often requested, encouraged housewives to use specially created recipes for ice cream to make everyday meals more attractive and be good hostesses on special occasions. A significant advantage of ice refrigerators was their ability to provide ice cubes for drinks and shaved ice for desserts and to make ice cream without freezing everything in the refrigerator. Before 1935, mechanical refrigerators did not possess separate freezer compartments so the only way to make frozen desserts in them was to lower the temperature of the entire refrigerator. The manufacturers of electric refrigerators, however, also put together recipe booklets showing housewives how to make special frozen desserts and ice cream, even though the directions could get complicated and there was a risk of freezing all the food in the refrigerator. The Frigidaire Corporation even set up an experimental kitchen to develop "refrigerator cooking" recipes.[26]

24. *Journeys: Eggs; Journeys: Fruits; Home Refrigeration of Fresh Vegetables.*
25. *How to Use a Good Refrigerator*, p. 8.
26. *Ice Cream Making*, pp. 2–6; Verna L. Miller, *Frigidaire Recipes* (Dayton, Ohio: Frigidaire Corporation, 1928), pp. 8–35.

The creation and demonstration of special recipes making use of ice became the catalyst for Pennington's expansion of the Household Refrigeration Bureau. At the end of 1923, she began searching for an assistant director by writing to Martha Van Rensselaer, chair of the Home Economics Department of Cornell University. Pennington offered $2,400 a year for a woman with "a good grounding in biology and chemistry . . . and a graduate in home economics from some college of recognized standing" who could visit schools, colleges, and clubs and "help prepare information to go out to teachers and home makers." Van Rensselaer replied that although she had no one to suggest, she hoped in the future to recommend a "Cornell woman" for this "very good opportunity." By 1925, Pennington had hired Margaret H. Kingsley as her assistant director, but this position was not officially recognized by the NAII until 1927. Pennington apparently hired Kingsley before the NAII allocated funds for the assistant director position.[27]

In 1927, the NAII officially recognized Kingsley's position, but Pennington kept pushing for more support. She wanted Kingsley to give public lectures on home refrigeration around the country, but the NAII refused to authorize any travel expenses. Undeterred, Pennington sent Kingsley to a conference at Columbia University on "the relation of the household arts teacher to food advertising and publicity as interpreted by home economics specialists in business" and billed the NAII for Kingsley's cab fare, which it eventually paid.[28]

That same year, Pennington also asked the NAII further to expand the activities of the Household Refrigeration Bureau by sponsoring the creation of a group of "home service workers," women with home economics training who would promote the use of ice in the home by giving public lectures on the construction and use of ice refrigerators and demonstrating new recipes using ice. Convinced that such public lectures would do "a tremendous amount of good for the industry," Pennington warned the NAII that "the industry cannot afford to overlook this matter." But the NAII was reluctant to allocate funds for this project.[29]

27. M. E. Pennington to Martha Van Rensselaer, December 26, 1923, and Martha Van Rensselaer to M. E. Pennington, January 2, 1924, both in Class of 1924 File, Alumni Records, College of Human Ecology, Division of Rare and Manuscript Collections, Cornell University Library. Kingsley listed her position as the assistant director of the Household Refrigeration Bureau in the 1925 membership list of the Home Economists in Business section of the American Home Economics Association. See A Forward Force . . . Home Economists in Business (Vienna, Va.: Home Economists in Business Section, AHEA, 1982), pp. 87–88. Since Kingsley is not mentioned in the NAII's proceedings until 1927, I assume that Pennington hired her unofficially while seeking funds for the position.

28. Proceedings of the Tenth Annual Convention of the National Association of Ice Industries (Chicago: NAII, 1927), p. 124; Proceedings of the Eleventh Annual Convention of the National Association of Ice Industries (Chicago: NAII, 1928), p. 80.

29. Tenth Annual Convention, p. 124.

In 1928, to overcome what she perceived as a unreasonable public prejudice against ice refrigerators, Pennington mounted an exhibit on the history
of refrigeration at the biennial convention of the Federated Women's Clubs
of America. To convince consumers that ice was the best means of refrigeration, the majority of refrigerators in the exhibit used ice. The success of the
exhibit helped Pennington gain the confidence of the president of the
Women's Clubs of Kansas, who invited the Household Refrigeration Bureau
to sponsor a series of talks to the women's clubs in her state. Pennington
sent Kingsley to Kansas for a month at the NAII's expense despite the association's insistence that it had no money for travel expenses. Kingsley gave
twenty-five talks to Women's Clubs and high school home economics
classes on "Refrigeration in the Home" and distributed 8,000 pamphlets.
She found the Women's Clubs quite wary of advertising and often reluctant
to let her speak. But she relied on Pennington's scientific reputation to reas-
sure everyone that the talks would be solely educational.[30]

That same year, the Household Refrigeration Bureau held its first training
school for home service workers. Fifty women took a week-long course under the direction of Margaret Kingsley. These women studied how to handle customers' complaints, give talks to groups such as women's clubs or
school classes, demonstrate "ice refrigerator cooking," cultivate consumer
contacts with the ice company, demonstrate the effectiveness of ice refrigerators for preserving a variety of food products, and cooperate with the
home service activities of other industries. Pennington and Kingsley held
a home service worker training school every year until 1931 but constantly
had to justify the expense to the NAII and to encourage ice companies
to hire their graduates.[31]

These newly trained home service workers for the ice industry competed directly with the home economists employed by the electrical and
gas industries and by public utilities. The National Electric Light Association urged its members that same year to establish home lighting departments staffed with specialists trained in home economics. The American
Gas Association had an ongoing program to encourage its members to hire
home service counselors who would "maintain close contacts with
schools and universities" by directing and advising faculty on courses in
home appliances.[32]

30. *Eleventh Annual Convention,* pp. 76–78, 86–88.
31. Margaret H. Kingsley, *Home Service Work for the Ice Industry* (Chicago: Nickerson &
Collins, 1931); *Eleventh Annual Convention,* p. 80; *Proceedings of the Fourteenth Annual Convention of the National Association of Ice Industries* (Chicago: NAII, 1931), p. 146. Sixty-five
women attended the school in 1931.
32. Nye, *Electrifying America,* p. 276; Frederick, *Selling Mrs. Consumer,* pp. 275–85; Jessie
McQueen, "The American Gas Association's Service through the Office of Its Home Service
Counsellor," *Proceedings of the First National Home Service Conference, March 6–8, 1930* (New
York: National Electric Light Association, 1930), pp. 44–46.

Pennington and Kingsley sought continuing support from the NAII by stressing that the presence of female home service workers would give a touch of class to the "rough and tumble, and very virile" ice industry. Ice manufacturing had traditionally employed only men because the work involved physical exertion and was done under difficult and sometimes dangerous conditions. Furthermore, the NAII was usually preoccupied with the "problem of ice deliverymen," who were often thought to be dirty, rude, and likely to cheat the customer by providing a slightly smaller block of ice than had been paid for. Because many ice deliverymen were recent immigrants or black men, the NAII worried that white middle-class women would be uneasy about allowing them entry into their kitchens. The NAII advocated training in manners and uniforms and white coats for ice deliverymen to make them seem more respectable, but the association also hoped that well-mannered, well-dressed female home service workers would counteract the deliverymen's negative image.[33]

Pennington and Kingsley also believed that home service work would provide challenging and well-paid employment for women as home economists. In practice, however, home service workers in the ice industry worked for small salaries and did not receive any commissions either for ice or for refrigerators sold as a result of their efforts. Since ice and refrigerators were sold by salesmen working on commission, the NAII feared that they would not accept the presence of home service workers if these women also competed for sales commissions. Consequently, the NAII barred home service workers from completing sales and ruled that even if a home service worker actually sold a refrigerator, her commission would go to the salesman who regularly worked the route. Ice manufacturing companies also often required home service workers to spend much of their time on routine clerical work, such as bookkeeping, to handle customers' complaints personally, and to check on the honesty and courteousness of ice deliverymen.[34]

Both the Household Refrigeration Bureau's pamphlets and the talks given by its home service workers concentrated on presenting the scientific principles underlying home refrigeration at the same time they subtly pushed the sale of ice refrigerators. The NAII, however, was not primarily interested

33. *Proceedings of the Fifteenth Annual Convention of the National Association of Ice Industries* (Chicago: NAII, 1932), p. 163; C. E. Whelan, "How Can We Secure Interest, and Retain Better Men for Ice Delivery," *Ice and Refrigeration* 52 (1917): 214; B. F. Schmidt, "Ice Delivery Men as Sales Force," *Ice and Refrigeration* 52 (1917): 202; N. H. Hardin, "Delivery Problems," *Ice and Refrigeration* 51 (1916): 277; C. S. Campbell, "The Ice Man in Relation to the Public," *Ice and Refrigeration* 51 (1916): 127; "Guardian of the Nation's Food Supply," *Ice and Refrigeration* 79 (1930): 185; "Newspaper Tells about Merits of Ice," *Ice and Refrigeration* 79 (1930): 186.

34. *Thirteenth Annual Convention*, pp. 125–30, 202.

in consumer education; it wanted increased sales of ice and refrigerators. Pennington realized that for her science-oriented, educational approach to sell ice effectively, ice refrigerators had to perform as well as, or better than, mechanical refrigerators. Because Pennington could not get much money for in-house testing of ice refrigerators at the Household Refrigeration Bureau, she encouraged the home economics departments of Cornell University and Columbia University to determine the temperatures required for keeping different foods and to monitor the various temperatures maintained by ice refrigerators over time under various environmental conditions. She convinced the NAII to give these two home economics departments $250 each and to provide ice refrigerators for the tests. Pennington was particularly interested in what materials made the best insulation, how much insulation was necessary, and how the overall size of the cabinet and the position of the ice within it affected the temperatures inside the unit.

In 1927, Pennington received an extra $5,000 from the National Association of Refrigerator Manufacturers to develop a standardized grading scale for ice refrigerators. She also helped design a comprehensive study of home refrigeration with the USDA's Bureau of Home Economics. Pennington worked closely with Louise Stanley, whom she had met at the New York section meeting of the American Society of Refrigerating Engineers, where both had spoken on home refrigeration. Pennington believed that such scientific research would lead to standardization, better insulation, and improved refrigerator design, all of which would greatly increase sales of ice refrigerators and make them more competitive with mechanical refrigerators.[35]

Mechanical refrigerator manufacturers countered by promoting the use of their particular brand names as synonyms for "refrigerator." In *Frigidaire Recipes*, the Frigidaire Corporation refers only once to "this modern home refrigerator" and instead uses "Frigidaire" instead. The company became so successful at establishing this brand name as a generic term for refrigerator that Pennington complained to the NAII that "Frigidaire . . . stands for everything in the way of a mechanical refrigerator. That is a marvellous trade-mark. I wish we had something in the ice industry that carried the same psychology."[36]

Pennington, frustrated by the continual shortage of funds from the NAII, warned its members at their 1930 annual meeting that "we are now at the parting of the industrial ways," but the NAII did not heed her warning, and extra funds were not forthcoming.[37]

Pennington wanted to conduct extensive scientific trials of all kinds of refrigerators and expand the activities of the home service worker training school because home economist Ada Bessie Swann, representing both the

35. *Sixth Annual Convention*, pp. 180–94; *Tenth Annual Convention*, pp. 124–25.
36. Anderson, *Refrigeration in America*, pp. 213–14; Miller, *Frigidaire Recipies*, pp. 1–3; *Eleventh Annual Convention*, p. 78.
37. *Thirteenth Annual Convention*, p. 192.

National Electric Light Association and the American Gas Association, organized the First National Home Service Worker Conference that year and did not invite home service workers from the ice industry. The ice manufacturers, however, remained blind to the threat from the electric and gas industries. That same year, an editorial in *Ice and Refrigeration* asserted that there would "continue to be an ample supply of new customers for ice" because ice would always be cheaper than mechanical refrigeration.[38]

As ice sales gradually declined from an all-time high in 1931, icemen returned to calling their refrigerators "*ice* or *iced* refrigerators," thereby acknowledging and accepting the presence of other kinds of refrigerators. The ice industry's retreat in language mirrored the growth in sales of its competitors, mechanical refrigerators, and the resulting decline in sales of ice.[39]

In 1931, Pennington left the Household Refrigeration Bureau to work for a more generous employer, the Institute of American Poultry Industries. With her departure, the directors of the NAII put the Household Refrigeration Bureau under the direct control of its Public Relations Department. It continued to send out the bureau's publications, but less than half as many went out in 1932 as in 1931. Although the number of pamphlets distributed did increase slightly over the next four years, it never reached the number sent out by Pennington. Most important, however, no new pamphlets were written or printed. By 1935, the NAII's supply of bulletins was exhausted.[40]

Pennington's departure came at the worst possible time for the ice industry. That same year, the National Electric Light Association launched a massive publicity campaign with a ten-page section in the *Saturday Evening Post* and a full-page advertisement in *Good Housekeeping*. Its sales campaign also included the creation of an Electric Refrigeration Bureau, which budgeted ten cents per metered customer for advertising. Furthermore, because electric refrigerators continued to be improved, the ice industry faced a market in which for the first time consumers could buy and operate an electric refrigerator for the same cost as an ice refrigerator. In spite of this serious competition, the NAII could not convince its members to contribute adequate funds for the Household Refrigeration Bureau.[41]

38. *Proceedings of the First National Home Service Conference*, pp. ii, 44, 57; "The Future of Ice," *Ice and Refrigeration* 79 (1930): 307–8.

39. Anderson, *Refrigeration in America*, pp. 202–23; Miller, *Frigidaire Recipes*, p. 7.

40. *Fifteenth Annual Convention*, pp. 160–67; *Proceedings of the Nineteenth Annual Convention of the National Association of Ice Industries* (Chicago: NAII, 1936), pp. 76–79, 163–76. The Institute of American Poultry Industries hired Pennington to help prepare a large exhibit on poultry and eggs for the 1933 Century of Progress Exhibition in Chicago. See Paul Mandeville et al., *Eggs* (Chicago: Progress Publications, 1933). I suspect that Kingsley also left the Household Refrigeration Bureau in 1931, but her departure (unlike Pennington's) is not recorded in the annual meeting proceedings. Kingsley worked for the Good Housekeeping Institute's Bureau of Food and Nutrition from 1935–1940.

41. Nye, *Electrifying America*, p. 276; *Nineteenth Annual Convention*, pp. 163–76.

The NAII did, however, hire Eleanor Howe as the new director of the Household Refrigeration Bureau. Howe was a home economist who had earned her B.S. from the University of Illinois in 1922, managed a school cafeteria in Detroit, returned to school to earn a M.S. from Columbia University in 1928, and been director of home economics at McCormick & Company in Baltimore from 1928 to 1933. She came to the notice of the NAII through her weekly Chicago radio program on home management. The NAII asked Howe to rewrite Pennington's pamphlets and specifically address the threat of mechanical refrigeration. In 1936, Howe changed the name of the home service workers to consumer service workers, a slight change that represented a major shift in philosophy. These "saleswomen in the ice industry" still engaged in "educational selling," but the new emphasis was on *selling*, not education. Howe promoted her recruits as home economics graduates "who can really go out and sell our product to Mrs. Consumer." But the ice companies remained reluctant to hire female service workers, and the NAII provided only grudging financial support so Howe left that same year to form a home economics consulting and publishing company with another home economist, Mary Wright Harvey. Although the Household Refrigeration Bureau continued to exist in one form or another until 1941, its efforts were always hobbled by the lack of support from the NAII. The ice industry never regained dominance of the home refrigeration market and slid into a slow decline until eventually the ice refrigerator vanished from American kitchens.[42]

The NAII successfully used home economics concepts in its advertising and home economists as home service workers to counter the vigorous sales efforts of the electric industry in the 1920s. But the NAII was eventually beaten at its own game; everything it did—educational selling through scientific pamphlets, appeals to maternal guilt, training home service workers, inventing special recipes, sponsoring research to improve refrigerator design, and making converts of home economics teachers—was done more successfully by the electric and gas industries.

For the individual ice manufacturing companies, the Household Refrigeration Bureau pamphlets and the trained home service workers represented unique opportunities to promote their product directly to women

---

42. *Nineteenth Annual Convention*, pp. 163–76; *Official Proceedings of the Twenty-Fourth Annual Convention of the National Association of Ice Industries* (Chicago: NAII, 1941), pp. 202–3. Howe formed Harvey & Howe with Mary Wright Harvey. This firm published *What's New in Home Economics* from 1936 onward and stayed in business until at least 1958. Howe also wrote *Household Hints for Homemakers* in 1943. Harvey earned her B.S. from Cornell in 1924 and lectured at commercial cooking schools in the northeastern United States from 1949–1951, produced home management shows for WKTV in Utica, New York, from 1951–1955, and became merchandising manager and dietitian for A. L. Mathias Company in Baltimore from 1955 until at least 1958 (*Who's Who of American Women*, vol. 1 [1958]).

and to advertise under the guise of providing educational material for classrooms. Blindly, the ice manufacturing companies refused to contribute sufficient money to support these activities and the NAII proved too weak a trade association to compel them. In contrast, the electrical manufacturing industry was much more cohesive and the National Electric Light Association had the clout to make its members contribute generous sums for national advertising campaigns.

Throughout her entire career, Mary Engle Pennington found satisfying work that allowed her to investigate and attempt to reform the American food distribution system. For Pennington, the Household Refrigeration Bureau represented the logical extension of her research on refrigeration in food processing and cold storage, as well as a way to educate consumers directly. Her thirteen pamphlets provided practical information on how to use an ice refrigerator and sound advice on safeguarding family health by its use. Her home service workers continued to work in the ice industry even after the NAII could no longer afford to sponsor their training. The NAII, however, convinced that neither electricity nor gas would ever replace ice for home refrigeration, continually hampered Pennington's efforts to improve ice refrigerators. The "Icemen" viewed the work of the Household Refrigeration Bureau in sex-stereotyped terms, as no more than selling to Mrs. Consumer by emphasizing a woman's responsibility to safeguard her family's health. After Pennington's departure, science took a backseat to public relations at the Household Refrigeration Bureau, but however much the NAII's and ice manufacturing companies' home economists urged Mrs. Consumer to buy ice, public relations alone could not substitute for product development. The NAII fell victim to its own shortsightedness and stereotypical thinking as the Frigidaire replaced the icebox.

13 Part of the Package: Home Economists in the Consumer Products Industries, 1920–1940

CAROLYN M. GOLDSTEIN

In June 1936, a group of home economists assembled to perform a play at an afternoon meeting during the American Home Economics Association's convention week. Representatives of the group's Business and Student Club Departments took time away from the busy annual meeting to observe a presentation of the dramatic work entitled "Experiment 63." Commissioned by these two departments and written by Charles Dillon, the play was intended to instruct home economics students about their opportunities for employment in the corporate business world. This line of work had apparently developed a glamorous reputation in recent years, and the professionals involved in it wanted to show potential newcomers the reality behind the image. The play received praise at the convention, which led to repeated performances at student club meetings in many of the nation's home economics colleges throughout the year.[1]

"Experiment 63" starred a home economist named Miss Welldone. During the course of the play, she experienced her first day on the job at the experimental kitchen of the Bigger and Batter Advertising Agency. She arrived

I would like to thank Anne Boylan, John Cheng, Jacqueline Dirks, Amy Hardin, David Hounshell, Jeanne Lawrence, Steven Lubar, Charles McGovern, Susan Smulyan, Susan Strasser, and Elizabeth White for their comments on earlier drafts of this essay.

1. Charles Dillon, "Experiment 63," typescript, January 1936; and Lillian B. Storms to Edna T. Amidon, August 17, 1936, Box 1, Home Economists in Business (HEIB), American Home Economics Association Archives, Alexandria, Va. (hereafter AHEA Archives). On Dillon, see *Who Was Who among North American Authors, 1921–1939* (Detroit: Gale Research Company, 1976), p. 432; and *Who Was Who in America* (Chicago: Marquis, 1950), p. 156.

on the job early in the morning only to discover that her predecessor, Miss Regulator, had quit after having a nervous breakdown in the kitchen.

Miss Welldone's assignment for the day was to create six "new," "fancy," and "inspiring" promotional recipes for the agency's Bingo Beans account. Before the day ended she produced a soup, a salad, a soufflé, baked beans, beans with pork chops en casserole, and bean loaf. Miss Welldone also completed other tasks, contributing to the product's promotion in many different ways. She provided eloquent descriptions of these dishes for the ad copywriter, assisted the photographer with his shoot, and gave health advice to Mr. Gastro, a man in the office suffering from stomach distress.

Maintaining her composure throughout these intrusions into what was already a busy day's schedule, Miss Welldone also deftly handled an unannounced visit from the "Man from Research Revelation," a consumer group conducting an investigation into Bingo Bean's labeling practices. "We've made an examination of your labels and we find that you do not mention the all-important fact that Bingo Beans make premature babies ill if more than one pound per day is fed," he announced. He then went on to explain that this omission threatened the "unsuspecting consumer who is already ground under the relentless heels of the industrial monarchs of America"; his organization was determined "to wipe out this evil" by exposing it to the public. Miss Welldone handled his aggressive accusations, presented in the script as extreme and irrational, with great care and patience. Refusing to make a statement under pressure, she cooperatively invited him back in the morning to receive answers to his questions.

Finally, Miss Welldone's last visitor was Mr. Bingo himself, who stopped by to see and taste the food she had prepared. The executive readily complimented her on her recipes. Thanking him, Miss Welldone offered him a suggestion about how to improve his product. "Have you ever thought of developing some fast cooking beans that wouldn't have to soak before being used?" she asked. Thrilled with the idea, he called it a "million dollar scheme" and exited, determined to make Miss Welldone's idea a reality. The play ended at the conclusion of the workday, when Mr. Batter asked the exhausted Miss Welldone to "go out to the suburbs tonight and talk to the girl scouts."

"Experiment 63" served as the means by which home economists in business informed their peers about the role they had been playing in America for about fifteen years: communicating between business and the public, arbitrating consumer relations in the marketplace. Although the play was written by an outsider, the context of the performance critically defined its significance. Home economists had commissioned the play and used it to represent themselves and their jobs at a professional annual meeting. Embedded in this representation was the assumption that they were objective professionals eliminating the extremes of "consumerism" by negotiating diplomatically and effectively with various parties. The play portrayed home economists as diligent, proud, and loyal employees who worked hard to provide high-quality products and service to their employers and to the community. It also suggested that women in such jobs made up for the incompetence of men in the corporate world. In sum, the business home economists who commissioned and performed this play argued that their profession made important contributions to both consumer products and consumer satisfaction.

A closer look at the play suggests that home economists operated in a world that was full of tensions, a world in which they engaged both their employers and consumers in daily struggles over the meaning of various products in modern American society. "Experiment 63" hints at some of the constituencies in this less than harmonious picture. The fate of Miss Welldone's predecessor suggests that jobs in business could be frustrating and that home economists exercised influence over producer-consumer relations only within closely circumscribed boundaries. The demands and imperatives of corporate employers represented the bottom line; home economists were never autonomous actors. Nor could they argue that they were the sole spokespersons for American consumers. The intrusion of the "Man from Research Revelation" signaled the growing influence of consumer advocacy groups such as Consumers' Research, which began challenging home economists' claims to represent consumers in the early 1930s. Finally, the limited contact home economists in these corporate jobs often had with consumers also undermined their commitment to understanding and speaking for the public; in the play, consumers themselves were markedly absent, except for the girl scouts. Yet the implied assumption that home economists could speak for consumers, regardless of how directly they were actually involved with them, recurred often in home economists' rhetoric.

The play provides a springboard to explore the relationship between home economists' professional ideals and their accomplishments in the industrial or business sector in the interwar period. To understand the complex ways that home economists' assumptions about their role in the marketplace intersected with their actual experience in commercial jobs, I will analyze them separately, beginning with an examination of the ideals that home economists carried with them into the commercial world. I locate their notion of professional service—to consumers, to corporations, and to American society at large—within the context of their affiliation with the American Home Economics Association, their educational background, and their previous work experience. Then I examine how, guided by the ideals of their profession, these business home economists tried to play a negotiating role between consumers and corporations. They mediated in the production and promotion of consumer goods through a range of activities In their efforts to do so, this small group of home economists became important in shaping the physical and cultural dimensions of an array of consumer products that emerged in the United States between the wars.[2]

IN characterizing the relationship between home economists and the rise of consumer capitalism in the early twentieth century, historians have relied heavily on the writings and career of Christine Frederick. An early spokeswoman for scientific management in the home, Frederick became known as the national authority on "Mrs. Consumer" in 1929, when she published *Selling Mrs. Consumer*, a book that instructed male manufacturers and advertisers on the importance of female buying power and how to manipulate it.[3] Many scholars have used Frederick to represent home economists as sellouts who became instruments of corporate control and then were duped into manipulating American consumers against their better interests.[4] At least one home economist, however, Anna Burdick of the Federal Bureau of Vocational Education, specifically disassociated herself from Frederick in a 1930 letter to Louise Stanley, chief of the Bureau of Home Economics at the United States Department of Agriculture. "I get quite wrought up over having women exploit their own kind," she exclaimed. In the margins of a newspaper clipping about Frederick, she asked: "Is Christine playing to the Gallery? Is she interested in Education or Exploitation?" Burdick was responding to Frederick's speech to the National Retail Institute in which she reiterated the main points of her book. Frederick's speech urged retailers to capitalize on women's natural "eye-appeal and instinct" and their "emotional desire for change," phrases that Burdick

2. For a full discussion of this argument, see Carolyn M. Goldstein, "Mediating Consumption: Home Economics and American Consumers, 1900–1940" (Ph.D. dissertation, University of Delaware, 1994). For more simplistic interpretations, see Laura Shapiro, *Perfection Salad: Women and Cooking at the Turn of the Century* (New York: Farrar, Straus and Giroux, 1986); and John Hess and Karen Hess, *The Taste of America* (New York: Penguin, 1972). For brief discussions of home economists in business, see Margaret Rossiter, *Women Scientists in America: Struggle and Strategies to 1940* (Baltimore: Johns Hopkins University Press, 1982), pp. 258–59; Susan Strasser, *Never Done: A History of American Housework* (New York: Pantheon, 1982); and Harvey Levenstein, *Revolution at the Table: The Transformation of the American Diet* (New York: Oxford University Press, 1988), pp. 156–58, 198.

3. Christine Frederick, *Selling Mrs. Consumer* (New York: Business Bourse, 1929). See also Strasser, *Never Done*, pp. 214–19; and Barbara Ehrenreich and Deirdre English, *For Her Own Good: 150 Years of Experts' Advice to Women* (New York: Doubleday, 1978), p. 180.

4. See, for example, Stuart Ewen, *Captains of Consciousness: Advertising and the Social Roots of the Consumer Culture* (New York: McGraw-Hill, 1976), p. 97; Dolores Hayden, *The Grand Domestic Revolution: A History of Feminist Designs for American Homes, Neighborhoods, and Cities* (Cambridge: MIT Press, 1981), p. 285; Glenna Matthews, *"Just a Housewife": The Rise and Fall of Domesticity in America* (New York: Oxford University Press, 1987), pp. 168–71; and Ehrenreich and English, *For Her Own Good*, p. 180.

underscored to indicate her disapproval.[5] Burdick's response to Frederick suggests that the interpretation of home economists as simple corporate tools, as well as the focus on Frederick as a spokeswoman for the home economics movement as a whole, obscures a less tidy picture of how home economists responded to the growing influence of the corporation over the private sphere. Although Frederick promoted herself as an expert in household matters and shared many activities with home economists in business—writing articles for women's magazines, testing products, and writing brochures as a consultant to various companies—she was not a graduate of a home economics college program.[6] Because of her training and her choice to affiliate primarily with advertising women throughout her professional career, Frederick operated apart from the larger group of home economists who were divided over the nature of their relationship with the consumer goods market. As the members of the American Home Economics Association struggled to resolve that relationship, they confronted issues of professional identity that Christine Frederick, as an outsider to AHEA, did not confront on the same terms.

By juxtaposing education on the one hand and exploitation on the other, Burdick framed a complex context in which home economists transported their tradition of nineteenth-century domestic reform into the burgeoning twentieth-century consumer society. Doing so entailed the messy process of sorting out the fluid categories of public and private, production and consumption, and what historian Warren Susman has termed the cultures of "character" and "personality."[7] For home economists who entered business, charting this gray borderland became a matter of professional identity

5. Anna Burdick to Louise Stanley, October 21, 1930, Folder: Federal Board for Vocational Education, 1929–32, Box 564, Record Group 176, Records of the Bureau of Home Economics and Human Nutrition, National Archives, Washington, D.C. (hereafter RG 176). For a copy of Frederick's speech, see "Mrs. Consumer Speaks Her Mind: How Women Look at Your Store," Folder 10, Box 1, Christine Isobel (MacGaffey) Frederick Papers, Arthur and Elizabeth Schlesinger Library on the History of Women in America, Radcliffe College, Cambridge, Mass. (hereafter CF Papers).

6. After receiving a general B.S. degree in 1906 from Northwestern University, where she studied advertising with Walter Dill Scott, Christine married business writer and editor J. George Frederick. Together they founded the Advertising Women of New York in 1912, an organization she spearheaded for many years. See "Career Chronology of Mrs. Christine Frederick," Folder 3, Box 1, CF Papers; Alumni Biographical Files, Northwestern University Archives; Caroline Shillaber, "Christine McGaffey Frederick," in Barbara Sicherman et al., Notable American Women: The Modern Period (Cambridge, Mass.: Belknap, 1980), pp. 249–50; and Ewen, Captains of Consciousness, 97. Susan Strasser makes a distinction between Christine Frederick and home economists. See Never Done, pp. 246–50, 256–57.

7. Warren Susman, "'Personality' and the Making of Twentieth-Century Culture," in New Directions in American Intellectual History, ed. John Higham and Paul K. Conkin (Baltimore: Johns Hopkins University Press, 1979). For a more recent discussion of these two cultures, see Richard Wightman Fox, "The Culture of Liberal Protestant Progressivism, 1875–1925," Journal of Interdisciplinary History 23 (Winter 1993): 639–60.

in the 1920s. Mary Keown, of the American Washing Machine Manufacturer's Association, was inspired by a vision that work in business would expand the profession's power base. She initiated the establishment of a separate section of the American Home Economics Association in 1920. Four years later, having formed the Home Economics in Business section, Keown and her colleagues invented a role for themselves simultaneously in the association and in the corporate world. They developed a professional ethic which held that home economists' social service and educational orientation, their training as scientists, and their natural intuition about the "woman's viewpoint" combined to qualify them as ideal interpreters or translators between consumers and producers. The idea of service proved fundamental to the rhetorical strategies these transitional figures used to establish their professional authority as expert mediators in the expanding consumer economy.

In the 1920s, as increasing numbers of home economists found employment in areas outside of teaching, they faced the challenge of combining a reform agenda with an occupational one.[8] This challenge entailed solving the problem of how to maintain standards and autonomy as they moved further out of the home and into the marketplace. They advocated an ethic of rational consumption which in one sense was compatible with corporate activities and priorities but in another sense was not. Home economists envisioned an ideal consumer society in which producers manufactured high-quality goods for healthful ways of living and consumers made systematic purchasing choices based on careful considerations of budget and long-term benefits. Through advice booklets, lectures, and radio programs, home economists in all fields sought to influence the dietary and financial practices of American homemakers. Their activities were compatible with corporate efforts to understand and control consumer demand for mass-produced clothing, appliances, and foodstuffs. At the same time, home economists remained wary of some of the manipulative means companies used to promote their products. For example, it was Christine Frederick's stereotyping of female consumers as essentially emotional, intuitive, and hence malleable that so offended Anna Burdick. And home economists remained leery of advertising. Burdick and her fellow home economics educators had trained with professors who, in the name of professional objectivity, disapproved of advertising in the classroom as "not quite 're-

8. Linda Fritschner, "The Rise and Fall of Home Economics: A Study with Implications for Women, Education, and Change" (Ph.D. dissertation, University of California, Davis, 1973). For comparison with other female professionals, see Nancy Tomes and Joan Jacobs Brumberg, "Women in the Professions: A Research Agenda for American Historians," *Reviews in American History* 10 (1982): 275–96; Robyn Muncy, *Creating a Female Dominion in American Reform, 1890–1935* (New York: Oxford University Press, 1991); and Nancy Cott, *The Grounding of Modern Feminism* (New Haven: Yale University Press, 1987), pp. 215–39.

fined'" and wrapped containers in paper to cover brand names.[9] Home economists did not agree about these issues, but Burdick's notion of home economics represents an ideal notion of service to which most home economists aspired.

Commercial work for home economists was nothing new in 1920: as early as the 1880s, domestic scientists such as Sarah Tyson Rorer had provided consulting services for business.[10] But after World War I increasing numbers of women trained in this field found permanent positions with food manufacturers, women's magazines, utility companies, banks, and retail establishments. By 1925, many corporations, often following the initiative of advertising firms or trade associations, had established home economics or home service departments to help them understand consumers and control demand for their products. That year the first list of members of the Home Economics in Business section of the American Home Economics Association included ninety-one women.[11] Of these, the largest group (38, or 42 percent) worked for such food companies as Washburn Crosby (later General Mills), Kellogg's, and Swift. Women's magazines employed the next largest segment of the membership (14, or 15 percent), with utilities following close behind (10, or 10 percent). By 1940, the section included over 600 members employed in more equal numbers by these types of firms. Food companies continued to employ the largest proportion, or 24 percent, of the membership fifteen years later. The relative number of women employed by utility companies grew to 103, or 17 percent. Another 12 percent managed restaurants or tearooms or worked for hotels, yet another 12 percent held positions as journalists with national magazines or local newspapers, and 7 percent listed themselves as independent consultants. Retail establishments such as department stores and grocery chains employed 4 percent, whereas manufacturers of household equipment hired 3 percent.[12]

9. Irene Hume Taylor and Mary Barber, quoted in "Report of Round Table Discussion Held Wednesday Morning, June 25, 1931," Box 1, HEIB, AHEA Archives.

10. On Rorer, see Emma Weigley, *Sarah Tyson Rorer: The Nation's Instructress in Dietetics and Cookery* (Philadelphia: American Philosophical Society, 1977), pp. 42, 116–17, 127, 141–42. On the Singer Manufacturing Company's practice of hiring women to demonstrate its sewing machines in the 1850s, see David Hounshell, *From the American System to Mass Production, 1800–1932: The Development of Manufacturing Technology in the United States* (Baltimore: Johns Hopkins University Press, 1984), pp. 84–85, 88.

11. "Membership List, Home Economics in Business Section, American Home Economics Association," Box 2, Home Economists in Business Archives, Westerville, Ohio (hereafter HEIB Archives). For a reproduction of this list, see *A Forward Force . . . Home Economists in Business* (Vienna, Va.: Home Economists in Business, 1983), pp. 87–89.

12. Members in 1925 also worked for banks, insurance companies, retail distributors, and as independent consultants. On the establishment and growth of the section, see Home Economics Women in Business Directories, 1927–40, Box 1, HEIB, AHEA Archives; Mary Keown to Edna White, May 18, 1920, Edna White to Mary Keown, May 21, 1920, Bess Rowe, "Report of the Committee Appointed to Present a Plan for Establishing Standards of Home Economics

Although they veered off the paths normally expected of them by administrators and professors, the early members of the Home Economists in Business section shared many assumptions with home economics educators about women's special duty and responsibility to serve society. Born in the 1880s and 1890s, they were of the same generation of home economists who extended the Progressive reform tradition into the 1920s and 1930s as teachers or extension workers. Educated in four-year college home economics programs—primarily at land-grant institutions—that placed a heavy emphasis on science, they graduated with knowledge of the basic chemical and physical principles of such subjects as textiles and nutrition.[13] Six out of nineteen members on the 1925 list for whom data on educational background are available had earned master's degrees in home economics, nutrition, or chemistry. Information about previous work experience is available for twenty-one, or slightly more than 20 percent of the total members; of these twenty-one, all but three worked in education, extension work, or some form of social service before taking commercial jobs. For example, Hannah Louise Wessling had worked for the federal government for about fifteen years before taking a position as director of home service at the Northwestern Yeast Company in Chicago.[14] Mary Keown, the founder of the Home Economics in Business section, started out in the extension service in 1916 and worked for four years for the American Washing Machine Manufacturers Association in the early 1920s. By the end of the decade she resumed extension work and continued what the *Extension Service Review* called "a long and distinguished career."[15] Margaret Sawyer left her job as nutrition director of the American Red Cross to develop a home economics department at the Postum Cereal Company (later General Foods) in 1924.[16]

These business home economists and their cohorts derived their concept of service from this educational and occupational context. As they moved into the social structure of the corporation and tried to distinguish themselves from other emerging groups of experts, home economists in business developed an ideological framework in which service and sales complemented, rather than contradicted, each other. This framework incorporated four basic components: first, that their work was educational; second, that

Work in Business," New Orleans, 1923, and Mary Keown, "A Summary of Three Years Work of the Home Economics in Business Section," 1924, Folder "History," Box 3, HEIB Archives; and Chase Going Woodhouse, *Business Opportunities for the Home Economist* (New York: McGraw-Hill, 1938).

13. Fritschner, "The Rise and Fall of Home Economics," pp. 83–89.

14. See "Questionnaire for Chemists," January 1920, File 272, Records of the Bureau of Vocational Information, Schlesinger Library (hereafter BVI).

15. "Mary Keown Will Be Missed," *Extension Service Review* 21 (October 1950): 175; *Progressive Farmer* 61 (January 1946): 35, 40.

16. Margaret Sawyer, "American Home Economics Association and the Health Program," *Journal of Home Economics* (hereafter *JHE*) 16 (December 1924): 683.

as women they could represent the "woman's viewpoint"; third, that they promoted science and objectivity; and fourth, that they were "interpreters" and "diplomats" in the consumer marketplace.

At the outset, home economists in business argued that their work would enhance the educational goals of the American Home Economics Association as well as the reputation of the organization and its members. From their vantage point inside the corporation, they could broaden and expand the audience for their messages about what they called the "art of right living" in American homes.[17] Consumers could learn from the experts about proper dietary habits and the safe, economical use of products. Describing her move to Borden's, Mary O'Leary explained, "I left the classroom, but not teaching."[18] One early vocational adviser to students interested in business careers pointed out that home economists were "missionar[ies] at heart."[19] Although this notion echoed and paralleled claims in the advertising industry that promotional material was of instructional value to consumers, it had a particular depth of significance for home economists who had themselves been teachers.[20] They openly recognized that the issue was ultimately a matter of financial resources: industry-funded materials could be important resources for the teacher or the home demonstration agent. As Jean Rich of the Royal Baking Powder Company put it, "The state, county, or city worker cannot do all the work, both from lack of time and lack of funds. The manufacturer on the other hand has the money."[21]

This educational mission could enlighten the business community as well as consumers, argued home economists in business. By educating manufacturers, they could elevate the standards of product quality and help orient banks, manufacturers, and utilities toward a more service-minded approach to the consumer. Some went so far as to say that working in business would improve products and lessen women's dependence on the male-dominated world of producers. For example, Martha Phillips of the North American Dye Corporation argued that a home economist in business "uses her knowledge to better the products upon which the application of the new methods and theories depend. We are more dependent than we sometimes realize on the manufacturing and business worlds for the products which make possible modern home making." The home economist's presence as a

17. For example, S. Agnes Donham, "The Educational Value of Business Organizations," speech delivered at the 1922 Annual Meeting of the AHEA, File 131, BVI.

18. Mary O'Leary, "Preparation for Business Home Economists as Contrasted with Preparation for Teaching," Folder: "Speeches, Annual Meetings, Etc.," Box 1, HEIB, AHEA Archives.

19. Genevieve Callahan, *Preparation for the Business Field of Home Economics* (San Francisco: Home Economics in Business Group of the San Francisco Bay Region, 1934), p. 8.

20. Roland Marchand, *Advertising the American Dream: Making Way for Modernity, 1920–1940* (Berkeley: University of California Press, 1985), pp. 8–9.

21. Jean K. Rich, "The Food Manufacturer and the Trained Woman," *American Food Journal* 18 (April 1923): 176.

"wedge" in the corporation, she envisioned, would be a "powerful force for betterment and uplift" and, she implied, would temper the hold that corporations had on American domestic life.[22]

This claim suggested that home economists charged themselves not only with instructing women but also with representing them as professional "typical" consumers. Despite the contradiction, insight into the "woman's point of view" constituted a second integral part of these women's professional ethic. As several business home economists agreed at a 1931 meeting, home economists were valuable to their employers because they understood the "viewpoint of the housewife."[23] By "housewife" they meant a specific formulation of a middle-class white woman who had high and rigorous demands for product quality. Interest in health and dietary issues, Mary Keown pointed out, was "a direct result of the work of home economics forces" in schools, colleges, extension agencies, and women's magazines.[24] Having constructed an ethic of well-informed, health-minded consumption in the first place, home economists viewed their representation of this particular group of consumers as a logical extension of their mission. That many home economists in business maintained close contacts with other home economists or women as part of their jobs, using the established networks of state extension agencies to disseminate their message, reinforced their identification with a white middle-class woman's perspective.

In their struggle to obtain professional legitimacy and to distinguish themselves from women in the advertising industry, the pioneers of the early 1920s constantly argued that their job could not be accomplished by just "any sensible woman." Manufacturers, Mary Keown explained, needed "not alone a woman's point of view . . . but the point of view of a woman thoroughly trained to know the housewife's problems and to understand the effective appeal to her."[25] Likewise, Jessie Hoover, a newly appointed home economist at Montgomery Ward in 1929, requested a letter of endorsement from the Bureau of Home Economics to impress upon the mail-order firm the value of home economics training as opposed to advertising training.[26]

22. Martha Phillips, "Home Economics in Business," 1922 speech to the AHEA annual meeting, File 131, BVI.

23. "Report of Round Table Discussion Held Wednesday Morning, June 25, 1931."

24. Mary E. Keown, "The Home Economics Worker in the Food Industry," *American Food Journal* 17 (November 1922): 24.

25. Keown, "The Home Economics Worker in the Food Industry." On adwomen, see Marchand, *Advertising the American Dream*, pp. 33–35; Jacqueline Dirks, "Advertisements for Themselves: Professional Women and the 'Woman's Viewpoint,' " longer version of her paper delivered at the Ninth Berkshire Conference on the History of Women, Vassar College, June 12, 1993; and Jennifer Scanlon, *Inarticulate Longings: The Ladies' Home Journal, Gender, and the Promises of Consumer Culture* (New York: Routledge, 1995), pp. 169–96.

26. Ruth O'Brien to Lenore Sater, February 12, 1929, Folder: "O'Brien, R.," Box 551, RG 176.

The term "home economics training" conveyed not only an education in home economics at a four-year college but also a third element of the business home economists' ideology: a belief in science and objectivity. Whereas home economists' ability to represent the "woman's viewpoint" seemed to make them naturally suited to projecting a human, friendly corporate image to the public, their scientific training in college qualified them to test and evaluate products objectively. With this background, home economists could learn about the scientific and technical aspects of goods at the point of production and thus educate consumers thoroughly about them. Martha Phillips, for example, explained that her job was critical to helping home-makers understand "why colors are, what colors are, and how and where best to use them."[27] S. Agnes Donham of the Society for the Promotion and Protection of Savings in Boston believed that home economists' experience with systematic fact-finding ensured that the company brochures they wrote met standards of truthfulness and clarity. "Definite instruction as to use," "clear, honest statements of results," and "few claims made without supporting fact" were the signature of a trained home economics worker.[28] Most important, Donham grounded her determination to resist sheer profit-making goals in her allegiance to an ethic of unbiased observation.[29] As she explained in a 1922 speech to the American Home Economics Association: "We must guard against over statement and against narrowness of outlook, developing our part of the work as broadly as possible, avoiding what was formerly called 'commercialism,' and creating, on a strong educational basis, good will for our respective firms, while we assist the homemaker to be a better home manager."[30] Mary Keown shared this allegiance. When she initiated the establishment of a separate business section of the organization in 1920, she told the organization's president, Edna White, that "so-called home economics specialists" had received much public attention but "have no home economics training and no real standards by which to measure themselves or their work."[31] Bess Rowe, field editor of the *Farmer's Wife*, argued similarly that home economists in business would "counteract false or misleading information" and the confusing demonstrations presented by unqualified women and men.[32] These home economists believed that unbiased fact-finding and science enabled them to resolve consumer issues by

27. Phillips, "Home Economics in Business."

28. *JHE* 14 (November 1922): 566–67.

29. For expressions of similar convictions by many corporate scientists, see David Houn-shell and John Smith, *Science and Corporate Strategy: Du Pont R&D, 1902–1980* (Cambridge: Cambridge University Press, 1988), chaps. 13 and 15; David Noble, *America by Design: Science, Technology, and the Rise of Corporate Capitalism* (New York: Oxford University Press, 1977).

30. *JHE* 14 (November 1922): 566–67.

31. Mary Keown to Edna White, May 18, 1920.

32. "Home Economists and the Business World," Proceedings of the 1922 Annual Meeting, *JHE* 14 (November 1922): 523–24.

protecting everyone involved in marketplace transactions—the consumer as well as the retailer and the manufacturer.

The synthesis of the female viewpoint with scientific training, home economists argued, qualified them for their unique role in the corporation: that of mediator and interpreter between the firm and its customers. Designating themselves as translators in this respect constituted a final dimension of their ideal notion of service. Home economists occupied, they believed, a strategic link between the manufacturers of equipment and the women who used it. Katherine Fisher, the director of the Good Housekeeping Institute, elaborated on this notion in a speech to the Home Service Bureau of the National Electric Light Association in 1928. For Fisher, if engineers were "statesmen," then women in the appliance field were "super statesmen." She characterized the "electrical women" who ran utility home service departments as "partner[s]" and "balance wheel[s]" to the industrial engineer who brought to the engineer's "attention the need for certain refinements which will mean added convenience to the user." Whereas an engineer developed a device, home economists instructed women about the proper way to "use it to advantage."[33]

Home economists in business often expressed their interpretive role through the metaphor of diplomacy which Fisher employed. Marye Dahnke highlighted the duality of her function in a 1937 autobiographical account of her tenure at Kraft since 1920: "Like the two-faced Janus, I must in my job look two ways at once. First of all, I must represent my company to the consumer. Second, I must represent the consumer's point of view to my company. Only in this way can I fulfill my function, both as a business woman and a home economist."[34] Home economists experienced a daily challenge of forging consensus and compromise. As one woman put it at a 1931 roundtable discussion of home economists in business, home economists understood "the value of cooperation and the dangers of 'high-hatting' any phase of her concern's work."[35] Rarely did they use oppositional terms to express this challenge, yet Dahnke admitted she preferred the "conflict of business" to the "rewards" of teaching.[36] The thrill and excitement of the commercial world drew in at least some women and kept them there. One occupational adviser stipulated in 1938 that a home economist in business must not only "be able to see both the business point of view of the employer and the home needs of the consumer, but also bring the two into harmony. She must be a happy medium between the

33. "The Woman in the Industry," *Electrical Merchandising* (hereafter *EM*) 39 (June 1928): 90–92.

34. Marye Dahnke, "A Business Career in Home Economics," *Forecast*, April 1937, p. 192.

35. Marjorie Heseltine, quoted in "Report of Round Table Discussion Held Wednesday Morning, June 25, 1931."

36. Dahnke, "A Business Career in Home Economics," p. 166.

professional and the commercial worker."[37] Understanding their role as a matter of "correlating" consumers' desires with corporate goals, home economists believed their gentle diplomacy would foster and maintain the inherent mutuality of interests between producers and consumers.[38]

Achieving this "harmony" often involved the emotional, interpersonal labor of channeling charm and grace toward the task of surrounding an array of new consumer products with what a utility home service manual called an "atmosphere of friendliness."[39] In this respect, home economists' mediating role between consumers and corporations constituted a kind of "emotional labor," to use sociologist Arlie Hochschild's term.[40] Home economists in business pioneered in "personality work," the phrase Suzanne Kolm uses to describe the work performed by stewardesses in postwar America.[41] Although business home economists' jobs varied widely, they involved interacting with consumers in a way that required channeling emotional energy into making companies appear human and responsive to their needs. "Personality," gendered as female in this context, was a cultural concept that allowed home economists to believe that they could see two points of view simultaneously and then reconcile them. Yet home economists were also rooted in Susman's culture of character—of self-control, duty, and honor—that stemmed from the reformist tradition of their field. With one foot in the world of "character" and another in the world of "personality," home economists blurred the boundaries between company and community for consumers and often for themselves.

THE rhetoric of diplomacy that home economists developed belied the fact they negotiated between two unequal parties. In practice, those who worked in business ultimately served corporations more immediately than they did consumers or their own professional goals. But because their professional ethic was predicated on a notion of themselves as diplomats in a

---

37. Woodhouse, *Business Opportunities for the Home Economist*, 118.

38. "Report of Round Table Discussion Held Wednesday Morning, June 25, 1931." Home economists' faith in the American corporate project—common among managers of the period—marked a change from the critical stance an earlier generation of home economists had taken in the Progressive era, but a common faith in the "good" corporations linked home economists across time. See Olivier Zunz, *Making America Corporate, 1870–1920* (Chicago: University of Chicago Press, 1990); and Alfred D. Chandler, Jr., *The Visible Hand: The Managerial Revolution in American Business* (Cambridge, Mass.: Belknap Press, 1977).

39. *Home Service: Helpful Suggestions for Organizing and Operating Home Service Departments* (New York: National Electric Light Association, 1930).

40. Arlie Hochschild, *The Managed Heart: The Commercialization of Human Feeling* (Berkeley: University of California Press, 1983).

41. Suzanne Kolm, "Labor Aloft: A Cultural History of Airline Flight Attendants in the United States, 1930–1978" (Ph.D. dissertation, Brown University, 1995).

marketplace and because they, like so many other groups of the period, understood the interests of producers and consumers as essentially the same, home economists' identity dovetailed nicely with corporate needs. Precisely because home economists felt professionally invested in marketing consumer goods, they were able to assume a comfortable position accommodating the profit-seeking aims of their employers. Their faith in big, "progressive" business, as well as their belief that they had something at stake in the process of producing foods and appliances suitable to American consumers, predisposed them to take cues from the emerging corporate culture, to participate in it, and even to shape it.

In this light, the story of the jobs they performed in business looks more complicated than scholars have previously portrayed it. Although home economists did not have the power to act as the objective diplomats they imagined themselves to be, they did fulfill an important set of mediating functions. In the interwar period, a time when the relationship between producers and consumers was changing and each group had new reasons to attempt to understand the other, home economists operated in the interstices. By virtue of their placement between production and consumption, business home economists embodied the reality and the difficulty of the two realms' interdepence, even though the emerging economic and social structures defined these realms increasingly as separate. Insofar as home economists provided, or seemed to provide, corporations and consumers with ways to communicate with one another, they performed important cultural and technical work.

The promise that home economists could tread the unfamiliar frontier where production and consumption intersected led manufacturers, utilities, and trade associations to hire them in the first place. For these firms, home economics seemed like a way to get closer to the consumer, to control demand more effectively at a time when managers were setting off a "marketing revolution."[42] The products that many of them made—whether lard substitutes or electric ranges and refrigerators—were new; whether people would buy them was not obvious or automatic. Advertising campaigns alone were not sufficient to guarantee public acceptance. These companies understood that there had to be a two-way street, that they had to do more to "read" potential markets and "listen" to consumers. Because man-

---

42. On the relationship between home economics and the system of direct selling at Procter & Gamble, see Oscar Schisgall, *Eyes on Tomorrow: The Evolution of Procter & Gamble* (Chicago: J. G. Ferguson, 1981), pp. 87–98. See also Michael Schudson, *Advertising, the Uneasy Persuasion: Its Dubious Impact on American Society* (New York: Basic Books, 1984), pp. 14–43; Susan Strasser, *Satisfaction Guaranteed: The Making of the American Mass Market* (New York: Pantheon, 1989); Richard Tedlow, *New and Improved: The Story of Mass Marketing in America* (New York: Basic Books, 1990).

ufacturers and advertisers assumed 85 percent of their clientele to be women, home economists would be effective in reaching homemakers.[43] In addition, because home economists had scientific training and practical experience as household managers, they seemed best qualified to explain clearly the use of a given product. Perceived as professional "typical" consumers, home economists promised their employers they would intuit the needs of other women as well as rationalize consumer behavior.

At the same time, manufacturers, utilities, and the trade associations to which they belonged found home economists useful in achieving a related goal, that of public relations. Popular criticism of the extent of economic concentration in these industries, especially in the utilities, as well as charges of false advertising, pressured leaders in the consumer products industries to go out of their way to promote positive images of themselves and the goods and services they sold.[44] Facing the new and expanding challenge of fostering public goodwill, they welcomed the professional image of home economists for two reasons. On one hand, home economists' scientific training qualified them to be objective standard-bearers and to provide educational service "free of commercialism."[45] Home economists' understanding of themselves as "missionaries at heart" was an asset to such firms.[46] On the other hand, that home economists were women seemed to make them naturally suited to projecting a human, friendly image of the corporation to the public, especially the homemaker.[47]

In the early 1920s, having a staff of home economists became a hallmark of the "progressive" company. But the home economists' place in the corporation was not clearly defined. Most firms did not expect immediate sales

43. Charles McGovern has found expressions of this assumption in the advertising literature as far back as the 1890s. See "Sold American: Inventing the Consumer" (Ph.D. dissertation, Harvard University, 1993), p. 30n55. See also Marchand, *Advertising the American Dream*, pp. 66–69; Cott, *Grounding of Modern Feminism*, p. 172; Schudson, *Advertising, the Uneasy Persuasion*, pp. 178–208; Ewen, *Captains of Consciousness*, pp. 159–76.

44. On public relations in the electrical industry, see David Nye, *Image Worlds: Corporate Identities at General Electric, 1880–1930* (Cambridge: MIT Press, 1985), pp. 135–47.

45. See "Heads Home Economics Department," *Cheesekraft* 5 (July–August 1925): 5, Kraft/General Foods Archives, Morton Grove, Ill. On the importance for employers that "workers enact their roles with conviction," see Robin Leidner, "Serving Hamburgers and Selling Insurance: Gender, Work, and Identity in Interactive Service Jobs," *Gender and Society* 5 (June 1991): 157.

46. Callahan, *Preparation for the Business Field of Home Economics*, p. 8.

47. See Frank B. Rae, Jr., "Buying Tomorrow's Good-Will with Today's Dollars," *EM* 21 (March 1919): 115–17; Tom J. Casey, "Common Sense Merchandising," *EM* 26 (July 1921): 30–33; and Clotilde Grunsky, "Always with a Smile!," *EM* 31 (March 1924): 4148–49, 4172. On issues of gender in the public relations field at the turn of the century, see Angel Kwolek-Folland, "Gender, Self, and Work in the Life Insurance Industry, 1880–1930," in *Work Engendered: Toward a New History of American Labor*, ed. Ava Baron (Ithaca: Cornell University Press, 1991), pp. 168–90.

results from the home economists they hired, although they did anticipate that the investment would pay off. Lacking a ready model, managers had to decide where to fit these women professionals into the structure of their firm and how to interact with them. Companies hired them to perform a new set of duties and to supplement those of male managers, advertisers, and salespeople. Sometimes companies took the initiative in establishing home economics departments; other times home economists literally carved spaces for themselves in corporations and trade associations. In most cases, managers and the women they hired looked for cues from one another as to the proper function home economists should serve. In the absence of fully developed departments of consumer and marketing research, home economists, like the protagonist in "Experiment 63," performed a range of functions. As Miss Welldone told a young home economics student, she could succeed in a business job "if you can be a diplomat and an artist and a copywriter and a nurse and an executive and a thousand and one other things, too."[48] Collectively, their spectrum of responsibilities included interpreting products to consumers, testing products for quality standards, interpreting consumers to corporate managers, and even developing or improving products.

A major part of their job was to interpret products to consumers. As directors of home economics, home service, or educational departments, they promoted food products, household equipment, or textile fabrics in a manner intended to explain products from the perspective of the homemaker or user. Home economists presented information through two major channels: published cookbooks, recipe booklets, and other brochures as well as demonstrations to public audiences. In both cases home economists helped pave the way for the acceptance of new products and the new ways of living that they implied.

The recipe booklets home economists wrote were technical manuals for the use of items ranging from leavening agents to the electric range. They provided "how-to" instruction about the narrowest as well as the broadest ways to employ a given product. The preparation of these texts gave home economists an opportunity to interpret goods according to their own values by choosing to place them in certain contexts rather than others. For example, by developing recipes specifying exact temperatures that took advantage of new control mechanisms on gas and electric stoves, home economists taught homemakers how to take advantage of these new features while also spreading the latest ideas about nutrition. They pointed out that the relative slowness of electric stoves in boiling water encouraged the more

48. Dillon, "Experiment 63," p. 20.

healthful practice of "waterless cookery," in which a minimum of water was used to steam vegetables so as to preserve vitamins.[49] In doing so, home economists made their expertise central to the use of a new realm of products, much as other types of technical guides worked to popularize the ideas of the experts who wrote them.[50]

Although food companies pioneered live cooking demonstrations that featured their brand name goods, by the late 1920s utility home service departments sponsored many demonstrations as well. When, in the 1910s, electrical dealers stopped selling appliances as novelties and shifted their focus to the "practical appeal" of toasters, ranges, and percolators, instructing consumers about the useful features of such devices became important. Selling this way, a member of the Philadelphia Electric Company's advertising department remarked, not only increased initial sales but also ensured "that the appliances sold will stay connected to the system and not be kept on the pantry shelf for occasional use."[51]

In the 1920s, home economists became part of a gendered division of labor in which women gave instruction about appliances and men sold them. Home service classes or "parties" created a neighborly cushion around male sales campaigns by introducing women to appliances in a pressure-free context. These demonstrations paved the way for visits from door-to-door salesmen and often helped close a doubtful sale afterward.[52] In addition to the twelve-part cooking lessons it offered, the home service department at Peoples' Gas, Light, and Coke in Chicago advised on canning, budget planning, and various other household matters. The lessons, radio programs, and "kitchens on wheels" became so much a part of the utility's operations that its managers designed special auditoriums for their branch offices as they were erected throughout the decade.[53] In large cities and small towns all over the country—wherever a power company was in operation—demonstrations by home economists increasingly became part of

49. Jane Busch, "Cooking Competition: Technology on the Domestic Market in the 1930s," *Technology and Culture* 24 (1983): 224–25; Florence Clauss, "How Can We Sell More Ranges?," *EM* 40 (October 1928): 62.

50. For a general account of the "modern how-to book" in this period, see Joseph Corn, "Educating the Enthusiast: Print and the Popularization of Technical Knowledge," in *Possible Dreams: Enthusiasm for Technology in America*, ed. John L. Wright (Dearborn, Mich.: Henry Ford Museum and Greenfield Village, 1992), pp. 18–33.

51. "To Cash in on the 'Kitchen Movies,'" *EM* 17 (February 1917): 59.

52. Florence Freer, "Home Service . . . Opens the Door," *EM* 47 (June 1932): 44–45.

53. "Gas Company Model Kitchen on Wheels," *Peoples Gas Club News*, October 16, 1922, p. 265; "Our Home Service Department," *Peoples Gas Club News*, May 16, 1923, p. 150; "Tuning in with Home Service," *Peoples Gas Club News*, February 1, 1924, p. 3. On the auditoriums, see "Our Home Service Department," *Peoples Gas Club News*, November 15, 1923, p. 355; "Opening Dates, Branch Home Service Auditoriums." All of these documents are located at the Peoples Gas, Light, and Coke Company Library, Chicago.

the shopping experience, although home economists rarely made sales themselves in the 1920s.

The audiences for these lessons ranged from sales representatives within the corporation to African American domestic servants. For the most part, however, home economists devoted their energies to establishing face-to-face relationships with consumers who most closely resembled themselves: white, middle-class American housewives, many of whom had studied home economics in secondary school or college. Some, like Marie Sellers, who left her editorial job at *Pictorial Review* magazine to take a job with Postum in 1926, were hired specifically to "build consumer contacts through home service directors in the public utility field, home demonstration agents, other manufacturers, and women's organizations."[54] Home economists were rarely given the formal task of surveying consumers or doing systematic market research, but in the process of cultivating a network of extension workers, teachers, and women's club members, many home economists brought back information from the field which helped interpret consumers to corporations.

In addition to serving as a conduit of information between manufacturers and consumers, several home economists performed an interpreting function behind the scenes by applying their scientific skills and expertise to testing products. At Sears, Roebuck and Company, Elizabeth Weirick emerged as a leader of the mail-order firm's testing laboratory.[55] Trained in chemistry at the University of Chicago in the 1910s, Weirick allied herself to the home economics profession soon after graduation when she took a job teaching chemistry at the Pratt Institute School of Household Science and Arts in Brooklyn, New York. While at Pratt, Weirick developed a course in textile and dye chemistry to train women for industrial positions. In researching the course, she spent a summer working in a New Jersey bleachery and later trained with J. Merritt Matthews, a professor at the Philadelphia Textile School, which prepared men for manufacturing positions and other careers in the textile field.[56]

54. "Once Upon a Time: A History of the Consumer Service Department," p. 2, Kraft/General Foods Archives. See also Mary Keown, "Winning the Support of Home Economics Leaders to Teach Electric Laundering," *EM* 29 (April 1923): 3256–57.

55. E. S. Weirick, "Sears Merchandise Testing and Development Laboratory," 1936; Elizabeth Weirick, "What Sears, Roebuck and Co. Are Doing to Give Their Customers the Best of Materials Obtainable and to Improve Their Service to These Customers," address delivered at a Joint Meeting of the American Chemical Society and the American Institute of Chemical Engineers, Purdue University, November 30, 1932; Elizabeth Weirick, "Control of Merchandise through Laboratory Inspection," Address to the Industrial Management Society, Chicago, January 11, 1940; and "Elizabeth S. Weirick Remembered," *Tower News*, April 16, 1976. All of these sources are located in the Sears Archives, Chicago, Ill.

56. Ellen B. McGowan to Emma Hirth, September 8, 1921, File 300, BVI.

In 1919 A. V. Mory hired Weirick to head the textile division of the product testing laboratory he had recently established at the Sears, Roebuck headquarters in Chicago. Within ten years, she became director of the Sears technological laboratories and guided them through more than a decade of growth and expansion. She enlarged the textile and chemical divisions and established new mechanical, electrical, home economics, and library divisions. By the time she retired in 1940, she had built the lab from just a few people to more than eighty scientists and technicians. Many of the laboratory's staff were women, attesting to Weirick's ability to use her authority to promote other women scientists and home economists.[57]

The lab provided factual and analytical information about the merchandise sold by Sears and, of course, aimed to boost the salability of the company's products.[58] Laboratory workers performed the necessary tests to uphold the company's guarantee that all articles listed in the catalog were described honestly. In this capacity, Weirick's labs acted collectively as a service bureau to Sears's advertising departments. They also cooperated closely with manufacturers and consumers. By testing products under household conditions, the lab helped Sears to select which merchandise to carry as well as to improve upon merchandise by making suggestions to manufacturers and working out standard specifications for buyers. The lab also conducted special research to develop new products or features. Supervising quality control of stock merchandise, writing instructions for care and use, and investigating customers' complaints were other responsibilities of the laboratory.

Weirick saw her responsibility in the lab as to use her scientific knowledge and training to promote the welfare of both her employer and its customers. Her 1936 policy outline specified that the lab existed for the purpose of "seeking accurate, unbiased, scientific information concerning merchandise or scientific facts." It promised "independent, unbiased results, free from [the] prejudiced influence of any department or person."[59] By translating technical knowledge to the consumer, Weirick and her department functioned as an intermediary between the firm and the homemaker. That home economists "would have to act as interpreters between the distributor and the consumer" was a point, she recalled at a 1931 meeting of the Home Economics in Business section, that she had had to "impress upon her company" at the outset, however.[60] In this respect Weirick

57. Among the women Weirick hired were Leone Ann Heuer, Laura Pratt, Mary Antrim Linsley, and Abbie Claire Dennen. See HEIB membership directories, 1925–40, AHEA Archives and HEIB Archives.

58. Weirick, "Sears Merchandise Testing and Development Laboratory," pp. 2–5.

59. Quoted ibid., p. 2.

60. "Report of Round Table Discussion Held Wednesday Morning, June 25, 1931."

61. Keown, "Home Economics in Business," *JHE* 16 (August 1924): 457.

echoed Mary Keown's earlier claim that business home economists, by mastering technical details, could eliminate dissatisfaction resulting from "misinterpretation" on the part of the manufacturer, dealer, or customer.[61] As part of her role as expert interpreter at Sears, Weirick forged ties with textile specialists at the United States Department of Agriculture's Bureau of Home Economics who were working to establish standard garment sizes for children and women.[62]

Several home economists participated in product development as part of their official duties. Margaret Mitchell, director of the test kitchen at the Wear-Ever Cooking Utensil Company, worked to develop new utensils starting in 1933. That year, at the suggestion and encouragement of an electric range manufacturer, the company began developing utensils suitable for use on an electric range. Utility companies had found that housewives complained about how high their first electric bill was after they had had a range installed. When a home service agent visited to find out what the problem was, "nine times out of ten she would find the trouble was due to improper utensils." Utilities hoped that fewer service calls would be necessary if they could make appropriate equipment available. Mitchell studied the sizes, shapes, and capacities of utensils the electric range manufacturers thought would be "efficient." Sales managers and home service agents of utility companies taught her how "proper utensils would simplify" their work and help sell ranges.[63]

Mitchell further surveyed editors of women's magazines and visited department stores as a "typical" consumer to find "efficient" pans for electric stoves. She deduced from her investigations that utensils for the electric range should have straight sides and perfectly flat bottoms, that they should exactly fit the range elements, that they should be of two-, three-, and four-quart capacity, and that a set that could be used both for surface and oven cookery would be ideal.

In addition, Mitchell met in a "long session" with Wear-Ever product development engineers. In the test kitchen she and her team checked samples "from every possible angle and given what would be equal to approximately six months use in a home." During this trial period, she recalled, "we made many changes" and "worked out styles and designs that gave them eye appeal and watched closely to make certain that any changes incorporated increased the practicability and beauty without changing the actual cost."[64]

After the trial period, Mitchell made the case for investing in "several thousand dollars of machinery" to build these utensils and sell them.

62. See, for example, Ruth O'Brien to Elizabeth Weirick, July 25, 1924, Folder: "Sears, Roebuck & Co.," Box 701, RG 176.

63. Margaret Mitchell, "Home Economists in the Equipment Field," 1937 speech, Folder: 1930s minutes, Box 1, HEIB Archives.

64. Ibid.

Placed on the market in June 1935, the products proved successful. By 1936, a year later, sales had increased fivefold, and utilities soon included the utensils with ranges in promotions. By 1937, Mitchell envisioned that "the day is not too far off when they will be just as much a part of the equipment of the range as the oven heat regulator is today." Although not all home economists were explicitly charged with developing new products as was Mitchell, many found ways to slip in new ideas or suggestions along the way.[65]

Eleanor Ahern's career at Procter & Gamble embraced a wide range of duties and illustrates the fluidity with which home economists moved within the boundaries between matters of production and consumption inside a given company.[66] Hired in 1924 as the first director of home economics at Procter & Gamble, Ahern worked there until her retirement in 1958. She came to the soap and shortening manufacturer with ten years' experience in a variety of home economics positions. Her first job after receiving a home economics degree from the University of Chicago in 1913 was as a high school teacher in West Chicago. Remaining in Chicago, she moved on to become the director of home economics for Wilson & Company, a meatpacking firm, and then spent three years as a dietitian at Michael Reese Hospital.[67]

Before hiring Ahern to develop a home economics department on a permanent basis, P&G had employed women and home economists beginning in 1911 for its pioneering advertising campaign for Crisco shortening. A small group of demonstrators traveled throughout the United States conducting week-long cooking schools. The firm also commissioned cookbooks of tested recipes by such well-known leaders in the profession as Marion Harris Neil. These women representatives participated in Procter & Gamble's pioneering strategy to create a continuous demand for its products by establishing brand-name identification among women consumers.[68]

Procter & Gamble's decision to establish a home economics department in 1924 was part of this overall marketing strategy. It is unclear which division of the company initiated the home economics department. At the outset, however, Ahern oversaw a new test kitchen and a laundry which were under the supervision of both the advertising division and the chem-

65. Ibid. For another example of a home economist who worked for an equipment manufacturer, see Regina Lee Blaszczyk's essay in this volume.

66. *Who's Who of American Women* (Chicago: A. N. Marquis, 1958); Schisgall, *Eyes on Tomorrow*; Eleanor Ahern, "A Short History of the Home Economics Department," 1958, R. K. Brodie, "Policy and Purpose of Home Economics Dept.," April 1, 1924, and R. K. Brodie to A. K. Schoepf, June 5, 1924, Procter & Gamble Archives, Cincinnati, Ohio (hereafter P&G).

67. *Who's Who of American Women*, p. 23.

68. Schisgall, *Eyes on Tomorrow*, pp. 11–12; Ahern, "A Short History of the Home Economics Department," pp. 2–4.

69. R. K. Brodie, "Policy and Purpose of Home Economics Dept.," April 1, 1924, and R. K. Brodie to A. K. Schoepf, June 5, 1924, P&G.

ical division.[69] She was responsible for working with advertising agencies on conceptual ideas, photography, layout, and recipe development for promotional programs. In her history of the home economics department, she credited herself with introducing the use of level measurements and a scientific attitude toward cooking into the company's recipe booklets. She also assisted with early market research efforts.[70]

To a large extent, however, Ahern's work in both laundry and bakery matters was directed by men associated with the production end of the firm. The test kitchen was located in the chemical division of the firm's manufacturing department at its Ivorydale, Ohio, plant. At this facility, Ahern collaborated with male engineers to tie the division's "experimental and research work" to consumers' needs and desires. While these men studied "food problems" such as fat absorption, the use of oil in salad dressings and mayonnaise, and rancidity, Ahern worked to develop optimal frying and baking temperatures as well as cooking processes. Ahern's regular consultation with the engineers on matters of food preparation required a thorough understanding of Crisco's physical and chemical properties.[71]

Ahern also devoted energy to improving the company's products. For example, in the late 1930s, Crisco faced competition from Spry, a Lever Brothers shortening product. Housewives apparently thought Spry creamed more easily than the Procter & Gamble product. Crisco sales dropped. The chemical division at Ivorydale insisted that its test, which consisted of dropping a plunger into cans of both products, showed no difference between the two. Ahern's team tested the actual behavior of the two products by timing women stirring them both with sugar. In this test, Spry indeed turned out to be easier. Based on the results of work in the test kitchen, Crisco engineers changed the manufacturing process to make a better, more competitive product.[72]

By virtue of her placement between these two parts of the firm, Ahern acted as a conduit between them. She also remained as close to as many representative consumers as possible to be on the lookout for new ideas. She combined her knowledge of food preparation in the home with that of company production processes to do more than just advertising; in her own eyes and in those of the company, she performed a function critical to the commercial success of P&G and its products.

70. Ahern, "A Short History of the Home Economics Department."

71. Brodie, "Policy and Purpose of Home Economics Dept."; "Food Problems," October 8, 1928, P & G Archives. The 1910s and 1920s were an important time for the development of vegetable oils for cooking. See David Wesson, "Some Phases of Progress in Vegetable Oil Production," in *Twenty-five Years of Chemical Engineering Progress,* ed. Sidney Kirkpatrick (New York: Institute of Chemical Engineers, 1933).

72. Ahern, "A Short History of the Home Economics Department," pp. 4–5.

Demonstrating products, testing them in laboratories behind the scenes, and suggesting ways to improve them were some of the ways home economists mediated. But just as the role of mediator within the firm offered home economists professional opportunity and often a great deal of power, it also relegated the women to marginal positions within the firm. Home economists' relative invisibility inside the firm contrasted with their extreme public visibility in the community. Because their authority derived from establishing connections between divisions rather than from expertise associated with a single division, their "translating" contribution remained hidden from upper management.[73] That such a product was invisible and that they were women dealing with other women were elements of a professional strategy that left them vulnerable.

Even in the mid-1930s, when more than five hundred home economists found employment in business, one home economics director remarked that her male colleagues still did not approve of women's presence in the firm. "However well a man may like women as women," she said, "I never knew one who did not prefer infinitely to work with men in business hours. They admit the value of women in this type of work but they are fundamentally opposed to women in an office." When they were tolerated at all, it was not because of their "sex appeal" to their "business usefulness." In this environment the writer acknowledged that she had to let men take credit for her ideas "in order to get them over." Those successful at influencing institutions understood that "the main object must be to put [our ideas] to work and to find satisfaction in seeing them succeed, even if they are changed beyond recognition."[74]

Yet the allure of high salaries made compromises and the long-term vulnerability of the group worthwhile for many individual women. Some, especially those who started home economics departments and remained directors for several decades, earned impressive salaries exceeding those of the average extension agent or teacher.[75] But these cases were more excep-

---

73. On the gendered nature of "translating" or instructional work in science and its relationship to the production of knowledge, see Sally Gregory Kohlstedt, "In from the Periphery: American Women in Science, 1830–1880," *Signs* 4 (Autumn 1978): 81–96.

74. Anonymous interviewee quoted in Woodhouse, *Business Opportunities for the Home Economist*, pp. 38–39.

75. Little evidence for individual women in specific firms is available, but vocational guides describe a market in which some home economists received large salaries but most earned salaries comparable to or slightly more than women in teaching or extension work. For 1929–30, Ruth Yeomans Schiffman claimed that women in charge of home economics departments could earn "up to $15,000." Home economists in "outstanding positions" with newspapers and magazines received "$10,000 or more." The $3,000 that fell on the high end of the scale earned by government home demonstration workers was more typical, however. See "An Outline of Opportunities in Home Economics," in *Careers for Women: New Ideas, New Methods, New Opportunities*, ed. Catherine Filene, 2d ed. (Boston: Houghton Mifflin, 1934), pp. 317, 320–21.

tional than typical. Although vocational adviser Genevieve Callahan noted in the height of the Depression that there was "theoretically no upper limit," she situated the median salary between $2500 and $5000. She explained: "There are a great many more $1800 salaries than $18,000 ones!" In a 1942 edition of her guide, Callahan declared home economics work in business "no gold mine."[76] Remuneration in business still either matched or exceeded that in teaching, but as another student of home economics occupations put it, "When one considers that the business year is fifty-two weeks instead of thirty-six, the larger salary does not seem so attractive."[77] The reality of high payment for some was an important but not the only factor that attracted home economists to commercial positions and kept them there.

By the late 1930s, home economists had acquired a place in most major consumer products firms. Yet although their different mediating roles added up to a substantial body of accomplishments, they did not necessarily result in harmonious relations between consumers and producers in the way that home economists, or even their employers, had initially intended or imagined. As the play "Experiment 63" suggested, both the professional ideals and the patterns of practical experience contained signs that, on the eve of World War II, a harmonious marketplace of rational consumers and producers had not been achieved.

Although home economists aimed to deliver their service to society with what Kraft home economics director Marye Dahnke called "all the composure of a hostess at tea-time," this ideology contained contradictions and tensions.[78] Their claims to professionalism and autonomy were precarious. On the most basic level, consumers' interests and corporate goals did not always coincide. Business home economists could maintain their commitment to education and objectivity only when employers hired them as scientists and when this definition of service was useful to their business needs. Nor did home economists have exclusive claim to being archetypal consumers. Consumers, furthermore, did not necessarily digest the ethic of rational consumption along with the products they purchased.

Soon after Anna Burdick articulated her thoughts on Christine Frederick in 1930, the experiences of the new decade challenged the ideals forged in the 1920s. Economic depression, the rise of consumer advocacy groups such as Consumers' Research, and the growth of marketing as a specialized field made visible the tensions between service and sales. Increased com-

---

76. Genevieve A. Callahan, *Preparation for the Business Field of Home Economics,* 2d ed. rev. (Washington, D.C.: American Home Economics Association, 1942), 18.

77. Laura Clark, "A Study of Occupations, Other Than Homemaking, Open to Women Trained in Home Economics," *Vocational Education News Notes,* March 1926, p. 12, File 127, BVI.

78. Dahnke, "A Business Career in Home Economics," 192.

79. On confrontations between AHEA and Consumers' Research, see Folder: Consumers' Research, Box: Executive Unit, AHEA Archives; and McGovern, "Sold American."

pany pressure on home economists to show their economic value in "cold figures" and competition from other groups proclaiming themselves "experts" about American consumers prompted growing concern and debate among home economists.[79] Many issues remained unresolved in the late 1930s as the defining characteristics of a "real" home economist became increasingly elusive.

More and more, home economists became torn over who they were to serve. As the utilities pressured them to move away from public relations and educational activities and more directly into sales, some home economists eagerly embraced the challenge to engage on a more commercial basis, while others tried to hold on to the goodwill and service orientation of the job as they had known it.[80] For example, after eleven years as a home service representative at the Brooklyn Edison Company, Beatrice Jackson found conditions "disagreeable" there in 1941. "As time goes on," she wrote, "our work becomes less and less of Home Economics and more and more of selling and so I feel I would do better elsewhere."[81] The disillusionment of Jackson and others signaled a disjuncture between "sales" and "service" created by new economic circumstances and a change that indicated a corresponding cultural imperative of "personality" over "character."

Jackson's response suggested that although home economists tried to preserve distinctions between selling and educating, those who chose business careers could not avoid the role of "Selling Mrs. Consumer" as outlined by Christine Frederick.[82] In the end, business home economists had to contribute to their employers' goals, regardless of the extent to which they served the public interest. But what was perhaps an inevitable and incommensurate confrontation between ideals of service and sales should not obscure the importance of these women's attempts to mediate between consumers and corporations. The role of industrial home economists in the production and marketing of consumer goods was complex. Upon close examination, home economists' participation in the world of commerce emerges as part of a dynamic way in which power companies, manufacturers of processed and packaged foods, and electrical appliance makers achieved a powerful influence in American life. For two decades, home economists, as women and as scientists, with one foot in the culture of "character" and another in that of "personality," filled a void in these firms.

80. Laurence Wray, "Cold Figures on Home Service," *EM* 53 (April 1935): 11, 35; "Come Off the Pedestal, Home Economists," *EM* 56 (December 1936): 10.

81. Beatrice Jackson to Flora Rose, March 20, 1941, New York State College of Home Economics Records, Division of Rare and Manuscript Collections, Cornell University Library, Ithaca, N.Y.

82. Frederick did, after all, share many assumptions with home economists, and her orientation to commercial goals had its limits. For example, she was opposed to overemphasizing color and style in product marketing. See Marchand, *Advertising the American Dream*, p. 159.

Managers found them useful in the delicate matters of human relations; at a time of cultural and economic transition, they helped the consumer products industries reach out to their customers. Home economists' professional strategy shaped and reinforced a relationship between manufacturers and consumers based on a gendered, white, middle-class construction of consumer society. For consumers, the presence of home economists in the marketplace meant that proper purchase of goods for the private sphere depended on advice from experts who projected a public, feminine ideal of "personality" and performance. In their jobs as home service consultants, food specialists, and product testers, home economists became integral to a cultural and technological system geared to producing consumer goods and values. Their knowledge, values, aspirations, and limitations became a part of the package.

REMINISCENCES | *Satenig St.Marie*

SATENIG ST.MARIE became the first woman vice-president in the JCPenney Company, where she worked from 1959 to 1987. As director of consumer affairs she was responsible for educational publications including the JCPenney *Forum,* a nationally distributed magazine aimed at Home Economics professionals. She developed programs designed to bring the voice of the consumer into the Penney Company, including one called Consumer Feedback. St.Marie recounts the three phases of her career, including her experiences in business and how she learned to "manage the boss."

Home economics was not on my horizon when I was growing up in East Bridgewater, Massachusetts, partly because there was no such program in our schools. My neighbor's daughter was a dietitian so I decided that was what I wanted to be. After enrolling in Simmons College in Boston and learning about the many opportunities in home economics, I changed my mind. Simmons required liberal arts for two years and concentration on your major for the next two. It was an excellent program.

I did not develop as a home economist until I started my first job. My career has been in three phases. The first was in the extension service, probably the most valuable time of my career in shaping me as a home economist. In school we learned subject matter, but it wasn't until I started to work in the extension service that I learned how to apply it and to understand that a home economist is a professional who focuses on the family, using her knowledge to help families help themselves. Extension also taught me how to be an administrator, how to manage resources to accomplish goals. It was a wonderful experience, and I always think of those years as the foundation of my career.

The second phase was my business career. Those are what I call the power years because I did have a lot of power. I had influence not only within the company but also, I think, in the profession. I began my career in the JCPenney Company as an educational consultant in the Consumer Services Department, grew into manager of educational and consumer

297

services, and finally became divisional vice-president and director of consumer affairs. Some people have said that home economists in business are not independent and they do what their boss tells them to do. Frankly, that surprised me because I don't know anyone who doesn't have a boss. Even the CEO has a boss, and that's the Board of Directors. But how you manage that boss and how you're able to get that boss to do what you think ought to be done, speaking in terms that are within his or her frame of reference, is what makes a difference. In my case, it was his frame of reference because when I started off in the Penney Company, I was the only woman on the professional level. Most of the men thought I was working because my husband couldn't support me, which was really funny because he is a dentist and probably earned more than some of them. They didn't know why I was there, but they tolerated me. At first, it did not seem that I would ever have a job with real responsibility. When I was thirty-five years old, my boss was promoted and a twenty-two-year-old boy, right out of college was brought in to be my boss. That was a blow. I had more experience and more education, but I was a woman, and who ever heard of a woman managing a department with a sizable budget? It just wasn't within their frame of reference. But reporting to this kid, after all *my* years of experience, wasn't in my frame of reference. That was a turning point for me. I decided to let him sink or swim on his own with only a minimum of help from me, and I prayed hard for a miracle. I believe in divine guidance because in a few months he was called into the service. Once he left, the men in the company decided to give me a chance to run the department. I didn't receive the salary and didn't get the title, but I was given the chance to manage the Consumer Services Department. They hesitated because they didn't believe a woman could manage all that money—it *was* a sizable budget. The rest is history. Not only did I manage that department, but I convinced the company to change the program that had been in place for a long time, We evolved from a program that developed educational materials for home economics teachers to use in sewing classes to one that focused on consumer education. The seventeen hundred Penney store managers who bought these materials from our department to give to teachers in their communities, as well as some of the teachers, had to be brought along to accept this new focus. Our program did not promote products. It was purely educational. Nobody in the company was telling me what to do. I was giving leadership to the company by providing one kind of service that our stores could give to the community, based on what I believed educators wanted and needed. Of course, I was lucky to have bosses who supported me, but I also had to know how to get them to understand that what I was trying to do was in the best interests of the company.

As an administrator, I had home economists working for me. One area in which they did not have enough strength was in understanding how to function within a political system. They did not know how to get the boss to do what they wanted done. They did not understand how to analyze the political hierarchy in the company, how to determine the power structure, or how to feed an idea into the system so that it was eventually presented by someone in a position of power as his idea. For example, as a woman in the company, I knew that I could never become the CEO, or even the President, but I knew which men were in the pipeline (because I developed my own grapevine) and planted my ideas with them. If I succeeded, they took full credit for it as their program that was in the best interest of the company, and I had the satisfaction of meeting my objective, which was to help educators, who in turn helped families in their communities. In my opinion, this is real power. To achieve it, you must have political skills and you must be willing to let others take credit for your ideas. You win some and you lose some, but professionally, it is stimulating and, at times, fun.

I can't say that there was a high point or a low point in my career because I had hitched my wagon to a star and expected some bumps as well as some smooth roads. Besides, my career isn't over yet. Certainly the day I was elected the first woman vice-president of the JCPenney Company was an exciting one for me. I wasn't even at the office. I was attending an AHEA meeting. It was a dream come true. And being appointed the first woman on many national committees and two boards of directors of companies was also a thrill.

Now I'm in the third phase of my career, which I call my creative phase. I retired from the Penney Company in 1987. I now work for myself, and it is absolutely great because I take on only those projects that appeal to me, ones that take advantage of my strengths and are fun. Since I enjoy administration, I found a wonderful small professional organization that needed my skills, the Antiques Dealers' Association of America, which I manage out of my office at home. Not only is it fun, but as a collector, I am learning much about antiques, which really are artifacts that reflect how families of another era lived. In addition, I always enjoyed creative writing but did not have much time to pursue this interest when I was in the business world. Now, as lifestyles editor of *Victorian Homes* magazine, I write a column for each issue on some aspect of Victorian life. I also had the thrill of proposing a book to a major publisher in New York and having it accepted. My book Romantic Victorian Weddings, *Then and Now* was published in 1992 by Dutton Studio Books. I hope there will be more books in my future.

One thread that runs through my career is that all of my jobs have involved some aspect of pioneering. First, in extension, I convinced the county agricultural agent to give us a budget, which the department had not had before. Then, of course, at JCPenney, I pioneered the role of women and became the first woman vice-president and now I am helping the Antiques Dealers' Association build a professional organization.

Two things that happened in society probably influenced my career the most. They were the consumer movement, which made many companies decide that they should have a consumer affairs director, and the women's movement, which put pressure on business to open up opportunities for women. Fortunately, I was in the right place at the right time.

14 Home Economics Moves
into the Twenty-First Century

VIRGINIA B. VINCENTI

During the last third of the century, society has changed dramatically and
so too has home economics. Since the 1960s the field has been in an almost
continual state of rethinking itself urged on by societal events and some of
its leaders. Dissatisfied with its place in society, the profession has continued to search for direction to enhance its image and status as well as to render it more powerful in addressing its mission.

This book provides a reinterpretation of home economics by historians
from outside the field, along with reflections of professionals from within.
It provides new insights about how and why home economics in the first
two-thirds of the twentieth century developed as it did, the circumstances
that created barriers to effective professional and disciplinary work of the
professional women in this primarily female field, and the positions they
took to survive.

This chapter adds to the stories told in the earlier chapters, bringing the
reader up to the dawn of the twenty-first century in relation to the profession's search for identity, the way in which it has grappled with race and
ethnicity, and its ongoing struggle to deal with the perceptions of a gendered field. Home economists have incorporated philosophical discussion
of such matters not only into their regularly scheduled professional conferences, but they have sponsored numerous special meetings to deal with
and established new organizations to strengthen the field. Leaders in the
American Home Economics Association (AHEA) initiated numerous opportunities for the association to examine itself and its place in society. Beginning in 1959 to celebrate the 50th anniversary of the organization, a
philosophy statement known as "New Directions" was developed which

reviewed the past and described the present work of the profession through education, research, social welfare and public health, dietetics and institutional administration, and business. It also identified challenges and made suggestions for the future.[1] In 1961, with the help of the U.S. Office of Education, the Federal Extension Service, and home economics units in land-grant universities, AHEA leaders sponsored a national conference in French Lick, Indiana, to address problems of articulation and differentiation in home economics subject matter at the secondary, college, and adult education levels. It explored the "'concept approach' as a possible way of identifying, organizing, structuring, and unifying significant subject-matter content in the field."[2] The conference resulted in workshops sponsored by the U.S. Office of Education to develop outlines of the basic concepts and generalizations in the subject matter specialties within the discipline of home economics.

From 1960–1965 administrators from higher education units with liberal arts backgrounds held what became known as the Lake Michigan Conferences in Chicago. As a result, in 1966 they established the National Council of Administrators of Home Economics (NCAHE). It was conceived as an organization for administrators from all types of degree-granting institutions—small and large, public and private, land grant, state, and parochial to strengthen home economics in higher education. In its early years it tackled the issues of declining enrollments, upgrading faculty, increasing the quality of research and publications, and clarifying the "blurred and indecisive image" of the field.[3]

Also in the mid-1960s administrators, specifically at state universities and land-grant colleges, had become concerned about the field's visibility and power within the National Association of State Universities and Land-Grant Colleges (NASULGC) after NASULGC in 1966 eliminated the Division of Home Economics and created a Commission on Home Economics within the Division of Agriculture.[4] Unhappy with this change in status, the members of the Division on Home Economics established their own organization which they named the Association of Administrators of Home Economics (AAHE).

1. Dorothy D. Scott et al., "Home Economics New Directions," *Journal of Home Economics* 51 (October 1959): 679–85.

2. *Concepts and Generalizations: Their Place in High School Home Economics Curriculum Development, Report of a National Project* (Washington, D.C.: American Home Economics Association, 1959), pp. 20–22.

3. Ardyce Gilbert, ed., *History of the National Council of Administrators of Home Economics, 1960–1990* (N.p., n.d.), p. 1.

4. Christian K. Arnold, ed., *Proceedings of the National Association of State Universities and Land-Grant Colleges*, 80th Annual Convention, November 13–16, 1966, p. 70.

In 1973 AHEA held the Eleventh Lake Placid Conference to develop consensus among members concerning the future direction of the field. In 1974 Daniel Yankelovich, Inc., completed its AHEA-commissioned study of the public's perception of home economics to provide a basis for the association to establish effective goals for a public relations campaign to improve the profession's image. Yankelovich found contradictory perceptions of home economics among employers in business, government, and academics. Some employers considered home economists to be active, skilled, and worthwhile contributors, while others considered them to be traditional and uncertain contributors to the employers' ultimate goals. The 1974 report recommended that the field further clarify its identity before trying to change its confusing polar-opposite public image.[5] In 1975 AHEA published "New Directions II," a two-page purpose statement, recommending a change in emphasis from tasks of home and family life to an ecosystem conceptualization of the field with humans as interdependent within a rapidly changing environment.[6]

A few years later, still searching for further identity clarification, the AHEA Future Directions Committee commissioned Marjorie Brown and Beatrice Paolucci to write *Home Economics: A Definition*.[7] Published in 1979, it is an in-depth philosophical essay that many home economists discussed at national and regional forums and at several state conventions as well as in college and university courses and seminars. Their new conceptualization, which Brown and Paolucci referred to as "home economics as a critical science", was based primarily on Jürgen Habermas's critical theory applied to culture. His theory critiques positivism while at the same time integrating empiricism, hermeneutics, and critical theory to determine how society *ought to be* rather than adapting to *what is*. The discourse prompted proponents of Brown and Paolucci's work to make numerous national presentations and develop publications critiquing unreflective acceptance of cultural norms and values and overemphasis on technical science as the primary means of addressing the mission of the profession and on how to integrate the new philosophy into practice. Over the next few years the Brown and Paolucci essay stimulated much reflection within the

5. "Home Economics Image Study: A Qualitative Investigation," Report prepared for the American Home Economics Association by Daniel Yankelovich, Inc., May 1974.

6. Gladys G. Vaughn, telephone interview, April 14, 1995. Vaughn served on the committee that developed "New Directions II." Gordon Bivens et al., "Home Economics: New Directions II," *Journal of Home Economics* 67 (May 1975): 26–27.

7. Marjorie Brown was professor of home economics education in the College of Education at the University of Minnesota and Beatrice Paolucci was professor of family ecology in the College of Human Ecology at Michigan State University. Both were highly respected within home economics as philosopher-scholars. Marjorie Brown and Beatrice Paolucci, *Home Economics: A Definition* (Washington, D.C.: American Home Economics Association, 1979).

field. To facilitate this process, the AHEA Future Development Committee wrote and distributed discussion outlines and leader guides to all state associations on issues of importance such as the profession's mission, ethics, specialization, and core curriculum. The Brown and Paolucci paper also inspired curriculum changes in institutions in both secondary and higher education from an emphasis on knowledge and skill development to an empowerment model with more concern for critical thinking and cultural critique. The greatest impact has been on home economics teacher education which welcomed a more integrative and less technical alternative.

To maintain the momentum started with Brown and Paolucci's joint work, Lois Lund, dean of the College of Human Ecology at Michigan State University, asked Marjorie Brown to develop a conceptual framework for the profession. Brown undertook this task in two steps. The first was to clarify how its history has led home economics to where it is was then and the second was to examine critically the basic ideas by which home economists understood their profession.[8] While Brown was writing, AHEA initiated an annual competitive commemorative lectureship to celebrate its seventy-fifth anniversary in 1984. It also was designed to stimulate critical thinking and to improve articulation of home economics and its relationship to society. Marjorie Brown, honored as the first lecturer in 1984 for her professional and intellectual contributions to the field, criticized home economics for conforming to existing society, dominated by individualistic goals strongly influenced by business and industry. She argued that the field still inappropriately subscribed to economic materialism, a nineteenth-century view, which contended that physical and economic conditions in society and in the home naturally precede political-moral, social-psychological, and cultural improvement. She also criticized the field for the resulting narrow understanding of the home in physicalistic terms, and for excessive adulation of empirical science and technology. In her view, one consequence was disloyalty to the profession's own aspirations, which created internal inconsistencies between what it espouses and what it does. In her presentation Brown criticized the profession for compromising its commitment to families so as to gain and keep positions in business and industry. Arguing that the field has been "blind and deaf to self-criticism," she concluded, "We cannot undo mistakes of the past, but we can correct them if we will." She challenged the profession to ask itself constantly, "Whose interests do we really serve?"[9] In 1985 Michigan State

8. Marjorie M. Brown, *Philosophical Studies in Home Economics: Basic Ideas by Which Home Economists Understand Themselves* (East Lansing: College of Human Ecology, Michigan State University, 1993), p. xiii.

9. Marjorie M. Brown, "Home Economics: Proud Past—Promising Future," AHEA Commemorative Lecture, *Journal of Home Economics* 76 (Winter 1984): 27, 48–54, quotations on p. 27.

University's College of Human Ecology published Brown's two-volume *Philosophical Studies of Home Economics in the United States: Our Practical-Intellectual Heritage*, and a third volume in 1993, subtitled *Basic Ideas by Which Home Economists Understand Themselves*.[10]

The self-examination continued. From 1984 to 1988 a small group of U.S. and Canadian home economists met annually in Chicago. The meetings stemmed from concern about the increasing emphasis on specialization within the field and the diminishing appreciation for and understanding of its integrative nature. Among those who supported this cause were extension administrators, teacher educators, faculty from several special-ties, but many from the specializations such as fashion merchandising/textiles, family science and child development, gerontology, hospitality management, dietetics/nutrition, housing/interior design, and family eco-nomics were either indifferent or unsupportive. By this time higher educa-tion units had adopted more than thirty names for themselves, either to emphasize its integrative nature or to accommodate the particular com-bination of specializations included in an individual unit. Nationally this proliferation of names exacerbated identity confusion rather than alle-viating it.

By the mid-1980s identity confusion was a problem within NCAHE and AAHE. Many home economics administrators participated in both organi-zations. Distinctions between the groups became blurred. Were both orga-nizations needed? A study was undertaken to examine the possibility of a merger, yet a subsequent vote in 1988 maintained the two entities, but with refocused missions. NCAHE broadened its membership eligibility and fo-cused on professional development for administrators. AAHE strengthened its connections with NASULGC because of its work related to legislation and funding affecting land-grant universities.[11]

By 1992 the identity problem within and outside the profession had be-come so problematic that five major professional home economics organi-zations appointed a joint task force that was charged with creating a process for examining the mission, breadth, scope, and name of the home econom-ics profession and with building consensus among the various home eco-nomics organizations on a name that would be deemed most appropriate for the profession in the years ahead. The work of the task force culminated

10. Marjorie M. Brown. *Philosophical Studies of Home Economics in the United States: Our Practical-Intellectual Heritage*, 2 Vols. (East Lansing: College of Human Ecology, Michigan State University, 1985), and Marjorie M. Brown, *Philosophical Studies in Home Economics: Basic Ideas by Which Home Economists Understand Themselves*.

11. Jennie C. Kitching and Lynda Harriman, "A Background Paper on [the] Association of Administrators of Home Economics and [the] Board on Home Economics, NASULGC," prepared for the 1995 Southern Region Program Leaders Committee meeting, August 1995, p. 6.

in a national meeting entitled Positioning the Profession for the 21st Century that convened in Scottsdale, Arizona, in October 1993.[12]

Through much reasoned discussion, the almost one hundred participants, representing all the specializations within the field from the five sponsoring organizations and several other associations "with vested interest in the well-being of the profession",[13] recommended a new conceptual framework, which included affirmation of diversity and of the field's use of alternative modes of inquiry in addition to that of empirical science. After much deliberation, they selected "family and consumer sciences" as the new name for the profession and "an integrative approach to the relationships among individuals, families, and communities and the environments in which they function" as its unifying focus. This new name was intended to move beyond the stereotypic connotations of the term "home economics" that have plagued the field and to communicate a broader focus than home—improvement of individual, family and community well-being; impact on the development, delivery and evaluation of consumer goods and services; influence on the development of policy; and the shaping of societal change, thereby enhancing the human condition.[14] Some of those who attended the conference felt it had created a new profession that not only built upon but transcended home economics. At their subsequent 1994 annual meetings, all five national associations voted to adopt the conceptual framework, and four voted to change their organizations' names to accommodate recommendations from the Scottsdale meeting. Thus the AHEA became the American Association of Family and Consumer Sciences (AAFCS). The exception was the Association of Administrators of Home Economics which changed its name in 1995 to the Association of Administrators of Human Sciences. Members believed this name to be more par-

---

12. Gladys G. Vaughn, telephone interview, April 14, 1995. The idea for this unity and identity conference, which it has been informally called, came from Virginia Caples, but it was implemented by Lynda Harriman, the next AHEA president. The five organizations represented on the task force were the American Home Economics Association, the Association of Administrators of Home Economics, the Home Economics Education Division of the American Vocational Association, the National Association of Extension Home Economists, and the National Council of Administrators of Home Economics. *Positioning the Profession for the 21st Century* (Alexandria, Va.: American Home Economics Association, n.d.). I also interviewed Coby Simerly, co-chair of the task force, April 13, 1995.

13. In addition to five key associations represented on the task force, the AHEA Council for Certification, twenty-six state associations of AHEA, and the W. K. Kellogg Foundation also supported the conference (*The Scottsdale Meeting: Positioning the Profession for the 21st Century, Proceedings* [Alexandria, Va.: American Home Economics Association, May 1994]). Participants also represented other organizations with vested interest in the profession such as Kappa Omicron Nu, the Association of School Administrators, National Council on Family Relations, and the American Dietetics Association (*Positioning the Profession*).

14. *The Scottsdale Meeting*, pp. A5, A6.

allel to and yet distinct from "agricultural sciences" with which home economics in land-grant institutions has been associated since the 1862 Morrill Act.

This endeavor has brought home economics full circle since the Lake Placid conferences at the turn of the century. It is also again adapting itself in order to gain acceptance as a field even though it focuses on the interests of women deemed less important than traditional male interests. It is now reemphasizing its more holistic conceptualization expressed in the term ecology which Ellen Richards proposed instead of home economics during the Lake Placid conferences at the turn of the century. Choosing a name for the profession was as difficult then as it has proven to be now, approximately ninety years later, because integrative, interdisciplinary, holistic ideas are not easily articulated in our analytically oriented culture and language.[15]

In addition to soul searching and redefinition, since the late 1950s, when the civil rights movement raised the nation's consciousness, home economics has made efforts to address racial inequality within the profession through a number of its professional organizations. Kappa Omicron Phi (KOΦ) and Omicron Nu (ON) honor societies led the way. In the 1958–1959 academic year Kansas State's ON chapter initiated its first African American student. In 1963 KOΦ and ON founded chapters in historically black colleges and universities.[16] The NCAHE, almost from its beginning in the early 1960's, has elected officers from historically black 1890 land-grant institutions and included in its conferences programs dealing with diversity and the recruitment of non-traditional and minority students.[17]

AHEA has given attention to racism, but progress has been slower than some had hoped. In 1962, when Florence Low became president, she ac-

15. Analytical thinking, which is a primary aspect of the scientific method, breaks ideas into parts or subconcepts. It is not focused on synthesis.

16. Omicron Nu's first black chapter was established at Howard University in 1963 and Kappa Omicron Phi's first was at Prairie View A&M University in 1963. A few years later, several other chapters were installed in historically black institutions. Dorothy Mitstifer, then executive director of Kappa Omicron Phi, recalled that the usual processes of moving freely on a college campus and the traditional installation ceremonies were hampered because of racial tension and segregation still in practice even after passage of the 1964 Civil Rights Act (Dorothy I. Mitstifer, KON Executive Director, telephone interview, March 21, 28, 1995).

17. Gilbert, ed., History of the National Council. Flemmie Kittrell of Howard University was elected secretary and Flossie Byrd of Prairie View A&M University was second vice-president (1969–1970), vice-president (1970–1971), president-elect (1971–1972), and president (1972–1973). Since then, several other administrators from historically black universities have been elected to different offices, and annual conference programming has given attention to diversity, including recruitment and retention of nontraditional and minority students.

knowledged racial tension within the organization and set out to ameliorate it.[18] Since the 1940s minorities could only be members-at-large,[19] not members of a state affiliate. This left them unable to rise through state leadership experiences to national offices. As a result of Low's leadership, in 1963 AHEA changed its by-laws, eliminating segregation in membership at the state and national levels.[20]

Since then four African American members have been elected to national office and ten resolutions have been passed to address the status of minorities in the AHEA/AAFCS and in the profession as a whole. In 1975 Dr. Gwen Newkirk, chair of the Department of Education and Family Resources at the University of Nebraska—Lincoln, became the first African American national president. In spite of this breakthrough, continuing minority dissatisfaction within AHEA and the profession as a whole prompted the passage in 1977 of a resolution reaffirming the need for equal opportunity.[21] Data were unavailable for 1977, but in 1979 statistics indicated that racial and ethnic minorities made up only about 5 percent of AHEA membership. To address this problem a subgroup of mostly black home economists in AHEA in 1980 established the Coalition for Black Development in Home Economics,[22] open to anyone interested in the organization's goal of creating a network of professionals to promote black participation in all aspects of the profession.[23] In 1982 Mildred Griggs, then associate professor in the Department of Home Economics Education and the Department of Vocational and Technical Education at the University of Illinois Urbana, became the second African American AHEA president. But in spite of this progress, by 1989 AHEA's minority membership had dropped to less than 1 percent. A resolution adopted at the annual meeting that year acknowledged that minorities had not received visibility

---

18. Florence Low, telephone interview, March 30, 1995.

19. Penny A. Ralston, "Black Participation in Home Economics: Review and Reflection," in *Empowerment through Difference: Multicultural Awareness in Education*, ed. Herma Barclay Williams, AHEA Teacher Education Section Yearbook 8 (Peoria, Il.: Glencoe, 1988), p. 29.

20. "Elimination of Racial Discrimination from All Facets of the American Home Economics Association," Resolution of the American Home Economics Association, adopted by the AHEA Assembly of Delegates, June 1963, in Archives of the American Association of Family and Consumer Sciences, Alexandria, Va.

21. "Minority Groups," Resolution of the American Home Economics Association, adopted by the AHEA Assembly of Delegates, July 1, 1977, ibid.

22. The Coalition for Black Development in Home Economics became national in 1984, renaming itself the National Coalition for Black Development in Home Economics. Irene K. Lee, president, provided a copy of the mission, goals, objectives, and general information about the organization.

23. The 1988 AHEA Teacher Education Section yearbook, *Empowerment through Difference: Multicultural Awareness in Education*, includes chapters about various cultures but provides little documentation of involvement in home economics of any ethnic group except African Americans.

commensurate with their contributions to the profession. According to the resolution writers, a resulting decline in the number of minorities choosing home economics at the undergraduate and graduate levels and in the number of those completing degrees diminished the pool of potential minority leaders. The resolution called for increased efforts to recruit and retain more minority females and males in the field.[24] It also called for minority and non-minority leaders to work collaboratively to develop opportunities for minorities to gain leadership skills.

The decline in minority representation in home economics, coupled with the prediction that by the year 2000 racial and ethnic minorities are expected to make up one-third of the U.S. population,[25] prompted the AHEA to launch Project 2000 in 1989 with a grant from the Office of Higher Education Programs of the U.S. Department of Agriculture (USDA). Its goals were to address the issues of recruitment, retention, and graduation of more minorities in the field, enhance academic programs to address the unique needs of diverse ethnic groups, establish networks to help minority graduates enter viable careers, establish a consortium of organizations to address the issues, collect benchmark data on minorities enrolled in specializations in home economics, and identify mechanisms for determining progress and future directions.[26] As a result of the project, the AHEA higher education community adopted guidelines for increased minority participation and held a summit conference in 1990 to address projected personnel needs for specializations within the field and to develop strategies and long-range plans for the recruitment, retention, and graduation of minorities in specializations.

In 1990 further support for racial equity was confirmed in yet another resolution calling for increased support for the 1890 land-grant colleges and universities (historically black) in their centennial year.[27] In 1991 Virginia Caples, then associate dean, School of Agriculture and Home Economics at Alabama A&M University, was elected the first AHEA president from an

24. "Minority Leadership in AHEA and Home Economics," Resolution of the American Home Economics Association, adopted by the AHEA Assembly, June 1989, Ibid.

25. Jane Coulter, "Maximizing Professional Talent for Millennium III," *Home Economics Forum* 6 (1991): 5.

26. Beverly Bryant, "A Report on Project 2000 for the Period August 1, 1989 to January 31, 1990," in Gilbert, ed., *History of the National Council*, p. 84; Gladys G. Vaughn, telephone interview, April 13, 1995.

27. "Centennial Celebration of the 1890 Land-Grant Colleges and Universities," Resolution of the American Home Economics Association, adopted by the AHEA Assembly, June 1990, Ibid. Land-grant universities funded in 1862 were not open to blacks in segregated southern states. In 1890 the Second Morrill Act of 1890 established the land-grant educational system for black Americans which has been among the primary ways black Americans have had access to higher education.

1890 land-grant institution. Two 1992 resolutions called upon the profession to work toward greater equality for minorities in society.[28] Penny Ralston, dean of the College of Human Sciences at Florida State University, was elected the first African American president to serve the organization (1996–1997) under its new name, American Association of Family and Consumer Sciences. In sum, between 1963 and 1993 AHEA has actively worked to eliminate discrimination and enhance opportunities for minority leadership in the profession.[29]

More than other ethnic groups, African American home economists themselves facilitated these changes. Ralston, who reviewed African American participation in the field from 1976 to 1986, argued that although home economists had been slow to acknowledge racism, in spite of "societal slippage [that] has occurred in Black achievements in the late 1970s and early 1980s, professional involvement by Black home economists has gone against this 'current'".[30] Acknowledging scholarly contributions and leadership accomplishments, Ralston concluded, "On the surface at least, one could argue that home economists have sustained the social movement of equality while societal values are shifting from this stance".[31]

It is difficult to get a clear picture of strides the field has made. Kappa Omicron Nu Honor Society (KON), created by a merger of KOΦ and ON in 1990, one of the members of the consortium created by Project 2000, published the summit papers on the status of minorities in the specialized programs in home economics in higher education. In calling for greater diversity in the field, the authors pointed to the inadequacy of data describing the status of minorities other than African Americans. Nationally disaggregated data on different minority groups in home economics/family and consumer sciences as a whole do not seem to be available from any of the field's organizations or the USDA. Only Ebro and Winterfeldt's article, "Status of Minority Recruitment, Retention, and Participation in Dietetics/Nutrition," published in the summit papers included the broad minority

---

28. "Education of Minority Children and Youth" and "Racism," Resolutions of the American Home Economics Association, adopted by the AHEA Assembly, June 1992, in Archives of the American Association of Family and Consumer Sciences, Alexandria, Va.

29. Other relevant resolutions adopted by the AHEA Assembly of Delegates are "Aging," adopted July 1971; "Aid to Handicapped and Families of the Handicapped," adopted June 1973; "Architectural Barriers," adopted June 1, 1976; and "Home Economics Education for the Immigrant," adopted June 1991.

30. Ralston, "Black Participation," p. 37.

31. Ibid. After Ralston's 1988 work went to press, Julia Miller was appointed in 1987 as the first African American dean of a home economics college at an 1862 land-grant institution, the College of Human Ecology at Michigan State University. Since then, three other African Americans have also been appointed to traditionally white higher education institutions: Esther Fahm, University of Wisconsin-Stout; Penny Ralston, Florida State University; Retia Walker, University of Kentucky.

categories Hispanic, Asian or Pacific Islander, American Indian or Aslaskan along with Caucasian and African American.[32] Although their data were too limited to show a real trend, they do indicate steady increases in the numbers (not percentages) of minority students enrolled in dietetics/nutrition programs in colleges and universities.

Continuing its efforts to increase diversity in home economics, in 1993 KON published *Leadership for a Culturally Diverse Society: A Professional Development Module* to encourage equity within the profession.[33] In 1994 and 1995 KON also awarded grants focusing on multicultural education in higher education, extension programming, and factors contributing to successful careers of African American graduates in housing and consumer economics.[34]

In spite of the increasing number of minorities in the profession since 1989, home economics was still below the national average for degrees granted to minorities. Nationally, 14 percent of all higher education degrees earned in 1991–1992 went to minorities.[35] That same year, home

32. The papers from the Project 2000 summit were published in Kappa Omicron Nu Honor Society's *Home Economics Forum* 6(Fall 1991) and 7(Fall 1994). They indicate that the dietetics/nutrition community has been more active than the other specializations in addressing the issue. As early as the 1970s, the American Dietetics Association (ADA) established incentives for its chapters to recruit minority members. In the mid-1980s, the Association established an affirmative action plan including an annually revised Minority Recruitment and Retention Plan. Although the number of minority members and leaders within the organization has increased, proportional membership has not improved. Data from the Federal Extension Service are also inadequate. They are not disaggregated to reveal the status of minorities in program areas such as home economics (Kirt Deville, Director of Civil Rights for the Federal Extension Service, telephone interview May 25, 1995). Inquiry into this matter has prompted a decision to return to collection of these data at the federal level. Ebro, Lea L. and Winterfeldt, Esther A. "Status of Minority Recruitment, Retention, and Participation in Dietetics/Nutrition." *Home Economics Forum* 7 (Fall 1994): 14–18. They gleaned the data from annual reports submitted to ADA by dietetic educators in November 1992.

33. Frances E. Andrews, Gwendolyn T. Paschall, and Dorothy I. Mitstifer, *Leadership for a Culturally Diverse Society: A Professional Development Module* (East Lansing, Kappa Omicron Nu Honor Society, 1993).

34. Grant proposals provided by Kappa Omicron Nu: "Factors Contributing to Career Success of African-American Graduates" by Sharon Y. Nickols, Carol B. Meeks, and Anne Sweaney; "Facilitating Multicultural Education in Collegiate Home Economics Programs" by Carol Darling, Bonnie Greenwood, and Sally Hansen-Gandy; "Facilitating Multi-Cultural Programming through the Family and Consumer Sciences Cooperative Extension Service" by Sally Hansen-Gandy, Carol Darling, and Bonnie Greenwood. Another home economics honor society, Phi Upsilon Omicron elected Eula Masingale as its first African American president from 1982–1984. It's journal, *The Candle*, has also published articles on diversity issues.

35. This includes all bachelor's, master's, and doctoral degrees conferred in 1991–1992 in higher education institutions to all minorities, not just to blacks. These data are from the U.S. Department of Education, National Center for Educational Statistics, Integrated Postsecondary Education Data System (IPEDS) in *Digest of Education Statistics* (Washington, D.C.: U.S. Department of Education, Office of Educational Research and Improvement, 1994). Minorities

TABLE 14.1 Women in predominately female professions, in percent

| Ethnic Group | Degree[a] | | | | U.S Citizen |
Field of Study	Bachelor's	Master's	Doctorate	White	Minority
Home Economics	89	83	76	74	8.0
Education	79	77	59	80	12.5
Library science	92	80	68	74	6.0
Health professions/ Related sciences	83	80	58	79	8.3

[a]*Bachelors, Masters and Doctoral Degrees Conferred by Institutions of Higher Education: 1991–92* (U.S. Department of Education, National Center for Education Statistics, Integrated Post-

economics conferred 11 percent of all its degrees to minorities.[36] However, when the percentage of home economics minority degrees conferred in 1991–1992 is compared to that in other traditionally female professions, home economics is not dissimilar. (See table 14.1.)

The public image of home economics as a gendered field has inhibited diversification. Recruitment to attract females into male-oriented professions have left traditionally female-dominated fields such as home economics with fewer professionals, particularly women of color.[37] At the same time, men have not expanded their career options at a similar rate into traditionally female fields. Consequently, home economics lost enrollments between 1970 and 1990. The actual number of men in the field increased slightly, but the profession remained primarily white and female. In public school programs, where most people form impressions of the field despite the breakdown in gender stereotyped curricula, there has been virtually no increase in the number of male home economics teachers,[38] but secondary home economics enrollments seem to be 40 to 50 percent males.[39]

---

included black, non-Hispanic, Hispanic, Asian/Pacific Islander, and American Indian/Alaskan Native.

36. One percent of all bachelor's, master's, and doctoral degrees conferred in 1991–92 went to students graduating from home economics programs (Bureau of Educational Research and Development, Office of Educational Research and Improvement, *Digest of Education Statistics 1994* Washington, D.C.: U.S. Government Printing Office, October 1994), pp. 279–82, 285.

37. Frances M. Smith, "Who Chooses to Study Home Economics?" *Journal of Family and Consumer Sciences Education* 87 (Spring 1995): 33–39.

38. Ibid., p.37.

39. According to Coby Simerly, then associate dean for instruction, College of Human Resources and Family Sciences, University of Nebraska—Lincoln, who was working on a study of enrollment trends in secondary family and consumer sciences programs in Nebraska, males were estimated to represent about 40 to 50 percent of the enrollment nationally. Personal interview, May 8, 1995.

Although the field of home economics created career opportunities for educated women early in the twentieth century, some have been lost and others have been maintained with difficulty, especially in higher education as Margaret Rossiter explains in her chapter. Another look at the story surrounding the McGrath and Johnson Report (referred to as the McGrath Report) reveals several important lessons. First, to avoid being caught off guard, it is important to anticipate how powerful adversaries might react to an action that women and minorities might take in support of their own interests. According to Helen R. LeBaron, then dean of the College of Home Economics at Iowa State University, the home economics administrators (Home Economics Division) asked the American Association of Land-Grant and State Colleges and Universities' (AALGSCU) executive committee in 1959 to fund a study of the "'problems, objectives, and future of home economics in their member institutions."[40] Some university presidents tried to use this opportunity to eliminate viable home economics programs from higher education institutions.[41] Although these leaders did not anticipate this move by the presidents, their response was savvy and at least partially successful. Second, we can learn from their success in changing the principal investigator, Earl J. McGrath's attitude toward home economics which seems to have come from avoiding unnecessary confrontation which was likely to have increased negativism toward the field. At the same time they were proactive in providing data that might otherwise have been suppressed if control of the situation remained in the hands of the adversary, in this case the university presidents and McGrath and Johnson of the Institute of Higher Education of Teachers College, Columbia University. Had the home economists not been so assertive, the report might have reinforced McGrath's initial negative perceptions of the field. The home economics administrators offered to cooperate fully. Even before McGrath could formulate questions, they supplied information that they wanted revealed.

Although the resulting report presented to the NASULGC Home Economics Commission (formerly the AALGSCU) Home Economics Division) on November 12, 1967,[42] was quite denigrating in part as Margaret Rossiter indicated earlier, it was positive in its recommendations about the future of the field. It was critical of federal and state legislation and agreements undergirding home economics education, extension, and research in the land-grant institutions for not providing enough "latitude or stimulation to

40. Helen LeBaron in Earl J. McGrath, "The Changing Mission of Home Economics," *Journal of Home Economics* 60 (February 1968): 85.

41. Marjorie East, telephone interview, April 10, 1995.

42. "Minutes, Executive Board Meeting, Association of Administrators of Home Economics in State Universities and Land Grant Colleges," January 19, 20, 1968. Thanks to Sharon Nickols for retrieving these minutes from the AAHE archival files kept at the University of Georgia, Athens.

enable home economics to meet the changing needs of the time. This . . . [was] particularly true of . . . the Cooperative Extension Service".[43] The report urged that a thorough review at the highest levels of government be conducted, including investigation of the confining relationships between county government and agrarian interests, to assure that home economics could and would redesign its programs and services to meet the needs of American society. McGrath concluded that such a review would "unquestionably show that large additional federal support is urgently required to allow home economics to fulfill its potentially rich variety of services needed to help raise the conditions of life among the urban poor in America and the impoverished throughout the world . . .With federal support, with the encouragement of the administrators responsible for the total institutional program, and with the imaginative planning of leaders within the field, there is no reason why home economists cannot in the future benefit the families of generations yet to come at home and abroad as fully as they have enriched the lives of countless Americans in the days which have passed".[44] The next June, McGrath spoke at the opening session of the AHEA annual meeting about the report that was "having such an impact on projections of future needs in home economics." He explained, "When the representatives of home economics and the officers of the Carnegie Corporation asked the Institute of Higher Education to undertake a study of home economics in the . . . [NASULGC institutions], I had some hesitation. . . . [Although] the Institute had made comparable investigations of a dozen or more other professional schools such as engineering, business administration, and nursing. In none of these, however, was there any question about the continuing existence of a particular . . . professional education unit which prepared practitioners for a specific occupation. No matter how radically some may have felt that a given kind of professional education ought to be reshaped, there was no suggestion that it ought to be abandoned or scattered among other educational units. With home economics it was different.

There were discouraging statements by some [AALGSCU leaders] who, even though they were not as well informed as one could wish, nevertheless were responsible persons. A few felt that although the home economics unit in our colleges and universities had performed service of unquestionable value in the past, their principal goals had been reached. The very reason for the continued existence of home economics units was, therefore, called into question.

[However,] the findings of this study indicate that there will be no lessening in the need for individuals trained in the skills of the home econom-

---

43. McGrath, "Changing Mission," p. 92.
44. Ibid. This is another area in which research is needed.

ics occupations. On the contrary, in the foreseeable future the demand for both generalists and specialists in the occupations related to home economics will continue to grow in response to internationalism, population shifts, and welfare trends. But if these new demands for additional persons in these occupations and in American society generally are to be met, extensive expansion and reorganization of education in the field of home economics are unavoidable."[45]

The third lesson revealed by this story is the power of collaborative political action. The home economics administrators worked together to determine how to most effectively use the positive aspects of the report to gain additional resources for university programs. The Home Economics Commission promptly submitted a request to the Senate of NASULGC and received $1,100 to "study, analyze and implement the findings of the McGrath report with dispatch."[46] A national invitational seminar of Home Economics administrators was held in the spring of 1968 in Chicago to do just that. Although the university presidents, who had planned to use the report against home economics, quietly filed it, home economics administrators worked hard to use it to increase support for higher education programs. The AAHE executive committee mailed the McGrath report not only to its membership but also to all NASULGC members.[47] The report was helpful in maintaining home economics in higher education and in some 1890 institutions, it even helped in obtaining increased support for units.[48] Even though the report did not have the full effect McGrath and the home economics administrators had hoped, without their intervention the intent of those university presidents who wanted to eliminate home economics in higher education probably would have been quickly realized.

In spite of this victory in the 1960s, not until the 1980s did home economists found opportunities in higher education administration beyond the level of dean of a home economics unit. In the 1980s and 1990s at institutions that combined colleges of home economics with other colleges, several home economists were appointed deans of these larger units. Only during the last decade, several home economists have obtained positions as

45. Earl J. McGrath, "The Imperatives of Change for Home Economics," *Journal of Home Economics* 60 (September 1968): 505–6.

46. Flossie Byrd, dean of the School of Home Economics at Prairie View A&M University, Home Economics Commission Report, p. 2, attached to the unpublished "Minutes of the Executive Board Meeting of Association of Administrators of Home Economics in State Universities and Land Grant Colleges," January 19–20, 1968, Chicago.

47. Naurine R. Higgins, "Minutes, Executive Board Meeting, AAHE, January 19, 20, 1968, p.3. Flossie Byrd, Chair of the national seminar held in Chicago in spring 1968, telephone interview, May 5, 1995.

48. Flossie Byrd, telephone interview, May 5, 1995.

chief academic officer at major universities and a small number have attained the position of university president or chancellor.[49]

In the corporate world, a few home economists such as Satenig St. Marie reached the level of vice-president as early as the late 1950s and 1960s. However, because these were staff positions, not administrative line positions, they did not break the "glass ceiling." In fact, some of the positions previously open to them in consumer services departments of large companies were eliminated. To circumvent these barriers home economists created entrepreneurial opportunities for themselves, expanding the range of careers available.[50] According to officers in the AAFCS Business Section, family and consumer sciences professionals are becoming entrepreneurs at a rapidly increasing rate and many are quite successful.[51]

Home economists have been politically active since Ellen Richards' day, but over the years experiences such as that surrounding the McGrath Report have prompted them to become even more proactive. For example, the Vocational Home Economics Coalition begins work five years in advance to affect reauthorization and appropriation of vocational education legislation. In addition many home economics professional organizations have set up legislative committees and provided legislative training for their members. NCAHE established an ad hoc legislative committee in 1975, making it a standing committee in 1979. It cooperated with other home economics organizations on legislative matters including the establishment of the Home Economics Public Policy Council (HEPPC) in 1985. HEPPC was a coalition addressing existing and proposed legislation and initiating legislative action in priority areas it identified annually. A basic premise underlying it was that what was good for one

49. Research is needed to identify the high-level positions women and men with home economics degrees have obtained in business and industry and government that were not open to them early in the 20th century. Research is also needed to determine how well home economists have done in getting women in high positions compared to other fields, especially other predominantly women's fields.

50. Examples of entrepreneurial careers of the members of the Business Section directory of AAFCS include educational materials developer, art director and food layout consultant, food photographer and stylist, producer of films and videos, including training videos, public relations and media relations consultant, media spokesperson, special events coordinator, contest organizer, educational tour organizer, nutrition analyst, customer satisfaction researcher, product design consultant for diverse ethnic groups, corporate health/lifestyle workshop consultant and presenter, child care center consultant, and financial services consultant who does lifestyle analysis for insurance and retirement planning (Joy Daniels, telephone interview, May 30, 1995).

51. AHEA Business Section vice-chair for marketing, Joy Daniels, telephone interview, March 31, 1995, and AHEA Business Section president, Pati Palmer, telephone interview, April 10, 1995.

segment of the field was good for all. The Government Relations Office of AHEA was to take the leadership. HEPPC was to seek funding for support of its efforts.[52] NCAHE also encouraged its members to attend the AHEA Legislative workshops in Washington, DC to teach professionals in the field how to influence legislation at all levels.[53] In 1979 Connie Ley's research on the political socialization of politically active home economists recommended that professional preparation stress public policy involvement to promote political participation.[54] In addition, in the late 1980s the AAHE and the NASULGC Commission on Home Economics (now the Board on Home Economics)[55] increased their political involvement.[56]

In January 1993 the Board on Home Economics hired a Washington firm to serve as a liaison to Capitol Hill. In 1994 the board established two priorities for that effort. The first was to bring together leaders in all aspects of the food system, including production, processing, distribution, retailing, consumption, health, safety, and environment, with congressional, senatorial, and federal agency staff to address public policy concerns cooperatively and holistically. The Food Systems for Consumer Health Workshop was held in Washington D.C. in December 1994. The second priority was to establish a human sciences institute to "bring a critical mass of human scientists, visiting scholars, and staff together at the national level, working closely with their colleagues in the states, to provide critical knowledge and expertise to administrators and policy makers at the national level".[57] Because legislative fragmentation is beginning to appear problematic to some federal legislators, home economics' integrative perspective may help to strengthen its clout if it continues to increase its public policy involvement.

The field has been and is likely to continue to be affected profoundly by state and federal legislation despite the current movement to reduce government. To increase the profession's legislative impact on block grants, AHEA held a public policy seminar in 1996 in Washington, D.C., including visits to legislators. Another public policy seminar was planned for 1997.

52. Gilbert, ed., *History of the National Council*, p. 30.

53. Ibid., p. 19.

54. Connie J. Ley, "An Exploratory Study of the Political Socialization of Politically Active Home Economists," (Ph.D. dissertation, The Pennsylvania State University, 1979).

55. When NASULGC approved by-laws changes to restructure itself in 1992, the Commission on Home Economics became the Board on Home Economics within the Commission on Food, Environment, and Renewable Resources. See "A NASULGC Chronology," fax from NASULGC, May 9, 1995.

56. Sharon Nickols, president of the Association of Administrators of Home Economics, 1992 and 1993, telephone interview, March 22, 1995.

57. Human Sciences Institute Design Team, "Human Sciences Institute: A Proposal," 1995, p. 3.

Many bills in addition to those discussed earlier in this book affect the work of the field. According to Brown and Paolucci, it is part of the mission of home economics/family and consumer sciences to "build and maintain systems of action [including but not limited to participation in the public policy process] which lead to . . . enlightened, cooperative participation in the critique and formulation of social goals and means for accomplishing them."[58]

Rethinking Home Economics has provided numerous examples of home economists who have recognized the need for change within society as well as within the profession. Unpaid home economists who volunteer in home and community settings and who hold at least bachelors' degrees, have advanced the field and its mission through their volunteer work, social activism, and philanthropy. Mary Ellen McFarland, president of the AHEA (1976–1977), and Martha Layne Collins, governor of Kentucky (1984–1987) provide notable examples. As family and consumer sciences moves into the twenty-first century, its effectiveness will depend on its ability to serve as an agent in the process of the "critique and formulation of social goals and means for accomplishing them."[59]

Stories told in this volume make clear that opportunities for educated professional women have been very limited in the twentieth century. Home economists, however, have created meaningful work for themselves that has also benefited society. Sometimes their plans succeeded and sometimes their efforts were thwarted, but home economists created new opportunities when the hegemonic forces in society sought to constrain them.

History is extremely important in helping us understand how home economics/family and consumer sciences came to be what it is today, but the past should not be used as a standard by which to measure the future. Depicting home economists as victims can disempower the field, whereas the stories of Marian Paul and other black South Carolina extension agents, the National Coalition for Black Development in Home Economics, and entrepreneurial home economists can inspire action toward social reconstruction. These women have found ways to fulfill their goals, not by playing the game according to the rules of those in power, but by finding alternative means of achieving success. A clear, positive vision for the future, based on critical self- reflection, sound reason, ethical principles, commitment, and the ability of the profession to implement its vision is extremely powerful in changing reality.

The field is now more aware that it has not been truly inclusive of people with diverse characteristics and experiences. As the United States population becomes increasingly diverse, home economists will need to

---

58. Brown and Paolucci, *Home Economics*, p. 23.
59. Ibid.

respond by preparing new professionals to work with diverse constituencies and to use interdisciplinary perspectives and diverse modes of thinking and interacting. The profession has a greater contribution to make in
transforming our culture *from* one based on the myth of equal opportunity
and mere adaptation to change *to* one that recognizes the interdependence
of all and the benefits of diversity and true collaboration in creating
change.

In 1990, Ernest L. Boyer argued that there is a trend toward more interdisciplinary, interpretive, and integrative scholarship that he believed is
"evidence that an intellectual sea change is occurring, one that is perhaps
as momentous as the nineteenth-century shift in the hierarchy of knowledge, when philosophy gave way . . . to science,"[60] Like many other fields,
including the humanities and nascent social sciences, the early home economics movement emulated empirical, natural sciences, which considered the scientific method to be the only valid mode of generating
knowledge, but the interdisciplinary and applied nature of its undertaking
left the field marginalized. However, according to Boyer, "Today, interdisciplinary *and* integrative studies, long on the edges of academic life, are
moving toward the center, responding both to new intellectual questions
and to pressing human problems."[61] Universities are being criticized for
not doing the very things home economics in higher education was held in
low esteem for doing, *integrating* knowledge and *applying* science. As a
field, home economics has long espoused interdisciplinary and integrative
approaches to inquiry and problem solving. Since Brown and Paolucci
questioned many assumptions held by the field, it has moved from a posi-
tivistic attitude about empirical science as the only legitimate method of
discovering knowledge toward a recognition of alternative modes of inquiry to guide teaching, research, and other functions of home economists
in settings other than higher education. Perhaps family and consumer sciences can now move in from the margin toward the center of the academy
and society.

However, until our culture becomes less gender-biased, we will continue
to have many societal problems that result from the marginalization of
women, their ideas and values. Some worry that women's studies programs
are encountering obstacles home economics has experienced throughout
the twentieth century.[62] Women's fields are likely to continue to have
gender-based problems into the twenty-first century. Although profession-

60. Ernest L. Boyer, *Scholarship Reconsidered: Priorities of the Professoriate* (Princeton:
Carnegie Foundation for the Advancement of Teaching, 1990), p. 21.

61. Ibid.

62. Lisa Bennett, "Warning Comes with Cornell Celebration of Women's Studies," *Cornell
95*, Winter 1995, p. 8.

als in home economics and the movement for gender equity in the larger society have not previously been collaborators, for societal changes to occur that are needed to bring women's concerns from the margin into the center, they must now work together. The third millennium calls for such bold thought and action.

Chronology of Events and Movements Which Have Defined and Shaped Home Economics

VIRGINIA B. VINCENTI

1841   Catharine Beecher contributes to the development of the domestic science movement by writing her *Treatise on Domestic Economy,* published 1841. It is the first comprehensive book on managing a home without servants, the first suitable text on the subject for public schools, and a source of energy-saving, scientific information for American women, eager to read it. Later editions also depict the Victorian ideal home and family that influence home economics pioneers at the turn of the century as they turn a movement into a profession. Her seminaries for girls are more intellectually rigorous than other contemporary female seminaries. Her teacher education programs for young women upgrade education for women, surpass the preparation that many male teachers receive, create a new career for women, and provide a means of financial independence, even though salaries are lower than those of male teachers.

1862   First Morrill Act is passed, providing federal lands to the states to be sold to support colleges of agriculture and mechanical arts.

1871   First course in domestic economy at the college level is offered at Iowa State.

1873   Kansas State begins its domestic economy curriculum.

           MIT grants Ellen Richards a Bachelor of Science degree, its first to a woman, but later refuses to grant its first doctoral degree to Richards because of her gender. Also in 1873 Vassar awards her a Master's degree based on her scientific thesis. She is the first American woman to earn an advanced science degree.

1874   Illinois Industrial University starts a domestic economy program.

1878   MIT appoints Ellen Richards an instructor and the American Association for the Advancement of Science designates her and another woman as their first female fellows.

1882   Ellen Richards publishes *The Chemistry of Cooking and Cleaning: A Manual for Housekeepers.*

1885   Domestic Science is introduced into the public schools in Boston.

1887   The Hatch Act is passed, providing $15,000 annually to each state to establish agricultural experiment stations. Such stations work closely with land-grant institutions to help farmers and to upgrade the nation's agricultural methods. Nutrition research is done at these stations.

Ellen Richards conducts the Great Sanitary Survey that modernized municipal sewerage treatment and develops the first water purity tables and water quality standards.

1890   The New England Kitchen food demonstration center opens in Boston to persuade the poor of the advantage of low-priced, nutritious food. Others soon follow in Providence, Rhode Island; New York City; and at Hull House in Chicago. They fail in their original intent because they ignore ethnic preferences.

The Second Morrill Act is passed, providing further endowment for colleges. Part of the funding is to be used for institutions for black students, leading to the creation of seventeen historically black land-grant colleges.

1893   The World's Columbian Exposition in Chicago asks Ellen Richards to set up an exhibit based on her experiments in nutrition at the New England Kitchen. She called her exhibit the Rumford Kitchen, named for Count Rumford of Bavaria, who first applied the term "science of nutrition" to the study of human food and food preparation.

1894   Ellen Richards is influential in developing the first nutritional school lunch program in Boston. Previously janitors prepared and served school lunches.

1899   The first Lake Placid conference on home economics is held, attended by eleven people. Conferences are held annually for ten years and culminate with the creation of the American Home Economics Association at the 1908–9 meeting. The definition of home economics formulated in 1902 is still widely used and quoted: "Home Economics in its most comprehensive sense is the study of the laws, conditions, principles, and ideals which are concerned on the one hand with man's immediate physical environment and on the other with his nature as a social being, and is the study *specially of the relation between these two factors."*

During the decade of the Lake Placid conferences the natural sciences dominate the curriculum, particularly the "Battle with bacteria and disease" which figures prominently in early home economics teachings, especially in work with the farm population and underprivileged. Child care occupies a minor place in the curriculum because the behavioral sciences are so new, but an emphasis on promoting a more enduring type of family life becomes a focus in home economics.

1901   Ellen Richards publishes *The Cost of Food.*

During the early 1900s increasing numbers of dietitians begin working with food, cookery, and diet therapy in hospitals (previously almost exclusively the male physician's realm).

Also during this decade support grows for state-backed practical education beyond the eighth grade because industrial America needed large numbers of skilled workers. The purpose of secondary education expands to include vocational education. Parents demand that high school girls be taught a greater variety of handiwork to prepare them for the work world of "home industries" or to establish their own homes. John Dewey emphasizes weaving, sewing, and cooking as life skills for both boys and girls.

1904   Ellen Richards publishes *The Art of Right Living.*

1909   Marie Cromer, schoolteacher and girls' club agent, establishes the first tomato club for girls in the United States. Agricultural Extension director Seaman Knapp believes farm women can be enriched by their daughters' participation in girls' club work, but does not favor employing women as agricultural extension agents.

         The American Home Economics Association and the *Journal of Home Economics* are established.

1910   Ellen Richards publishes *Euthenics: The Science of Controllable Environment.*

         Smith College grants Ellen Richards an honorary Doctor of Science degree.

1911   Ellen Richards dies on March 30.

1912   *The Life of Ellen H. Richards: 1842–1911,* by Caroline Hunt, is published in June and is in a second printing by November.

         In South Carolina, two white women become home demonstration agents. No evidence indicates that these women worked with black farm women.

1914   The Smith-Lever Act is passed, specifying the creation of the Agriculture Extension Service to provide farm women with education in home economics and men with education in agriculture.

1916   Dietitians begin to take on a managerial role as food administrators. From the 1890s to this time, they served primarily as instructors in practical cookery for nurses or as supervisors for preparation of special meals.

1917   The Smith-Hughes Act is passed, establishing federal support for vocational education.

         The American Dietetic Association is founded and mandates completion of a two-year home economics course to become a dietitian.

1917–19 As part of the war effort, home economists teach the nation the rules of substitution—beans for meat, dark bread for white bread—and to increase consumption of fresh fruits and vegetables, which could not be shipped abroad to soldiers during World War I. The Cooperative Extension Service is highly involved in this work through 1919.

1918   The American Home Economics Association sets goals to establish and maintain instruction in elements of home management for elementary and high school girls and appropriate home economics instruction for boys.

1919   In South Carolina, black women are first hired in the home demonstration service. Until 1928 South Carolina's black assistant agents work under white women agents instead of directly under the supervision of the black land-grant colleges.

In South Carolina, the Cooperative Extension Live-at-Home program is established and continues until 1930 so agents' work can bring better living and community conditions to African Americans, and thus decrease black migration to northern industrial centers.

1920   The home economics section is added to the American Association of Land-Grant Colleges (later known as NASULGC).

Home economists seek to enlist men as well as women in parent education classes during the 1920s and 1930s. Some fathers are receptive to child study work, but others resent any effort to persuade them to help more with parenting.

The definition and objectives of home economics begin to shift from an emphasis on housework to greater attention to home and family. For example, parent education classes for men as well as women stress child study. Also, state agriculture extension services begin collaborating with home economics departments at several colleges to transmit knowledge about children to homemakers, and continue to do so through the 1940s.

1923   The National Association of Ice Industries hires Mary Engle Pennington as the director of its Household Refrigeration Bureau to promote the use of home refrigerators cooled by ice and to beat competition from electric refrigerators.

1924   The AHEA creates its Home Economics in Business section to act as interpreter, translator, and mediator between consumers and producers.

The AHEA first supports the parent education movement at its annual convention. A survey of curricular needs of college-educated women shows that 80 percent of the respondents requested a child study component in the home economics programs.

1925   Eloise Davison, Professor of Home Economics at Iowa State, becomes the first representative of the AHEA on the Committee on the Relation of Electricity to Agriculture (CREA).

Home economists lobby successfully to have the Land-Grant College Association recognize child care as a key element in the home economics curriculum.

1926   The AHEA opens its convention floor to commercial displays.

Food corporations begin employing home economists to create recipes and nutritional information for other home economists in classrooms, for those writing in newspapers and magazines.

For membership in the ADA a dietitian is now required to complete a four-year degree with a major in foods and nutrition.

1930   All black South Carolina agents hired after 1930 are required to hold a college degree. The Rosenwald Fund, endowed by a Sears and Roebuck executive, begins funding regional summer institutes for black extension workers.

Marian B. Paul is appointed the State Supervisor of Negro Home Demonstration in South Carolina. She advocates not only improving the standard of living for rural families but also helping them become independent and self-supporting by instructing them about marketing, economical management, home ownership, better education, and keeping their children in school. She retires in 1959.

1931   Extension service home economists begin cooperative work with New York State administrators of the newly formed Temporary Emergency Relief Administration (TERA) in educating families on relief about nutrition and emergency food budgets. Between 1932 and 1935 they collaborate to offer education to those on relief in New York State and to sponsor subsistence gardens and canning centers to effectively maintain their health. Home economists in the state become accepted by the public as experts in human nutrition with valuable skills. Such cooperation continues through 1938.

1936   The George-Deen Act boosts home economics by authorizing equal appropriations for home economics and agriculture. It results in more equitable funding for home economics in relation to other vocational education areas. However, the Depression diminishes the Act's intended effect because the funds are not available as appropriated.

1939   The Rural Electrification Administration (REA) and the U.S. Department of Agriculture become part of an extended network of public and private agencies that bring electricity to rural people. Home economists play significant roles in this network well into the 1950s. They train and work with extension agents and are hired by utility companies to make home visits to customers to demonstrate how to run and use electric appliances and cook with electricity. Electric manufacturers seek home economists' advice on the design and marketing of appliances.

By this time home economists have established a place in most major consumer products firms. Increasingly they become torn over whom to serve, consumer or firm. In the 1950s availability of such positions begins to wane.

1941   Agnes Faye Morgan, chair of the Department of Home Economics at the University of California, Berkeley, is appointed to serve on President Roosevelt's First Nutrition Congress.

Home economists participate in the war effort by operating canning kitchens and performing other emergency functions until 1945.

1943   The USDA Bureau of Home Economics becomes the Bureau of Human Nutrition and Home Economics.

1945   The Rural Electrification Administration encourages its local cooperatives to hire home economists because of the post-war consumer boom. Home economists' loyalties are divided between professional ideals to enlighten adults and REA's purpose of educating rural folk to use more electricity.

1946   The George-Barden Act is passed, making it possible for home economics teachers to supervise home and community projects. It helps to give home economics a status more equal to that of traditional subjects.

Agnes Faye Morgan becomes the first woman member of the Committee of Nine to administer cooperative research funds for state agriculture experiment stations. She serves in this capacity until 1950.

1958   The National Defense Education Act is prompted by the Russian launch of Sputnik I in 1957. The law stresses science, math, and foreign languages, challenging home economics, an elective in secondary schools.

1959   Fifteen members of the AHEA Committee on Philosophy and Objectives worked for three years to produce "Home Economics New Directions" with input from the Gull Lake Workshop (1958) that included representatives from the American Dietetics Association, American Vocational Association, National Education Association, and the Home Demonstration Agents.

Five members from the land-grant administrators' group worked as a committee to produce a companion publication: *Home Economics in Land-Grant Colleges and Universities.*

1960s   Home agents have to consider the changing trends that affect African American lives when designing their programs. Mechanization alleviates some of the drudgery of farm life and the need for some forms of manual labor, but the need for enlightenment from economic, educational, and social bondage remains. When South Carolina integrates its extension service, some of the projects and organizations for black home demonstration are absorbed, but most are eliminated.

Feminists criticize scientific experts in home economics for fostering restrictive roles for women.

Specialized programs (home economics teacher education; family economics and home management; family relations and child development; food, nutrition and dietetics; textiles and clothing; housing, furnishings, and equipment; institutional administration; and home economics communications) emerge in response to public and consumer interest and demand. The 1960s see a rise of specialized programs in colleges and universities that continues to the present.

1961   An accreditation committee of seven begins its work together of nearly a decade to produce a plan and criteria for the accreditation of undergraduate programs in home economics. The proposal was adopted by the AHEA Assembly of Delegates in 1967.

With the help of the U.S. Office of Education, the Federal Extension Service, and home economics units in land-grant universities, AHEA holds a national conference in French Lick, Indiana, to address problems of articulation and differentiation in home economics subject matter in its specialization. Sixty-five home economists meet for five days to identify the basic concepts and generalizations in the discipline of home economics.

Report of the U.S. Commission on Civil Rights on Public Higher Education recommends federal funds be disbursed only to public institutions of higher education that do not discriminate by race, color, religion, or national origin.

1962   Florence Low, AHEA President, acknowledges racial tension within the organization and sets out to eliminate it.

1963   AHEA changes its by-laws to permit minorities to hold state membership. This replaces their restriction to only member-at-large status, a policy in place since the 1940s that had left minorities unable to rise through state leadership experiences to national offices.

Amendments to the Vocational Education Act are passed. After Helen LeBaron is appointed to a White House panel, funds are included in the Act specifically for home economics research.

The Vocational Education Act does provide categorical funding for home economics, but it reduces funds for homemaking education or family life education and sets aside at least 10 percent of the funds from the Smith-Hughes and George-Barden Acts (sections incorporated within The Vocational Education Act) after 1965 to be used for home economics-related occupational training. For the first time, the vocational legislation spells out clearly that in addition to the regular program for unpaid useful employment in everyday life, home economists had to begin training students for gainful employment outside the home.

1965   Prompted by a reorganization of the NASULGC, the Division of Home Economics forms a new organization, the Association of Administrators of Home Economics (AAHE). Its purposes were to maintain a liaison with the proposed commissions and councils of the larger organization; to work with other organizations and agencies with similar purposes to strengthen the contributions of home economics within the states, nationally, and internationally; and to provide opportunity for home economics administrators to work together to determine and consider the larger problems in society and their influence on family members as individuals and consumers; and to determine contributions resident instruction, research, and extension can make to the solution of such problems.

1966   The first South Carolinian African American agent successfully wins a protest of unfair treatment in the extension service. The Civil Rights Act of 1964 gave the agents an effective weapon with which to defend their rights.

The National Council of Administrators of Home Economics is established by administrators from higher education units with liberal arts backgrounds for administrators of all types of degree-granting institutions (small and large; public and private; land grant, state and parochial) to strengthen home economics in higher education.

1968   *The Changing Mission of Home Economics* by Earl J. McGrath is published in the *Journal of Home Economics.* The executive committee of the American Association of Land-Grant Colleges and State Universities (AALGCSU), later renamed the National Association of State Universities and Land-Grant Colleges, had commissioned outside consultants

McGrath and Jack T. Johnson (from the Institute of Higher Education at Teachers College, Columbia University) to study home economics curricula, extension services, and research and to define the future role and scope of home economics in land-grant institutions.

Amendments to the 1963 Vocational Education Act provide additional funding for handicapped and disadvantaged students, vocational counseling, vocational school construction to increase programs offered, and program evaluation. Through the Act's categorical funding for home economics education, it strengthens the position of home economics in the schools.

1970   *National Goals and Guidelines for Research in Home Economics* by Jean Schlater is published from a study sponsored by the Association of Administrators of Home Economics to identify priorities for research in home economics. The publication reflects "the continuing commitment of home economics to the family and to the interaction between man and his near environment."

1970s   In projects to improve the diets of poor ethnic people, home economists encourage people to use culturally familiar foods. The Home Economics Bureau of the New York City School Board begins encouraging teachers to feature cultural recipes in classrooms.

1971   The AHEA is accepted as an accredited agency by the National Commission on Accrediting.

1972   Title IX of Civil Rights Act is passed, prohibiting sex discrimination in all educational programs.

1973   Feminist Robin Morgan, author of *Sisterhood is Powerful,* is invited to address the AHEA annual meeting in Denver. She criticizes the field, claiming its main emphasis is to reinforce the institution of marriage, the nuclear family, and manipulation of women as consumers (euphemistically called consumer protection). These being the primary areas targeted by radical feminists, she declares, "I am here addressing the enemy."

In response to Robin Morgan's accusations, AHEA establishes the Women's Role Committee to explore the relationship of home economics to changing concepts of women's roles.

The Eleventh Lake Placid Conference is held to develop consensus among members concerning the future direction of the field.

1974   *Home Economist Image Study: A Qualitative Investigation* is published. The AHEA had commissioned an outside marketing consultant (Yankelovich, Inc.) to study the public's perception of home economics and provide data for a planned public relations program. The survey concludes that the profession of home economics suffers from "a fractionated series of unrelated identities."

1975   AHEA publishes "Home Economics New Directions II," a statement of purpose and priorities for the home economics profession. It reiterates the 1959 definition and basic mission, but emphasizes an ecosystem framework for the field.

1976   Following the Vocational Education Act amendment that is passed this year, the home economics profession begins to gear its work seriously toward males.

1979   AHEA uses *Home Economics: A Definition* (1979) by Marjorie Brown and Beatrice Paolucci as the focus of a series of dialectic discussions to clarify the basic mission and philosophy of the field.

1980   A group of mostly African American AHEA home economists establishes the Coalition for Black Development in Home Economics, open to anyone interested in the organization's goal of creating a network of professionals to promote black participation in all aspects of the profession.

            The Science and Education Administration of the U.S. Department of Agriculture conducts a study (1980–81) resulting in *New Initiatives in Home Economics*. This report proposes new programs in home economics research, extension, and higher education.

            The American Home Economics Association's Future Development Committee designs the first of a series of discussion outlines on issues in home economics. From 1980–1985 the topics include mission, specialization, career orientation, and ethics as well as guidelines for discussion leaders. These are distributed to all state associations.

1984   Honored for her professional and intellectual contributions to the field, Marjorie Brown gives the first AHEA commemorative lecture celebrating the organization's seventy-fifth anniversary. In it she criticizes her profession for conforming to existing society, for viewing the home in physicalistic terms, and for excessive adulation of empirical science and technology. She intends it to stimulate critical thinking and to improve articulation of home economics and its relationship to society.

            A small group of U.S. and Canadian home economists meets annually through 1987 in Chicago. This group, which called itself the International Interest Group on Integration in Home Economics, sponsors several additional conferences in Knoxville and Baltimore to discuss how integration within the field could be strengthened.

1985   The first volume of *Philosophical Studies of Home Economics in the United States: Our Practical-Intellectual Heritage* by Marjorie M. Brown is published.

            A conference on integrated undergraduate core curriculum entitled "Integration in Home Economics" is held at the University of Tennessee, Knoxville during October to consider ways to strengthen the field's preparation of new professionals.

1988   The International Interest Group on Integration in Home Economics sponsors another conference on integration in home economics prior to the Baltimore AHEA convention.

1989   AHEA launches Project 2000, funded to enhance academic programs to meet the needs of diverse ethnic groups, establish networks to help minority graduates enter viable careers, establish a consortium of organizations to address diversity issues, collect data on minorities enrolled in home economics specializations, and identify mechanisms for determining progress and future directions.

1991   The New York Council for the Humanities and the Cornell University College of Human Ecology sponsor a conference entitled "Rethinking Women and Home Economics in the 20th Century" in October. Participants explore the history of roles home economics and home economists have played as well as the effects the profession has had on the American society.

1992   Five major professional home economics organizations, American Home Economics Association, Association of Administrators of Home Economics, Home Economics Education Division of the American Vocational Association, National Association of Extension Home Economists, and National Council of Administrators of Home Economics, appoint a taskforce charged with creating a process for examining the mission, breadth, and scope of the profession, and building consensus among home economics organizations for a name deemed most appropriate for the profession for the twenty-first century. The outcome is the Scottsdale meeting in 1993.

1993   The second volume of *Philosophical Studies of Home Economics in the United States: Basic Ideas by Which Home Economists Understand Themselves* by Marjorie M. Brown is published.

"Positioning the Profession for the 21st Century," a conference stressing unity and identity which involves representatives of home economics professional associations, meets in Scottsdale, Arizona. The conferees develop a new conceptual framework describing the field's purpose, focus, and mode of operation. The group also recommends that organizations in the field consider changing their names and the name of the profession to family and consumer sciences. The conceptual framework is to provide a meaningful and functional holistic guide for the work of the field and the development of intellectual and ethical congruence between the field's philosophy and its practice.

1994   American Home Economics Association, Home Economics Education Division of the American Vocational Association, National Association of Extension Home Economists, and National Council of Administrators of Home Economics change their names to the American Association of Family and Consumer Sciences, the Family and Consumer Sciences Education Division of AVA, National Extension Association of Family and Consumer Sciences, and Council of Administrators of Family and Consumer Sciences, respectively, to include the new name recommended at the 1993 Scottsdale conference.

1995   The Board on Home Economics within the National Association of State Universities and Land-Grant Colleges votes to change its name to the Board on Human Sciences because it believes this name will serve the profession better in the agriculturally oriented environment in which it functions within NASULGC.

Suggested Reading

Appel, Toby. "Physiology in American Women's Colleges: The Rise and Decline of a Female Subculture." *Isis* 85 (1994): 26–56.

Apple, Rima D. *Mothers and Medicine: A Social History of Infant Feeding, 1890–1950.* Madison: University of Wisconsin Press, 1987.

Barber, Mary L., ed. *History of the American Dietetics Association, 1917–1959.* Philadelphia: J. B. Lippincott, 1959.

Baritz, Loren. *Servants of Power: A History of the Use of Social Science in American History.* Middletown, Conn.: Wesleyan University Press, 1960.

Baron, Ava, ed. *Work Engendered: Toward a New History of American Labor.* Ithaca: Cornell University Press, 1991.

Beeuwkes, Adelia M., E. Neige Todhunter, and Emma Seifrit Weigley, eds. *Essays on the History of Nutrition and Dietetics.* Chicago: American Dietetics Association, 1967.

Bremer, William D. *Depression Winters: New York Social Workers and the New Deal.* Philadelphia: Temple University Press, 1986.

Briscoe, Sherman. "Negro Home Demonstration Agents Doing a Remarkable Job." *Extension Service Review* 21 (1950): 88–9.

———. *A Way to Better Rural Homes: South Carolina Demonstration House.* U.S. Department of Agriculture, Extension Service Circular 505, April 1956.

Brown, Deward Clayton. *Electricity for Rural America: The Fight for the REA.* Westport, Conn.: Greenwood Press, 1980.

Brown, Marjorie M. "Home Economics: Proud Past—Promising Future." AHEA Commemorative Lecture, *Journal of Home Economics* 76 (1984): 48–54, 27.

———. *Philosophical Studies in Home Economics:* Vols. 1 and 2. East Lansing: Michigan State University College of Human Ecology, 1985 and 1993.

Brown, Minnie M. "Black Women in American Agriculture." *Agricultural History* 50 (1976): 202–12.

Brunner, Edmund de Schweinitz. *Rural America and the Extension Service: A History and Critique of the Cooperative Agricultural and Home Economics Extension Service.* New York: Bureau of Publications, Teachers College Press, Columbia University, 1949.

————. *Rural Trends in Depression Years: A Survey of Village-Centered Agricultural Communities, 1930–1936*. New York: Columbia University Press, 1937.

Cotton, Barbara R. *The Lamplighters: Black Farm and Home Demonstration Agents in Florida, 1915–1965*. Tallahassee: U.S. Department of Agriculture in cooperation with Florida Agricultural and Mechanical University, 1982.

Cowan, Ruth Schwartz. *More Work for Mother: The Ironies of Household Technology from the Open Hearth to the Microwave*. New York: Basic Books, 1983.

Cravens, Hamilton. *Before Head Start: The Iowa Station and America's Children*. Chapel Hill: University of North Carolina Press, 1993.

————. "Child-Saving in the Age of Professionalism, 1915–1930." In *American Childhood: A Research Guide and Historical Handbook*, edited by Joseph M. Hawes and N. Ray Hiner. Westport, Conn.: Greenwood Press, 1985.

Danbom, David B. *The Resisted Revolution: Urban America and the Industrialization of Agriculture, 1900–1930*. Ames: Iowa State University Press, 1979.

Duffy, John. *The Sanitarians: A History of American Public Health*. Urbana: University of Illinois Press, 1990.

Eagles, Juanita A., Orrea F. Pye, and Clara M. Taylor. *Mary Swartz Rose, 1874–1941: Pioneer in Nutrition*. New York: Teachers College Press, 1979.

Ehrenreich, Barbara, and Deirdre English. *For Her Own Good: 150 Years of the Experts' Advice to Women*. 1978. Reprint. New York: Doubleday, 1989.

Eppright, Ercel S., and E. S. Ferguson. *A Century of Home Economics at Iowa State University*. Ames: Iowa State University Home Economics Alumni Association, 1971.

Fox, Richard Wrightman, and T. J. Jackson Lears, eds. *The Culture of Consumption: Critical Essays in American History, 1880–1980*. New York: Pantheon Books, 1983.

————. *The Power of Culture: Critical Essays in American History*. Chicago: University of Chicago Press, 1993.

Fritschner, Linda Marie. "Women's Work and Women's Education: The Case of Home Economics, 1870–1920." *Sociology of Work and Occupations* 4 (1977): 209–34.

Gilkes, Cheryl Townsend. "Successful Rebellious Professionals: The Black Woman's Professional Identity and Community Commitment." In *Black Women in American History: The Twentieth Century*, edited by Darlene Clark Hine. Brooklyn: Carlson, 1990.

Graham, Laurel. "Lillian Moller Gilbreth: Extension of Scientific Management into Women's Work, 1924–1935." Ph.D. dissertation, University of Illinois, 1992.

Haney, Wava G., and Jane B. Knowles, eds. *Women and Farming: Changing Roles, Changing Structures*. Boulder: Westview Press, 1988.

Hoffschwelle, Mary S. "Rebuilding the Rural Southern Community: Reformers, Schools, and Homes in Tennessee, 1914–1919." Ph.D. dissertation, Vanderbilt University, 1993.

Hoy, Suellen. *Chasing Dirt: The American Pursuit of Cleanliness*. New York: Oxford University Press, 1995.

Hughes, Thomas P. *Networks of Power: Electrification in Western Society, 1880–1930*. Baltimore: Johns Hopkins University Press, 1983.

Jellison, Katherine. *Entitled to Power: Farm Women and Technology, 1913–1963*. Chapel Hill: University of North Carolina Press, 1993.

Kanter, Rosabeth Moss. *Men and Women of the Corporation*. New York: Basic Books, 1977.

Kessler-Harris, Alice. *A Woman's Wage: Historical Meanings and Social Consequences*. Lexington: University Press of Kentucky, 1990.

Kwolek-Polland, Angel. *Engendering Business: Men and Women in the Corporate Office, 1870–1930*. Baltimore: Johns Hopkins University Press, 1994.

Ladd-Taylor, Molly. *Raising a Baby the Government Way: Mothers' Letters to the U.S. Children's Bureau, 1915–1932*. New Brunswick: Rutgers University Press, 1986.

Leavitt, Judith Walzer. *The Healthiest City: Milwaukee and the Politics of Public Health Reform.* Princeton: Princeton University Press, 1992.

Lofton, M. C. Joelle Fignole. *Bittersweet Perspectives on Maryland's Extension Service.* Princess Anne, Md.: School of Agricultural Sciences, University of Maryland Eastern Shore, University of Maryland System, 1990.

Lyford, Carrie Alberta. "Home Economics in Negro Schools." *Journal of Home Economics* 15 (1923): 633–37.

McGrath, Earl J., and Jack T. Johnson. *The Changing Mission of Home Economics: A Report on Home Economics in the Land-Grant Colleges and State Universities.* New York: Teachers College Press, 1968.

Margolis, Maxine L. *Mothers and Such: Views of American Women and Why They Changed.* Berkeley: University of California Press, 1984.

May, Elaine Tyler. *Homeward Bound: American Families in the Cold War Era.* New York: Basic Books, 1988.

Meckel, Richard A. *Save the Babies: American Public Health Reform and the Prevention of Infant Mortality, 1850–1990.* Baltimore: Johns Hopkins University Press, 1990.

Meikle, Jeffery. *Twentieth-Century Limited: Industrial Design in America, 1925–1939.* Philadelphia: Temple University Press, 1979.

Miller, Roger. "Selling Mrs. Consumer: Advertising and the Creation of Suburban Socio-Spatial Relations, 1910–1930." *Antipode* 23 (1991): 263–301.

Moffitt, Marie Clapp. *The Growth and Development of the New Homemakers of America.* [N.p.]: M. C. Moffitt, 1977.

Muncy, Robyn. *Creating a Female Dominion in American Reform, 1890–1935.* New York: Oxford University Press, 1991.

Nerad, Maresi. "Gender Stratification in Higher Education: The Department of Home Economics at the University of California, Berkeley, 1916–1962." *Women's Studies International Forum* 10 (1987): 157–64.

Neth, Mary C. *Preserving the Family Farm: Women, Community and the Foundation of Agribusiness in the Midwest, 1900–1940.* Baltimore: Johns Hopkins University Press, 1994.

Neverdon-Morton, Cynthia. *Afro-American Women of the South and the Advancement of the Race, 1895–1925.* Knoxville: University of Tennessee Press, 1989.

Nye, David. *Electrifying America: Social Meanings of a New Technology, 1880–1940.* Cambridge, Mass.: MIT Press, 1990.

Palmer, Phyllis. *Domesticity and Dirt: Housewives and Domestic Servants in the United States, 1920–1945.* Philadelphia: Temple University Press, 1989.

Poppendieck, Janet. *Breadlines Knee-Deep in Wheat: Food Assistance in the Great Depression.* New Brunswick: Rutgers University Press, 1986.

Powers, Jane Bernard. *The "Girl Question" in Education: Vocational Training for Young Women in the Progressive Era.* London: Falmer Press, 1992.

Ralston, Penny A. "Black Participation in Home Economics: Review and Reflection." In *Empowerment through Difference: Multicultural Awareness in Education,* edited by Herma Barclay Williams. AHEA Teacher Education Section, Yearbook 8. Peoria, Ill.: Glencoe, 1988.

Rose, Flora, et al. *A Growing College: Home Economics at Cornell University.* Ithaca: New York State College of Human Ecology, Cornell University, 1969 (esp. Esther Stocks, "Part II: A Second Page, 1940–1965").

Rossiter, Margaret. *Women in American Science: Before Affirmative Action, 1940–1972.* Baltimore: Johns Hopkins University Press, 1995.

———. *Women Scientists in America: Struggles and Strategies to 1940.* Baltimore: Johns Hopkins University Press, 1982.

Rothman, Sheila M. *Woman's Proper Place: A History of Changing Ideals and Practices, 1870 to the Present.* New York: Basic Books, 1978.

Rury, John. *Education and Women's Work: Female Schooling and the Division of Labor in Urban America, 1870–1930.* Albany: State University of New York Press, 1991.

———. "Vocationalism for Home and Work: Women's Education in the United States, 1880–1930." In *The Social History of American Education,* edited by B. Edward McClellan and William Reese. Urbana: University of Illinois Press, 1988.

Schlossman, Steven L. "Before Home Start: Notes toward a History of Parent Education in America." *Harvard Educational Review* 46 (August 1976): 436–67.

———. "Philanthropy and the Gospel of Child Development." *History of Education Quarterly* 21 (1981): 275–99.

The Scottsdale Meeting: Positioning the Profession for the 21st Century, Proceedings. Alexandria, Va.: American Home Economics Association, 1994.

Senn, Milton J. E. *Insights on the Child Development Movement in the United States.* Chicago: Society for Research in Child Development, 1975.

Sklar, Kathryn Kish. *Catharine Beecher: A Study in American Domesticity.* New Haven: Yale University Press, 1973.

Smith, Ruby Green. *The People's Colleges: A History of the New York State Extension Service in Cornell University and the State, 1876–1948.* Ithaca: Cornell University Press, 1949.

Strasser, Susan. *Never Done: A History of American Housework.* New York: Pantheon Books, 1982.

———. *Satisfaction Guaranteed: The Making of the American Mass Market.* New York: Pantheon Books, 1989.

Vallance, Theodore. "Home Economics and the Development of New Forms of Human Service Education." in *Land-Grant Universities and Their Continuing Challenge,* edited by G. Lester Anderson. East Lansing: Michigan State University Press, 1976.

Wajcman, Judy. *Feminism Confronts Technology.* University Park: Pennsylvania State University Press, 1991.

Weigley, Emma Seifrit. "It Might Have Been Euthenics: The Lake Placid Conferences and the Home Economics Movement." *American Quarterly* 26 (March 1974): 79–96.

———. "Professionalization and the Dietitian." *Journal of the American Dietetics Association* 74 (1979): 317–20.

Williams, James Mickel. *Human Aspects of Unemployment and Relief: With Special Reference to the Effects of the Depression on Children.* Chapel Hill: University of North Carolina Press, 1933.

Contributors

RIMA D. APPLE is Professor at the University of Wisconsin–Madison, where she holds a joint appointment in the School of Human Ecology and the Women's Studies Program. She has published extensively in the history of science and medicine, focusing on the roles of women. Her most recent book is *Vitamania: Vitamins in American Culture* (1996).

KATHLEEN R. BABBITT teaches U.S. and women's history at St. Lawrence University. She completed her Ph.D. in U.S. history at the State University of New York at Binghamton in 1994. Her dissertation is titled "Producers and Consumers: The Rural Women of New York State and the Cooperative Extension Service, 1900–1940." One chapter, "The Productive Farm Woman and the Extension Home Economist in New York State, 1920–1940," was published in *Agriculture History* (Spring 1992).

REGINA LEE BLASZCZYK is Assistant Professor of History at Boston University. She received her Ph.D. from the University of Delaware, where she was a fellow in the Hagley Program in the History of Industrial America. Before studying for her doctorate, she spent ten years as a researcher at the Smithsonian Institution's National Museum of American History. Her chapter on Lucy Maltby is drawn from her book, *Imagining Consumers: Manufacturers and Markets in Ceramics and Glass, 1865–1965* (forthcoming).

JOAN JACOBS BRUMBERG is Professor of History in the Department of Human Development and Family Studies in the New York State College of

Human Ecology at Cornell University. She teaches about the history of home economics in a popular Cornell course on the history of women in the professions. She is the author of the prize-winning book *Fasting Girls: The Emergence of Anorexia Nervosa as a Modern Disease* (1988). Her latest book is *Our Girls: Growing Up in a Female Body, An Intimate History* (1997).

MARJORIE EAST, Professor Emerita at Pennsylvania State University, received her Ph.D. in home economics from Teachers College, Columbia University. She taught at Simmons and Antioch colleges and worked for Houghton Mifflin. From 1958 to 1980 she chaired the Department of Home Economics Education at Pennsylvania State University, retiring in 1980. East served as president of the American Home Economics Association from 1972 to 1973. In 1984 she was awarded an honorary Doctor of Laws degree from Framingham State College in Massachusetts.

CAROLYN M. GOLDSTEIN is a historian of technology interested in gender and American consumer culture. She received her Ph.D. in history from the University of Delaware, where she was a fellow in the Hagley Program. She has held research fellowships from the Smithsonian's National Museum of American History and the College of Human Ecology at Cornell University. She is currently a curator at the National Building Museum in Washington, D.C.

JULIA GRANT is Assistant Professor of Public Affairs at James Madison College, Michigan State University. She holds a Ph.D. in American studies from Boston University. She received a National Academy of Education Spencer Postdoctoral Fellowship for 1996–97. Her book on mothers and the child development profession is entitled *Raising Baby by the Book: The Education of American Mothers, 1890–1960* (forthcoming).

CARMEN HARRIS is an instructor in history at the University of North Carolina at Asheville. Her dissertation from the history department at Michigan State University examines the role of South Carolina's African American extension agents in the transformation of the state's social and political institutions.

RONALD R. KLINE is Associate Professor of the History of Technology in the Department of Science and Technology Studies at Cornell University. He is author of *Steinmetz: Engineer and Socialist* (1992) and articles on the history of engineering education, electronics, and the relationship between science and technology. He is currently working on a social history of the telephone, automobile, radio, and electric light and power in the rural United States from 1900 to 1960.

LYNN K. NYHART is an Assistant Professor in the Department of the History of Science and in the Women's Studies Program at the University of Wisconsin–Madison, where she teaches the history of modern science, the history of biology, and biology and gender. She is the author of *Biology Takes Form: Animal Morphology and the German Universities, 1800–1900* (1995).

HAZEL REED, Professor Emerita, received her Ph.D. from Cornell University's College of Home Economics. During the Depression of the 1930s she worked as an extension agent in New York State. In 1949 she returned to Cornell in extension administration, where she worked until her retirement in 1967. She died in Ithaca, New York, January 4, 1997.

LISA MAE ROBINSON is currently teaching in the freshman writing program of James Madison College at Michigan State University and is a Master's student in the School of Information at the University of Michigan. She received her Ph.D. in the history and sociology of science from the University of Pennsylvania. Her current research is on the scientific career of Mary Engle Pennington and on Pennington's mentor and Ph.D. supervisor, Edgar Fahs Smith.

MARGARET W. ROSSITER is the Marie Underhill Noll Professor of the History of Science in Cornell University's Department of Science and Technology Studies. She is editor of the journals *Isis* and *Osiris*. She wrote *Women Scientists in America: Struggles and Strategies to 1940* (1982) and a sequel, *Women in American Science: Before Affirmative Action, 1940–1972* (1995).

SATENIG ST.MARIE received her degree in home economics from Simmons College in Boston. She worked for the JCPenney Company from 1959 to 1987, holding the position of director of consumer affairs. St.Marie became the first woman vice-president at the Penney Company. She retired from the company in 1987 and works as a writer and editor for *Victorian America.*

SARAH STAGE is Professor and Chair of Women's Studies at Arizona State University West in Phoenix. She is the author of *Female Complaints: Lydia Pinkham and the Business of Women's Medicine* (1980) and is currently working on a book entitled *Women and the Progressive Impulse,* which deals with the careers of Ellen Richards, Grace Dodge, Margaret Dreier Robins, Katharine Bement Davis, and S. Josephine Baker.

GENEVIEVE J. WHEELER THOMAS graduated from Spelman College's home economics department. In the midst of the Depression of the 1930s she worked as a home economics educator in Georgia and Florida. At Florida A&M she served as dean of home economics. She retired in 1977 and lives in Tallahassee, Florida.

NANCY TOMES is Associate Professor of History at the State University of New York at Stony Brook. She received her Ph.D. in history from the University of Pennsylvania. She has published widely on the history of psychiatry, nursing, and public history. Her chapter is drawn from *The Gospel of Germs: Men, Women, and the Microbe in American Life, 1870–1930*, a forthcoming book on the popularization of the germ theory of disease in turn-of-the-century America. She coauthored with Joan Jacobs Brumberg the pathbreaking article "Women in the Professions: A Research Agenda for American Historians" in *Reviews in American History*, (June, 1982).

VIRGINIA B. VINCENTI is Professor of Family and Consumer Sciences and Associate to the Dean for Special Projects, College of Agriculture, at the University of Wyoming. Her dissertation was "A History of the Philosophy of Home Economics" (1981), and she wrote a chapter entitled "History as a Mode of Inquiry for Home Economics" in *Alternative Modes of Inquiry in Home Economics Research* (1989). She has also written articles on home economics history and on issues related to professional development, including "Home Economics in Higher Education: Communities of Convenience or Purpose?" *Home Economics Research Journal* 19(2): 184–193.

Index